TRIAL OF
THOMAS JOHN LEY

AND

LAWRENCE JOHN SMITH

(The Chalk Pit Murder)

EDITED BY

F. TENNYSON JESSE, F.R.L.S.

Author of "Murder and Its Motives," &c.

LONDON   EDINBURGH   GLASGOW
WILLIAM HODGE AND COMPANY, LIMITED

MADE AND PRINTED IN GREAT BRITAIN
BY
WILLIAM HODGE AND COMPANY LIMITED
LONDON, EDINBURGH, AND GLASGOW

1947

TO

MOIRA TIGHE

"TIGER"

MY FELLOW WORKER

IN

THE CHALK PIT

AND

EVERYTHING CONCERNED WITH IT

WITH LOVE AND THANKS

PREFACE

My thanks are due to the Lord Chief Justice of England, the Right Hon. the Lord Goddard, in consenting to read over his charge to the jury. I also must thank Mr. Anthony Hawke, Sir Walter Monckton, K.C., Mr. Derek Curtis Bennett, K.C., Dr. Eric Gardner, and Dr. Keith Simpson. In view of the fact that no shorthand transcript of the second half of the Closing Speech for the Crown was available, Mr. Anthony Hawke kindly recast this part of his speech from his notes at my request. The proceedings in the Court of Criminal Appeal have been reproduced by permission of the proprietors of *The Times,* and I am indebted to the editor of the *Motherwell Times* for the photograph of Mudie. I am grateful to Detective-Sergeant Ernest Frank Cox, of the Surrey Constabulary, and to his colleagues at the Oxted Police Station, who were most courteous. Mrs. Evans, of 3 Homefield Road, Wimbledon, was my informer as to the daily life of her lodgers, and it is to her that I am chiefly indebted for the light that was thrown upon the protagonists in this trial from what may be called a human—and humane—point of view.

F. Tennyson Jesse.

CONTENTS

CONTENTS

x

LIST OF ILLUSTRATIONS

INTRODUCTION.

On the 29th November, 1946, the body of a murdered man was found in a chalk pit near Woldingham in Surrey. Round the man's neck was a loose cord tied with a half-hitch, so that it only had to be pulled slightly upwards to strangle him. On the neck of the corpse was a deep mark which might have been made by such a cord, had it been so employed. The body was that of John Mudie, a barman employed at the Reigate Hill Hotel. His murderers had been careless enough to leave his visiting card in his pocket.

In spring and summer the place is screened by the thick leafy green of the trees that grow so profusely in Surrey. But there is no ever-green, not so much as one hollybush. The chalk pit is extremely slippery and grass slopes rise perpendicularly on either side. There was nothing in November to conceal Mudie's body except bare twigs and good luck. The trees were free of any leaf and the shallow grave at the end of a sort of corridor of bushes looked like the remains of an army latrine. The army had camped in these parts, as it had all over England before the end of the war. The trench seemed to have been dug much earlier than 1946 with a spade; it was deepened in the middle, probably with the pickaxe brought by the murderers. It was about a foot and a half across and a foot deep, neither long nor deep enough to cover a body. Yet it was in this ill-disguised spot that the body of Jack Mudie was found.

A Mr. Walter Coombs who lived at Woldingham happened to be passing by after his work for the day was over, and saw something that he guessed to be the body of a man. He did not go up to it or touch it, he went home and called his father who accompanied him back to the chalk pit. Neither man altered the position of the body; the older man raised one of the trouser legs in order to see the flesh and to make sure it was a dead man lying there. The chalk pit is not in winter the haunt of picknickers or of lovers. One approaches it by a sharp turning off a good secondary road. Mr. Coombs and his son went to the Surrey Joint Police Force* at Oxted, and P.C. Hearn went back with them, arriving at about

---

*Since 1st April, 1947, the Surrey Constabulary.

Ley and Smith.

4.45 p.m. The body was lying upon its right side but with the feet sticking out over the end of the trench or grave. It was clothed in a blue chalk-stripe suit of what is known as the "Demob. type." An overcoat was twisted over the dead man's head, inside out. A rope was wound twice outside the overcoat. The rope was tied by two loose half-hitches, not very tightly. One end of the rope went under the body and the shorter end of the rope came from the neck under the left arm and was tried with another half-hitch.

P.C. Hearn untied the forearm first and then the rope from the man's neck, the rope in which there were the two half-hitches. He was then able to pull off the overcoat, and he noticed that the rope continued round the man's neck and that there was a piece of rag lying there that smelt of polish. This rag was still wet at the time that the police officer found it. It may have been merely wet with rain; it had been raining heavily and all the ground round the base of the chalk pit was inches deep in mud. Yet the soles of Mudie's shoes were clean, so he could not have walked to the place where his body was found. He must have been carried. This is a most important point, for a pickaxe was lying nearby, a pickaxe that, like the french polisher's rag, was eventually traced to a house in Beaufort Gardens, S.W.

Police-Constable Hearn at once informed his superior officer, Detective-Sergeant Cox, of the discovery of the body.

Here the fates began to take a hand in the murder. On the 27th November, 1946, two landscape gardeners on their way home from work at a nearby property were bicycling along Slines Oak Road. These men were a Mr. Clifford Tamplin and a Mr. Frederick Smith, and as the road rises sharply by the chalk pit they had descended from their bicycles and were walking up the hill. To their surprise, for on a November evening it was a place where few would like to linger, they saw a car inside the entrance of the chalk pit parallel to the main road.

It is a great mistake to imagine that a countryman notices nothing. He notices far more than a townsman about whose head circumstances seem to be perpetually whirling. It was an event for Tamplin and Smith to see such an unlikely thing as a car on the lip of the desolate chalk pit and they paused for a moment. They

Introduction.

might not have paid any more attention if they had not seen a man who was further up a steep bank beyond the car; a man who, at sight of them, at once ran down, jumped in the car, and, reversing with some difficulty in the thick mud round the chalk pit, got on to the road and drove away. Clifford Tamplin and Frederick Smith were honest witnesses and they never pretended to have agreed upon the index letters of the car number; it was dusk of a November evening, and the time for observation was short. But they were so certain that they had seen a car at that deserted spot on 27th November, that when they heard a body had been found there on the 30th, they at once, being good citizens, informed the police of the incident.

They both agreed that the car bore the number 101 and as it drove quickly past them they saw that it was a dark saloon. They were not quite sure of the make—one of them thought it was a Ford.

These two witnesses not only could not agree about the index letters of the car, but at an identification parade later on, each chose a different man as the driver thereof. One chose Lawrence John Smith, a foreman joiner, who was working for a Mr. Ley at 5 Beaufort Gardens, S.W. Identification is one of the worst forms of evidence. One realizes this, remembering the cases of Oscar Slater and of Adolf Beck, also the not un-humorous incident when one of the witnesses at the "Moat Farm" trial identified the criminal, first amongst the jury, and then proceeded to choose the Shire Hall keeper.

But what is important about the matter of Frederick Smith and Clifford Tamplin noticing this dark saloon car, the number of which was 101, was the fact that they noticed it on the day before Mudie was murdered. Now, one Lawrence John Smith had hired a car for a week; it was a dark Ford saloon of which the number was 101. For some inexplicable reason—since it is impossible to look inside a man's brain—somebody or other had driven such a car to that deserted chalk pit on Wednesday, 27th November, 1946. Nothing shook these two honest men, the landscape gardeners, in cross-examination. They might perhaps have forgotten the whole affair if the man, whoever he was, had not run so quickly down the dangerous and greasy slope to the car, jumped into it,

Ley and Smith.

reversed with difficulty owing to the sticky mud, and driven off. It is, to say the least, a coincidence that a man drives to the lip of an abandoned chalk pit, and that a dead body should have been deposited there the next evening. What is there to conclude except that whoever had gone to the chalk pit driving such a car, had gone for the purpose of finding a quiet and unfrequented spot? In summer either of two reasons, both normal, for which a quiet spot is sought, might have obtained, but not in winter.

There is no getting away from the fact that the body of Jack Mudie was found in that chalk pit on Saturday evening, 30th November. There is no getting away from the fact that he was decoyed up to London on Thursday, the 28th November. There is no getting away from the fact that a dark saloon car, No. 101, was there on the Wednesday evening, and John Lawrence Smith had hired just such a car on the Monday of that week. For the murder of Mudie, Thomas Ley, John Lawrence Smith, and John William Buckingham, an army deserter, were arrested.

Buckingham turned "King's evidence," but Ley and Smith were found guilty on the clearest possible evidence and sentenced to death. This sentence was confirmed by the Court of Criminal Appeal.

Ley was the brain, if such it can be called, which designed the whole affair. Smith was the hand which at least helped to carry it out. There is a curious weakness in the people of England which causes them to dislike, when the brain which designed the crime has been found to be insane, hanging the man who obeyed the primary directions. It seems to me, a mere layman, that anyone who is prepared to commit a felony in which there is at least danger of death to the victim, should be executed; as long as there is capital punishment in England. A man who is capable of putting in deadly danger another human being and thereby assisting in the actual murder of that human being is just as guilty whether his employer be sane or a paranoiac. Smith is none the less guilty because Ley is in Broadmoor, a most comfortable spot, where a man of means can have a private room, if there be one un-occupied, can have a batman, if there be a fellow-prisoner willing to serve him (and it is amazing what snobs are to be found among criminal

Introduction.

lunatics) and, save for the sunken walls—which he cannot see—in that lovely garden, believe himself to be in a comfortable country house.

Ley is supposed to be the richest prisoner ever sent to the Criminal Lunatic Asylum. But the fact that Ley was a rich man had only helped him in his career of dishonesty, it had nothing to do with his reprieve. I merely mention this because in some other countries justice can be bought. In Great Britain no judge can be bought with money, nor yet by "a ribbon, star or garter . . . a great man's smile, a seat in Parliament, a tap upon the shoulder from a courtly sword, a place, a party or a thriving lie. . . ." Mr. Pecksniff thought these things might have been worth acceptance by any man making his way up, but even Mr. Pecksniff would have known that justice is not for sale in what has been called this "land of hypocrites" of which Mr. Pecksniff is himself the supreme example. Dickens knew better than to make Mr. Pecksniff fall into such an error.

The story first told about what was known as "The Chalk Pit Murder" was an extremely curious one, and it remained curious until the end. The leading character, if one may so describe him, was Thomas John Ley.

Smith, "Snug the Joiner," was an ordinary enough little man to look at. It was suggested he had ambitions to change his way of life, to go out to South Africa, or to buy a business of his own. He was a quiet lodger at the house where he had a room at Dulwich.

Ley had held an important Government position in Australia in former days. He had been the Hon. Thomas Ley, Minister for Justice of New South Wales. He was born in England and had gone out to Australia at the age of eight. He began life selling newspapers in the correct romantic manner, then became a junior clerk and stenographer to one of the most respectable and oldest firms of solicitors in Sydney. Yet although he became a partner he was never particularly liked. He married and had a family. In the early 20's of this century he became interested in politics and stood for the local state electorate of Kogarah, a Sydney suburb that is partly industrial and partly "white collar." His firm did not like any partner of theirs taking an active part in politics, so the partnership was dissolved and he joined with another solicitor, but the firm did more company promoting than law work. Ley organised a team whose effort was to sweep the Hurstville municipal poll, and push through his policy of rating unimproved land values. This was fairly good going for a young man in his twenties.

In 1917, at the age of 36, on a policy of electoral reform and more Australian participation in the war, he captured Hurstville. Then he broke with his leader, became unofficial head of the Progressives (equivalent to the Conservatives over here) and won his seat again with a big majority. He had formed the coalition that defeated the Dooley Government in 1922, and had come within an ace of leadership, when he was made Minister of Justice. He filled this important office successfully, and showed a sense of values. He handled the Marriage Amendment Bill and the Liquor Bill, and, as he entered his forties, he competed with Hughes as the dominant figure in Australian politics. It is one of the most curious facts of this case that Ley was quite a good Minister of Justice, although while holding this responsible office he unloaded some disreputable shares upon one of his colleagues. He was nominated for the federal electorate of Barton, which included his own state electorate.

Now we come to one of the most odd matters connected with Ley. A certain man put up against him announced that he was withdrawing from the contest and, whether truly or not, the word went round that he was withdrawing because Ley had paid him to do so. Nevertheless he did stand, but Ley was elected, though a little later the accusation was made that Ley had offered a bribe, and a political agitation, not unnaturally, took place.

The High Court of Australia, which deals with matters affecting the Federal House, was to make an inquiry. The man whom Ley was supposed to have paid never turned up at the inquiry, and the case lapsed for lack of evidence. The usual rumours ran around New South Wales. Some people said that Ley's political opponent had been paid by Ley to leave Australia. Certainly no trace of him has ever been found. Other people said that Ley had tried his hand at murder—and tried it very successfully.

It must be admitted that Ley was most unfortunate in the fate

Introduction.

of his friends. He had a business association with a Mr. Goldstein, whose lifeless body was recovered shortly after dawn on 3rd September, 1928, from the foot of Coogie cliffs. One Mr. Puddifoot, sentenced to three years' imprisonment in September, 1923, for the manslaughter of a boy whom he had criminally assaulted, was released on Ley's order nineteen months later. Ley may, owing to the curious workings of his mind, have taken a fancy to shorten Puddifoot's sentence. There is no proof of any guilt on the part of Ley in any of these deaths, and coincidences occur in real life of which no one would dare to write in fiction.

Most of Ley's co-members of the Cabinet are now dead, but those still alive seem to remember him as a "smarmy" sort of individual, although they admitted he administered his department well. The great thing to remember about Ley is that few people liked him. True, he was a teetotaller, even an ardent one; he was nicknamed "Lemonade Ley," which may have accounted for some of the dislike he met, but although he did well in politics, was hail-fellow-well-met and what might be called a good sort, he still was not liked. That he did well in politics is not surprising, doing well in politics is not necessarily to be beloved, and when the head of the Government went on a trip to Europe, Ley thought he was going to be made Deputy Premier. He was only left in his former position, and left Australia, probably for that country's good, to go to the Riviera and to England. His share-pushing in Australia had not been looked upon favourably.

Before Ley left Australia, a friend of his went to England, and when she came back, so rumour has it—and I am merely quoting Australian rumours—she showed a very important member of the National Party a letter from her husband telling her that the wife of the man who had disappeared and the wife's sister had both come to Ley's house to demand news of him and had refused to leave, and that Ley had finally had to call the police to cause them to be evicted from the drawing-room. It is very probable that the man who had disappeared was in some matrimonial or financial trouble and that he might have accepted money to leave the country and escape his home obligations. That, however, since the murder of Mudie, has not been the common opinion in New South Wales. The absurd notion remains that it is easier to bury a body in the

Ley and Smith.

great spaces of Australia than in little England. But such notions remain in the realm of speculation.

An interesting point is that a large framed photograph of Ley hangs in the Justice Department together with all the other holders of the office of Minister of Justice. When the Chalk Pit Case "broke" various people approached the present Minister and asked him to have it taken down, but he said it must remain as part of the historical sequence, in which he was perfectly right. It would be of interest to know whether a footnote will be placed below it to say that this particular Minister of Justice is in Broadmoor.

Ley was a man whom you or I might have met at dinner and considered pleasant, educated, full of knowledge, though perhaps a little pompous. Yet because under his smooth exterior Ley was mad, Jack Mudie is dead. Ley was a vain old man, he was corrupt. He had never found anything in life he could not buy. And for an entirely idiotic foolish jealousy he bought Jack Mudie's death. He bought it as plainly and clearly as though he had lived in some dictator state, as plainly and clearly as though he had been a member of the Council of Ten in Venice and had wished an enemy to be removed. He did this in modern England; because he found tools to his hand whose price was slightly higher because of modern economics. He did this while he spoke amiably to his fellow men and women, while he took taxi-cabs and omnibuses, while he ate in popular restaurants, while he played gin-rummy with his ex-mistress, while he went to and fro on his lawful occasions. It was as though a shadow man had lived amongst us, a man whom no one would have dreamed of suspecting of anything ill, but a man nevertheless whose heart was the heart of his great prototype, Cain. Unlike Cain, he had a bank balance, and therefore it must have seemed to him that the urgencies by which he was impelled were easier to arrange.

He was mistaken, but that does not alter the fact that through his arteries, making his strange heart beat, his strange brain think, ran that same envious blood which actuated the earliest of murderers. The blood of Cain runs through the veins of every one of us. It doubtless ran through those of Abel, although Cain got his blow in first. There is no one of us who at one time or another has not wished another human being dead. Even in love "deep as

Introduction.

a well" there lurks the seed of hatred, which may come to bloom in love's very waters.

There may seem to us no question of what sane human beings call love in Ley's case, but hatred can grow even without love. Ley, competent, gifted and rich, was so bemused by these qualities that he thought he could choose between the good way and the bad way. He chose the bad way deliberately. He could buy it as he had bought everything else. Abel was fortunate to be the murderee and not the murderer. But there is a very fine hair line between the two.

There are many of us who have a certain amount of sympathy with Cain; he was (and I do not for a moment put this forward as a cause for sympathy) a vegetarian, but at least his pathetic little offering to the Almighty was made from the vegetables that he grew. Abel started right in with the idea of blood sacrifices, and "brought the firstlings of his flock and all the fat thereof, and the Lord had respect unto Abel and his offering but unto Cain and to his offering he had not respect." For once the housewife may be on the side of the Lord. There is extremely little we would not do nowadays for cooking fat. But the Lord, as he is presented in Genesis, was not of modern opinion. Therefore when Cain lost his temper and slew Abel he started a long line of descendants against whom not only God's hand but Man's hand is for ever raised. The voice of our brother's blood cries from the ground; if thoughts were deeds we should all bear the brand of Cain. He wandered forth saying that his punishment was greater than he could bear, although the Lord had been merciful and had set a mark upon him to prevent anyone who met him from killing him. There is a certain resemblance between this and the difficulty which ex-prisoners have in getting an honest job of work. Nevertheless we have to remember that Abel was not a killer save of innocent sheep, and that Cain was a killer of his brother.

Ley's sheep were shareholders whom he had cheated, and from this exercise, not unknown to many of our great men to-day who have happened to have had luck, he graduated to killing. Cain, perhaps annoyed with the blood-thirstiness of Abel, became himself the prototype of all killers. At least we can say that Cain knew what he was doing. Ley's plots, Ley's killing, were as stupid and

Ley and Smith.

baseless as that of the carrot fly in the vegetable garden. And the activities of the carrot fly at least benefit the fly, though not the carrot or what is nowadays called the "consumer."

We come now to the most interesting matter that there is to be found in this tangled story. What was it that brought together three such different men as the Hon. Thomas Ley, ex-Minister for Justice of New South Wales; Smith, a foreman joiner; Buckingham, a deserter who turned King's evidence, and Jack Mudie, an ordinary harmless young man whose bad luck it was that he should have been picked upon for a kidnapping that ended in death?

The answer is to be found in that strange character, Ley. To Smith two or three hundred pounds was a fortune. We all have our temptation point, and Smith's was set very low—he came into it simply because of Ley's nature. He lived no fantasy life such as Ley lived, such as every murderer in essence must live, whether he be mad or not. Smith was merely a greedy, hard-bitten little man who was willing to engage in an act of violence for money.

Ley, an insanely jealous man, had had for some twenty years a mistress, Mrs. Brook, who was at the time of Mudie's death sixty-six years of age. Ley had met her and befriended her in Australia. She was a widow, her husband having died untimely from being stung by bees. She became his mistress, and when he left Australia, she came to England with her daughter. For some ten years before the trial there had been no question of any sexual intercourse between them, but she acted as his housekeeper. There is no doubt she was afraid of Ley, though not too afraid to be an honest if reluctant witness at the trial.

Mrs. Brook's daughter married in England a respectable young man, son of an ex-golf club steward, called Barron. The young Barrons took a flat at the house of a Mrs. Evans in Homefield Road, near Wimbledon Common. Young Mrs. Barron fell ill and had to go into hospital for an operation. At Ley's own suggestion, Mrs. Brook went to Mrs. Evans's house to look after her son-in-law and be near her daughter.

Mrs. Evans, whose house is a grey brick Victorian villa which she lets out in rooms, is in herself a most unusual person as well as having been an excellent witness. Her chief interest in life is music and she plays beautifully. Her lodgers, amongst whom was

xxii

Introduction.

Jack Mudie, were men who went out to work, so she was enabled to give most of her time to the practice of her art. Young Mrs. Barron when in health was no trouble, as she looked after her own flat. There is no doubt about Mrs. Evans's opinion both of Mudie and of Ley.

Of Mudie she says he was a harmless decent young man, anxious to get on in the hotel world, and pleased when he got his job at the Reigate Hill Hotel. He had been barman at the "Dog and Fox" at Wimbledon, and doubtless thought he was stepping up in the world when he went from its human warmth to the studied refinement of the Reigate Hill Hotel. Mudie was kindly and thoughtful. He did not forget his landlady and came up twice to have tea with her. His bed-sitting room in Wimbledon, painted a pale sea-green with a divan bed, looked out on trees. He was companionable and evidently treated Mrs. Evans as a friend—which she was. When she had a severe attack of rheumatism he used to bring her tea and run her errands. Mrs. Evans did many things for him, such as a young man living on his own cannot do for himself, keeping his room tidy, seeing to his washing and all the rest of the tiresome matters which have become more and more difficult since the war has ceased: "Jack Mudie looked very like Bing Crosby," Mrs. Evans remarks nostalgically.

Of Mr. Ley, Mrs. Evans has an equally positive opinion. He was enormously fat at the time he came to see her and he sat overflowing one of the armchairs in her living-room, and not only made all the coarse remarks which were attributed to him by the Crown, but made them with an unpleasant leer. She took a dislike to him which she has naturally seen no reason to change.

On his second visit to Homefield Road to see Mrs. Brook, Ley seized Mrs. Evans and gave her a resounding kiss, an attention which somewhat startled poor Mrs. Evans, and which she would have preferred to have done without. He also produced two pound notes and said: "This is for the Cause." He knew that Mrs. Evans was interested in institutions for the blind and gave piano recitals at two of them in the neighbourhood. She duly sent £1 to each saying what at the time she thought was true—that the money came from "a gentleman who was interested in the Cause." Yet Mrs. Evans, as people who let flats have to be, is a shrewd judge of character. None of the young men who lived in her house, she is certain, was wishful to approach old Mrs. Brook with any fell intent, and indeed did not do so. Knowing Jack Mudie's ambitions, Mrs. Evans naturally thought when Ley said to her that he would like to help the young man, that he meant to get him on in the hotel world. She did not at that time realize that the bluebottle suspicions of Ley, settling first here and then there, had finally decided that poor Jack Mudie was the best resting place.

Mr. Romer, another lodger, a respectable married man who went home to his wife and children for the week-ends, was not called as a witness; he, like the dead Mudie, had nothing to do with Mrs. Brook. And young Mr. Barron certainly had no notion of assaulting his aged mother-in-law. Yet at one time Ley had settled on Mr. Romer as the villain in the case and wanted to arrange a meeting with him. Romer replied courteously that he would be delighted to see Ley, but accompanied by his two brothers—who happened to be good boxers. Nothing more came of that approach from Ley.

At the time that Ley had picked on young Mr. Barron, a curious incident occurred. Mr. Barron, senior, was rung up at his office by his son, who said that Mrs. Brook had invited him to tea at 5 Beaufort Gardens, the house which Ley was converting into flats and where he lived. Young Barron added: "It can't have been Mrs. Brook, it must have been her maid, she spoke in a most uneducated voice," and he therefore asked his father's advice as to what to do. Mr. Barron, senior, said: "Don't touch it with the end of a barge pole," or words to that effect, and later on the son telephoned to say he had taken his advice. When Mr. Barron, senior, asked Mrs. Brook whether she had indeed sent such an invitation she replied indignantly that she was not living at Beaufort Gardens but at a room in West Cromwell Road, and that she had no knowledge whatever of the affair.

Young Mr. Barron was more fortunate than poor Jack Mudie, for at 5 Beaufort Gardens, Ley was lying in wait with some physically powerful friends ready to attack Mrs. Brook's son-in-law had he in all innocence arrived for tea.

While Mrs. Brook was staying at Wimbledon to be near her sick daughter she met Mudie once. Mrs. Evans introduced them,

Introduction.

when Mrs. Brook was sweeping the stairs from her daughter's flat and Mudie happened to come out of his room. Mrs. Evans made some remark about Mudie being a bachelor, and Mrs. Brook replied jokingly: "Well, he won't be one long with such beautiful blue eyes." And that was the whole of the relationship between Mrs. Brook and young Mudie. Mrs. Brook has suffered much. She could not marry Ley who was married already, she was a widow, she may at one time have been attractive, she became afraid of Ley, too afraid even to leave him.

So there we are back again at our first question: Why did Ley have this jealous obsession about an old woman with whom he had ceased to have sexual relations? We are all, as we know, born the slaves of our genes, we are more or less the servants of our glands. Ley was at one time, to judge by his photographs, enormously fat; when the present writer saw him in Court he was normal in size, distinguished-looking, white-haired. This does not mean that he was innocent of killing a fellow human being, but it does mean that something was terribly wrong with his physical outfit, and when one says "physical" one means mental as well, for body and mind are so tied up together that it is quite impossible for the layman (and extremely dangerous for the expert) to say which influences the other the more. This does not deter the experts, who seldom fail to be sure of their judgments (and to disagree).

Ley had accused Mrs. Brook of an adulterous relationship with her own son-in-law, and with the unfortunate Mudie who had met her once upon the stairs. Beset with suspicions, Ley went to the Royal Hotel, Woburn Place, the London hotel where his wife always stayed on her visits from Australia, and addressed Mr. Minden, the hall porter, in those curious words: "Do you know a man with a car who can look after himself and keep his mouth shut?"

Now, Buckingham was a friend of Minden's, and Minden had frequently rung him up when a hire car was necessary for clients staying at the Royal Hotel. Therefore he replied that he thought he did know such a man. According to Minden, Ley then said to him: "My wife sends her compliments and says she is not coming back to England." Since she had been resident in the hotel, off

xxv

Ley and Smith.

and on, for some years, Minden was naturally not surprised when
Ley put something in his hand. After Ley had gone, Minden
found that the envelope contained ten one pound notes. Minden
had waited on Mrs. Ley for a very long time, had sent ten trunks
of hers to Australia and assumed that the present was from Mrs.
Ley, although it came from her husband. Mr. Ley, incidentally,
had never stayed at the hotel, though he came there nearly every
day to see his wife. At all events it was obvious that Mr. Ley
was a lavish spender, and Minden saw no reason why his friend
Buckingham should not get any money that was going.

Buckingham telephoned the number and spoke to Ley, arranging to meet him at the Royal Hotel the following evening. This
appointment was carried out. Ley told Buckingham about two
ladies who were being blackmailed by a man who had seduced
them. He was cautious, and did not at that time give the names
of the ladies. He merely said he would introduce Buckingham to
another man who knew about the case. This man was Lawrence
John Smith, the foreman joiner at 5 Beaufort Gardens, the somewhat derelict house where Ley lived in a certain degree of squalor,
and which he was converting into flats.

Thus the fantastic series of meetings began between
Buckingham, Smith, and Ley. The following evening Ley introduced Smith to Buckingham at the Royal Hotel. Ley went away,
leaving Buckingham and Smith together. According to
Buckingham's evidence, Smith said that he knew, through working
at 5 Beaufort Gardens, that Ley had got into contact with a young
lady who had been seduced by a man. Pressed by the Lord Chief
Justice, Buckingham enlarged upon this slight statement and
admitted that Lawrence Smith had told him that Ley had got into
contact with two ladies who had been blackmailed, that they were
mother and daughter, the mother having been seduced as well as
the daughter, and that a certain man was blackmailing both women.
This extraordinary affair appeared to have taken place at Wimbledon, but at the time no particular address was given to Buckingham.
Ley had already said to Buckingham that he wanted to "get something on this man" and Smith corroborated this statement. How
Buckingham, a total stranger, was to "get something on" this

Introduction.

mythical man was not mentioned, nor did the fantastic suggestion seem to strike Buckingham as odd.

The word "legal" played a great part in this trial. Mr. Minden had asked Ley at the first meeting whether the affair was legal; since Ley was a solicitor, he concluded it was. Everyone seemed to know that it was a queer business, but that if it was "legal" it would be all right. Mrs. Bruce, a friend of Buckingham's, when asked to decoy Mudie up to London from Reigate, asked whether the affair were "legal." There is a strange half world, by which I do not mean the equivalent of the French *demi-monde,* which exists throughout England, where men and women may be bought for matters that are just within the law, and so : "Is it legal?" are the first words that spring to their lips.

The plot rapidly progressed, and it must have become obvious to Buckingham father, Buckingham son, who was also engaged in the affair, who helped his father in the car-hire service and was a witness for the Crown, and to Mrs. Bruce and Smith that it was not "legal" to kidnap a man, gag him, and tie him up.

At a later stage, after the first meetings of this strange trio, Ley Buckingham and Smith, Ley told Buckingham that he had had to "fetch" Mrs. Brook from Wimbledon at 2.30 on the morning of 19th June. He took her away in a hired Daimler and a state of distress.

The Lord Chief Justice extracted from Buckingham that Ley had spoken to him about money, that he had said he would get a year's salary if he did what he was told. These golden dreams floated round the Royal Hotel, and to Buckingham and Smith they bore the veritable stamp from Eldorado. Monies, and big monies, were paid both to Buckingham and to Smith, but the end of Jack Mudie was an ill-dug grave in a chalk pit, that of Smith in a convict prison and that of Ley himself in Broadmoor. There is an old legend common to most countries, of fairy gold that turns to dead leaves, and it may be said that this legend was true of everyone concerned in this case.

After Mrs. Brook had been "fetched" at that fantastic hour in the morning from Wimbledon by Ley, she went to live in a room in West Cromwell Road. Nevertheless, though Ley was perfectly aware of this fact, he still brooded over his jealousy of

Ley and Smith.

Mudie. He began an absurd correspondence with the young man.

Ley was a director of many companies, and one of these was Connaught Properties, Ltd. Mrs. Brook was a co-director and her signature, therefore, had to appear with his when cheques were needed by the company. Three cheques were needed, according to Ley, and there is no reason to doubt this, for the payment of salaries in the month of June.

Ley, who had himself taken Mrs. Brook away from Wimbledon, yet sent the three cheques which required her signature to young Mudie at Homefield Road. He sent them with a covering letter in which he said:

"Dear Sir,

Mrs. Brook telephoned last afternoon that she was going to the country about some arrangements in regard to the convalescence of her daughter who is still in hospital, and, as we want some cheques signed and returned to us not later than Friday next, we asked for her instructions. She directed us to send the cheques to her in your care, with a request that if she did not reach Holmfield Road by 4 p.m. on Thursday, to ask you to be good enough to seal up the enclosed envelope and post it to her new flat at 5 Beaufort Gardens, London, S.W.7, so that we can send on Friday morning by taxi and obtain them. We enclose stamped addressed envelope addressed to her, and marked as she directed 'Strictly Private,' her instructions being that we were not to open the envelope on any account until she returned on Friday morning. Thanking you in anticipation for your help in the matter. We are, yours faithfully,

(Sgd.) G. H. BAKER, p.p. Secretary."

Most of this letter was a lie. Mrs. Brook had no flat at 5 Beaufort Gardens. That was where Ley was living. She was living in the room in West Cromwell Road whither he had taken her. She knew nothing about the sending of the cheques to Mudie and had given no instructions whatsoever.

What Ley hoped was that if by any incredible chance Mrs. Brook had signed the cheques, that would be proof that she was "carrying on" with Mudie. But the bewildered Mudie could make neither head nor tail of the affair, had no notion why Ley should have written to him, why he should be asked to give cheques to

Introduction.

Mrs. Brook to be endorsed, but he was a sensible young man and he took these cheques to Mr. Barron, senior, the father-in-law of Mrs. Brook's daughter. Mr. Barron, whose head was screwed on, if one may allow oneself the expression, extremely well, took the cheques to the office of Connaught Properties, Ltd., and insisted on getting a receipt for them. Ley, who was by then so obsessed by jealousy that he could not tell a hawk from a handsaw, when he did not at once receive the cheques back, told his solicitors to write to Mudie demanding their return, and two letters from these solicitors were found in Mudie's room at the Reigate Hill Hotel whither he had gone as barman. Ley then went down to the Reigate Hill Hotel and saw Mudie, who told him what he had done with the cheques, namely that he had handed them to Mr. Barron. Ley insisted on taking Mudie all the way to Wimbledon to see if Mr. Barron could verify this story. Naturally, Mr. Barron did verify it. Ley's own account to Mr. Barron was that he had sent the cheques to Mr. Mudie as "a bit of private detective work on his own." There is no action which Ley did in this fantastic story for which there could have been any motive whatsoever. When Ley went down to the Reigate Hill Hotel it was, as far as we know, the only time he ever met Mudie. Mrs. Brook had only met Mudie once on the stairs at the house of Mrs. Evans.

The trial was so extraordinary, so beyond reason, that, speaking for myself, I should not have been surprised if everyone in Court had turned, as they did in *Alice in Wonderland,* into a pack of cards, and Alice, who in this case might have been anyone of the jurors, the talented counsel, or, more likely still, the Lord Chief Justice, would have beaten them away quoting the immortal words : "Why, they're nothing but a pack of cards."

We have Ley, a man who had risen to a high position in Australia, worrying himself about whether an old lady was having an affair with any one of three young men (one of whom was her own son-in-law) and the other two men were almost unaware of Mrs. Brook's existence.

Ley was obsessed with sex. He may have been impotent, and this may have caused his mind to dwell more and more upon the subject. Yet his obsession was such that it caused him to go to the infinite trouble and pains of suborning Smith, the joiner, the

Ley and Smith.

Buckinghams, and through them, Mrs. Bruce; of spending large sums of money to get a young man who was a total stranger up to his own house in London where he could murder him. And of these incredible series of events he could, or would, only say that he knew nothing. The man who died was innocuous, and had nothing to do with the strange outfit represented first by Ley and then by Smith and Buckingham, an outfit in which Mrs. Brooks, her son-in-law and—for we may be sure she did not escape from suffering—Mrs. Brook's daughter, were all innocently involved. Mrs. Bruce, Buckingham's friend, may have merely thought that she was asked to help in a chivalrous enterprise. Two women were being blackmailed, and of all crimes blackmail is the most evil. There can never have been so many people who had nothing to do with each other whose lives and status in life were so entirely different, brought together for no reason whatsoever save a total lack of reason. As a rule it is the motive of a murder that makes it interesting. It is the total lack of motive in this tangled tale which makes it of supreme interest.

Buckingham's first scheme to get Mudie to London was that he should go with his son to the Reigate Hill Hotel, pretend to be drunk, and that Mudie, as barman of the hotel, should be asked to assist him into his car. They could then manœuvre Mudie inside the car and drive off with him. Ley was not so mad that he did not see that this was a dangerous proposition. Jack Mudie was young and vigorous, and might have struggled and called for help. Buckingham then suggested that his friend, Mrs. Bruce, a visiting cook, should go down to the Reigate Hill Hotel, pose as a lady of means, and make friends with Mudie and ask him if he would come up and act as barman at a cocktail party she was giving. She went down and did make Mudie's acquaintance. Mudie said that he would like to make a little extra money, and Thursday would be the best day for him as it was his half day off.

Therefore, on Thursday, 28th November, 1946, two cars set off for the Reigate Hill Hotel. One was a Wolseley belonging to Buckingham, one was a dark saloon Ford, numbered 101, which Smith had hired at the beginning of the week from a garage in Beauchamp Place. Jack Mudie was waiting for Mrs Bruce, and young Buckingham, whom he thought was her chauffeur.

Introduction.

The cars went back to London, Mudie and Mrs. Bruce being driven by young Buckingham in the Wolseley, while the Ford saloon, with the elder Buckingham and Smith in it, went on ahead and arrived at the front door of 5 Beaufort Gardens. Mudie was driven to the back door, Mrs. Bruce got out of the car and gave a Yale key to young Buckingham. He opened the door. She went in. Mudie followed her. Mrs. Bruce then made a pretence of wishing to speak to her chauffeur and left the house, closing the door behind her. Mudie was then seized upon by Buckingham, senior, and Smith, and Mrs. Bruce and Buckingham, junior, went to "The Crown and Sceptre" and had a drink, which they must have badly needed. They were joined about five minutes after by Buckingham, senior, but not by Smith.

In most cases of murder one can truly say that even when murderers are sane they are never normal. The fantasy world guides them, it is to them the real world, as real as an exhibition may appear to a child. Yet it is but lath and plaster and paint. In this fantasy world Ley lived. Now, this does not apply to Smith who had no fantasy world but who merely wanted money to go to South Africa. In this he differs from Ley. There is not, there cannot be, the smallest doubt that Smith knew that he was engaged in an affair which was, to say the least of it, criminal, or that he was engaged in an affair which might bring death to Mudie. It is possible that he did not realize the very sensible old British Law that anyone who undertakes to play a part in a major felony that may endanger life, is guilty of murder if the victim die even though he die by accident.

It is an extremely good law as long as capital punishment exists at all in the land. No one can possibly have made that expedition to the Reigate Hill Hotel, have seized upon Mudie in 5 Beaufort Gardens and helped to tie him up, without knowing that he was committing a felony. It is of no importance whether Ley or Smith killed Mudie. The one was the brain, the other the tool, but let us hope there are few of us who would be the tool in such a plan. Smith, according to his landlady, was a decent sensible fellow, but there is no doubt that he carried out the task assigned him by Ley of bringing up Mudie to London to be a cocktail mixer at a mythical party. Whose was the hand matters not. What matters

Ley and Smith.

is that if a man be prepared to undertake a dangerous and unlawful affair and death result, it is murder.

As Buckingham, of whom not much can be said in favour, turned King's evidence, there is nothing more to be observed except the Lord Chief Justice's clear direction to the jury that anyone would have expected these two men, Buckingham and Smith, who had come into large sums of money for men in their positions, to have celebrated that night. Smith did not. Buckingham, whose lady friend, Mrs. Bruce, played Delilah to the unconscious Samson of poor Mudie, was not an intelligent witness, but she and Buckingham and Smith agreed in various matters. They all, for instance—and this is a most important point—swore that Buckingham went off with Mrs. Bruce to do a round of public-houses and that Smith never turned up. Not only that, but Smith had said to Buckingham "I'm driving to Leicester to-night in my car." Why did he say that when he was not driving to Leicester until the following night?

The Lord Chief Justice, with great firmness, and, if I may be allowed to say so, acumen, at once noticed this point against Smith. True, the defence had brought in Smith's landlady to say he had taken a bath on Thursday night, the 28th November, and was in bed about eleven o'clock, but even she could not say he had gone to Leicester on Thursday. Her evidence was honest, but it still placed Smith at Dulwich. But what was Smith doing between— let us say—ten minutes to seven in the evening, when he had been left with Ley and the pinioned and gagged Mudie, and the time that he went back to his lodgings in Dulwich? He may, of course, after having committed the crime—for kidnapping and assaulting a man by tying him up against his will are both crimes—have just gone out into the night and had a drink here or a drink there entirely by himself, and then slowly found his way back to his lodgings. But—and although negative evidence is poor evidence— there also is nothing to show what he did between seven and half-past ten that night. Taking the time—not summer time nor what I have heard called "God's time," but simply a matter of hours— it is quite possible that Buckingham, having played his part, went off with Mrs. Bruce to have a drink, leaving Smith with Ley and Mudie. And there was sufficient space in whatever time there

Introduction.

was, to drive a dead body to the chalk pit and get back to Dulwich. There is nothing to show that Ley and Smith could not at once have put the body into the hired car (101) and taken him down and tossed him into that chalk pit, which, as we know, had been explored by some man, whether Smith or another, a day earlier, in a car of which the registration number was 101, and which was a dark saloon. There is a point where coincidence ceases to be coincidence and becomes a terrible pattern of facts.

Ley was undoubtedly the killer . . . with his mind if not with his hands. He had lived for many years not only a life both in Australia and in England of financial dishonesty, but had also lived a fantasy life as regarded Mrs. Brook. No one who saw Mrs. Brook would have considered her guilty for one moment of anything save being afraid of Ley. She was not a young woman, she was not the sort of woman of whom some would have said: "Yes, I know she is sixty-six, but she is so smart and so elegant one would take her for not more than fifty." She was quite frankly sixty-six. She obviously suffered when giving her evidence; she had obviously been terrorized by Ley for very many years. It appears that in his curious fashion he was faithful to her, every night of his life when he was not giving Smith dinner he took Mrs. Brook out to dinner. In a hundred years' time people will say: "How wicked to have convicted Ley, he was obviously mad." But he was not mad under the M'Naughton Rules, he was merely obsessed. He did not plead, as he should have, "Guilty but Insane." He was a man of fantasy, and he moved in fields of fantasy. Rich, old, vain, dishonest, he had never found anything he could not buy. He had bought Buckingham and Smith, as he had bought anything else he wanted during his career. He probably believed that he was telling the truth and there is no more dangerous witness than the man who thinks he is telling the truth in the face of all the evidence against him. That is to say, dangerous to himself but not to the prosecution. Ley had throughout his life (and he had quite a good brain) believed he could, in common parlance, "get away with it." He had always got away with it, though not always with a clean garment as regarded his company-promoting activities. If a company promotor were forced to wear a white robe, or even

Ley and Smith.

a grey one, Ley's would have been found to have been extremely dirty.

What then was his motive in wishing Mudie killed?

Now, it is surely unnecessary to say that it is no part of the Crown's duty to prove motive, just as it is no part of the duty of the prisoner's counsel to prove his innocence. We come back then to the only question that really matters: "What was Ley's motive in murdering that decent and ordinary young man, Jack Mudie?"

Ley was insanely jealous of Mrs. Brook. She may have been swept off her feet by that attractive big shot the Hon. Thomas Ley. What we do know is that he persuaded her to allow him to become her lover, and that she was afraid of him.

There was an extremely good speech once made, probably the best speech ever made by anyone on the face of this earth (and I am not forgetting Gettysburg) by someone who said: "Let him who is without sin amongst you first cast a stone." There I think we can leave Mrs. Brook, though her desire to be inconspicuous was not helped by her leaving the Old Bailey in a large hired Rolls Royce. Indeed, this unfortunate choice of a vehicle drew upon her much more notice than she would have suffered had she employed a humble omnibus or even a taxi-cab.

Sir Walter Monckton had the most difficult part when he defended Ley. His client denied absolutely that he had ever known Mudie or had anything to do with him. He presented a "blanket" innocence. He looked distinguished, he spoke quietly. He had lost his vast adipose deposit. He simply said in the witness box that he had never heard of Mudie, never met him, that (like Pranzini of unholy memory) he was *pour rien dans cette affaire.*"

It would have been a most extraordinary coincidence if Smith and Buckingham and Mrs. Bruce had agreed, as they did agree, to bring the unfortunate Mudie to 5 Beaufort Gardens, if they had not heard about him from Ley. They had nothing against him; indeed who had anything against him? We must accept the fact that Ley's glands or his mind, whichever way one looks at it, had made him insanely jealous of an elderly woman, and that he suspected man after man in his quest for vengeance. We can accept the fact, as indeed we are bound to accept it on the highest medical authority, that Ley was a paranoiac. We are not bound

Introduction.

to accept the same of Smith. Many of us want to go to South Africa. Many of us would like to live there. But to accept £500 for committing a criminal act—and to kidnap a man and to tie him up forms a criminal act—is, I trust, beyond most of us.

Smith in evidence said that his wages were £7 10s. a week, and that he also had a lodging allowance amounting to £1 and a travelling allowance. He had served in the Royal Air Force during the war and had a gratuity of £32 odd when he came out. He said that he had thought about going to South Africa and also to New Zealand.

He admitted that Buckingham's first scheme which involved the question of pretending to be drunk had been turned down by Ley, but that Buckingham's second scheme of decoying Mudie up to Beaufort Gardens was accepted. He admitted that Ley had told him that he wanted Mudie left at Beaufort Gardens tied and gagged. Therefore he knew that the bringing of the innocent Mudie up to Beaufort Gardens involved a dangerous and unlawful act. He admitted that Ley had two bundles of bank-notes which he had asked him to count. That he did, and found the bundles contained £200 each. He added that Ley had said: "This is here for you when you bring Mudie in. You will be able to collect your money and go right away." He admitted that he met Mrs. Bruce through Buckingham, senior. That until then he had never met her and that he had never met Mudie at all and had no grievance against him. He admitted that he bought a clothes-line early on the day that Mudie was murdered. It was a clothes line exactly similar to that with which Mudie was bound. He admitted that when the workmen went away in the evenings from 5 Beaufort Gardens, the doors of the basement and the front area were locked and bolted so that it would be impossible for anyone to get in, unless he were let in or had a key. He admitted that when Mudie came in through the back door he grabbed him round the waist while Buckingham put a rug over his head. He told a different story from Buckingham in that he said when Buckingham was "jumping" Mudie along the passage, the former stumbled and fell upon Mudie. He said that he had arranged with Buckingham that after they had delivered Mudie according to

Ley and Smith.

contract they would go to "The Crown and Sceptre" in Brompton Road and have a drink.

This part of the programme was not carried out. Smith's story of why he stayed behind was that Ley told him that "his end had slipped up; that he would like me to hang on for a moment or two. That he was having somebody come there to help him to get a statement."

Smith insisted that by this he took Ley to mean that he wanted him to hang on—the use of the word "hang" was most unfortunate. After Mudie had been tied up, according to Smith, Ley said: "There is no need for Buckingham to stay. Let him push off." Ley then handed Smith an envelope saying: "Put this in your pocket. I've got Buckingham's here." Smith continued: "I told Buckingham that Ley wanted me to hold on as his people hadn't turned up. I told him that I didn't want to, as I had made arrangements with Buckingham to go and have a drink afterwards. I heard the car pull up at the back door and we again took up our positions."

Smith did not deny that he saw Ley give Buckingham his envelope, that he took his own, that he let Buckingham out of the back door. From thereon, his story as given in examination-in-chief was that Ley had said to him his friends were arriving, that he, Smith, had heard steps so he went out of the door in the front area while Ley went up the stairs to the front door. Smith also said that he went and had a look at "The Crown and Sceptre" to see if Buckingham's car was there, which it was not. He then went to the public-house nearest his own lodgings, and went home. He swore that he went home at about a quarter to ten or ten o'clock, when he took a bath and went to bed in Dulwich, not in Leicester. He did not go there for the week-end until the next day, when he went in the hire-car with the number 101. Smith swore that he had no part in taking Mudie's body to Woldingham, that he had not been there on the day before the murder. So whatever car was seen at the chalk pit, although its number happened to be 101 and it was a dark saloon, it cannot have been his hire-car. . . .

Smith's evidence was peppered with the two terrible words "actually" and "definitely." When asked whether the car at the

Introduction.

chalk pit on the 27th had been his, he said "Definitely not." When asked what he was going to do with the car he had hired on the previous Monday he said "Nothing particular at all, actually," and added, "I was definitely going to Leicester for the week-end." He persisted that he was using his car for his work until he wanted it for the week-end, but "There was a 'bus, definitely." It seems curious that he should have hired a car when there was a 'bus to take him to his work. He denied that Ley lent him the money and insisted that he had enough money himself, though he had to admit that he knew that a large sum of money was coming from Ley.

The Lord Chief Justice pounced:

"Were you hiring this car," asked the learned judge, "for the purpose of effecting what Ley wanted you to do?" Smith replied: "No, not actually at all."

However, Smith had to admit that he had not used the car on the Monday and Tuesday of the week he had hired it, but had kept it in a garage in Goose Green. He also said that during the day of Wednesday, 27th November, the car stood outside 5 Beaufort Gardens; and there remained the insuperable difficulty of the fact that he left the car outside his lodgings on the nights of Wednesday, 27th, and Thursday, 28th, with no corroboration as to the time he had parked it there. On the late afternoon of Wednesday, the 27th, a car with the number 101 was seen at the chalk pit, and on the Thursday, Mudie's body was deposited in the chalk pit.

Smith said that he was quite aware that in hiring the car he had "definitely" signed his name to a document which had the number of the car upon it. He returned the car to the hire service from which it came on the Monday when he came back from Leicester, the day he saw Ley again, at Beaufort Gardens, the 2nd December. Smith swore that all Ley said to him was that everything had gone off quite all right and that Mudie had been "dropped" at Wimbledon. He did not, apparently, have the curiosity to ask by whom he had been dropped—or exactly where. The subconscious is a curious thing, and Wimbledon was the last place that Smith, for his own sake, ought to have mentioned, but

Ley and Smith.

he knew that that was where Mudie had been living before he went to the Reigate Hill Hotel.

He went on to tell a story of wishing to buy a car, but being unable to afford to, which is not unnatural considering his wages, and that Ley offered him the money to buy one and lent him £300 on the 4th December. Smith, however, did not buy any car, although he says he made one or two inquiries. But he was keener on going abroad than anything else, and so, according to his own statement, came to the conclusion that he would not need a car. He opened an account with Ley's cheque for £300, but on the 9th December took the money out and paid it back to Ley through Miss Ingleson, Ley's secretary.

Mr. Curtis Bennett asked: "What did you say to him?" and Smith replied: "I told him I had no use for the money and thanked him for it and I was thinking of going abroad and did not need the money."

Mr. Curtis Bennett pressed the matter further: "I suppose the suggestion was that you were paid that £300 for being a further party to the murder of Mudie? Any truth in that?"

"None whatever," replied Smith firmly.

"Were you a party to a murder plot at the price of £200 or the price of £500 or any other price?"

"Never."

"When," said Mr. Curtis Bennett, "I said £500, I was adding the £300 on to the £200. Was your idea to go abroad and avoid the consequences of this?"

"Definitely not," replied Smith.

"Is all you have told us true?"

"Definitely," said Smith, using his favourite word.

Mr. Curtis Bennett did the best he could for Smith, and it was a very good best, and on the whole he did not have quite such a difficult job as Sir Walter Monckton did in trying to put over Ley's blanket defence of innocence, but the whole affair was very much like the three-cornered duel in *Midshipman Easy*. Since there were two prisoners, it meant that the counsel of each prisoner could discredit his learned friend's client, and added to that there were Mr. Anthony Hawke and his junior for the prosecution.

Smith never denied, and Mr. Curtis Bennett made a great point

Introduction.

of this, that he was "definitely" responsible for getting Mudie to Beaufort Gardens. Naturally Sir Walter, who was appearing for Ley, suggested to Smith that it was quite untrue that Ley had anything to do with the affair at all. Our sympathies can be with Sir Walter, he could not plead "Guilty but Insane" because his client refused to do so.

The cross-examination of Smith by Mr. Anthony Hawke was deadly :

"Did you know Mudie at all?—Not at all."

"Had you any interest in Mudie?—None whatever."

"Did you know until you were told that he was at the Reigate Hill Hotel?—I did not know anything about him until told by Mr. Ley."

"Did Buckingham?—As far as I know, no."

Definitely and actually, that was apparently all that Smith knew, and though his evidence did not quite chime with Buckingham's, it was not the complete ignorance that Ley presented.

Now, when Smith gave this evidence, Ley had already given his. It is not very interesting, for it consists of a denial of everything. Ley, so he swore, had not been in the house that night. . . . He had dined at the Cumberland and spent the evening playing gin-rummy with Mrs. Brook in her room in West Cromwell Road. He had never mentioned Mudie to either Smith or Buckingham. This blanket denial did not aid Sir Walter Monckton, who had to do his best for a client who lied quite steadily and blandly, whereas Smith did confess to certain things such as the kidnapping and tying up of Mudie, in both of which matters he was confirmed by Buckingham.

There is only one delightful little sentence in Ley's evidence. He described how when he had gone down to see Mrs. Brook at the flat of her daughter in Mrs. Evans's house on one occasion, a certain incident had occurred; this was on the 8th June. "I arrived at the house rather early," said Ley, "and walked in with someone who was opening the door and was under the impression that I was going to give her some surprise that she would welcome. When I got to the top of the hall I heard her voice and another man's voice, both of whom seemed to be very happy and she was calling him 'Arthur.' I went down stairs and closed the door

Ley and Smith.

because I was quite satisfied from what I had heard that I was not wanted, and I pushed the bell, ringing the electric bell in the flat. Mrs. Brook put her head out of the window and she looked transfigured, very white, and she said she was boiling an egg."

This exquisite non-sequitur deserves to be remembered. The transfiguration of physical passion being explained away by the boiling of an egg is one that surely only the brain of a madman could conceive, but at least it has the quality of being unique. The passion is, quite rightly, denied by Mrs. Brook. The egg remains in suspension. But it is a very decorative rococo detail, delightful in its unreality.

The circumstance that would have hanged both Ley and Smith, if Ley had not been proved by three of the best doctors in lunacy we possess to be a paranoiac, was chiefly that fatal car numbered 101. The next matter was Ley's absurd correspondence with young Mudie about the signature to cheques by Mrs. Brook, and the third was the paying out of large sums of money to Buckingham and Smith. It may also be argued, and very reasonably, that Ley's "blanket defence" of complete innocence did him no good at all. It was proved beyond a doubt that he had told Smith about Mudie, and that he had engaged, through Minden, the porter of the Royal Hotel, the hire-car owner, Buckingham. It was proved beyond a doubt that Buckingham and Smith, young Buckingham and Mrs. Bruce, took part in the decoying of Mudie up to London. None of them, save for Ley, would ever have joined in a foul and dangerous conspiracy. Yet Ley persisted that he had never mentioned the name of Mudie to anyone of them, and that he knew nothing about it! Why, then, did Buckingham, senior, Buckingham, junior, Bruce and Smith all conspire to bring Mudie up to 5 Beaufort Gardens? You may have one coincidence, but three or four or five are too many.

There never was a crime more stupidly conceived or more badly executed, except that it did bring about the death of Mudie, which was Ley's aim.

Buckingham, senior, Buckingham, junior, Mrs. Bruce, were all involved in the case. Buckingham, terrified when he found that murder had been done, went with Mrs. Bruce to Scotland Yard. Smith did no such thing. There are many people willing to

Introduction.

commit what we might call a little illegal act who are, quite rightly, especially in England, terrified of a murder charge, and there is no doubt that the Buckinghams and Mrs. Bruce were horrified when they heard of the discovery of Jack Mudie's body. They all three, about a fortnight after the murder, when the crime was bruited abroad in the papers, told of their share in it, though naturally not admitting that they had guessed the greatest crime of all had been contemplated when they played their parts and took their money. Indeed, why should anyone of them have thought anything except that the rich Ley was telling the truth when he said Mudie was blackmailing the two women and that he wanted a signed confession? To entice a man, to tie him up and gag him . . . yes. But murder is something so terribly apart, so far from the life even of a Buckingham, that one may well imagine it chills the heart and stimulates the conscience, which latter may be described as a lively sense of self-preservation.

One of the most interesting points in the trial was when the Lord Chief Justice disallowed expenses in the case of Mrs. Bruce, Buckingham, senior, Buckingham, junior, and the hostile witness, Miss Ingleson, who was Ley's secretary. There is not the smallest suggestion that these people took the notorious blunt instrument and hit Mudie on the head with it. But there is far more than the suggestion, there is the certainty, that Smith connived at bringing Mudie up to the flat in Beaufort Gardens, that Mrs. Bruce did the same (perhaps thinking the whole thing was not serious) and that Buckingham helped, afterwards turning King's evidence. This last is an established fact. The hostile witness was the personal secretary of Ley who was quite obviously determined not to incriminate him further than was possible. It is clear that if the oath is of any consequence whatsoever to the witness, the truth, the whole truth, and nothing but the truth should be told. The fact that the Lord Chief Justice disallowed expenses in these four cases needs no comment.

No account of "The Chalk Pit Case" is complete without a description of Cruikshank, one of the most extraordinary witnesses ever seen in any Court of Law. It is easy for those who know nothing of the anxiety of defending a man for his life to cavil at the decision made by Sir Walter Monckton to call Robert John Cruikshank, but those who knew the issues involved, the terrible

Ley and Smith.

weakness of the defence, that absurd blanket innocence of Ley, will sympathise with Sir Walter Monckton.

Cruikshank, according to his own account, was a married man with two children. He was a man of many occupations. He had been a steward on board a ship, he had worked in war factories, he had been a clerk. After he was discharged from this last occupation as redundant—and redundant seems a mild word to use in connexion with Mr. Cruikshank—he tried to get back to Australia where he had been once before. Eventually he found himself living with his children in a hotel in Berne, in Switzerland.

Cruikshank came by air from Berne on the afternoon of the 28th November. He could not say how he got a passage, but merely that the 'plane in which he travelled was to the best of his belief an unauthorized 'plane. He declared that he did not know the name of the man who took him over, and that he was merely coming to bring over a parcel, in other words that he was engaged in smuggling between Switzerland and London. He swore that he did not know where he landed in England or who met him in a car and drove him into London to hand over his packet. According to his story, one thing was certain, he was in Berne at four o'clock on the Thursday afternoon and that he was there again at seven o'clock on the Friday morning. At about eight o'clock on the evening of Thursday, 28th November, Cruikshank (according to his own account), having a few hours to spare before catching another 'plane (also presumably unauthorized) back to Switzerland, decided to call upon Ley. He had heard of Ley some time before, in some bar, as a rich man who might help him to get back to Australia. He went to 5 Beaufort Gardens, up to the front door, and hammered at it with his hand. He got no answer, and went down the area steps to the basement door. This he found open.

Again he hammered with his fist. He again got no answer. He wondered whether if the house were empty there might not be an opportunity for him to commit a felony? He pushed the door open and went in. He swore that he did not see any lights in the house from the time he arrived to the time he left. He went through the basement, and finally found himself in a small room. He tried to get a light from his lighter, he merely succeeded in getting a flicker, but he saw what appeared to him to be somebody in a chair, somebody who was tied up. He stood for a couple of moments there and heard "some sort of a moan or grunt." He went across to the person tied in the chair, felt some ropes, and started pulling at them. He was not sure where the ropes were, they were round the legs and there were some round the top part of the body. According to his own account he just pulled at them in a sort of frenzy. He noticed that the man had some sort of gag round his mouth, but made no attempt to pull it off. Cruik-shank's own account was:

"Well, I was just trying to collect my thoughts. I was thinking all sorts of things. I was thinking about probably somebody up-stairs who was going to come down and beat me up. I thought it was the caretaker, all sorts of thoughts entered my mind, and some sort of noise happened. I don't know whether it was a car, whether it was a hot water pipe. I have got no idea at all . . . my nerve just snapped and I got out of the place as quickly as I could. . . . There is one sentence in my statement which might make other people believe otherwise, but never at any time did I think this man was in danger of death. . . . I want you to understand that at the time this occurrence happened I was already worried. I had lost my home; I had lost my money, my children were in Switzerland. . . . I cannot describe clearly what happened afterwards. I got out of the place and made my way to Sloane Square. . . ."

Sir Walter Monckton asked him: "Tell me, did you tell any-body about this at the time?" Cruikshank replied: "No . . . but one thing you have got to bear in mind with everything I say is that in 1938 I have been informed . . . I believe there was a warrant out against me by the police in London, something to do with get-ting rid of furniture before I had sold it. . . . That was one of the reasons that I have been hesitant in this matter. I can only say that I have never made any secret of the fact that I've got a criminal record. . . . I just told my wife I knew something about the case. On several occasions I read about it. My trouble is I must contradict something which you have got in writing, which is I was frightened I had killed the man. Well in a sense that is true and in another it isn't. I didn't know I had killed him and yet there was . . ."

Ley and Smith.

Again came one of the bleak queries from the Lord Chief Justice :

"Are you coming here to confess to killing this man?"

"Oh no," said Cruikshank, "but if there was a possibility, if he was bound in such a way . . . I can't say how it was done."

"Well," continued the Lord Chief Justice, "you said you pulled some ropes on his arms. That wouldn't kill him."

From his own evidence that same evening, Cruikshank appears to have taken his 'plane, authorized or unauthorized, back to Berne. Cruikshank was a quarrelsome witness. He contradicted himself as such witnesses do, and eventually said that he could not swear that Mudie was alive, but that he had formed that opinion. He made a mock valiant effort at playing the hero when he said : "I have never made a secret of it, I haven't got a good record, my word is nothing. I am just an outcast, I have had convictions. I didn't want to get mixed up in it, it is nothing to me what happens in this case. By coming forward I have brought upon myself suspicions of being bribed and corrupted. I have an impossible story to tell, I have got no story to tell, I have got no witnesses, I have put myself in great danger by going into this box."

In his summing up the Lord Chief Justice said : "With regard to Cruikshank, that man whom we know as an ex-convict, came and told you his story which you may or may not believe to have any truth in it at all. It is not uncommon, you know, that people of bad character come and tell these various stories. . . . It is not for me to express any opinion as to the wisdom of his being called, but you know he tells you he saw a man sitting bound in the room and he saw him with the aid of a cigarette lighter which he had got in his pocket and he said he fumbled with the cords. Well, supposing he did, how could that have mattered? . . . Members of the jury, you probably have formed your own opinion about it, but I should have thought you had not very far to seek. If an ex-convict of that description sees a man in trouble, who, according to the evidence, has been willing to give £300 to one, £200 to another, might he not have thought that if he, finding that man in trouble, comes forward and tells some story that might help him afterwards, he might also be a recipient of this man's bounty?"

There, I think, we can leave Mr. Cruikshank, always with the

Introduction.

qualifying remark that he was the most fantastic witness that this editor has ever heard trying to put over a story in the witness box of any Court in the world.

Let us, now we have read the whole story, think for a minute about the personalities involved in this terrible affair.

It may well be asked why the trial of Ley and Smith should be of such great interest in the history of English criminal law, since as a rule it is the relationship of the murdered person to the murderer that gives human interest to any trial on the capital charge. "The Chalk Pit Trial" is of interest, as I have said, exactly because of this lack of reason and also because of a strong Lord Chief Justice and the brilliance of counsel both for the Crown and the Defence. Ley was a man who as far as could be discovered was perfectly certain that he could succeed in whatever he did. He had a good brain and yet he put up that absurd defence of complete ignorance. It is easy to say that his brain had degenerated, but we still have the fact that from his early youth he had used his brain for making money in an illicit manner, and so come to believe that there was nothing he could not buy. He was an ardent teetotaller, probably because his egotism did not need any aggrandizement; he was the great "I am." He was a man who could always succeed, whether it were with company promoting, with legal or illegal proceedings, or with stocks, and yet there was within him that tainted spot which encouraged him to continue with whatever his business of the moment might be. It was the tainted spot that grew bigger than the man himself. It is easy to say that he was mad, that he was a paranoiac, and both these things are true. It will probably be a hundred years before mankind has begun to find out very early in a child's existence that this tainted spot exists.

That Ley was an egoist goes without saying, a murderer is always an egoist, and no fradulent company director really thinks he can possibly fail, he is the clever man, the man who always imposes himself upon society, the man who even when he has not been liked has been believed. Few fraudulent company directors

xlv

Ley and Smith.

commit murder. Few murderers have the intelligence to be fraudulent company directors. Ley must have known within himself that he had the gifts both of taking money and taking life, and when at last justice caught up with him he probably felt himself a much aggrieved man. A double criminal such as was Ley is extremely rare. We get the multiple killer, we get the clever fraud, but the two things in conjunction are seldom found.

Smith was more normal than Ley. He was greedy and heartless and avid of money. Unluckily Ley had a deep purse. Buckingham was not a scrupulous man and proved to have deserted after Dunkirk. He is now serving his punishment. Mrs. Bruce has retired into obscurity for all this editor knows. Mrs. Brook is living retired from the world in a house that Ley had bought her in a London suburb, with her daughter and son-in-law and the son-in-law's parents. They only ask to be left alone.

It would seem incredible, were it not true, that all these people, the guilty and the innocent, should have come together in the fatal knot of death about someone who was completely guiltless, and never knew what it was all about.

Now we come to the innocent bewildered murdered man—"the forgotten man," for once a man is dead it is in his murderers the public are interested.

Jack Mudie was exceptionally unlucky not only in the fact that he was murdered but in the even more terrible circumstance that he was murdered for nothing—and that he was unsuspecting. The mind of a distorted man had seized upon him for a victim. This man had money enough to employ human tools. It is easy but horrible to imagine Jack Mudie's feelings when he went on a dark night into the back way of 5 Beaufort Gardens. Mrs. Bruce went on ahead of him and called him to come in. She said she had to have a word with the driver and went out. Mudie then had a rug thrown over his head, he was trussed up, pulled, or, as they said, "jumped" along the passage by Buckingham and Smith and met his death in the chair of a little room that was used as an office. He must have been terribly bewildered as to what it was all about.

xlvi

Introduction.

He knew nothing about Ley except from the curious affair of the cheques. He knew nothing about the Buckinghams or Smith. He was merely asked to make a little extra money by shaking the drinks at a cocktail party. This meant nothing to him whatever until it meant his death. Strong young men are not easily killed, and it is—in the true sense of the word—awful to imagine Jack Mudie sitting trussed up in that chair with a gag in his mouth, terrified as any man in his position would have been terrified, awaiting the hand of the strangler. The hand of the strangler came, and poor Jack Mudie, that decent, ordinary fellow, left 5 Beaufort Gardens as a corpse, though he had come into it as a young, strong, vital man. If there is anything to add to the terror of being murdered, one can surely say that there is the terror of being murdered when one cannot imagine why.

He had come to London in all good faith, he was called in at the back door and at once assaulted, bound up and eventually strangled. If he had any last thoughts they must have been of the most bemused. Whether he saw Ley or not we do not know, the rug was taken from off his head, the gag was thrust into his mouth and he then was killed by the rope round his neck pulled with "a certain degree of suspension." Hanging, except at official hands, is not a merciful business. A man who is hanged in England dies because his neck is broken, generally at the third cervical. But poor Jack Mudie sat in the chair unable to cry out, still wondering what it was all about and killed slowly by a rope from "a slight degree of suspension." True, the murderer who is hanged suffers the torments of the damned during his time of waiting, and the torments consist of knowing that a term has been set to his natural life. This was not Jack Mudie's fear. His fear must have been that of someone caught up in a nightmare who knew nothing but who yet must have realized that he was in deadly danger. He must have known from the moment that he was "jumped" along the corridor with the rug over his head and the ropes about him that there was something very strange afoot. Nobody employs a

xlvii

Ley and Smith.

barman to shake cocktails and treats him in this manner. Therefore this strangeness must have struck the poor young man's heart
with a sense of doom. He had wandered into a nightmare and the
nightmare was coming true. There is the terrible innocence of
death on his face when it was photographed in the chalk pit.

Thus the sorry story comes to an end, a stupid story, a wicked
story, and a mad story. Nothing can bring Jack Mudie back to
life; his murderers have been fortunate. Many innocent people in
the case have been unfortunate in that they were inextricably connected with it. Jack Mudie was not an important person, but he
had just as much right to live as the greatest amongst us. Through
no fault of his own he lost that right—and indeed his very
unimportance points the moral though it may not adorn the tale.

There is no one, not even a criminal, who has not the right to
the protection of the law and the right to be treated decently by
society, just as there is no one, not even a professional prostitute,
who has not the right to choose with whom she wishes to spend the
night. It is just as possible to rape a prostitute as to rape an
innocent woman. The right of choice, the right to be an individual
is, or at least so we have thought in England, a right that we all
share.

F. TENNYSON JESSE.

July, 1947.

P.S.—The Hon. Thomas John Ley was sent to Broadmoor on
5th May, 1947. He died there of a seizure on 24th July, 1947.
Anyone who cared for him must be glad that he is out of
his misery. The taxpayer will naturally feel, and quite rightly,
a certain relief. Yet it is always possible to feel a certain
sympathy with the man whose brain, from early youth, bore the

Introduction.

equivalent of the rotten speck within the fruit; which eventually influenced him far beyond his own understanding.

Ley leaves behind him a trail of unhappiness, but which one of us is there who dares say that he was responsible for leaving that trail? We still know too little and those of us in full possession of our faculties are few who can say with truth that we have caused no suffering.

Leading Dates in the Ley & Smith Case

1946

	End of May or early June, Mrs. Brook went to her son-in-law's flat at Wimbledon.
12th June	Ley fetched Mrs. Brook away from Wimbledon at 2.30 a.m.
19th June	Ley wrote letters to Mudie *re* Connaught Property cheques. About
7th August	Ley went to see Mudie at Reigate Hill Hotel. About
Late Autumn	Ley met Minden, porter at the Royal Hotel, Woburn Place.
,,	Ley met Buckingham.
,,	Following evening, Ley introduced Smith to Buckingham.
,,	Few evenings later, further meeting at Royal Hotel between Ley, Smith and Buckingham.
16th November	Ley withdrew £250 in cash from his account.
25th November	Ford saloon car No. 101 hired by Smith.
26th November	£300 in cash withdrawn by Ley from his account.
27th November	A car No. 101 seen in Woldingham chalk pit.
28th November	Mudie decoyed from Reigate to London in car numbered 101.
28th November	Mudie murdered.
30th November	Mudie's body discovered in Woldingham chalk pit.
2nd December	Smith returned hire car No. 101 to owners.

1

1946

4th December	£300 transferred to bank account of Lawrence John Smith by cheque from Ley.
9th December	£300 withdrawn from his account and handed back by Smith to Ley via Miss Ingleson.

1947

19th March	Trial of Ley and Smith began at Central Criminal Court.
24th March	Ley and Smith found guilty and sentenced to death.
21st April	Appeals dismissed.
2nd May	Application for fiat to appeal to the House of Lords refused.
5th May	Ley reported insane and removed to Broadmoor. Smith's sentence commuted to penal servitude for life.

THE TRIAL

WITHIN THE

CENTRAL CRIMINAL COURT,
OLD BAILEY, LONDON,
WEDNESDAY, 19TH MARCH, 1947.

Judge—

THE LORD CHIEF JUSTICE OF ENGLAND.
(RT. HON. LORD GODDARD.)

Counsel for the Crown—

MR. E. ANTHONY HAWKE.
MR. HENRY ELAM.
(Instructed by the Director of Public Prosecutions.)

Counsel for the Prisoner Thomas John Ley—

SIR WALTER MONCKTON, K.C.
MR. PHINEAS QUASS.
MR. S. GERALD HOWARD.
(Instructed by Messrs. Wontner & Sons, London.)

Counsel for the Prisoner Lawrence John Smith—

MR. DEREK CURTIS BENNETT, K.C.
MR. MALCOLM MORRIS.
(Instructed by Messrs. Freeborough & Company, London.)

A   I

First Day—Wednesday, 19th March, 1947.

The CLERK OF THE COURT—Thomas John Ley and Lawrence John Smith, you are charged with the murder of John McMain Mudie on the 28th November, 1946. Thomas John Ley are you guilty or not guilty?

The PRISONER LEY—Not guilty.

The CLERK OF THE COURT—Lawrence John Smith are you guilty or not guilty?

The PRISONER SMITH—Not guilty.

A Jury was empanelled and sworn.

The CLERK OF THE COURT—Members of the jury, the prisoners at the bar, Thomas John Ley and Lawrence John Smith, are charged with the murder of John McMain Mudie on the 28th November, last. To this indictment they have severally pleaded not guilty, and it is your charge, having heard the evidence, to say whether they or either of them be guilty or not.

Mr. HAWKE—My lord, there are some photographs in this case which I shall have to refer to in my opening address. Would it be convenient if they were handed up now and for them to be proved at the proper time?

The LORD CHIEF JUSTICE—Yes, Mr. Hawke.

Opening Speech for the Crown.

Mr. HAWKE—May it please your lordship, members of the jury, as you have heard these two men stand in your charge indicted with the murder of a man named Mudie on 28th November last year. I appear with my learned friend, Mr. Elam, for the Crown. The defendant, Mr. Ley, who is the one furthest from you in the dock, is defended by my learned friends Sir Walter Monckton, Mr. Quass, and Mr. Gerald Howard. Mr. Smith, the one nearest to you, is defended by my learned friends Mr. Curtis Bennett and Mr. Morris. Members of the jury, at about half-past three on the afternoon of 30th November a man named Coombs, who lived at

3

Ley and Smith.

Mr. Hawke

Woldingham, in Surrey, was walking home, and his way took him past a chalk pit which stands abutting on a road called Slines Oak Road, which leads from the main Croydon-Westerham Road to Woldingham. As he passed by the entrance to the pit he saw what appeared to be a bundle of rags on the ground, but a closer inspection indicated that those rags were covering the body of a man. The police were at once informed, and at half-past four on that afternoon Constable Hearn, of the Surrey Police, went to the spot, and found the body.

If you, members of the jury, would look at the second photograph in your book, you will see on the right hand edge as you look at it a white mark. That white mark here (indicating) shows you the spot where this body was found, lying as you see on the edge of the pit. It was lying in a trench, in a partly dug grave. There was a loosely tied rope round the neck outside the overcoat that was covering the body. The constable pulled the coat away, and he then found underneath a piece of rope loosely tied round the neck, and also a piece of rag round the neck which was likewise loosely tied. This you will see in the third photograph in your book.

The body was subsequently found to be the body of a man called John Mudie. John Mudie was at the time of his death employed as a barman at a hotel called the Reigate Hill Hotel at Reigate, in Surrey. He was living at the hotel at the time. He left the hotel, as you will hear, on the afternoon of 28th November and he never came back, and his bed was not slept in that night.

The inquiry, and it must be perhaps an inquiry of some length, which you have the burden of conducting, is an inquiry into what happened between 28th November, that Thursday afternoon when this man was alive and well and going about his duties in the hotel, and the discovery of his body on the late afternoon of Saturday, 30th November, some 12 miles from Reigate where he lived and worked.

Members of the jury, he had been strangled. In the opinion of Dr. Eric Gardner, the consulting pathologist of Weybridge Hospital, who saw the body shortly after its discovery, and who later conducted the post-mortem upon it on 1st December, the cause of death was asphyxia mainly due to the rope round his neck having been drawn tight round the neck. If you look—and this is the last time I shall trouble you—at the last photograph in the book, No. 4, you will see round the dead man's neck the deep marks which indicate that the rope, which at the time his body was found was loose, had been drawn tightly round his neck at some time. Dr. Gardner, as I told you, found that the cause of his death

4

Opening Speech for the Crown.

Mr. Hawke

appeared to be asphyxia due to strangulation. The head of the body and the neck also provided evidence that this man had been violently handled before his death. In Dr. Gardner's estimation death had taken place about 48 hours before. It is a calculation which must always be elastic, but that is Dr. Gardner's view, and if that is so of course it indicates that this man met his death some time in the evening or in the early part of the night of 28th November, the previous Thursday.

One further fact emerged, and it is a fact of considerable importance in connexion with this case in the light of subsequent information which came to hand and which will be the subject of evidence before you. It was found that whereas the ground surrounding the body was wet and muddy, and the clothing was stained and smeared with mud, caused of course by contact with the ground, the shoes, the uppers of the shoes and the soles of the shoes, were perfectly clean. There was no evidence at all that this man had walked to the place where his dead body was found, and you may think that it is a reasonable inference that he had met his death elsewhere and been placed after his death in this trench where he was found. If this is right—and indeed the Crown will invite you to say when you have heard the evidence, that there is no doubt about it—that he was in fact transported to and dumped in this pit where he was found, then, of course, the question arises, how came it that this man who lived and worked at Reigate should have been found dead 12 miles away from that town in a chalk pit where his body had apparently, as I say, been deposited.

Another and a vital question arises out of that, the question where did he die. Members of the jury, it is the case for the Crown that he died in London, that he died as a result of being strangled or in some way asphyxiated after being gagged and bound and violently handled. It is the case for the Crown that the acts which caused his death were performed in a Kensington flat, which is part of a house then being converted into flats, No. 5 Beaufort Gardens, which some of you may know is a road which leads out of the Brompton Road, that these acts were done in this house to which he was decoyed on the night of 28th November, and decoyed there by persons suborned for the purpose by the defendant Ley. These persons occupy different places. One of them, Smith, is in the dock, the others in their different capacities are witnesses— a man called Buckingham, this man Buckingham's son, and a woman named Mrs. Bruce—and it is necessary for the proper unfolding of this story to you that the Crown should rely in part on the evidence of those witnesses. Members of the jury, they can hardly command respect. They are persons who, as the Crown

5

Ley and Smith.

must put them before you, were apparently quite willing for money paid to them by Ley, to take their different parts in a plot which lured this man Mudie to London and to the place where he met his death.

One of them, the older Buckingham, was actually arrested and charged himself with being concerned with these two defendants in the murder, but he was discharged before the learned magistrate in the Lower Court, no evidence being offered against him. He will stand in the witness box and give his evidence, upon oath, and give you his version of this matter on behalf of the Crown. The Crown ask you to treat these persons with the caution that they must all deserve. You will no doubt wish to see whether you can find independent evidence of these persons which corroborates them, which indicates to you that what they are telling you is the truth. I say at once, and I think it is right that I should say it, that up to the moment when Mudie was slumped in a chair at 5 Beaufort Gardens, trussed up, gagged, and bound with a rug over his head, Buckingham's account of what happened—how this man was brought to London, how he was treated when he got there—is corroborated line for line and letter for letter by the defendant Smith himself. That is not to be taken as evidence against Mr. Ley, his co-defendant. What Smith has said in the statement, unchecked and untested by any cross-examination or investigation by persons who have Ley's interest in hand, cannot of course be evidence against Mr. Ley, and the prosecution do not put it forward as such.

The LORD CHIEF JUSTICE—You will not use any prefixes, Mr. Hawke.

Mr. HAWKE—If your lordship pleases. Members of the jury, that it is evidence against Smith there can be no question, and it is evidence, of course, of great weight. There is other evidence also which supports the evidence which Buckingham will give. There was a green rag found around the neck of this body. At the time we are investigating work was being done at 5 Beaufort Gardens converting the house into flats, and Smith was the foreman in charge of that work. This green rag, according to Dr. Gardner, could have been used as a gag, and Smith says in his statement that it was so used. That piece of rag is in fact some of the rag that was used at Beaufort Gardens by a french polisher who was working at No. 5 during the time that we are considering, the latter part of November and the early part of December. You will hear also that some three feet away from the body where it was found there

6

Opening Speech for the Crown.

Mr. Hawke

was a pickaxe in some bushes. That pickaxe had been used, as you will be told, at Beaufort Gardens for the purpose of mixing concrete. So you see articles found by the body came from this house in London.

I think it is proper, perhaps, to mention here that Smith says in his statement that for his part in this matter he was paid £200 by Ley in notes. He says that he gave £30 of it to Buckingham and spent £130 of it on clothes and presents. Buckingham also says that he was paid £200 in notes which were handed to him by Ley in a packet just before he left Beaufort Gardens on this night of 28th November. You will hear that there were two cash withdrawals from Ley's banking account at the Midland Bank, Sloane Street, of £250 in cash on 16th November and £300 in cash on 26th November. These are all facts which independently tend, you may think, to corroborate the evidence which you will hear.

It may be when the evidence has been laid before you that you will have no doubt at all that Mudie was brought to 5 Beaufort Gardens on 28th November, that he was there subjected to the treatment which resulted in his death, and that some time between 28th November and 30th November, when his body was found his body was conveyed to that desolate chalk pit and left in this half dug grave. Further you will have to ask yourselves, I think, when you have heard this evidence, whether you have any doubt at all that the instigator and the financier of the plot which led this man to London was the defendant Ley.

I think it is therefore now the time that I should bring before you the story as it must be unfolded in evidence of how and why Mudie was brought to 5 Beaufort Gardens on the night of 28th November. It is a very extraordinary story. It must start, I think of necessity (I hope I shall not put anything irrelevant before you) some distance back in time before this date. It is founded, it would appear, upon an unreasoning jealousy which this man Ley felt in connexion with a woman named Mrs. Brook. Mrs. Brook is a widow, 66 years of age. During her married life she lived in Australia, and there she met the defendant Ley, who also lived there. After her husband's death she and her daughter came to England. Ley was already in England at that time, and there is no doubt that Mrs. Brook and Ley lived together at various addresses after she, Mrs. Brook, came to London. Mrs. Brook's daughter married a man named Barron, and she lived with her husband, Mr. Barron, at No. 3 Homefield Road in Wimbledon in a flat. At the end of May or early in June, 1946, that is to say last year, Mrs. Brook's daughter, Mrs. Barron, went into hospital for

Ley and Smith.

an operation, and while she was there Mrs. Brook took over her flat, and occupied it.

Now among other people who were living at No. 3 Homefield Road at this time was this man Mudie. At that time there were two other men also living in the house, but perhaps fortunately for them they do not enter into this story in any great detail. Mudie at that time was employed as a barman at a public house called "The Dog and Fox," at Wimbledon, that is before he went to the Reigate Hill Hotel. According to Mrs. Brook (and she is supported in this by her landlady, Mrs. Evans), she met Mudie on one occasion and one occasion only. She met him one day on the stairs. She was introduced to him for a moment, by Mrs. Evans, and she passed the time of day. Mudie appears, so far as anybody knows, to have been a perfectly harmless and decent individual, but for some reason Ley got it into his head that he was engaged in an intrigue with Mrs. Brook. There appears to be no foundation whatsoever for any such suspicion, but reason apparently did not operate with Ley where Mrs. Brook was concerned. I say that because he actually accused her of being her son-in-law's mistress, and he made similar accusations about a person named Romer who was a person lodging in 3 Homefield Road at this time.

It appears that suspicion so preyed upon his mind that on 12th June he actually drove down to Wimbledon in the middle of the night, the early hours of the morning, arriving at half-past two, and he removed Mrs. Brook from the house, and took her to London. His suspicions from being at first quite indiscriminate with regard to Mrs. Brook focussed upon this unfortunate man Mudie. That is evidenced, I think you will feel, by the fact that Ley actually when he was at 3 Homefield Road, in the middle of July having, as I have already told you, removed Mrs. Brook from the house in the previous month, saw Mrs. Evans, the landlady, said he had found that Mudie had been in the flat with Mrs. Brook, and he added some such phrase as "Poor old thing, she can't keep the pace," obviously suggesting that Mudie and Mrs. Brook were having an intrigue together at 3 Homefield Road.

By this time the idea of the association between Mrs. Brook and Mudie was becoming an obsession with this man. There was an incident which occurred in June which you may think shows to what extent this is true and to what lengths even as early as that date this obsession was leading this man. Ley, among other things, is a director of a company called Connaught Properties, Limited. Mrs. Brook was a co-director, and her signature was required when cheques had to be drawn on the company's account. In the middle of June three cheques were required by the company, Ley says

8

Opening Speech for the Crown.

Mr. Hawke

they were for the payment of salaries, and they required Mrs. Brook's signature. On 19th June, which is the week after Ley had routed Mrs. Brook out of 3 Homefield Road at half-past two in the morning and brought her back to London, and when in fact he must have known perfectly well not only that she was in London, but also exactly where she was, so the prosecution invite you to infer, he sent these three cheques which required Mrs. Brook's signature with a covering letter, to, of all people, Mr. Mudie. The covering letter is quite a short one, but I think you may be interested to hear it. It reads as follows:

"Jack Mudie, Esq., 3 Homefield Road, Wimbledon, S.W.19. 19th June, 1946. Dear Sir, Mrs. Brook telephoned last evening that she was going to the country about some arrangements in regard to the convalescence of her daughter who is still in hospital, and as we want some cheques signed and returned to us not later than Friday next, we asked for her instructions. She directed us to send the cheques to her in your care, with the request, that if she did not reach Homefield Road by 4 p.m. on Thursday, to ask you to be good enough to seal up the enclosed addressed envelope and post it to her flat at 5 Beaufort Gardens, London, S.W.7, so we can send up on Friday morning and obtain them. We enclose stamped envelope addressed to her, and marked as she directed 'Strictly Private,' her instructions being that we were not to open the envelope on any account until her return on Friday morning."

Members of the jury, it is sometimes dangerous to speculate as to what objects prompt otherwise seemingly harmless performances, but why this man, knowing as one would imagine, and certainly knowing according to what Mrs. Brook says, where she was—she was in fact in a flat in West Cromwell Road, London—should go through this extraordinary performance of sending these three cheques to her at Wimbledon is a speculation of some difficulty. And the only assignable object you may think of this action of his was that if Mrs. Brook had by any chance signed the cheques, it would show that she was visiting and associating with Mudie either in Wimbledon or in London behind Ley's back. This plan, if it was such, misfired completely, because Mudie, who, one imagines, was completely mystified by the whole business, very properly took these cheques to Mr. Barron, who was the father of Mrs. Brook's daughter's husband, and Mr. Barron in turn took the cheques to the offices of the Connaught Properties and got a receipt for them.

9

Ley and Smith.

Mr. Hawke

There is an interesting sequel to this extraordinary performance, because it did bring Ley for the first time so far as any evidence is available into direct contact with this man Mudie, whom he appeared to be suspecting so strongly at this time, because not having received the cheques back he first of all caused his solicitors to write to Mudie demanding their return, and two letters from these solicitors were found in Mudie's room at the Reigate Hill Hotel after his death; and secondly, when there was no answer to these letters he decided to go down to Reigate himself. According to his own statement, this was on 7th August, or about that date. He went down to the Reigate Hill Hotel. He saw Mudie. Mudie told him what he had done with the cheques. He said he had handed them back to Mr. Barron. Ley then took Mudie all the way over to Wimbledon to see Mr. Barron and verify this story. Mr. Barron did verify it and Ley pronounced himself perfectly satisfied.

Members of the jury, I have indicated to you, and it is a matter entirely for you, what the object of that queer business may have been. You may think that some support for that theory is furnished by a later observation which Ley made to Mr. Barron, when he said that he had sent the cheques to Mr. Mudie as a bit of private detective work of his own. I have, I hope rightly, related that incident at some little length, for it may be relevant you may think for two reasons. In the first place it shows what Ley's state of mind towards Mudie was as early as the midsummer of 1946, last year, and in the second place you may think it shows to what lengths even as early as that this obsession of his was taking him. Ley has said that this occasion when he went to the Reigate Hill Hotel and saw Mudie is the last time, and the only time that he saw him.

That is the whole question, and I think now we come to the last act, the last act, incidentally, which ended in the finding of Mudie's dead body. In the late autumn or the early winter of last year Ley called at a hotel in Woburn Place, called the Royal Hotel. He used to be a frequent visitor at that hotel, and he knew the hall porter, a man called Minden, very well. He saw Minden on this occasion and asked him if he knew anybody who had a car who could keep his mouth shut and look after himself. If he did, said Ley, then that man, whoever be might be, could earn a year's salary in a few weeks. The result of that conversation was that Minden got in touch with Buckingham. Buckingham has a business, part of which consists in the letting out on hire of a Wolseley car. As a result of Minden getting into touch with Buckingham, Buckingham rang up Ley, and he then met Ley by

Opening Speech for the Crown.

appointment at the Royal Hotel in Woburn Place that evening.
Ley introduced himself as a retired solicitor. He told Buckingham
that he had come into contact with a lady who was being blackmailed, and that he would introduce him to a man who would
tell him all about the details of this matter. He asked Buckingham
to meet him the next evening, and the next evening he introduced Buckingham to Smith, and left the two of them together.
They went to a café, and while they were eating there Smith
repeated to Buckingham the story which Ley had told him the
previous night of this woman being blackmailed. He also added
that she was a young woman in Wimbledon. He improved on the
story by saying that this young woman's mother was also being
blackmailed, that the person who was blackmailing them was a
person who had seduced both of them, and therefore was in the
position to extract money from them on threats of exposure. He
told Buckingham that Ley as a solicitor wished to try and deal
with this blackmailer.

Following upon that interview there was a further meeting at
the hotel some days later. Ley and Smith were both present on
that occasion. Ley confirmed the story that Smith had told, and
he added that he had actually once had to go to Wimbledon and
collect the mother who was being blackmailed, the elder of the two
women, and take her away to the Cromwell Road flat. I indicated
a little while ago that you might like to find corroboration of any
evidence that Buckingham may have to give. You may think that
corroboration of some force is to be found in those words that
Buckingham says Ley spoke to him about him having to go to
Wimbledon and collect the elderly lady and bring her to London,
and put her in the Cromwell Road flat. I say that because, so far
as Ley is concerned, I am not in a position to indicate, nor is it any
province of mine to do so, what he may say in the future. I can
only tell you what he has said up to date, and Ley up to date has
said there is not a word of truth in this story from Buckingham
or Smith. He says that he never met Buckingham at the Royal
Hotel. He says that he knew Buckingham merely as the owner of
a car which he let out for hire. He says that he knew Smith
simply as the foreman who was engaged upon the work at 5
Beaufort Gardens. You will know when you have heard the
evidence that he did go down to Wimbledon, and I have told you
in what circumstances, and that after that Mrs. Brook did stay
in the Cromwell Road, and you may like to ask yourselves at some
later stage how on earth Buckingham could have known that unless
one person and one person only had told him so. This part of the
story, of course, as it must of necessity, depends to a great extent

Ley and Smith.

upon the evidence and upon the word of this man Buckingham. Ley denies it from beginning to end, or has done so up to now.

It is interesting, perhaps, to know what Smith says about it. Smith has made a long statement in this matter. It is Exhibit 20, and no doubt it will be read to you at the proper time. I do not propose to trouble you with it except by reading small extracts from it unless my learned friends desire otherwise. The effect of it as regards this part of this story is this. Smith has said that Ley became very friendly with him while he was working on this work at Beaufort Gardens, and that they had many meetings of a social kind. They had dinner together on several occasions, and during their conversations he says that Ley confided in him about this blackmail, and the desire to get the blackmailer to London. Eventually, says Smith, Ley told him that he had found a man who might be able to bring this about, and in this way Smith, according to his own version of this matter, became introduced to Buckingham by Ley at the Royal Hotel. So far as Smith is concerned, he agrees, as I have I think indicated to you before, that every thing that Buckingham says occurred in the early stages of this matter did occur.

Members of the jury, I think I have digressed a little. I left these three discussing this blackmail affair at the Royal Hotel. There were several further meetings between Buckingham and Ley and Smith. It is unnecessary for me to give the details of what occurred at them. You will hear them. It is impossible for me to give you the dates upon which they occurred, but they were occurring as October passed and as November went on its way. In the course of those conversations Ley said that he had discovered that this man, the blackmailer as he said, was working at the Reigate Hill Hotel, and the three of them then proceeded to discuss ways and means of getting this man to London. The result of these discussions was that finally a scheme was decided upon, a scheme which culminated in No. 5 Beaufort Gardens on the night of 28th November, and the scheme was this. There was to be a cocktail party at Beaufort Gardens, and of course at the cocktail party the services of a barman would be useful. Consequently Mudie was to be invited to attend this party in that capacity. In order to achieve this of course the services of other people were required. The two people whose services were engaged, the two who were added to the team, were young Buckingham and a woman called Mrs. Bruce, who is a friend of Buckingham senior, and who is the wife of a 'bus driver, a cook-housekeeper. Neither young Buckingham nor Mrs. Bruce were told the whole story. All they knew was that it was necessary

Opening Speech for the Crown.

that Mudie should be got to London and taken to Beaufort Gardens. Mrs. Bruce was to be a lady of means who would actually invite Mudie to come along and act as barman at this cocktail party in Kensington.

The greatest possible pains were taken to see that this did not misfire. Mrs. Bruce made two journeys to Reigate. Once she went with Mr. Buckingham senior alone, and once she went with the two Buckinghams. She had a good look at Mudie. She eventually got acquainted with him, and finally, after that had been achieved, and the trap had been nicely baited, Thursday, 28th November, was fixed for the date of the cocktail party. You will hear that all this time Ley was being informed about the progress of events, and his final instructions were, Thursday the 28th having been fixed, when he learned that the fish had been hooked, that he was to be landed at No. 5 Beaufort Gardens, and there he was to be tied up, forced to sign a confession, and given money and got out of the country. Those were his final instructions to Buckingham and to Smith, and every word of this is corroborated by Smith.

I think it is convenient here, and I think it may be as well to have it in your minds, to refer you to one part of Smith's statement, because it is peculiarly relevant to this part of this story which I am endeavouring to unfold to you now. It is not evidence against Ley as to what occurs in this statement, but it is evidence against Smith, and I am bound to draw your attention to it as evidence against him. I had told you that Thursday, 28th November, had been fixed. This bogus cocktail party was ready as a bait for Mudie. Mrs. Bruce had got to know him, and everything was ready. This is what Smith says: "I told Ley the following morning the full details that Lil . . ."—that is Mrs. Bruce— ". . . had arranged to pick up Mudie outside the Reigate Hill Hotel at half-past six. Buckingham and I discussed that Lil should be given a key to the back door of 5 Beaufort Gardens, and that she should come in with Mudie, Buckingham and I waiting inside the door to tie him up. This was not what Mr. Ley wanted. He really wanted us to tie Mudie up on the way so that he would not be able to create when he arrived at the house. On Thursday, the 28th, in preparation for Mudie, I purchased a clothes line from Farmer Brothers, Montpelier Street, next to the 'Crown and Sceptre,' for 9d. or 1s. It had two rings on it." That was found on the body, members of the jury. I did not bother you with that when giving details about the body, but that was in fact so. "The assistants there know me very well as I often go in to buy stuff for the job where I worked. I told

Ley and Smith.

Buckingham that I bought this and that I would have a rag handy in the house."

So that is Smith's version, and, as he says in this statement of his, the necessary apparatus for tying up this wretched man was purchased by him on the morning of 28th November, in the shape of this rope. You will also hear—I have not read it to you— that in his statement he refers to the necessary apparatus for gagging the man. He says at the end of his statement that the piece of cloth which had been found round the dead man's neck was actually a piece which he got from Beaufort Gardens and had given to Buckingham, and that Buckingham had used it for the purpose of gagging Mudie when he arrived.

Members of the jury, there appeared to be only one more thing to do to get everything ready, and that was to provide some transport. You see, Mrs. Bruce was to bring Mudie to London. She was to be driven by young Buckingham, because Mudie knew them by this time as a lady with a motor car and her chauffeur. Mrs. Bruce had been down to Reigate twice, and she had got to know Mudie and she had young Buckingham with her, and she was going down to Reigate again to fetch Mudie, but of course it was necessary that Smith and Buckingham should be on hand to see that everything went all right; and so another car was wanted. This was arranged, as you will hear, during the few days which preceded 28th November. Some days before that Thursday—and I cannot tell you the exact date—Ley rang up a firm which hires out motor cars, called Howard's Car Hire Service, in Beauchamp Place, just round the corner. He spoke to Miss Brittain, the receptionist, and he asked if she had got any cars which they would hire for a person to drive himself. He said he wanted the car for a friend of his called Smith for whom he could vouch. He arranged that Smith his friend should call on the following day at this firm's premises. Smith did so, as you will hear. He looked at a car, and he asked that the manager, Mr. Normanton, should go round to see him, Mr. Normanton being out at that time. He went there twice to Beaufort Gardens, and the second time he saw Ley and Smith together, and Smith said that he had decided that he was not going to take the car which he had already seen. But as you will hear, a day or two later Mr. Normanton found he had got an 8 h.p. Ford. He informed Smith accordingly, Smith said that he thought the car would suit him, and on Monday, 25th November, he hired that Ford car for a week. He told Normanton that he wanted to use it mostly for driving round London, but that on Thursday, 28th November, he might be going for quite a long journey. That car had a registration number of course. The

14

Opening Speech for the Crown.

index letters were "F G P" and the number was 101, and those figures 101 I would most respectfully ask you to bear in mind, because they become, you may think, important in connexion with a matter which I must introduce to you at a later stage.

So you see, by 28th November, all was ready. The ground had been reconnoitred, the actors knew their parts, one of them, incidentally, Buckingham, you will hear had been paid £10 on account of salary at this time, the properties had been got ready, the rug, the rope and the gag, and of course the victim was waiting at the other end. On the evening of 28th November two cars left London, one of them the Wolseley, driven by Buckingham, and the other one the Ford, driven by Smith, and he had young Buckingham as his passenger. They stopped at Putney and picked Mrs. Bruce up, and so they went down to Reigate. Just before they got into Reigate the two Buckinghams changed places. Young Buckingham took over the Wolseley. At the Reigate Hill Hotel, Mudie, by appointment, was waiting in the forecourt of the hotel. He stepped into the Wolseley, and he was driven back to London on what was his last journey.

Members of the jury, there is no need for me to give you any details of that return to London. All I need tell you is that Smith and Buckingham arrived at Beaufort Gardens first. They entered by the front door, of which Smith had the key. Ley was waiting for them. The time was about a quarter to seven. Smith and Buckingham then repaired to the basement, and it is into the basement that the back door, the door at which Mudie was due to be deposited, opened, and there in the basement Smith pointed out to Buckingham the positions that they were to take up. Buckingham was to take up his stand just inside the back door in a room to the left of the back door which formed, of course, a very convenient place for anybody to hide. Smith was to take up his position in a recess which was a yard or two farther along the passage where the wall turns back. Smith was to get himself behind there. That having been arranged, Smith went upstairs, collected the rug, came down, and handed it to Buckingham. They took up their positions and they waited. The back door opened and Mudie stepped in.

I do not think that I can do better than to give you Smith's own words as to what happened then. I will begin with a moment or two just before Mudie stepped into the back entrance with Buckingham and Smith waiting for him : "We took up our positions. Buckingham was to throw the rug over Mudie's head when he entered the door. I was then going to help him to tie him up. He had the rug and I had the rope. Mr. Ley was standing on the

Ley and Smith.

stairs leading to his flat, and he called me and said: 'Will you hang on a little while as my end has slipped up.' By this I took it he wanted me to hang on after Mudie had been tied up, as he said: 'There is no need for Buckingham to stay. Let him push off.' He then handed me an envelope, saying, 'Put this in your pocket; I have got Buckingham's here.' I knew the envelope contained the money. I told Buckingham that Ley wanted me to hold on as his people hadn't turned up. I told him that I did not want to as I had made arrangements with Buckingham to go out and have a drink afterwards. I heard the car pull up at the back door, and we again took up our positions. The door was opened and I heard Lil say what we had already arranged she should say: 'Excuse me, I want to speak to John,' meaning the younger Buckingham. I saw Mudie come past the angle where I was standing and the back door closed. I put my arms round Mudie's chest, holding his arms down, standing in front of him whilst Buckingham came up behind and threw the rug over him. He then held his arms down with the rug over his head whilst I tied Mudie's ankles and then wound the rope round his body, taking in his left arm but leaving out the right, holding it tight over the top of the rug. I tied the rope in the middle of his back, taking it down to his ankles again and then back. The reason why I left out his right arm was purely incidental because it was raised level with the back of his head and Buckingham was holding it. If I remember rightly, his left hand was in his overcoat pocket. Buckingham helped him along the passage by jumping him, and at the door of the room we were going to take him into, he fell forward, with Buckingham on top of him. Buckingham picked him up and helped him into the room and sat him down on a swivel chair which was beside the desk where Ley had told us to put him. Buckingham asked me if I had got a gag, and I hunted round and went into the front room where I found a piece of cloth which I knew was a french polisher's rag, hard in pieces from the polish, and gave it to Buckingham. He pulled the rug back from Mudie's face and tied the gag round his mouth. Both of us went out of the room, and Ley came down the stairs and stood at the bottom where we met him. Ley handed an envelope to Buckingham. He shook his hand and said: 'Don't contact me or telephone me for some time.' I then let Buckingham out of the back door, and as Ley had asked me to stop behind, I went and stood with him in the passage."

So you see, members of the jury, that agrees (with one important exception) word for word with what Buckingham says happened in that flat that night. The important exception is that Buckingham

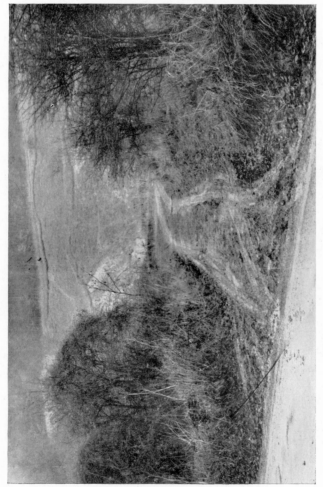

The Chalk Pit, Woldingham, Surrey, from the road.   Photograph No. 1 of photographic exhibits

Opening Speech for the Crown.

Mr. Hawke

says that while he was there Mudie did not fall down, and he was not gagged. Smith, on the other hand, as I have read to you, says he did fall, and he was gagged. It may be you will think, and it is a matter for you of course, that Smith's is the more probable version. At all events, according to both of them, there was Mudie at this time trussed and helpless and deposited in this chair in the room at the end of the passage. Smith and Buckingham—this is the evidence you will hear from Buckingham—their work having been accomplished, stepped into the passage. Ley was standing on the basement stairs. He handed Buckingham a package with the words, "Thanks very much. Don't contact me again." Smith opened the back door, and Buckingham passed out into the alley behind that place.

There really Buckingham passes out of this story, but for the sake of tidiness I might finish with him and leave him. He made his way to "The Crown and Sceptre," the public house opposite, where his son and Mrs. Bruce were waiting for him. They went from there to another public house. They finally went to Putney, and finished the evening at Mrs. Bruce's flat at midnight. In the car, Buckingham says, on the way from one public house to another, he felt in his pocket for the package and found that it contained £1 notes. That is the package which had been given him by Ley at the bottom of the stairs. He gave £30 to Mrs. Bruce, £10 to his wife, £25 to his son, kept £15 for running expenses, and paid the rest into his bank. He says he never saw Ley again, and it may be that that is perfectly true, but he did see Smith. He saw Smith on 1st December at "The Crown and Sceptre," when Smith informed him that Ley was very pleased with the way things had gone, and said that Mudie had been given money and gone out of the country.

I think it only remains to say that on 14th December, that is to say, about a fortnight later, Mrs. Bruce saw in the paper an account of the finding of this man's body in the chalk pit. She communicated with Buckingham at once, and later that day they went round to Scotland Yard. Members of the jury, there I leave Buckingham, and you may think nothing becomes him so much as his leaving, and just return to No. 5 Beaufort Gardens, because you will remember that in the narrative that this evidence supports, we left Smith and Ley, as far as any evidence goes, alone in that flat with this man tied up and gagged and placed in this chair in the room at the end of the passage. As to what happened afterwards, so far as there is the word of only one of them, it is right that I should draw your attention to that. It is again what Smith says, and it is the last matter I shall trouble you with in

B   17

Ley and Smith.

connexion with this. He says—and you will remember that I left them alone in this flat together—"Ley asked if we had any difficulty in picking Mudie up, and I told him that everything had gone off all right; I said that I thought our plan was the best in not tying Mudie up whilst we were in the car. Ley and I stood talking for about ten minutes, during which time neither of us went in to see how Mudie was. I could see from Ley's attitude that he was expecting someone to call. I heard somebody coming up the stairs to the front door, and Ley said: 'All right, you can go now.' I went out by way of the basement door at the front, and when I got to the top of the stairs I could not see anyone. I heard the front door close, and I came to the conclusion that someone had gone into the house, although I did not see anybody or hear any voices. My car was at the front of the house, and I got in and drove along to Brompton Road. I could not see Buckingham's car outside so I did not stop at 'The Crown and Sceptre.'"

I do not think I need trouble you with any more of that, and I omit any further reference to this statement, as I think I should do in fairness to the other defendant, against whom it cannot possibly or conceivably be evidence. Smith says that the next day he went down to Leicester, and later he was told that Mudie had been dropped at Wimbledon. Members of the jury, we know that he had not. He had been dropped at a chalk pit in Surrey, 20 miles odd from London and 12 miles from Reigate, and he was dead by strangulation when he was found there, and death, in the opinion of the pathologist who examined him, took place approximately 48 hours before the finding of his body on the night of 30th November.

It may be said, and it can properly be said, that Smith's statement is a document conspicuous for its frankness up to a point. The question is: Does it contain the whole of the truth? He admits, as Buckingham does, being a party to a plot whereby a man was kidnapped—I think it is a fair word to use—trussed and gagged, but clearly implicit you may think in his version of the facts is the suggestion that no more was suggested or contemplated than just to tie this man up and put him in a chair and that, he says, he was to be induced, whilst he was helpless, to sign a confession of some kind, and then be paid off.

As I said before, we know that that was not so. The evidence will prove it, and there can be no question about it. The case for the prosecution, as I have indicated to you—and it is a case which, of course, the prosecution must prove; no burden whatever lies upon the accused person, there is no need for me to tell you that—

Opening Speech for the Crown.

Mr. Hawke

is that Ley's jealousy prompted this conspiracy, a conspiracy which was to end as it did, according to the evidence, with the victim of that plot helpless in his hands. What was the purpose of it? Was it just to frighten him into signing some confession, or was it contemplated—and this may be a most important question, which I venture to submit very humbly, members of the jury—that such treatment was to be meted out to this man as might result in serious bodily injury being done to him, because Buckingham, you see, if he is telling the truth, left Mudie trussed, gagged and help-less in this chair. He left Ley and Smith at that time you may think alone with this man in the position that he was. Can it be proved that anything happened after Buckingham had passed out of the back door, and out of this affair? This man was found dead two days later strangled 20 odd miles from London, and some person or some cause had pulled that rope tight round his neck so that he died of strangulation, and someone, some person, conveyed him from London to Woldingham and left him in the pit.

Now if some violence as might cause serious bodily harm was contemplated to this man when he got to 5 Beaufort Gardens, it would be necessary, you may think, to make sure that no evidence of such an event should remain. If that is right, it would be neces-sary of course to have a plan ready to ensure that no such evidence was available at the spot where this man had been dealt with, and to remove any traces of the fact that any bodily injury such as might be contemplated had occurred in any place which either of these two had anything to do with.

There is evidence of such a plan, and it is independent evidence. It is evidence of a very interesting kind, you may think, which, if it is accurate, may throw some light upon the question. It will be purely a matter for you, and I speak with respect before my lord and under his direction, but it may throw some light upon what was contemplated in that house that night. I want to carry you back one evening only, from 28th November to the 27th, Wednesday evening. On that evening, between half-past four and twenty minutes to five, two landscape gardeners, one called Smith and the other called Tamplin, were wheeling their bicycles along the road which abuts and adjoins the chalk pit, and as they passed the entrance to the pit they saw a man standing on the hill up the side of it, looking round. This man apparently saw them, and apparently saw that they were looking at him, because he suddenly broke into a run. He ran down the slope, he ran down to a car which was behind some bushes at the edge of the road near the entrance to the pit. He got into the car and he made three or four efforts to reverse out of the pit. He finally succeeded and got to the road, and he drove

Ley and Smith.

off past Smith and Tamplin as they stood leaning on their bicycles. Well, members of the jury, it was getting dusk at this time. It was a November evening. Obviously identification of an individual at such a time and in such circumstances would be most unsatisfactory as a proof of that individual's identity. It is fair that I should say at once that Smith and Tamplin were called upon to attend an identification parade, which was held at Brixton Prison on 13th January, to see if they could pick out the man they had seen on the edge of the chalk pit on 27th November, and Smith, this landscape gardener, picked out somebody altogether different. Tamplin did pick out this Smith here as the man he had seen, but he said he only recognized him by the back of his head. Members of the jury, the Crown would ask you to attach absolutely no importance whatever to any personal identification of an individual in any such circumstances.

If it stopped there I should not have troubled you with this evidence, but it does not stop there; indeed, you may think very far from it. Whatever Smith or Tamplin may disagree about as to the appearance of this man whom they saw, they agree about one thing, and that is the number of the car that he drove. They did not get the index letters of it, but they got the number, and the number was 101. You will remember that I did indicate to you that these numbers 101 might have some important bearing upon this case. True that these two men cannot tell you what the index letters of the car which drove away from the pit that evening were, but you know Smith had hired a Ford car on 25th November, the Monday, with the index letters FGP and the number 101. Smith assisted, we have got his own word for it, in this violent assault upon Mudie in London on 28th November, the Thursday. Mudie's body was found in the chalk pit on Saturday, 30th November. Somebody with a car with the number 101 was reconnoitring that chalk pit on Wednesday, the 27th. Members of the jury, sometimes it has been said that facts by undesigned coincidence are capable of proving a proposition with the certainty of mathematics. Is it just a coincidence that the car which stood at the entrance of that chalk pit bore the same number as the car which Smith had been using all the week, and which he returned, as you will hear, to the person who hired it to him, on 1st December? If that man was Smith, or if it was Smith's car, why was that chalk pit being reconnoitred on the afternoon not after but before the date on which Mudie was to be brought to London according to this plot? Somebody—if you think this was the car, and you may have no doubt about it—was reconnoitring that place, a place to which this man was eventually conveyed, and

Opening Speech for the Crown.

where he was found dead from strangulation on 30th November, the Saturday. You will remember what Smith says in his statement, that he had been told that Mudie had been dropped at Wimbledon. I venture to say now that you will have to consider whether that statement of Smith's tells you the whole truth about this matter.

I have only to add this, members of the jury, and then I will lay the evidence before you with the assistance of my learned friend. If bodily violence was intended upon Mudie, if Ley and Smith (and it may have been other people were in that house), but if Ley and Smith or either of them knowingly inflicted upon him bodily injury such as was calculated to cause him grievous bodily harm or death, then, subject to my lord's direction to you upon the law, if that is proved against them or either of them, the person against whom it is proved is guilty of murder.

Evidence for the Prosecution.

KENNETH ALFRED BLANDFORD, sworn, examined by Mr. ELAM— I am a detective-constable of the Surrey Joint Police Force. On 1st December, 1945, I went to a chalk pit in Slines Oak Road, Woldingham, Surrey, and took two photographs of the chalk pit. Later on the same day I went to Oxted Mortuary and took two more photographs of a body of a man. Exhibit 8 is a book containing copies of the four photographs I took. I am accustomed to taking photographs, and the untouched negatives are in my possession. The first photograph in the book shows the entrance to the chalk pit taken from the road. The second photograph shows part of the chalk pit a bit higher up from the road. Before I had actually taken that photograph I had seen a body lying there. The body was removed before I took that second photograph. I myself hung up the white sheet which can be seen on the right of the second photograph. That was exactly over the spot where the body had been lying. The third photograph is a photograph I took at the mortuary. A police-officer, Shoobridge, was there and pointed the body out to me. The third photograph shows the head and shoulders of that body with a rope and some rag. The fourth and last photograph in the book shows the head and neck of that body with marks on the neck.

Cross-examined by Mr. CURTIS BENNETT—Just take the first photograph. The path in the foreground we have seen. There is

Ley and Smith.

Kenneth A. Blandford

a considerable gap between the foreground and the back, that is the hollow of the chalk pit?—Yes.

The bit that is pale in colour at the back is extremely steep, is it not?—Yes.

The climb up?—Yes.

If the members of the jury will look at the white sheet on the second picture and now turn back to the first picture where the entrance to the chalk pit is shown, they will see, will they not, that that part on the first picture is away to the left?—Yes, it is roughly level with the edge of the picture.

To the left hand of the picture behind the bushes?—Yes.

We can see it a little bit from the picture also, that if you are coming up from the road to the trench or to the white sheet it is a very steep grassy slope, is it not?—It is fairly steep; you can see the actual incline in the second photograph.

It is actually steeper than it looks, is it not? It is a very steep grassy climb?—I would not say very steep.

Did you walk up?—Yes, I did.

It is quite plain that from the entrance to the chalk pit from the road in picture No. 1 you could not see the trench or the white flag or sheet, or anybody in the trench, could you?—No.

If the jury would look at picture 2. You could see the road there right down at the bottom near the trees?—Yes, that is right.

Where the car is?—Lower down than the car.

The car is not on the road, my lord. (To witness) About how far would you say it was from the road to where the flag is on the second photograph?—Well, I should estimate it roughtly at 100 yards.

And all uphill?—Yes, all uphill. That is a pure estimate, of course.

By the LORD CHIEF JUSTICE—Is this a frequented road, or is it rather remote and out in the country?—It is well out in the country.

Is there much traffic along this road?—I cannot say.

ADAM M'HARDY, sworn, examined by Mr. ELAM—I am a police-constable, No. 271, "B" Division, and on 3rd January, 1947, I went to 5 Beaufort Gardens and took some measurements. I produce Exhibit No. 1 as a plan and copies of the measurements I took. I am accustomed to the preparation of such plans and it is drawn to scale. On the right of the plan is shown the ground floor of 5 Beaufort Gardens.

Standing on the footway, seen at the bottom of the plan, can

Evidence for Prosecution.

you go into No. 5 Beaufort Gardens either up the steps in the porch and in the front door or in through the area gate, down the steps of the area, and in through the basement?—Yes.

I am going to the top left of the plan, the other side. Is that Brompton Place, and can you also get into 5 Beaufort Gardens from Brompton Place?—Yes.

Under the "mp" of Brompton Road is there what I may call the back door?—Yes.

By the LORD CHIEF JUSTICE—Beaufort Gardens itself is a cul-de-sac, is it?—Yes.

Examination continued—Is Brompton Place?—Yes, it is also a cul-de-sac.

Over that back door there is something written to identify it. What do you see written there?—"Old Air Raid Shelter."

Coming in through the back door do you go down three steps? —Yes.

As you are going in on the left is there a small room and a door-way on the immediate left as you come in?—Yes.

A little further on, on the right as you come in, is there, so to speak, an angle formed by the wall and a door sticking out? —Yes, the passage bends.

Going further along that passage, as if you had come in through the back door, is there a room marked "Room Partly Furnished" on the left hand side?—Yes.

The LORD CHIEF JUSTICE—I do not think there is any harm in my asking this question. It will be proved in due course. Just indicate what room it is we are concerned with.

Mr. ELAM—Yes, my lord, *that* room, and we are also concerned with the first door-way on the left of the back door as you come in. (Indicating.)

The LORD CHIEF JUSTICE—The door of the room marked "Containing Telephone"?

Mr. ELAM—Yes.

Examination continued—What sort of locks and how many are there on the back door?—There are two locks. On the back door in Brompton Place there is a Yale lock and also a mortise.

Ley and Smith.

Adam M'Hardy

Cross-examined by Mr. CURTIS BENNETT—With regard to that back door, the Yale lock is the usual type of lock and the usual Yale key operates it?—Yes.

The mortise lock is the old-fashioned lock, a permanent lock sunk in the door?—Yes.

Which can be opened either by a key from inside or outside?—Yes.

If you had a key for this Yale lock, and not for the mortise lock, and the mortise lock was shut, you could not get in?—No.

The passage-way leading from the back door to the recess is a stone floor passage-way, is it not?—Yes.

In the room partly furnished, the one with which we are dealing, behind the door on the left hand side there is a big table or desk, is there not?—Well, when I went there all the furniture that was in the room seemed to me to be in the centre of the room.

Was there a big desk table there?—It was more or less covered. There was what might have been either a desk or a table.

Was there also a swivel chair?—I did not see it.

You did not look for it?—No, I did not specially look for it.

From the other end going down the plan and across the recess, if you want to go out of the area door you can go through a room into the kitchen, out in the area and up steps, and then you are on the ground floor?—Yes, at the pavement level.

WALTER TOM COOMBS, sworn, examined by Mr. ELAM—Do you live at Woldingham, in Surrey?—Yes.

On 30th November last in the afternoon were you going home? —Yes.

Do you know a chalk pit off Slines Oak Road?—I do.

Did you go near or through that?—Yes, at about 4 o'clock.

Was your attention attracted to anything in the pit?—Not in the pit, by the side of the pit. I saw what I thought to be the body of a man in a trench.

Did you go up to it?—I did not go close.

So it follows that you did not touch it?—No.

Did you go home and call your father?—Yes, I did.

Did you go back to the same place?—We both went back together.

Was the body then touched?—No.

But you were satisfied that it was a body?—Yes.

Were the police informed?—Yes.

Is there much habitation near this chalk pit, houses and that sort of thing?—No, not in the vicinity of the chalk pit.

Evidence for Prosecution.

Walter T. Coombs

Do you get a lot of traffic along Slines Oak Road, do you know?
—A moderate amount, I think.

By the LORD CHIEF JUSTICE—Where does that road lead from
and to?—From the main Croydon-Westerham Road to Woldingham village.

Cross-examined by Sir WALTER MONCKTON—When you came
back again with your father did one or other of you then touch the
body?—My father raised one of the trouser legs.

In order to see what it was?—In order to see the flesh.

Otherwise you did not either of you interfere with the body at
all?—No, sir.

CYRIL VICTOR HEARN, sworn, examined by Mr. HAWKE—I am
an officer in the Surrey Joint Police Force, and on 30th November,
1946, I went with the two Coombs to the chalk pit, arriving there
at about 4.45 p.m.

Did you find a body lying in the trench?—I did.

Just look at the photograph (handed). Is the white mark there
on the right (indicating) the place where the body was found?—
That is correct.

You walked up from the path, did you?—Yes, from the left of
the photograph.

How far up is it?—Not more than 200 yards from the road.

How was the body lying?—It was lying on its right side.

Was it on the surface of the ground?—It was in the trench
with the feet protruding over the edge.

What depth was this trench?—Roughly about 18 inches; it was
a shallow trench.

What clothes had this man got on?—He had a blue chalk-stripe
demob. suit on.

He had an overcoat on?—Yes. The overcoat was twisted
inside out and pulled up over the man's head.

Did you see any rope?—Yes. The rope was wound twice outside the overcoat round the man's head.

Was it tied or loose?—It was tied with two loose half-hitches,
not very tightly.

Was it round his body?—No. One end of the rope went under
his body, and the shorter end came from his neck round to his
left forearm and tied with another half-hitch. This end of the
rope was not longer than six inches.

Did you untie any of it?—Yes. I untied the forearm first round
the wrist.

Ley and Smith.

You untied that knot?—Yes.

Then did you untie the other end?—I untied the rope from round the man's neck, the two half-hitches.

You were then able to ease off the overcoat?—Yes, and I did so.

When you got the overcoat off, did you notice anything round his neck?—Yes, the rope continued round his neck and there was also a piece of rag there.

Was it a piece of rag like that? (Exhibit 13 handed to witness)—That is the rag, sir.

Does it smell of polish?—Yes.

Did you smell it?—Yes, it smelt of varnish.

Just look at Exhibit 12. (Handed to witness.) Is that like the rope that was round the body?—Yes; it was wet at the time.

I take it that when you found the rope round the neck and this rag, they were not tied tightly then?—No, they were very loose.

Was the ground wet?—Yes, it had been raining heavily.

I suppose that would make it muddy, would it not?—Yes, very muddy.

You found a card in the man's pocket, did you not, with the name "Mudie" on it, and you informed your superior officers?—I did.

Mr. HAWKE—The next witness is Mr. Mudie. He was conditionally bound over. May his deposition be read, my lord?

The LORD CHIEF JUSTICE—Yes. Members of the jury, this is just a piece of formal evidence with regard to the identification of the body by the man's brother.

The CLERK OF THE COURT—"Joseph Grant Mudie, of 20 Nethergate, Kinghorn, Fifeshire, on his oath sayeth: I am a plumber. John McMain Mudie was my brother. He was a married man with one child. On 3rd December I went with Sergeant Shoobridge to Oxted, and there identified the dead body of my brother. (Signed) Joseph Grant Mudie."

EUPHEMIA MARY M'GILL, sworn, examined by Mr. ELAM—I am single and work at the Reigate Hill Hotel. I know a man who also worked there called Jack Mudie. He was a barman and I got quite friendly with him.

Do you remember when you last saw him alive and well at the hotel?—The last time I saw him was between 2.30 and 3 in the afternoon of 28th November.

Evidence for Prosecution.

Euphemia M. M'Gill

On the same evening at about 10 p.m. did you go up to see if he was in his bedroom?—Yes.

Was he there?—No.

Have you ever seen him again?—No.

Was the bed turned down or did it look as if anybody was going to occupy or had occupied it?—It had not been slept in.

PERCY WILLIAM GOLDSWORTHY, sworn, examined by Mr. ELAM—I am a french polisher, working for a firm called C. A. Flood. I know No. 5 Beaufort Gardens because I work there.

Did you go there about 14th November, 1946?—Yes.

How long did you stay there working?—Till mid-day, 5th December.

Will you look at that piece of rag, Exhibit 13. (Handed to witness.) Is that similar to what you used to polish with on those premises?—Yes, it is the same piece of rag.

NORMAN LESLIE HOLMES, sworn, examined by Mr. ELAM—I am a bricklayer by occupation, and in December, 1945, I was working in Connaught Place. After I had worked there I went to work at No. 5 Beaufort Gardens.

When about did you start working at Beaufort Gardens?—The first time I went to Beaufort Gardens was in December.

And after that?—After that about February.

Would you look at Exhibit No. 17. There will be evidence where this was found. It is a pickaxe; have you seen that before? (Handed to witness.)—Yes.

Where?—The first time I used it was at Connaught Place.

And then?—On the Monday after the Victory Celebrations I took it to Beaufort Gardens.

Did you use it at Beaufort Gardens?—Yes, for mixing concrete.

About when did you finish your job at Beaufort Gardens?—I finished the Friday before August Bank Holiday Monday.

When you went away from that job did you take the pickaxe with you?—No, I left it at the house.

Cross-examined by Sir WALTER MONCKTON—Is this the ordinary sort of pickaxe used in mixing concrete? You used a similar one on other jobs, I suppose?—Actually no, that was the only pick we had at that time.

But at other jobs since then, you have done jobs with another pickaxe?—Not since I left London.

By the LORD CHIEF JUSTICE—Do you generally use a pickaxe for mixing concrete?—No, sir, not generally.

27

Ley and Smith.

Francis B. O'Hagen

FRANCIS BERNARD O'HAGEN, sworn, examined by Mr. ELAM—Are you a plasterer's labourer?—Yes.

Sometime about March, 1946, did you go to work at 5 Beaufort Gardens?—Yes.

Do you recognize that pickaxe, Exhibit No. 17? (Handed to witness.)—Yes.

Did you use it at 5 Beaufort Gardens?—Yes.

Who was your foreman on the job there?—Laurie Smith.

Do you see him in Court here?—Yes.

How long did the job go on for?—I worked there for about nine months.

Did he leave before you, or you before him?—He left sometime round about Christmas last year, before me.

Cross-examined by Mr. CURTIS BENNETT—He left sometime in the month of December?—Yes.

This may be very important indeed. Did Smith usually arrive at the job about 8.30 in the morning?—Round about 8 o'clock sharp.

Would he leave round about half-past five?—Yes, well, sometimes after that.

After five?—Yes.

That would be what he would usually do, work from eight to five?—Yes.

Take your mind back to 27th November, which was a Wednesday. It is some time ago now. Are you able to remember anything about it at all?—I am not sure.

That week started on Sunday, 24th?—Yes, I worked there that week and that week-end.

During that week, as far as you can remember, was Smith on his job between eight in the morning and five in the evening?—I cannot remember.

That is a perfectly fair answer. As far as you can remember was he behaving as usual during that week?—Yes.

Although you cannot remember specifically, if Smith said to you, "I was on duty until after five on the 27th at Beaufort Gardens" you would not disagree with it?—No, I would not.

The probability is that he was?—Well, I just could not say.

Quite apart from that week, used Smith to come to his work and go away from it in a motor car?—Sometimes.

ERNEST FRANK COX, sworn, examined by Mr. ELAM—I am a detective-sergeant, Surrey Joint Police Force, stationed at Oxted.

Evidence for Prosecution.

Ernest F. Cox

About 6 p.m. on 30th November, 1946, I went to the chalk pit in Slines Oak Road.

Did you go to a shallow trench?—Yes.

Was there the body of a man lying in that trench?—Yes.

Did you find something near the trench in some bramble bushes?—A pickaxe. I identify Exhibit No. 17 (Handed to witness.) as the pickaxe.

When you saw it did it appear to have been used recently?—No.

About how far was it from the trench where the body was lying?—About three feet from the feet end of the trench.

Look at Exhibit No. 12. (Handed to witness.) Was there some rope round the neck of the body and do you produce it?—Yes. It was loosely tied round the neck of the body.

After the body had been taken out of the trench, did you find another piece of rope?—Yes, a piece about four feet in length at the feet end of the trench.

Is Exhibit No. 18 a similar rope? (Handed to witness.)—Yes, that is right.

Was that round the neck?—No, that was under the feet at the feet end of the trench. It was concealed until the body had been removed, when I could see it.

About mid-day on 1st December, 1946, did you go to a room at the Reigate Hill Hotel which you understood had been occupied by the deceased previously?—Yes.

Did you find there two letters, Exhibits Nos. 14 and 15? (Handed to witness.)—Yes, these are the two letters. I took possession of them.

The LORD CHIEF JUSTICE—These are the letters, members of the jury, written by solicitors on behalf of Connaught Properties. It will be proved that the prisoner Ley is a director of Connaught Properties, and these are letters written by a firm of solicitors acting on behalf of Connaught Properties. They were found in Mudie's room.

The CLERK OF THE COURT—Exhibit 14 is dated 25th July, 1946, and addressed to—

"Jack Mudie, Esq.,
   3 Homefield Road,
      Wimbledon, S.W.19.

Dear sir,
   On the 19th June, 1946, our clients, Connaught Properties, Limited, sent to your care a certain letter addressed to Mrs.

Ley and Smith.

Ernest F. Cox

Byron Brook, one of their directors, in an envelope enclosed, addressed and ready stamped. Our clients asked that you might be good enough, if Mrs. Brook had not then returned to your address, to seal and post it back to Mrs. Brook. According to Mrs. Brook you did not do this. Instead our clients' chairman understands from her that you telephoned that you would not do so because it might involve your signature coming into our clients' possession. If this is correct our clients cannot understand your attitude, because your signature was not asked for, nor was it necessary in order to seal and post the letter already addressed and fully stamped. We understand that Mrs. Brook has assured the chairman of the company that she has not received the envelope with the company's cheques in it. Do you intend to retain it? Our clients know that you received the communications, because, according to our instructions, without their authority you went to the trouble of seeking out the father-in-law of Mrs. Brook's daughter, Mr. Thomas Barron, and gave copies to him. It is incomprehensible to us that you should after five weeks refuse to return to our clients their cheques which were intended for Mrs. Brook, and have not been passed on to her. Unless the cheques are returned to our clients by mid-day on Monday, 28th inst., our instructions are to proceed in accordance with counsel's advice for recovery thereof. In that case we shall be glad to have from you the name of the solicitors who will accept service on your behalf in any process issued. A copy of this letter has been sent to Mrs. Brook.

Yours faithfully,"

Then the signature of the firm appears.

Mr. ELAM—Exhibit 15 is in similar terms, my lord. The one is addressed to Wimbledon and the other to Reigate.

Dr. ERIC GARDNER, sworn, examined by Mr. HAWKE—I am a qualified doctor and Consulting Pathologist at the Weybridge Hospital. At quarter-past nine on the night of 30th November, 1946, I visited the chalk pit at Woldingham along with Superintendent Roberts and other police officers. I went to the place where the body was lying in the trench, and although I did not make a detailed examination at that time I estimated the man had been dead about 48 hours.

Evidence for Prosecution.

Dr. Eric Gardner

You went again on the following morning, 1st December, at half-past nine?—I did

On that occasion did you make a more detailed examination?— I did.

At the trench, of course?—Yes.

You examined the clothing, I suppose. What sort of state was the clothing in?—Well, there were mud stains on it and mud smears.

We have heard from the police-officer who was there the previous night it was muddy and wet. I suppose those stains and those smears were consistent with contact with the wet earth?— Yes, the mud stains were consistent with contact with the wet earth when the body was stationary, and the mud smears when the body was being moved on the muddy soil.

By the LORD CHIEF JUSTICE—As if it had been dragged, you mean?—Yes. You could see that quite easily, because the pebbles in the muddy clay had imprinted the clothes where they had been in stationary contact with them, but the clothes were mud-smeared where the body had been dragged over the wet clay.

Examination continued—Pebbles which would be on the way to the trench?—The pebbles were in the clay that had been dug out from the trench. The rest of the clay on the side of the hill was the ordinary chalky stuff; where the trench had been cut the soil was yellow clay with stones in it.

Did you look at his shoes?—I did. They were perfectly clean.

All over, both the uppers and the soles?—Principally the soles. They were quite clean.

Would that be consistent with this man having made his own way to this trench?—No, it is quite inconsistent with him walking in the vicinity.

There was a rope round his neck, was there not?—Yes.

How was that?—It was tied very loosely round the neck in a half-hitch, and then the two ends that came away, I do not know if you want this now, entered a complicated knot, and one continued and encircled the body.

Was there another piece of rope round the body?—No, there was this one long piece round the body, and there was a four-foot length loose under the body.

Mr. HAWKE—I think it would be easier if the witness described how these ropes were.

Ley and Smith.

Dr. Eric Gardner

By the LORD CHIEF JUSTICE—Have you a fair enough recollection, if an officer stood up, for you to put the rope round him and show the jury how it was?—Yes, my lord.

[The witness demonstrates with the aid of the Chief Inspector.]

The WITNESS—*This* is the far end (demonstrating). *Here* is the noose that was round the neck. (Demonstrates and places noose round the Chief Inspector's neck.)

By the LORD CHIEF JUSTICE—Let the jury see that. Is that a slip knot?—It is an ordinary straight-forward half-hitch. Like this. (Demonstrates with handkerchief.) The two strands leaving the half-hitch are both encircled a hand's breath further on by a loose length of the distal end of the rope tied in a very tight clove-hitch. One strand then continues for only another 30 inches, the other comes back and encircles both strands in another half-hitch between the half-hitch of the noose and the clove-hitch, and then continues on to pass round the body. I saw it beneath the legs and entangled in the feet. This piece (witness holds up a four-foot length of rope) was lying under the body, and it appeared as if the main rope had been cut in two places to release the body so as to get it into the trench.

By the LORD CHIEF JUSTICE—As if the body had been trussed up?—Yes.

So that when the rope was cut the body was released?—Yes.

Examination continued—There was actually another small piece of rope close to the head, was there not?—Yes.

Have you got that piece there?—It is quite a small piece and was lying close to the head on the ground.

Did you also find the piece of green material, Exhibit No. 13, loosely round the neck?—Yes.

By the LORD CHIEF JUSTICE—There were two rings on the rope, were there not?—Well, every laundry rope has a terminal ring and that ring had been threaded on to the running portion. I do not think it is of importance.

Examination continued—I was asking you about the piece of cloth round the neck, which I think you have in your hand.

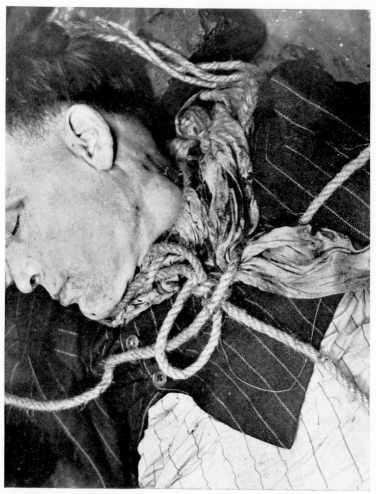

Photograph No. 4 of photographic exhibits showing the tying of the noose round the neck

Evidence for Prosecution.

Dr. Eric Gardner

That was loosely tied when you found it?—It was tied in a reef knot and actually was lying loosely, like that. (Demonstrates.)

Supposing it were folded double, what would be the effect? (Witness demonstrates.)—If it were folded, so that it passed over the mouth, and the two ends were crossed over at the back of the neck and then brought forward and tied in front, it would act as a gag. If it then slipped and were pulled off over the head, it would open out to a loop the size I found.

Could it have been used as a gag, do you think?—Oh, yes.

In that form?—Yes, as I have demonstrated.

Then the body was taken away to the Oxted Mortuary?—Yes.

Did you make a post-mortem examination?—Yes, on Sunday morning at about 11 o'clock. Dr. Keith Simpson was there at the same time.

What did you find on the body?—There were small abrasions above the left eyebrow with bruising on the outer angle of the left eye and on the centre of the forehead, and there was another rather heavier bruise on the front of the right hip bone.

Did you examine his brain?—Yes.

What did you find there?—On the right side there were two bruises on the front of the brain (pointing). One was on the front and undersurface of this lobe of the brain (frontal lobe), and there was another on the front of what is called the temporal lobe. But in my opinion the important observation was that the brain fluid was rather deeply blood-stained.

What conclusion did you draw from that?—The conclusion I drew from that was that there had been an injury to the head, a blow, causing concussion, and I looked upon the blood-stained fluid as the result of concussion of some severity.

What about the intestines? Were there signs of injury there? —There was very deep congestion of the intestine and there was hæmorrhage in the stomach and upper part of the small intestine. The mucous membrane of all the intestines was so congested that it looked like crimson velvet.

What does this internal bleeding indicate?—I interpreted it and the deep congestion as evidence of some violence such as might have been caused by a blow or a knee striking the abdomen.

Could such a condition be caused by a man having fallen down with somebody on top of him?—Very easily.

So you found a marked injury to the brain, which you have described?—Yes, and also to the abdomen.

By the LORD CHIEF JUSTICE—I would just like to know this. You say that may have been caused by somebody falling down on

Ley and Smith.

top of him. That might take place, for instance, at a game of rugby football, but you would not expect to find all these signs of which you have told us then, would you?—Well, my lord, I have quite recently met with a sudden death on the football field from a similar accident.

These marks that you have spoken of stretched from the head, and then there were all these intestines, which seemed to show that considerable violence had been caused to this body?—I thought so.

During life?—I thought so.

Such as with a man after he was beaten up?—I thought it suggested a thoroughly rough house.

Examination continued—These injuries that you have described are all before death?—Yes.

With regard to this injury to the brain which you said from the internal evidence indicated unconsciousness, was the bruise you described on the forehead, at first sight, consistent with the force necessary to produce unconsciousness?—No, not under ordinary circumstances.

Supposing this man at the time he struck his forehead had a rug over his head, or something of that kind, would that have made a difference?—Yes, for then he could have struck his head heavily without causing severe bruising to the skin but at the same time damaging the brain.

By the LORD CHIEF JUSTICE—It was consistent with a rug being over the head at the time it was struck?—Yes. He may have been struck or fallen on any part of his head, but I would point out the position of the bruises on the front of the brain are in a characteristic position resulting from a fall or blow on the back of the head.

Examination continued—So far you have described injuries which you say in your opinion were caused before this man died?—Yes.

Were there any other injuries as well?—There was a mark round the neck.

There is a mark shown clearly round the neck in the photograph which no doubt you have seen. Could that have been caused by a rope being drawn tightly round the neck?—Yes.

What in your opinion was the cause of this man's death?—Asphyxia, mainly, and presumably, from the tightening of the rope.

Strangulation?—Yes.

34

Evidence for Prosecution.

Dr. Eric Gardner

There were injuries also in other parts of the body, were there not?—There was an injury here on the eighth and ninth ribs, and they were broken.

Did that appear to have happened before death or after?—I thought the indications were after death, because the bruising resulting from these two broken ribs was so very slight, and was practically confined to the muscle tissue which was torn where they were broken.

Did the marks of the rope drawn tight look as though they may well have caused death?—Yes, and they must have been made before death because above them there were hæmorrhages in the skin of the face and the whites of the eyes were just a mass of blood.

Was there any other mark on the neck apart from the rope marks?—There was just an indication of the two loose ends going upwards.

Was this man wearing a collar?—Yes.

Was there any mark apparently connected with the collar?— There was a very conspicuous mark on the left side corresponding with the top edge of the collar, suggesting somebody's hand in the collar on the right side of the neck pulling very hard. The left edge had cut right deeply into the skin, and there were quite a lot of hæmorrhages under the skin beneath that mark. So that was an injury before death.

It is possible to tell, is it not, with some accuracy how long it has taken for a person to become asphyxiated? I mean whether it has happened suddenly or gradually?—Yes.

What is your view about this case?—There were a lot of hæmorrhages on the heart and on the surface of the lungs and the great vessels of the chest were distended with very dark fluid blood, and that all pointed to what one calls a slow asphyxia.

You said there was evidence that he might have been gagged?— Yes.

I suppose that would contribute?—Yes, certainly it would.

It must follow from your evidence, Dr. Gardner, that in your opinion this man was dead when he was put in the trench?— Oh, yes.

I know that sounds rather an obvious question, but that is your opinion?—Yes

Is it possible to tell at all how long before?—It is quite certain from the position of the body as I saw it that the body was put in the trench before rigor mortis started, and that begins in four to six hours after death, in ordinary cases. It might be a little delayed

Ley and Smith.

Dr. Eric Gardner

here, because rigor mortis comes on more slowly after an asphyxial death, but I think four to six hours is reasonable.

Your view is that at the time you examined that body at quarter-past nine on 30th November, it had been dead about 48 hours?—Yes, rigor mortis was complete and was just beginning to pass off in one area, in one area only.

Cross-examined by Sir WALTER MONCKTON—Dr. Gardner, in your view were the long pieces of rope both being used for trussing up the dead body?—When I saw them they were obviously being used for that purpose.

I want to ask you first of all about the bruises of which you have spoken. There were, I gather, small bruises, as you have described them, on the brow, on the left eyebrow, on the outer angle of the left eye?—Yes.

And the front of the left hip?—Yes.

As I gather from you such marks of injury did not guide you by themselves to your conclusions? You did not think them of great importance?—No.

They might, I suppose, have been caused either in a scuffle or if the body of a person was entangled in a rope and fell?—Yes, they were not important.

I don't think you told us before about the fall or blow on the back of the head. You did not take that into account?—I have reached that in this way. There is evidence from the blood-stained brain-fluid of some injury on that man's head, and the bruising in front of the brain on those two areas I have described is suggestive that he did fall or was struck on the back of the head, which might have been protected, perhaps by a rug.

First of all, objectively, you are not telling us that there was an indication on the back of the head of a blow?—No. There was nothing to see there. He may have fallen on a carpet—as well as being protected by a rug.

It is what you would conclude from the two other things taken together?—Yes.

I want to come now to the condition in which you found the brain. You called it a rather deeply blood-stained brain fluid from which you drew a conclusion of concussion?—Yes.

It is true that in a case of asphyxia you get some indication of hæmorrhage on the surface of the brain?—I do not quite agree.

I will put it to you in these words: are the cerebral vessels particularly liable to asphyxial injury from a rope round the neck? —No, I don't think they are.

Yes?—No, I don't think they are.

Evidence for Prosecution.

Dr. Eric Gardner

Is it true that you do get hæmorrhages over the surface of the brain, and into the ventricle of the brain, and from the stomach in cases of asphyxia?—I have never seen it in the stomach.

Have you seen it into the ventricle of the brain and over the surface of the brain in cases of asphyxia?—No, I have not.

What we had in this case, the hæmorrhages which you observed in the eyes and on the face, would you describe them as asphyxial? —I would describe them as a result of the noose tightening round the neck, and so interfering with the return of the blood from the head to the heart.

What I want to put to you quite clearly is this: in a case of asphyxia—whether it is caused by suspension; whether it is caused by accident; or whether it is caused by what you have been describing—do you not see in many cases hæmorrhage on the surface of the brain, or into the ventricle of the brain?—I have not seen them. I know this is a very important point, and if I may be allowed, I should like to quote one of my cases to you in order to explain my answer. It is the record of a man who was asphyxiated, and whose jugular veins were completely obstructed by very heavy pressure across the front of the neck so that none of the blood in the head could return to the heart through them. As a result the small vessels in the skin of the face not only congested but actually burst so that the face was black from hæmorrhage into the skin. The white of the eyes was blood-shot and oozing and the scalp was separated from the skull by a blood clot. It was a condition exactly similar to Mudie's, only more so, but there were no hæmorrhages on the brain surface, nor was the brain fluid blood-stained; on the contrary, the brain was paler than normal, for its blood finding the usual passage through the jugular veins blocked, had returned to the heart via a set of veins around the spinal column, known as the vertebral veins, thus avoiding even congestion of the brain. (Witness produced notes and photograph.)

By the LORD CHIEF JUSTICE—This particular photograph you are showing, is that of a case which came within your personal knowledge?—Yes, and I took the photograph myself.

Cross-examination continued—There you have got the face gone completely black?—Yes, that is hæmorrhage in the skin.

Perhaps I may put to you, this work, with which you are more familiar than I. Moritz in "The Pathology of Trauma," at page 179, says: "The hæmorrhages which are characteristically small occur most commonly in and beneath the pericardium, endo-cardium, pleura pia ependyma and in the substance of the brain,

Ley and Smith.

Dr. Eric Gardner

lungs and heart muscle. The cerebral vessels are particularly susceptible to asphyxial injury." That is right, is it not?—Well, I have seen a very large number of asphyxial cases and I have not noticed that.

Could we agree that it is fair to say that it is common in cases of asphyxia that the small vessels of blood in the body do tend to burst owing to the swelling?—Certainly, in the chest, when there is obstruction to the free entry of air.

What I am seeking to say to you is this: amongst asphyxial appearances the surface of the brain may very often be discoloured by hæmorrhage. That is what we want to put to you quite clearly?—No, I certainly have not met that.

I have to put it to you upon instructions and I will pass from it in a minute. You see the conclusion I am seeking to draw from this is, if I be right in suggesting that it is common in cases of asphyxia that the surface of the brain would have this discolouration from hæmorrhage, then it would not be right to attribute it in a particular case to a blow or trauma?—Except in so far as there is evidence of the trauma.

By the LORD CHIEF JUSTICE—The evidence, as I understand it, was of a concussion?—Yes, from bruising of the brain.

Cross-examination continued—What I was seeking to put to you was that the symptoms you there discovered could be attributable to asphyxia without assuming a concussion—discolouration of the brain fluid?—Well, I am not conversant with marked discolouration of the brain fluid from asphyxia.

The LORD CHIEF JUSTICE—Have you ever come across it?—I don't think I have.

How many cases of asphyxia have you seen?—I do about 1000 post-mortem examinations a year, and I have done that for a good many years.

That does not mean 1000 asphyxial cases a year?—Oh, no, but amongst these there are of course a large number of asphyxial cases.

Cross-examination continued—Of course, Dr. Keith Simpson is someone else who has a considerable experience of this, has he not? —Yes.

And was present with you on the occasions when you were examining the body?—Yes, but I don't think he noticed the staining of the fluid.

Evidence for Prosecution.

Dr. Eric Gardner

Well, that may or may not be. I want to put to you one more passage upon which I hope to get your view. This is Professor Glaister's "Medical Jurisprudence and Toxicology," at page 132, where he is dealing with internal post-mortem appearances. Perhaps you would help me with the first word—"Petechial"?—Minute hæmorrhage.

"Petechial hæmorrhages, due to capillary injury, are commonly present on the costal, pulmonary, and pericardial pleura, pericardium, heart muscle, endocardium, and substance of the brain." Would you agree with that?—I have often seen hæmorrhages in the substance of the brain, and I have looked upon them more as leakage of blood through blood vessels which have been damaged by lack of oxygen, rather than oozing from extreme congestion.

You say that as to the substance of the brain and as to the surface of the brain?—I think I would limit it to the substance of the brain.

Now, I want to ask you a question or two about the signs you noticed in relation to the abdomen. Am I right in saying that there was no sign of injury to the abdomen wall or to the back of the abdomen?—No, none.

Is it right too that at the autopsy the discolouration in the abdomen was so slight as to be barely visible?—No. I consider that the discolouration of the intestines was one of the most intense degrees of discolouration I have ever seen.

What I suppose was done was that some portion of the discoloured bowel was taken out from the lower abdomen?—No, the entire intestine was taken out and opened.

When it was taken out did you notice that it, having been hanging down, had got locally congested and discoloured?—No, it was universally congested.

Was that congestion and discolouration something which could have happened after death?—No. If it had been post-mortem discolouration and the man had been lying on his right side after death, then the dependant part of the intestine would have been very dark, and the blood would have drained out from elsewhere.

Do you commonly get in asphyxial cases slight effects from the congestion of the bodies?—Well, yes, slight.

So that in such a case you are not driven to interpret what you find as indicating a blow?—No, I was driven to a suggestion of a blow by the intensity of the congestion, from the depth of the colour.

You appreciate, do you not, that I am suggesting that there was no deep-seated injury?—There quite definitely was, because I took the entire intestine out. I opened it from one end to the other, and

39

Ley and Smith.

Dr. Eric Gardner

from one end to the other the mucous membrane was like crimson velvet.

You think that that could be accounted for by a fall?—I think it could be accounted for by a blow on the abdomen, causing what is called reflex congestion of the intestine, which has been fully described by Sir Bernard Spilsbury.

Could it be caused by a fall? If he fell against some object would he injure the abdomen in that way?—I think if I fell from here on to that sharp edge I could give myself a blow that could completely knock me out from causing intense congestion of my abdominal contents.

I want to turn, if I may, to something else. In the course of your evidence you spoke about the looseness of the noose. It is right, is it not—I think the photographs probably show it—that there is an indication from the mark on the neck that he was pulled up at some stage; I think the third or fourth of the photographs give you the best indication?—There was an indication of some tension upwards.

I was going to ask you about that. When you first went into this matter did you take the view that the rope marks which we see illustrated there, rising to an open angle under the left ear, indicated that the deceased was suspended by it?—You will see in my report the words I used were, "Some degree of suspension."

In fact there was some degree of suspension?—Yes.

Did you take the view that from the position of the rope mark and the open angle under the left ear, there was no doubt that the deceased was suspended by the rope?—No, I did not take that view because if you put it that way you have got to assume the deceased hanging by it. That is what you mean, is it not?

Yes?—Well, then, I never subscribed to that.

Did you in your original report make use of something such as I have been putting?—No, I said, "Some degree of suspension."

Did you not say in your original report that there was no doubt the accused was suspended by it, meaning the rope?—I cannot remember.

I would be extremely grateful to you if you would look?—(Witness consults notes.) There was no doubt—I mean as the examination went on, for it took place over two or three days—that he was never fully suspended by that rope.

Did you take this view when you were first told to make a report that the cause of death was asphyxia through strangulation, when suspended by a rope round the neck?—Partially suspended, I agree.

Evidence for Prosecution.

Dr. Eric Gardner

Which view did you express at that time, that the asphyxia was when partially suspended?—You are going a long time back, you know.

But you see it was a time when you felt yourself able to report about the cause of death, and I am asking you whether that was not a view you then held and whether it was not a reasonable view?—I said reading from notes the mark indicated that there had been some form of suspension, but there had been no drop.

By the LORD CHIEF JUSTICE—You did not think he had been hung, in the ordinary sense?—No, I did not.

You mean you could have a man lying on his back with a rope round his neck and that rope could have been pulled up?—You have put it exactly. Right from the beginning I took the view that he had not been hung, but I did agree that if the rope were fixed when the noose was round his neck and if his body were sagging against the fixed rope, then that could have produced the condition I found. In my report to the police I said: "The rope mark differs in no way from that commonly seen in self-hanging, but I am not satisfied that death was due to suicide."

Cross-examination continued—So that as far as the rope mark went you could not have drawn any other conclusion with certainty?—No, the rope mark round the neck was an indication of some degree of suspension.

Were you led finally to a different view, in part by the way in which the knot was tied?—Partly. I said I had never seen a suicide hang himself with a noose tied in a single half-hitch.

It is right, is it not, that the knots are very often very complicated in cases of suicide?—Yes.

And in cases of murder you infrequently find complicated knots. I mean, a complicated knot is something which one often sees in suicide, whereas someone that is just doing a strangulation does it without any sign of many knots?—Yes, but I think a murder by a rope round the neck is very rare.

I want to put one more matter to you on this aspect of the case, as to the length of time which the asphyxiation took. The state which you were able to discover was one which would be reached in two or three minutes?—Yes.

And might have been a good deal less?—Well, if you are going to have a good deal less you are going to have a good deal less congestion.

I suggested to you what I had to say about the method of tying the knot; what I had to say about the cause of asphyxiation, &c.;

Ley and Smith.

did you also rely on the suspicious disposal of the body?—I looked upon the injury to the abdomen and the blood-stained brain fluid as indicating a degree of injury after which he would be unable to hang himself.

So what you were merely relying on were the signs we have already discussed?—No. The rope mark was visible right round the neck pressing on extremely vital centres, and I think you know if a body is suspended with a rope pressing on these very vital centres in the neck death is pretty quick. It was quite slow in this case, and therefore a death from pure hanging with the whole weight of the body on the rope, to my mind, was out of the question.

You thought that because of the period of time?—That was one of the points.

It would not be right if you are looking at the medical symptoms in this case to take into account the position where the body was eventually found. Do you think that you could be led in part to your conclusions by your suspicions because of the way the body was disposed of?—No, I had plenty other than that to go on.

You see what I am putting to you is this, that subject to what you have said about the abdomen, if you look at the appearances which you have got they are symptoms which did not necessarily drive you to a conclusion that this death was the result of foul play at all. You cannot tell whether it is suspension, whether it is suicide or accident, or foul play?—He died from asphyxia after receiving injuries of an extremely grave character, definitely bruising the brain, here, and here (indicating) and causing a condition in the abdomen that I have never seen before.

So far as the bruising is concerned, I think we have agreed that it is not of prime importance?—The bruising on the brain was.

You meant the bruising when you dealt with the discoloured fluid?—I mean the front lobe of the brain, here (indicating), was definitely bruised, and there was another area of the brain, here, that was also bruised; and those bruises must have been the result of some injury.

And an injury caused either by a blow or a fall?—Yes.

Cross-examined by Mr. CURTIS BENNETT—Is this right, "In my opinion, about four hours, possibly longer, had elapsed between death and the body being placed in the trench"?—Yes.

What would you put as the minimum time which must have elapsed between death and this body being put in the trench? About four hours?—I think, considering it was death from asphyxiation, you must have a minimum of about four hours.

42

Evidence for Prosecution.

Dr. Eric Gardner

At least four hours?—Yes.

Might it have been much longer?—No, not much longer.

Let us try it at the other end of the scale?—Four to six.

Four to six—or seven?—Four to six.

Or seven?—Possibly seven; sometimes you get freak conditions.

You don't wish to be unfair. Would you say four the minimum and seven the most?—I should say four to six hours, with the possibility of freak restriction, with the possibility of it being seven hours. Why I say that is you may get a freak extension because the time of onset of rigor mortis may be considerably altered, if the man is quite fresh, or tired.

That you cannot tell?—That I cannot tell, but four to six.

So that freak conditions might have applied in this case for all you know?—With an absolutely tied up man the rigor mortis would come on earlier.

Re-examined by Mr. HAWKE—I have a copy of your report here. After saying the cause of death, in your opinion, was strangulation by a rope round the neck, you go on to say death was undoubtedly due from slow strangulation, from constriction of the neck, from the rope found round it?—Yes.

And the marks of that rope indicated some form of suspension? —Yes.

There had been no drop?—No.

Did you mean by that, there was no evidence that he had hung from a height?—Yes.

That is consistent with what you told my lord, possibly that the rope had been jerked up——

By the LORD CHIEF JUSTICE—Or pulled up when his body was sagging?—Or if the body was on a couch and unconscious and sagging with the end of the rope fixed.

I was going to ask you that. Supposing this man's body was trussed up and tied, and in a sagging position, when unconscious in the chair, and the rope then——?—If the loop of the rope were over the knob of the chair and the body were sagging against it, you have got the ideal position.

MAGGIE EVELYN BYRON BROOK, sworn, examined by Mr. HAWKE —You are living in Wimbledon now, are you not?—Yes.

You used to live in Australia when you were married?—Yes.

You are a widow now, Mrs. Brook?—Yes.

How old are you?—Sixty-six.

I think that your husband died many years ago?—Yes.

Ley and Smith.

Maggie E. B. Brook

Did you leave Australia when your husband died?—Yes.

Did you know Mr. Ley in Australia?—Yes.

When you came back to England from Australia, after your husband died, did you renew your acquaintance with Mr. Ley here?—Yes.

Did you live with him in different places in England?—Yes.

You have a daughter?—Yes.

Did she come back to England from Australia with you?—Yes.

She is married, is she not, to a Mr. Barron?—Yes.

Did she live with Mr. Barron, her husband, at a flat in Wimbledon at No. 3 Homefield Road?—Yes.

Did she have to go into hospital for an operation during last summer?—Yes, that is true.

Did you go and take over her flat at Homefield Road when she went into hospital?—Yes, I did.

Did Ley know that?—Yes.

Did you ever meet a man called Mudie?—Once only.

He was at that time lodging in this house, was not he?—Yes.

Can you tell me roughly when that was—May, or June or what?—I don't seem to remember.

Perhaps you could fix it by the time your daughter went into hospital?—I remember the time she came out; it was 12th June. I think I met him the day before Victory Day.

That would be early in June?—Yes.

I do not want to tie you down to an exact date, but about that date?—Yes.

How did you come to meet?—I was sweeping down the stairs from my daughter's part of the house, which was the top, and the landlady was talking to him at his door which was at the bottom of the stairs. I was sweeping down, and she called down and introduced me to him and I spoke to him there. That was the only time I spoke to him.

Incidentally, the landlady's name is Mrs. Evans, is it not?—Yes.

The landlady introduced you to Mr. Mudie, who stood at his door?—That is right; he was standing at his door at the time.

Were you outside yourself?—No, I was at the foot of the stairs coming down; I was about the second step of the stairs coming down.

By the LORD CHIEF JUSTICE—Where was his room, on the ground floor, or the first floor? Do you remember?—On the first floor, it would be, because my daughter has the top floor.

44

Evidence for Prosecution.

Maggie E. B. Brook

Examination continued—That you say is the only time you saw him?—That is the only time I saw him ever.

Now, while you were in your daughter's flat, were you in communication with Ley in London?—Oh, yes.

By telephone? Did he come and see you, or what?—We used to go out to dinner, I think, nearly every night.

He used to take you out to dinner?—Yes.

Did he drive down to Wimbledon and pick you up?—No, just came out by 'bus or whatever he came by.

By 'bus or underground, and then he took you out to dinner? —Yes.

Did he speak to you on the telephone at all while you were down there?—Yes.

By the LORD CHIEF JUSTICE—Did he ever talk to you about your being friendly with other men?—After I left, not before.

After what?—After I left 3 Homefield Road.

Examination continued—Not before?—No, I don't think so before.

Let us come to when you left then. How did you come to leave this flat?—Mr. Ley rang me up and was very, very annoyed on the telephone and asked me if I would come back.

What time of the day was it when he rang you up?—I think it started at about 10 o'clock at night.

Did he ring you up more than once during the night then?— Yes.

What was he ringing you up about?—He accused me of being familiar with my son-in-law.

Is that what he was annoyed about, as you say?—Yes.

How did it end then?—He then called for me, and I packed up and he called for me and I went back to 16 Knightsbridge Court.

What time did he call for you?—About two or half-past.

In the morning?—In the morning.

How did he come—by car?—By car.

You had packed up, and you came back to London with him, did you?—Yes.

At that time?—Yes.

Did he say when he called why he had knocked you up at this time of night to go back to London with him?—Yes, I have told you.

The same thing, was it?—Yes.

Was he jealous of you at the time?—Yes, he was jealous; more in a protective way he was jealous of me.

45

Ley and Smith.

By the LORD CHIEF JUSTICE—More what?—In a protective way, if you can understand that—to look after me.

He didn't want anybody else to look after you: is that what you mean?—Perhaps that was it.

Examination continued—You went back in the car with him to London, did you?—Yes.

To Knightsbridge Court, you say?—Yes.

Was that where he was living at this time?—Yes, but most of the furniture was out, you see; we were moving, and most of the furniture was out, had been taken out.

Where were you moving to?—Well, the furniture was being stored. He was moving down to the National Liberal Club because our lease was up.

Your lease at Knightsbridge Court?—Yes.

By the LORD CHIEF JUSTICE—Had you been living with him at Knightsbridge Court?—We had been living there.

Then you went down to your daughter's flat?—To be nearer when she went for an operation into hospital.

He brings you back to Knightsbridge Court and most of the furniture has been already moved?—Yes.

He was going to live at the National Liberal Club?—Yes.

Examination continued—Did you spend the rest of the night at 16 Knightsbridge Court?—Yes.

Where did you go next day?—I went to West Cromwell Road.

Had you got a room there, Mrs. Brook?—Well, previous to that, before I knew my daughter was going into hospital, I had found a room for myself there, when we had to move out of the flat, you see. Then I had to ring up and give it up, so when this happened I rang straight there and asked could I still have the room there, which I got.

I follow. You went straight back the next day to this room in West Cromwell Road?—Yes.

Did Ley know that you had gone there?—Yes.

What was the number?—Fourteen.

I think you have actually said it before, but I am not quite sure—the date on which you came back to London?—Yes, I remember that. I left Wimbledon at half-past two in the morning of the 13th, and went to West Cromwell Road in the morning of the 14th.

In other words, you came away in the middle of the night of 12th June?—Yes.

And went to West Cromwell Road next day?—On 13th June.

Evidence for Prosecution.

Maggie E. B. Brook

How long did you go on staying in this room in West Cromwell Road?—I stayed there, I think, until 23rd December. I think that is correct.

So that from 13th June to 23rd December you were in this room and Ley knew you were there?—Yes.

You told me that he had made these suggestions about you and your son-in-law?—Yes.

That was the reason for you being taken away on the night of 12th June?—That was the reason, I think.

Or the reason you were given. Did he at any time subsequent to that make suggestions about anyone else?—I don't remember.

Well, who else was lodging at Homefield Road besides your daughter and your son-in-law and this man, Mudie? Was there anybody else there?—There were, but I didn't know anyone. I didn't know their names.

Mrs. Brook, I wasn't suggesting for a moment that you did. I wanted to know whether you knew other people were there?—I think Mrs. Evans had the rooms full.

You met this man Mudie once?—Yes.

On the occasion you have told us about?—Yes.

Did you ever hear mention of any other man who was living there?—No, I didn't, not at the time I didn't.

Did you ever hear a rumour?—Not till after I left.

After you left and you were in West Cromwell Road did Ley make any suggestion to you about any other people in this house? —Yes, about Mr. Romer.

What did he say about him?—Well, I think the same thing. That you had been familiar with him?—Yes.

Did he ever mention Mudie after you left?—Yes.

What did he say about him?—I think he asked me if Mr. Mudie had been blackmailing me.

What did you tell him?—No.

Did he say anything else about Mudie?—I think he said the same about Mudie as he said about the other two.

In other words, you mean he accused you of being familiar with Mudie as he suggested with the other two?—Yes.

Was this just an isolated accusation or was it continually being made?—Well, I think he kept up about my son-in-law for some time.

By the LORD CHIEF JUSTICE—Kept up about what?—Kept up about my son-in-law.

47

Ley and Smith.

Maggie E. B. Brook

Kept up about your son-in-law?—Yes; then it was Mr. Mudie for some time, and then those two were dropped; then it was Mr. Romer for some time.

Had you ever accused Mr. Ley at any time of being responsible for Mudie's death?—No, never.

Cross-examined by Sir WALTER MONCKTON—Mrs. Brook, did you first get to know Ley in about 1921 or 1922, when your husband was still alive?—My husband died 24 years ago, if you reckon that back. I couldn't. I am sorry.

It was just before his death, was it not?—Yes, he came over with a letter of introduction to my husband.

After your husband's death which, as you say, was some 24 years ago, did you and Ley come together?—Yes, he looked after all my business concerns for me.

He helped you, did he not, with money?—Yes, he did.

You and your daughter in those days?—Well, he helped me with money by investing, advising me about investments.

He did himself help you by buying for you at his expense debentures in a Sydney hotel company, and shares in another company?—Yes, I think he did.

I don't want to trouble you about any details, but did he find in that way something like between £4000 and £5000 which he put aside for you after you came here?—No.

Not as much as that?—No, definitely not.

I am suggesting, you know, that about 24 years ago, soon after your husband's death you and he lived together?—We did up till about 10 or 12 years ago.

During the period you were living together in that full sense sexually, was he paying for your living expenses? I suppose so?—No, not then because I was getting my money over from Australia.

But he took a house for you and with you?—He would pay the rent, yes.

And though you think it was not as much as £4000 or £5000, did he put money aside in your name?—Yes.

I don't want to take that in any way in detail, but before you came to England in succeeding years did he take you to America and Canada?—Yes.

And then through Europe from Australia, from the East? Well; if you don't remember, I won't trouble you. Did he leave Sydney in Australia about the end of 1929?—I do not remember; maybe.

Something like that?—Yes, that is right.

Evidence for Prosecution.

Maggie E. B. Brook

You followed in the next year with your daughter?—I think that is right.

Then you were together, and did he take a house in Wimbledon which he conveyed over to you?—Yes, but——

Somewhere in Worcester Road, Wimbledon?—I think that needs a little explanation. When I first came over I brought over a certain amount of money of my own. That money I lent to Mr. Ley to get a start with, which I think explains the house.

You lent it?—Yes.

That is how it started?—Yes.

Let me take you nearer the time. During the war I think the house in Wimbledon was let, was it not?—Yes.

Then was it in 1942 that you came together to 16 Knightsbridge Court of which we have heard?—It might be about that. I think so.

Did you live there until 1946?—Yes, we did.

Would it be right to say, from what you said a moment ago, that for the whole of that period and for some time before you had not been living together as though you were man and wife?—No, not for 10 or 12 years.

That had stopped for 10 or 12 years?—Yes, that is correct.

You explained to my lord, and I need not trouble you with it therefore, that when your lease in Knightsbridge came to an end in June, 1946, or thereabouts, you could not find a flat immediately, and it was then you first heard of 14 West Cromwell Road?—Yes.

It was then that he went off to the National Liberal Club?—Yes.

At that time, in the middle of 1946, he was converting the property at 5 Beaufort Gardens into four self-contained flats?—Yes.

The idea was that you were going to have one of them?—Yes, that is right.

At, I think, a nominal rent?—Yes.

That brings you to the end of May or June, 1946, and that is the time when you were at 3 Homefield Road, I gather, for something like a fortnight, not much more?—Not even that long.

There did occur during the time you were there something which upset him?—Yes.

He heard something?—Yes, well, I don't know——

But something upset him?—Apparently so.

If you were to come together again he wanted to find out about it?—Yes, that is right.

He took you away, you have told us, on or about 12th June; I think you say in the middle of the night?—Yes, that is right.

Ley and Smith.

Maggie E. B. Brook

You did ring him up that night, did you not? He used to ring up, having taken you out to dinner and gone home, or having had dinner with you and gone home?—Yes, one or other. He rang up to say good-night; it may have been one or the other.

Did you on that occasion, when that conversation took place, say you were packing?—Not until I saw there was going to be trouble.

You saw that and you said you were packing?—I said I would pack up and get out of here.

You were packed?—Yes, I was packed at two o'clock.

When he came?—In the morning.

He had first suggested you should try 14 West Cromwell Road? —No, I had found that place before.

Did he suggest that?—No, I had found that place before.

I think he took you there next day?—Yes.

Well now, you remember, do you, about some cheques which he sent—we have heard about them this morning—cheques which he sent to you, care of Mudie?—I didn't know anything about it until after.

You did not know anything about it until after?—No, not a word.

You remember there was an episode about the cheques?—I remember there was.

After the incident of the cheques, did Ley refer to Mudie any more as someone about whom he entertained any suspicion?—No, after that he started on Mr. Romer.

So at that time he had stopped as far as Mudie was concerned? —Apparently he had stopped.

Had he given you to think at this time he was complaining about Mudie earlier, that he was afraid you were giving money to Mudie?—Yes.

He was worried, was he, because you would not let him see your bank passbook as you used to do?—Yes, he was.

By the Lord Chief Justice—Did he ever give any reason for suspecting you were giving money to Mudie?—There could be no reason, my lord.

Did he ever give you any reason?—No.

Mudie was a man to whom you had spoken once by saying "Good morning" on the stairs?—That is all.

And he made accusations that you had been familiar with him? —Yes.

You have told Sir Walter Monckton that he seemed to think you had been giving money to Mudie?—Yes.

Evidence for Prosecution.

Maggie E. B. Brook

Did he ever tell you anybody had told him that, or when he was making the accusation did you never ask him why he suspected such a thing?—No, I just indignantly denied it.

Cross-examination continued—Mrs. Brook, did he say that he had heard that Mudie was wanting to set up in a small hotel business and he thought that he was asking for money for it?—Yes, he did say that.

You said that in the past he had looked after your money affairs and advised you about them?—Yes, he always advised me about my investments.

Tell me this. Apart from this episode of which you have spoken, during the time you have been together have you been happy together?—Yes.

I just want to get this. Some time in November of this last year, did Ley take on a housekeeper for Beaufort Gardens?—Yes, at the end of November.

A Miss Lane?—Yes.

Do you remember—this was before November of last year—going to Mr. Brashier's office, the solicitor?—Yes, I do.

You know him well?—Yes.

I think that Mr. Barron, senior, Mr. Thomas Barron, went too? —Yes.

Was there a discussion then about the moneys which had been set aside by Mr. Ley for you and what was to be done with them? —There was.

I think he wanted these moneys and property to be held by you for your life and by him afterwards, and then as you might jointly appoint?—Yes, that is so.

I think that Mr. Barron suggested that it had all been coming to you absolutely and therefore that ought not to be done?—It was all coming to me absolutely.

Mr. Barron was saying that. I take it you agree with me. But Ley was taking the other view : it was for you to hold for life and then he?—Yes, he did at that time.

He was annoyed when you failed to agree about that?—He was annoyed.

Was it after that that he appointed the housekeeper of whom I have spoken?—Yes.

I wanted to ask you about 28th November. That is the day on which all this that you have heard so much about is said to have taken place?—Yes.

Tell me, did you dine with Ley night after night normally?— Yes.

Ley and Smith.

Maggie E. B. Brook

Had dinner together?—Yes.

Can you remember the day of which I am speaking, 28th November?—Yes.

On that day had you been to 5 Beaufort Gardens with Ley in the afternoon?—We had afternoon tea at 5 Beaufort Gardens.

After tea did you go off together, start off together?—We did.

Did you go down Beaufort Gardens into Brompton Road?—Yes.

And walk along until you got somewhere near Harrods?—Yes.

Was Ley looking for a taxi for you?—Yes.

I think you could not find one?—No.

Did you get on to a 'bus?—I got on a 74.

Did Ley tell you where he was going?—To the club.

Where did you go?—I went to West Cromwell Road.

When did you next see Ley?—About a quarter to eight that night.

A quarter to eight the same night?—Yes.

Where did you see him?—At West Cromwell Road.

He came to your place?—Yes.

Did he tell you where he had been?—To the club.

Did he tell you about his having taken a taxi to the club and it had broken down?—Yes.

And that he had to get another one?—Yes.

Did he tell you about whether he had eaten anything or not at that time?—No.

Did you have something together?—Yes, we had some sandwiches and coffee.

How did you pass the evening?—Played gin-rummy.

When about did Ley leave your flat?—About the usual time; eleven, or a quarter past.

During the week in which the 28th occurred did you dine with Ley on other nights of that week?—Yes, I did.

Where did you dine? Always the same place?—Mostly, either at the Cumberland Hotel or the Knightsbridge Restaurant.

It was the Grill of the Cumberland, was it not?—The Grill Room.

Was that where you were dining during that week in which the 28th November occurred?—Yes, it would be.

Was there any other night that week upon which you did not dine together?—No.

On that particular night, though he did not dine with you, he came round and had sandwiches and you played gin-rummy?—Yes.

Evidence for Prosecution.

Maggie E. B. Brook

Did he play his usual game?—Well, he must have because I don't remember.

You don't remember any difference in his play that night?—No.

Cross-examined by Mr. CURTIS BENNETT—Mrs. Brook, would you give us about what time it was you left Ley and caught the bus?—It must have been about a quarter to five.

He said he was going to the club. Is that the National Liberal Club?—That is so.

The next time you saw him, as you have told us, is 7.45 p.m. at West Cromwell Road?—Yes.

How far would that be from Beaufort Gardens?—It is a 2d. 'bus ride, if that gives you any idea.

That was the only night that week that you had not dined with him?—That is so.

You say he had been to the club?—Yes, I left him to go to the club in Brompton Road.

That is what he said?—Yes.

If he had come from Beaufort Gardens, getting to you about a quarter to eight, he might have left a few minutes before?—Left where?

Supposing he was coming from Beaufort Gardens to your home in West Cromwell Road, it would have taken a few minutes?—It would have taken a little while. He would have to find a 'bus or taxi.

Ten minutes?—Maybe.

I should have thought less. Quite a short time?—You have got to wait for a 'bus or a taxi. You might wait——

I agree the chances are you might have to wait quite a time. You may or may not have to wait?—You may.

It would not take long, would it?—No, not very long.

Re-examined by Mr. HAWKE—When he told you that he thought that Mudie was setting up in a hotel business, did he tell you where he had got his information from?—No, I don't think he did. I don't remember him ever telling me so.

Did he say that somebody had told him that Mudie had asked for money from you?—I am sorry. I cannot remember that.

You see, according to you there was no beginning of truth in this because you had only met the man for a moment?—Yes.

I suppose you were a little surprised to hear this, were you not?—A little angry.

Ley and Smith.

Maggie E. B. Brook

Well, perhaps angry. Did you ask him where he got this entirely misplaced information from?—No, I don't think I did. I simply said: "That is not true."

By the LORD CHIEF JUSTICE—Is that all you said to him? He was accusing you of familiarity with this man Mudie and suggesting that Mudie had been borrowing money, or getting money, out of you, a man you had only spoken to once in your life just to say "Good morning." You must have asked him how he got that information, did not you?—I don't remember.

Is that not what any woman would do, or any man as far as that goes?—Well, I think we did argue and argue and argue about it.

Did he never tell you anything? You say that he had accused you first of all of misconduct with your son-in-law?—Yes.

Did you ask him who had accused you of it? Just try and think?—I am trying to think. No, I don't remember. I remember him saying once he could bring five people forward to prove it, and I said, "Well, bring the five people forward. I would like to face them." That is all I can remember about it.

Re-examination continued—Did he by any chance say he was in a position to bring anybody to prove that you had been familiar with Mudie?—No, I don't remember him ever saying that.

Or prove Mudie was trying to get money out of you?—No. It really all does sound so stupid, I know, but I don't think he did.

I wonder if he said that about your son-in-law, whether he said anything of the same kind about the other people?—Well, I think he just made accusations.

By the LORD CHIEF JUSTICE—Just tell me this, Mrs. Brook. How is it you remember exactly what you did on 28th November? What was there that fixed that date in your mind?—I can tell you that exactly, my lord.

Tell me then?—Because on 23rd November he engaged his housekeeper, and then he said to me would I come down every day and show her how to run the house or give her advice. That is how I remember that, and I went every day excepting one day down there, and I think that the one day I didn't go down to look after him was Tuesday or Wednesday, and that was the only day that we didn't go out to dinner.

Which day of the week was it?—The 28th was the only day.

Which day?—Thursday, and either Tuesday or Wednesday I didn't go and have afternoon tea, but every other day I was down there having afternoon tea.

Evidence for Prosecution.

Maggie E. B. Brook

You didn't have afternoon tea with him that day?—Yes, but one day I didn't—either Tuesday or Wednesday I didn't have afternoon tea. That is the only day I wasn't there.

Is that the reason for remembering you met him at Harrods and that he came and had sandwiches with you on the 28th?—Because that was the only day, and every other day we had gone out and every day practically I had been down to——

How do you remember it was the Thursday you did not go out to dinner and not Wednesday?—Well, I remember now. It has all come back to my mind, my lord. I remember because that was the day he always went to the National Liberal Club. It was always on the Thursday. He met his friends there. That is why I remember it.

When were you first asked to remember if you could what happened on Thursday, the 28th?—I think to-day.

Is this the first time you have been asked?—Yes.

You see, Sir Walter Monckton cross-examined you and then said he was going to ask you something, and then he proceeded to ask you about 28th November. I think that is so. I think you must have told your solicitor or somebody about 28th November. I want to know when you first were asked about it?—I told it to-day when I told Mr. Monckton.

It seems very odd. How soon after 28th November did you know there was a question of murder?—I saw it in the paper, I think, towards the end of the next week.

How soon did you know that Mr. Ley was accused of murder? —Well, I was down at 5 Beaufort Gardens when Inspector Shoobridge came down on the Saturday morning to question me.

That was on 5th December?—It might have been.

Did you not tell anybody when you knew this man you had been living with was accused of murder, that you could account for his movements on that night?—Oh no, I didn't.

BLANCHE MOORE EVANS, sworn, examined by Mr. ELAM—I am a widow, living at 3 Homefield Road, Wimbledon, and I let certain rooms at that address out into flats for tenants.

Now about May of last year, 1946, who was living in, and who had you let off the top flat to, at this address?—A Mr. and Mrs. Barron.

Mrs. Barron was a Miss Brook before she was married?—Yes.

Did you know a man, Jack Mudie?—He came to stay in my house, on the second floor—one room only.

Ley and Smith.

Blanche M. Evans

When he was staying with you was he working as a barman at a licensed house near?—Well, he wasn't at the time he came but he eventually did get a job there.

"The Dog and Fox"?—Yes.

Can you say when about Mudie left your flat, roughly?—He came on 29th May and was there six weeks. I cannot remember off-hand the date—I did give it, but I have forgotten it for the moment. Now I come to think of it, I believe it was 3rd July.

We can work it out. Do you remember Mrs. Barron went to hospital for an operation?—Yes.

That was May, was it not?—Yes.

After Mrs. Barron had gone to hospital did Mrs. Brook come to your flat?—Yes.

Did she, so to speak, take over your daughter's flat?—Well, she stayed there while they were away. There was no case of taking over.

To be near the hospital?—Yes, that is right.

She was there about ten days?—Ten days exactly.

Were you actually there when Mrs. Brook left your flats—when she went away?—Yes.

We know that was in the early hours of the morning of the 13th. Before she actually left your place did somebody come and fetch her, or go with her in the car?—I can't say, I did not see them go.

You did not see them?—No. I heard of it.

Had you seen the accused, Ley, at all?—Yes, on two occasions.

Was that before Mrs. Brook left or afterwards?—Afterwards.

How did it come about you saw him for the first time?—He rang me up and wanted to know what had happened to Mrs. Brook on this Thursday morning; he wanted to see me.

Do you know what day he rang you up?—I think it was Friday.

Of the same week?—Yes.

Did you agree to see him?—Yes.

Did he come?—Yes.

When was that?—On the following Sunday at 12 o'clock.

By the LORD CHIEF JUSTICE—This is all in June, I understand? —Yes, my lord—Sunday, 16th June.

Examination continued—Did he tell you what he had come to see you about?—Yes, he said he wanted to know what happened in the house on the morning of that Thursday.

When Mrs. Brook had gone away?—Yes.

Evidence for Prosecution.

Blanche M. Evans

Did he say any more about it to you, and did you?—Oh yes, I told him I did not know what had happened.

By the LORD CHIEF JUSTICE—Did you know anything had happened?—I did not know anything had happened at all; I wasn't up at 2.30 in the morning.

Examination continued—Did he ask you anything about Mrs. Brook?—Yes, he said she had rung him up at that time and she was in a very agitated state of mind and said would he fetch her away immediately.

Did he tell you or did you ask him what she was agitated about?—I said I wanted to know what was the matter, why she was agitated.

What did he say?—He said that she said that all men were beasts. That is the expression he used.

Anything else?—No, I don't think so.

Did he say whether he had gone over to Wimbledon himself that night?—He said he came and fetched her away, took her away.

Who else was living in the house at that time?—Two other gentlemen; Mr. Mudie, of course, Mr. Wynn and Mr. Romer.

Did Ley ask you who was living at the house?—Yes.

Did you tell him?—Yes.

Having told him who was there, did he say anything about your tenants?—Yes, I imagine I mentioned Jack Mudie, and he said, "Jack," he said, "she is always mentioning his name."

Did he say any more about Mudie?—He asked me what kind of a man he was.

Mrs. Evans, when he asked you what Jack Mudie was like what did you say?—I said he was a very nice man, and so he was.

By the LORD CHIEF JUSTICE—No one has told us yet. Can you give us any idea about how old Mudie was? I understand he was quite a young man?—Well, he was 35—of course, I did not know his age; he looked quite young—thirtyish.

Examination continued—Did you say anything about Mudie ever meeting Mrs. Brook?—Yes.

Would you tell my lord and the jury what?—I introduced Mudie to Mrs. Brook on the landing outside the bathroom, and he only talked to her about five minutes.

Were you there all the time?—Yes, I introduced them.

Ley and Smith.

Blanche M. Evans

Did you say that he had met her at any other time?—Not to my knowledge.

Did you tell Ley that?—Yes.

What did he say when you told him that?—This was the second occasion, of course, he told me this. Then he said: "Oh, they had high jinks at the flat upstairs, and," he said, "of course" —to put it broadly—"She couldn't keep the pace."

When you told him about you having introduced Mrs. Brook to Mudie once and so on, did Ley seem satisfied? Did it seem to end the matter, or what?—He sort of turned it off, as it were.

How?—Well, I was rather flabbergasted at what he said, and he saw that and he said, "Oh, I would like to meet this young fellow and apologize to him. I feel very sorry that he is involved in an affair like this," kind of apologetic, I took it, of course.

You told us you saw Ley twice—once on Sunday, 16th June. Do you remember when the other occasion was, or how long there was in between?—As far as I remember there was a fortnight in between, I could not be absolutely certain.

Were you expecting to see him the second time? I mean, did you know he was coming?—No, he 'phoned up again.

And came after that?—Yes, that is right.

What was said? I am talking about the second occasion now, though it may not matter particularly what occasion. What else did he say when he came to see you?—He asked me if I would make an appointment to meet this Mr. Mudie, and he said, "I would like to meet him," and he felt very sorry for him; he had sons of his own and would like to help him.

Help him in what way, did he say?—He did not say. I rather gather financially, as he was a man who seemed interested in——

After the second occasion, did you ever see Ley again?—No.

Cross-examined by Sir WALTER MONCKTON—I am not sure which occasion it was, but when Ley came down to see you did he say anything about an idea that perhaps Mudie wanted to go into the hotel business?—I told him that.

You told him you thought Mudie did want to?—Well, he was in the hotel business, yes.

When he talked about finance had you in mind that it might be help, perhaps, with the hotel business?—Yes, I did not suggest to Mr. Ley that he should give him money.

By the LORD CHIEF JUSTICE—I think you said you told him Mudie was in the hotel business. That might mean he was a

Evidence for Prosecution.

proprietor or potman. Did you say in what way?—That he was in the hotel business.

That is what you said, he was in the hotel business?—Yes, that is right.

Cross-examination continued—Was it in connexion with that that Ley said he would like to see and help him?—Well, it was after that, of course.

Re-examined by Mr. HAWKE—Did you tell him that Mudie had been asking Mrs. Brook for money to set him up?—No, I never mentioned that.

Did you say anything like that?—Nothing whatever.

Nothing that could possibly be construed like that?—Nothing whatever, I never mentioned money like that.

THOMAS HENRY BARRON, sworn, examined by Mr. ELAM—I live at Wimbledon and have a son who married Miss Brook. They lived at 3 Homefield Road, Wimbledon. I myself have known Mrs. Brook for about eight or nine years.

Do you know the accused, Ley?—Yes, the first I met him I think was about five years ago.

Do you know a man called Jack Mudie?—Yes.

Did you see him many times, or only occasionally?—I saw Mudie four times.

We know he was a tenant of a flat underneath your daughter's flat?—That is right, 3 Homefield Road. He had just a room on the first floor.

Did you see him at Homefield Road?—Yes.

Would you look at Exhibit 4, please. (Handed to witness.) Have you seen that before?—Yes, this is a letter dated 19th June which Mudie handed to me at Homefield Road, or showed me.

Do you know when he handed it to you?—The Sunday after he received it—23rd June.

Did he also show you Exhibit No. 5?—Yes, at the same time.

Did he also show you three blank cheques?—That is right; at the same time.

And did he show you an envelope, Exhibit No. 6, at the same time?—Yes, that is right.

Did you take possession of the cheques?—No, Mudie sent them down by my daughter-in-law two or three weeks afterwards.

By the LORD CHIEF JUSTICE—We have not had Exhibit No. 4 read. It is a long time since Exhibit No. 5 was read, so, as

Ley and Smith.

Thomas H. Barron

Exhibit 5 shows how Exhibit 4 came to be in existence, I think you had better read Exhibit 5 to the jury, then Exhibit 4.

Mr. ELAM—Exhibit 5 reads:

"Jack Mudie, Esq.,
 3 Homefield Road,
  Wimbledon, S.W.19.

19th June, 1946.

Dear sir,
 Mrs. Brook telephoned last afternoon that she was going to the country about some arrangements in regard to the convalescence of her daughter, who is still in hospital, and as we want some cheques signed and returned to us not later than Friday next, we asked for her instructions. She directed us to send the cheques to her in your care with the request that, if she did not reach Homefield Road by 4 p.m. on Thursday to ask you to be good enough to seal up the enclosed addressed envelope and post it to her new flat at 5 Beaufort Gardens, London, S.W.7, so that we can send up on Friday morning by taxi and obtain them. We enclose stamped envelope addressed to her and marked as she directed, 'Strictly Private,' her instructions being that we were not to open the envelope on any account until she returned on Friday morning. Thanking you in anticipation for your help in the matter.
 We are,

Yours faithfully,

(Sgd.) G. H. BAKER,
p.p. Secretary."

Exhibit 4:

"Connaught Properties, Limited,
82 King William Street,
London, E.C.4,

19th June, 1946.

Mrs. M. E. Brook,
 c/o J. Mudie, Esq.,
  3 Homefield Road,
   Wimbledon, S.W.19.

Dear madam,
 We refer to you telephone message, and, as the cheques are essential for wages to-morrow, payable on Friday, we

Evidence for Prosecution.

have sent the cheques, under separate cover, addressed as directed. We trust they will reach you safely and you will be able to let us have them back signed either from Wimbledon or 5 Beaufort Gardens, not later than Friday morning, the 20th instant. If you care to telephone we will send someone to Beaufort Gardens, but you will appreciate that the distance from here to Wimbledon might make a special journey awkward. The only other Director available is Mr. Ley or we should not worry you at this time.

Yours faithfully,

(Sgd.) G. H. BAKER,
p.p. Secretary."

The envelope, Exhibit 6, a foolscap envelope, reads: "Strictly Private. Not to be opened except by the addressee." The addressee is Mrs. Byron Brook, 5 Beaufort Gardens, Knightsbridge, N.W.7.

Examination continued—What happened to the cheques, Mr. Barron?—After Mudie sent them down to me I took and handed them over to Mr. Baker personally and obtained a receipt for them—which is Exhibit No. 7.

Is Mr. Baker the secretary of Connaught Properties, Limited? —Yes.

The receipt reads, "Connaught Properties, Limited, 82 King William Street, London, E.C.4. Tel.: SLOane 8603. 29th July, 1946. Received from Mr. T. Barron blank cheques Nos. 739, 740 and 741. (Sgd.) G. H. Baker." Is that correct?—That is right.

You got that the day you handed over the cheques to Mr. Baker?—Yes.

After you had done that did you see Jack Mudie again?—I saw him again at Wimbledon, I should think a fortnight after the cheques had been returned.

That is about a fortnight after 29th July?—Yes.

Was he alone?—Yes.

Had you the receipt, Exhibit No. 7, for the cheques with you?— Yes, I showed him the receipt.

Did you see Mudie again after that?—Yes, he came up with Ley and another man to my flat.

By car?—By car, yes.

With Ley and another man whom you did not know?—I don't know the other man, no.

Ley and Smith.

Thomas H. Barron

Did Ley say anything?—He said he had come to see me about the cheques, as he understood I had a receipt for them. I got the receipt from the safe and showed it to him and he was perfectly satisfied.

Mudie was there?—Yes.

Did he then go away?—Yes.

Did you see Ley after that anywhere?—Not after that, no.

At the interview—I am going back for a minute—was anything said about letters?—No, nothing at all.

Did Ley say anything to you at that interview or meeting about these cheques, or why they had been sent?—No, he did not. I told him that when I returned them to Mr. Baker I had asked him to notify him, Ley, that they had been returned. He said he hadn't received them; they hadn't been delivered; they hadn't been returned.

Did he say why they had ever been sent like that?—No.

Did you ever go to the solicitors' office and have an interview there?—Yes, Mr. Brashier's office.

Was Ley there?—Yes.

Was something said about these cheques and letters there?— Well, during the course of discussion I expressed an opinion, and I showed Mr. Brashier the letters and said I had the cheques at home, or copies of the letter.

Did Ley say anything then about these letters?—Yes, he said he had sent them to Mudie.

Did he say why he had done so?—He then said, a little private detective work of his own.

Did you ever see Ley at or near 3 Homefield Road, Wimbledon? —Yes, on 25th September.

Did you speak to him then?—Yes.

Did he say why he had come?—He asked me if I knew anybody by the name of Romer living at Homefield Road. I said I did not know anybody of that name. He said it was a Major Romer, and he had come to see him as he had been associated with Mrs. Brook.

Did he say anything more about Romer?—Well, then he said that he exonerated my son because he had found out he had mistaken him for another man, whose name was Arthur, and then he mentioned Romer's name again.

By the LORD CHIEF JUSTICE—Had he previously made a complaint to you about your son?—No, he had not, but he then said he had exonerated my son because he had mixed him up with a man named Arthur.

Evidence for Prosecution.

Examination continued—What did you say when he said he had exonerated your son?—I said I never knew of anything he had to exonerate him for.

As you have said, you had never heard about that before?—Not from Ley.

Was there any more about Romer and Mrs. Brook?—Well, he said he went to the flat at 3 Homefield Road on 8th June and found them locked together for two hours.

Locked together—whose room?—In my daughter-in-law's, where Mrs. Brook was staying.

Did you or he say any more?—I asked him how he remembered the date; he said he made a note in his diary.

Then did you part company?—Yes, Romer drove up in his car and they went inside the house, and we left.

MAGGIE EVELYN BYRON BROOK, recalled, further examined by Mr. HAWKE—Would you just look at Exhibit No. 4, please. (Handed to witness.) Have you ever seen that letter which is addressed to you?—No, I don't remember it at all.

Now, would you just look at Exhibit 5?——

By the LORD CHIEF JUSTICE—Read that letter carefully. You see who it is addressed to—"Jack Mudie." Do you see that?—Yes, I see that.

Did you ever direct anyone to send cheques for you to Mr. Mudie?—Never, my lord.

Did you ever give Ley or anybody at Connaught Properties Mudie's name as a place to which to send documents to you?—Never, my lord.

The LORD CHIEF JUSTICE—Members of the jury, we no longer are obliged to keep juries locked up in murder cases, but I need hardly say you will take great care not to speak to anybody about this case and tell me if anybody approaches you about it.*

The Court adjourned.

---

* This relaxation in the segregation of a jury does not apply to Scotland where juries are still kept strictly to themselves during the entire procedure of a capital charge.

Ley and Smith.

Second Day—Thursday 20th March, 1947.

THOMAS HENRY BARRON, recalled, cross-examined by Sir WALTER MONCKTON—There are three interviews of the defendant Ley about which I want to ask you a little to see that I have got it right. The first of them is the episode of the cheques. There were two interviews, were there not, at Mr. Brashier's office, or was it only one? —One.

That was the interview where the matter of the cheques was finally disposed of?—Yes.

The interview where they were finally disposed of was later or before?—Later.

That is what I wanted first to get. There was an interview at Mr. Brashier's office—would that be in July?—About 10th July.

Was the subject matter of that interview the question of a settlement of monies and property which Mrs. Brook had got from Ley?—I do not know what the interview was really about. Mrs. Brook asked me to go there to look after her interests and that of her daughter.

You know, do you not, that the interview was in relation to property which had been got for Mrs. Brook by Ley?—There was some financial matter, but what it was I did not know.

See if you can remember this. Was the conversation on this line, that Mrs. Brook was saying: "These gifts to me were absolute gifts, out and out "?—I think she did.

And Ley was saying, on the contrary, that he had given them to her on the understanding that she would have the properties for life and he would have them after her death?—I don't remember him saying that.

At any rate, on the question as to whether they were absolute gifts or conditional in that sense, there was a marked difference of opinion between them?—Yes.

At the end of the interview he went away saying he was angry about it?—He said he would drop the whole matter.

Did he say he had finished with her at that time?—Yes.

That was 10th July, for which I am obliged. Then the other interview in relation to the cheques would be in August?—In August last.

That was the one which finished that. He saw the receipt?— He saw the receipt and said he was satisfied.

And then the third interview about which I want to ask you was where he spoke to you about Mr. Romer?—Yes, that was on 25th September.

Evidence for Prosecution.

Thomas H. Barron

That was the one in which he said he had muddled up the two Arthurs?—He had mistaken my son for another man named Arthur.

Your son being named Arthur too?—Yes.

By the LORD CHIEF JUSTICE—What are you by profession?—A welfare officer.

JOSEPH MINDEN, sworn, examined by Mr. HAWKE—You are the head porter, are you not, at the Royal Hotel in Woburn Place?—That is correct.

Do you know the defendant, Ley, as a visitor to the hotel?—Yes.

Do you remember late towards the end of last year Ley coming to see you at the hotel?—Yes.

I should think it was somewhere in September?—Somewhere about that period—possibly August.

What did he come to see you about then?—Well, he went to the letter box to see if there were any letters, presumably; then he came up to me and said: "I want a man with a car, a man who can keep his mouth shut."

By the LORD CHIEF JUSTICE—Was that as early as August?—Possibly September; I am afraid I cannot pin it down particularly.

Anyway, he asked you if you knew a man with a car who could keep his mouth shut?—A man who could look after himself and keep his mouth shut.

Examination continued—What did you say?—I thought it was a rather strange thing to ask, but as I knew that Mr. Ley had been, or was, a solicitor, it might be in pursuit of his duties, so I asked him straight away if it was legal, and he said it was.

You knew he was legal, and you thought it had something to do with his business?—Yes, exactly.

And he told you it was legal?—He said it was.

What did you say then?—I asked him: "Well, if I get anybody will he be amply repaid?" or, "Well paid"—words to that effect, in so far as I did not know what the job would be.

What did he say to that?—He said that he could earn a year's salary in a matter of weeks.

Did you know of anybody who had a car, who could keep his mouth shut?—Well, I did not know about the mouth shut, but I frequently give out jobs to people who have private cars, particularly to Buckingham as he was working for the Company—well, not for the Company.

E   65

Ley and Smith.

You thought of Mr. Buckingham?—Yes.

Did Ley tell you how you were to communicate with him if you did find somebody?—Yes, he just gave me a telephone number on a piece of paper.

Can you remember the number?—It is either Kensington 5991 or 9551.

You say you thought of Mr. Buckingham?—At that particular moment I never thought of anybody, but subsequently Buckingham came into the hotel to see if there was any work. I spoke to him and gave him the telephone number that Ley had given me.

Did you see Ley again after that?—Yes, I saw him at the hotel twice in the lounge.

Was he by himself when you saw him or with anybody else? —He came in on his own and met Buckingham in the lounge.

You saw him and Buckingham in the lounge of your hotel?— In the lounge on two occasions.

Can you give me any idea as to what time we are reaching now?—Somewhere in November, I should think—the latter end of October or November.

Would it be fair to say towards the end of October or the beginning of November?—Somewhere in that period. I am afraid I cannot really say definitely.

About that time you saw the two of them twice together in the hotel?—Yes.

Did you ever see anybody else with him?—Not actually with Mr. Ley, no.

Did you see anybody else with Mr. Buckingham?—Yes, on another occasion another man came in.

Who?—Well, it is rather difficult.

Can you see him now?—It seems to me it was the defendant, Smith.

On that occasion, when you saw Buckingham with someone who might have been Smith, did either of them speak to you?— I believe now that as Buckingham walked into the hotel hall he mentioned, "This is Mr. Smith."

He just said in passing, "This is Mr. Smith"?—Yes.

Did he say what they were there for?—No.

Did they just come and sit down?—They sat together in the lounge.

Did Buckingham say why he was sitting down with Smith in the lounge?—No, he gave no reason for that.

Did you have any further conversation at any time with Ley after this?—On the very last occasion I saw him, yes, and one other occasion towards the end of November.

Evidence for Prosecution.

Joseph Minden

Did he come to the hotel?—Yes.

Had he told you he was coming?—Yes, he 'phoned me up and said he was coming to see me.

Towards the end of November?—Yes.

Did he ring you up on one day and see you the same day, or the next day, or what?—That is what I have been trying to think. I believe now, although at one time I said he 'phoned me up the previous evening, it was the same morning as he 'phoned me that he came to see me.

That does not matter much. I only wanted to try and get the day of the week. Can you tell me the day of the week?—I think it was a Friday.

A Friday at the end of November?—That was my idea, that it was a Friday; certainly the end of the week and the end of the month.

And having telephoned, he came to see you at the hotel. What did he say?—He said, "My wife sends her compliments"—his wife was in Australia then and I had known her very well—"and she says that she is coming back to England very shortly but we will not be staying at the hotel. We propose to get a flat together."

She had in fact been resident in the hotel?—For many years.

For some time up to the early part of last year?—That is correct, yes.

And this was just to send her compliments and say she was not going to stay there this time?—That was the impression I got, yes.

Was that all that happened?—No. He put something in my hand.

What was it?—Well, it was paper money, but I did not realize what it was until after he had left. After he had gone I saw it was ten one-pound notes.

He handed you £10?—Yes.

Was that the last time you saw him?—Absolutely.

Cross-examined by Sir WALTER MONCKTON—At the time this money was given you, was the conversation a conversation in which he was saying his wife was not coming back?—Yes, that is what he said.

And it was his wife whom you had known well in the past as a resident in the hotel?—Yes.

Ley himself you had known by sight?—By sight for about four years, every day.

But I gather you had not had conversations with him?—No.

67

Ley and Smith.

Joseph Minden

Never?—Never—just passing the time of day and, "Good morning."

By the LORD CHIEF JUSTICE—Did he ever stay in the hotel?—He never stayed over night. He came nearly every day to see his wife and have coffee with her but he never stayed.

Cross-examination continued—When she was not there did he come to see about her letters and cables?—Yes.

And you saw him from time to time?—I saw him twice actually before he spoke to me.

I suppose Mrs. Ley was a person with whom you were quite well acquainted?—Yes.

And it would not be an astonishing thing to you if she should, through Mr. Ley, make a present to you?—That is what I rather expected.

Especially as she was not coming back again?—May I elaborate that? I had sent two trunks of hers off to Australia, and I used to pay her newspaper bills and one or two things, and she said she would come back and see me on a certain day; but unfortunately she could not get back and went without seeing me.

Was it not £5 instead of £10?—No, quite definitely ten one-pound notes.

Buckingham is a man you have known very well for a long time?—Yes.

For a lengthy number of years?—Oh no, for 18 months.

You have known him very well?—Well, I used to give him work, yes.

What I suggest to you is that that conversation which you said you had with Mr. Ley in which you say he said he wanted someone who could keep his mouth shut and look after himself and that it was legal and that the man would be well paid, in the expressive way you put it, never took place?—Oh but it did, quite definitely.

You quite understand what I am putting to you, so that there is no doubt?—I quite understand, but I would like to emphasize definitely that it did take place.

Am I right in this, that from that time onwards you saw Mr. Buckingham frequently?—Yes.

In the lounge and in the hotel?—I saw him every day. He used to come and see if there was any work, any private hire jobs going.

Was he the person for whom you got most private hire?—Most of the people I used to put on to him, yes.

Evidence for Prosecution.

Joseph Minden

You only saw Ley with him once, did you not, in the lounge?—Twice.

When you were asked before did you not say this: "I saw Ley in the hotel lounge with Buckingham on one occasion sitting down in an arm chair"?—Yes, on the second time he came in Buckingham was waiting for him, and I assumed they met in the lounge; they must have done.

But you did not see them?—No. I saw Buckingham there and then Mr. Ley went in.

The question was whether you saw them sitting together in the lounge on one occasion or on two?—Well, on one occasion, but they were definitely together the second time. Buckingham was already in the lounge waiting for Mr. Ley to arrive, and Mr. Ley did arrive and went into the lounge; he could not have missed him in those circumstances.

I am only trying to get what you saw. You never saw them together except on one occasion, but you saw him once go into the lounge where you knew Buckingham was?—That is it.

And there were no other conversations that you had with Mr. Ley other than those you have told us of?—That is all, absolutely.

Cross-examined by Mr. CURTIS BENNETT—With regard to Mr. Smith. How many times do you say you saw him at the Royal Hotel?—Once.

Only once?—Yes.

That was with Buckingham, was it?—Yes.

What time of day was it?—That was about four o'clock I think; somewhere round the region of tea time.

Can you give us any idea how long Smith stayed there?—No, because I went off home and I never saw him go off.

You know they went off together, he and Buckingham?—I could not say that.

That is the only time you have seen Smith there?—Once at Scotland Yard.

The only time you saw Smith there?—Yes; I never saw Smith after that.

JOHN WILLIAM BUCKINGHAM, sworn, examined by Mr. HAWKE—Your full name is John William Buckingham?—Yes.

By the LORD CHIEF JUSTICE—Are you willing to give your evidence?—Yes.

Ley and Smith.

John W. Buckingham

Examination continued—You have a business of letting out a car for hire, have you not?—Yes.

Where do you carry it on?—From Mostyn Road and from St. John's Wood.

What cars have you got?—A Wolseley, at the moment.

Did you have a Wolseley last year?—Yes.

Does your son assist you in that business?—Yes.

You do work for the Royal Hotel in Woburn Place, amongst other people, do you not?—Yes.

You did last year?—Yes.

And you, of course, know as he has told us, the hall porter, Minden?—Yes.

Did Minden have a conversation with you some time last year about a car?—Yes.

Did he give you anything when he spoke to you?—He gave me a telephone number.

As a result, did you ring up that number?—Yes.

What was that number?—Kensington 5199.

The LORD CHIEF JUSTICE—It is very difficult to remember telephone numbers over a long time; he seems to remember that there were two nine's and a five and some combination of five, nine and one.

Examination continued—I suppose the main thing is who answered the telephone when you rang up. Who did you speak to on the telephone?—A lady's voice on the telephone, and then a man who made himself known as Mr. Ley.

Was any arrangement made between you and Mr. Ley?—Yes, we made an arrangement to meet at the Royal Hotel the next evening.

Did you go to the Royal Hotel the next evening and meet Mr. Ley?—Yes.

This man here?—Yes, that is right.

What was said when you met him?—He told me that he was an ex-solicitor and that in the course of his business had come in contact with two ladies who were being blackmailed.

Did he tell you anything more about them at the time?—No, he seemed very cautious of what he was telling me, and he said that he would introduce me to another man that knew about the case.

Did he introduce you to another man?—Yes, the following evening at the Royal Hotel.

70

Evidence for Prosecution.

John W. Buckingham

Did anything further pass between you?—No, I do not think so.

He just said what you have told us about two women being blackmailed and that he would introduce you to a man who knew about the case?—Yes.

That was all that happened that first time, was it?—Yes.

By the LORD CHIEF JUSTICE—Did he not say he wanted you to do anything, or wanted a car?—He said that it was time that he wanted to get something on this man to stop the blackmailing.

Examination continued—Did he say anything to you about a car then?—No, not on that occasion.

That was all that passed between you then?—Yes.

And the following evening he introduced you to this other man in the Royal Hotel?—Yes.

Who was the other man?—Mr. Smith.

When he introduced you to Mr. Smith did he stay with you or did he go away?—No, Mr. Ley went away.

He went away and left you together?—Yes.

Did you have a talk together, you and Smith?—Yes, in the café opposite the Royal Hotel.

While you were there I suppose Smith talked to you. What did he say?—He told me that he knew Mr. Ley through working at his house as a builder's foreman, and that Mr. Ley got into contact with a young lady that had been seduced by a man.

By the LORD CHIEF JUSTICE—Ley told him what?—Ley had told me that he had got in contact with two ladies that were being blackmailed.

You said something about "seduced"?—Yes—well, the young lady had been seduced by a certain man, and also the mother, and the man was blackmailing them.

Examination continued—Did he say where it was that these two women had been seduced and were being blackmailed?—Yes, at Wimbledon.

Just "Wimbledon," or some house in Wimbledon?—At that time it was just "Wimbledon."

That this was going on in Wimbledon?—Yes.

You say Ley had told you that he wanted to get something on this man?—Yes.

Did Smith say anything about that?—Yes. He said that Ley wanted to try and get some evidence against this man.

Ley and Smith.

John W. Buckingham

It is a little hard at the moment to see what this has got to do with you. Did Smith say anything about that?—He wanted me to help in trying to get something on him.

That is what Smith said at this last meeting?—Yes.

Is that the effect of the conversation between you two that evening?—Yes.

Was anything else said of any bearing on this?—No, I do not think so.

By the Lord Chief Justice—Did he tell you how he wanted you to help to get something on this man?—No, it was just that he wanted to try to get something on him. He just gave me the outline of the case, that the women were being blackmailed, and they would like to get something on the man.

Examination continued—Did he explain how you were to help to get something on the man?—No, not at that time.

Did you see Smith again?—Yes.

Did you see Ley again?—Yes.

Both together or separately?—Together; on one or two occasions.

Let us take the first one. You saw them together after this interview you had with Smith?—Yes.

Where did you see them?—At the Royal Hotel again.

Was that shortly after this conversation with Smith in the café?—Yes, it would be about the same week.

Did Ley say anything to you then about the conversation you had had with Smith a few days before?—Yes, he verified the story that Smith had told me about the ladies being blackmailed.

Did he mention Wimbledon?—Yes. He told me that the young lady was living at Wimbledon, in a flat at Wimbledon, but he never gave me any definite address.

Did he say where the elder woman was?—No, I do not think he did, not on that occasion.

Did he on any occasion mention the elder woman?—Yes.

Was that at a later conversation?—Yes, I think it was when I met Mr. Ley on his own.

On a later occasion you met Ley alone and he said something about the elder woman. What did he say?—He said he had to go up to Wimbledon to fetch Mrs. Brook and take her to Cromwell Road, as she was in such a distressed state.

He mentioned the name then, did he—Mrs. Brook?—No, he never mentioned any names at all to me.

You are speaking of what you know now?—Yes.

Evidence for Prosecution.

John W. Buckingham

He did not mention the elder woman's name or the young woman's name?—No name was mentioned to me.

He said he had had to bring her back to Cromwell Road did he?—Yes.

That was at a later conversation when you were alone with him, was it?—Yes.

Had you at this time heard where you came in?—No.

I mean, what it had got to do with you?—Well, I was in a quandary myself about that.

Did you ask?—Yes, but I was just put off that they just wanted to find something on him or get something on him.

Was it indicated to you how you were to help to get something on him?—No, not at that time.

By the LORD CHIEF JUSTICE—Was anything said to you about money, whether you would be paid?—I cannot remember if it was exactly at that meeting, but they told me I would get a year's salary.

Do you remember who told you?—Mr. Ley.

Examination continued—I take it from what you are saying that there were various meetings between you and Ley?—Yes.

Always at the Royal Hotel?—Yes. Can I explain? You see there were such big lapses. For some weeks after this first meeting I never heard from either of them.

By the LORD CHIEF JUSTICE—About which month was it that you had your first meeting? How long before the time that you drove a car down somewhere?—I should say two months.

About how many meetings did you have with Ley?—I met him often, nearly every week.

Where?—Various places; mostly at the Royal Hotel.

Where else?—He came to my house, and we met in different public-houses.

Examination continued—Some time elapsed, you say, before you saw Ley again, after the conversation you have been telling us about?—Yes.

How did it come about that you came into contact with him again?—A telephone message was left at my house.

What was the message?—Making an appointment for me to meet Mr. Ley at the Royal Hotel on the following morning, which I did.

Ley and Smith.

John W. Buckingham

That was a special appointment?—Yes; I was late on that occasion and Mr. Ley had gone leaving a message with Minden to tell me to ring again to Ley's.

Did you ring again?—Yes, and made a further appointment which I kept the next morning.

At any rate you did eventually meet him?—Yes.

At the Royal Hotel?—Yes.

How long was that before the day that you drove down to Reigate?—In the region of about a fortnight, about two weeks.

Was that the occasion that you had a special appointment by telephone to meet Ley?—Yes.

Then I suppose he had something to tell you?—Yes.

What did he say?—He said that he now had something on the man; he had enough evidence on the man to make him sign a confession, and that he would like him brought up to London to be left in his presence to sign this confession.

Did he tell you who the man was?—Yes.

What did he say about him?—He said that he was a barman working at Reigate Hotel.

Did he tell you his name?—Yes, I think he did on that occasion.

What was the name?—Mudie.

Did he say why he was telling you that he wanted this man brought to London—what you were to do about it?—He wanted me to go down with Smith to get Mudie and to take him to a place in London so that he could sign a confession.

Did you know Mudie?—No.

Had you ever heard of him before?—No.

Did you know the Reigate Hotel?—Yes, I had known it passing by.

Did he say how you were to get this man whom you had never seen to come to London with you?—Well, he said that he wanted him tied up and left in his presence; that is all.

Were you alone with him when this conversation was going on, or was anybody else there?—I think I was alone with him at this time.

He said this man was to be tied up and brought to London. Who was to tie him up?—Me and Smith.

Were these instructions to you; I mean, was that what he told you you had got to get on with?—Yes.

Were you willing to do it?—Well, I done it.

Was any inducement given to you at this interview to make you willing to do it? Were you given any money?—Yes. He

Evidence for Prosecution.

gave me £10 at the Royal Hotel but I do not know if that was on that particular occasion.

But at one time at the hotel when he was talking to you he gave you £10?—Yes.

Of course, that was not more than a year's salary?—No.

Were you given any promise about that?—No.

Were you prepared to do this for £10?—Well, I was not thinking actually of the money at all at the time.

Perhaps we had better deal with this at once; did you get some money for this in the end?—Yes.

How much did you get?—£200.

Had you been informed you were going to get £200?—No.

You were going to get more than a year's salary?—Yes.

Were you expecting to get a substantial sum?—Yes.

And this was £10 on account?—Yes.

You and Smith were to tie this man up and bring him to London?—Yes.

I suppose then you saw Smith?—Yes.

When did you see Smith; was it immediately after this interview?—We were seeing one another all the time.

I do not suppose for a moment you could give the exact date, but shortly afterwards you saw Smith?—Well, I think Smith might have been there at the same time when those arrangements were made.

I did ask you that and you said no. Try to carry your mind back?—Yes; I think Smith was there at the actual time in Beaufort Gardens.

By the LORD CHIEF JUSTICE—Wait a minute. Have you got to Beaufort Gardens now? Did you have an interview with Ley at Beaufort Gardens?—Yes, me and Smith; I think that is where the arrangements were made.

The arrangement about tying up was made at Beaufort Gardens?—Yes.

And who had taken you to Beaufort Gardens?—Smith.

Had you been to Beaufort Gardens more than once before the day that you took Mudie there?—Yes.

Examination continued—Is the conversation that you have been telling me about then a conversation which took place between the two of you at Beaufort Gardens?—Yes.

Very well; that is clear. Did it follow various other meetings? —Yes.

When you had seen Ley alone—Yes, that is right.

75

Ley and Smith.

John W. Buckingham

Then you and Smith discussed how you were to tie this man up and bring him to London?—Yes.

Presumably he would not be very keen on it himself. What were you going to do?—One arrangement was that I go down, or we go down, to Reigate in my car, for my son to pretend that he was a chauffeur and I to act drunk, and my son was to ask Mudie to assist me into the car and we were going to bundle him into the car and drive away.

That was the first suggestion. Did that scheme come off?—No.

Why was that?—Because on that night I had the car stolen.

Your car was stolen on the very night when this scheme was involved, was it?—Yes.

Was that the Wolseley?—That is right.

You must have got it back fairly quick?—Yes.

Was it used for a job?—Well, I do not know, but the police informed me the next day that they had found it.

It was found abandoned somewhere and you got it back?—Yes.

That did not last long?—No.

Was that the only reason, the fact that you had not got a car that night, that you did not go down to Reigate and pretend to be drunk?—Yes. Then Smith put that idea up to Mr. Ley.

That is what I wanted to know. Smith passed this scheme that you and he had concocted to Ley, did he?—Yes.

Was it approved of?—No, definitely not.

So something else had to be thought of?—Yes.

Had you got your car back all right the next day?—Yes.

Did you and Smith then discuss further ways and means of getting Mudie to London?—Yes.

Was Ley present on this occasion?—No, not on this occasion.

What was the next idea?—I took Smith to Putney, where I knew some friends, and I divulged more or less to them the scheme that I was on, the job of work that I was on.

You call it "a job of work"?—Yes.

By the LORD CHIEF JUSTICE—Who did you introduce him to?—Mrs. Bruce.

Examination continued—Mrs. Bruce is a friend of yours, is she, and lives in Putney?—Yes.

With Mr. Bruce, who is a 'bus driver?—Yes, he is a friend of mine.

What is Mrs. Bruce?—A housekeeper and cook.

You took Smith down there to introduce him to them. What for?—Well, on the first occasion it was just to have a drink, and

Evidence for Prosecution.

in the course of the evening it came up about Mudie blackmailing these ladies, and the scheme was then made about Mrs. Bruce going down and inviting him to come up to London.

By the LORD CHIEF JUSTICE—You introduced Mrs. Bruce and evolved a scheme that Mrs. Bruce should invite Mudie to come to London; is that it?—Yes.

Examination continued—I suppose it is obvious really that she did not, but did Mrs. Bruce know Mudie?—No.

How was she to get this man to London?—The scheme was to pretend there was a cocktail party, and Mrs. Bruce to act as a lady of means and invite Mudie up to a cocktail party.

Was Mrs. Bruce to get into touch with Mudie first to get to know him, or something, and later on to ask him to come up for a cocktail party?—Yes.

She was to pose as lady of means?—Yes, with a chauffeur.

Which car was to be her car?—The Wolseley.

With a chauffeur?—Yes.

Who was to be the chauffeur?—My son.

So Mrs. Bruce, the lady with the car, was going down to Reigate with her chauffeur to the Reigate Hill Hotel to ask Mudie to come up to London to act as barman for this cocktail party?—Yes.

Was it considered advisable to go and look at the ground first?—Yes.

Did Mrs. Bruce go down to Reigate?—Yes.

Who with?—I drove them down, but I never went into the bar.

I suppose the idea still was that you were going to help in the tying up when the time came, was not it?—Yes.

So you would not want to go into the bar?—No.

But you went down with Mrs. Bruce and your son and they went inside and you stayed outside?—Yes.

Did you both go down—you and your son—more than once?—Yes; I think my son went on two occasions.

And you went each time, did you?—Yes.

When this plan was arranged that you were to get this man to London by this means, was Ley informed of it?—Yes.

Did you tell him?—No, Smith told him.

By the LORD CHIEF JUSTICE—In your presence?—Yes, I think it was in my presence, my lord.

Did you ever discuss it with Ley himself? Did you ever tell him what you proposed to do?—Yes.

Ley and Smith.

John W. Buckingham

Examination continued—Did he approve of it?—Yes. On that occasion I offered to give him Mrs. Bruce's telephone number, but he did not want to know anything about the telephone number.

I think perhaps I have gone ahead a little in asking what you said about the visits to Reigate. Just to go back; when the scheme was told to Ley, did you receive anything?—Yes, £20.

Who gave it to you?—Smith.

What did he say when he gave it to you?—He got it from Mr. Ley for expenses.

And it was after that that you went down a couple of times to the Reigate Hill Hotel to have a look at the place and so that Mrs. Bruce could get to know Mudie?—Yes.

Well, she managed that, did she not?—Yes.

What was the final arrangement when Mrs. Bruce had made Mudie's acquaintance? When she had made Mudie's acquaintance, what was the final plan?—That she was to bring him up on the Thursday night to her flat in London.

By the LORD CHIEF JUSTICE—To bring him up to where?—To London.

To a flat?—To her flat in London.

And where would the flat be?—Beaufort Gardens.

Mrs. Bruce was to represent that that was her flat, you mean?—Yes.

Examination continued—Perhaps now you can give a date. What was the day?—28th November.

Who fixed the date?—Well, actually Mudie himself fixed the date. He said——

He said that day would suit him to come up to London?—Yes, because that was his half-day.

Was that information, that Thursday was the day that would suit Mudie, relayed to Ley?—Yes.

When he knew that Thursday the 28th was the day, did he give any final instructions?—Yes, that Mudie was to be brought to the basement through a back entrance.

And what then?—He was to be tied up and I was to leave Mudie then.

He was to be tied up where, inside the house?—Yes.

When he had come through the back door, do you mean?—Well, actually he wanted him tied up on the road.

Who did?—Mr. Ley wanted him tied up on the way.

Evidence for Prosecution.

John W. Buckingham

Did you agree with that idea?—No. Me and Smith thought it would be better when he got to the place to tie him up there.

By the LORD CHIEF JUSTICE—I suppose you thought it risky to have him tied up in the car?—We did not see any point in tying him up.

Examination continued—You had been keeping well in the background. You had not been in the bar at Reigate?—No.

You did not want to meet Mudie, did you?—No.

Nor did Smith?—No.

But you and Smith were to do the tying up, you told us?—Yes.

You did not agree with the idea of tying him up in the car on the way up?—No.

So where was he to be tied up—what was finally decided?—When we got back to Beaufort Gardens me and Smith got back first.

Do not hurry on. I want to know what was arranged. Where was he to be tied up?—In Beaufort Gardens.

After he had come in at the back door?—Yes.

Who gave those instructions finally?—Smith.

Did Ley say what was to be done with him when he was tied up?—Yes.

What did he say?—He was to be placed in the centre room by the table, or by a desk there with the papers.

Where was the room?—The centre room in the basement.

Had you seen it?—Yes.

You had a look over the basement, had you?—Yes.

Who took you over?—Mr. Ley and Smith.

Was that all? Was he just to be left in the chair?—Yes, as far as I was concerned they told me I was to leave right away.

Did Ley say why he was to be left tied up in this chair by the table?—Yes, I understood that he was going to get him to sign a confession.

Did he tell you that?—Yes.

Did he indicate how you were to get in by the back door?—Yes. That either Mrs. Bruce or my son was to open the door and let Mudie in, pretending that he was coming into a flat.

Yes, but I suppose it might be locked. Was there any arrangement about the key?—Yes. Smith gave me the key which I handed to Mrs. Bruce.

That was the key of the back door, was it?—Yes.

Ley and Smith.

John W. Buckingham

By the LORD CHIEF JUSTICE—Was it a Yale key or a mortise lock?—A Yale key.

Examination continued—And you gave it to Mrs. Bruce?—Yes.
So it was fixed up that you were going down on the 28th, on the Thursday?—Yes.
Did you go down to Reigate on the 28th?—Yes.
Who did you go with?—I drove down so far with Mrs. Bruce.
In your own car?—Yes.
Did you pick her up on the way, then?—Yes, at Putney.
Did Smith go too?—Yes, he went in a Ford car.
Did anybody go with him?—My son.
So the two cars left London?—Yes.
The Wolseley you were driving, and your son and Smith in the other?—Yes.

By the LORD CHIEF JUSTICE—Do you happen to remember the number of the Ford car?—No, it was dark.

Examination continued—Did you know where Smith had got the car?—No.
All you knew was that he had a Ford car?—Yes, a Ford 10 h.p.
You picked up Mrs. Bruce in Putney and went down to Reigate?—That is right.
And the Ford as well?—Yes.
I suppose you were more or less going along together?—Yes.
Did you arrive at Reigate like that?—Well, no, the top of Reigate Hill.
You went as far as the top of Reigate Hill. What happened at the top of Reigate Hill?—My son got in the Wolseley and I got in the Ford car.
I suppose your son was assuming the role of chauffeur, was he?—Yes. The reason why the two cars went was that my son did not know the road, and we proposed that I should show him the way back—lead the way back.
It was not just to make sure that nothing miscarried?—No.

By the LORD CHIEF JUSTICE—On the top of Reigate Hill you stopped, your son got into the Wolseley and you got into the Ford?—Yes.
So you arrived at Reigate, your son driving Mrs. Bruce?—That is right.
And you were driving Smith?—I drove the Ford.

JOHN WILLIAM BUCKINGHAM, Senior

Evidence for Prosecution.

John W. Buckingham

Examination continued—And you arrived at Reigate Hill Hotel?—Yes.

What did you and Smith do at the Reigate Hill Hotel?—Nothing. We just turned round and came straight back.

Ready to go back to London?—Yes.

It was to be left to your son and Mrs. Bruce to bring Mudie back in the Wolseley?—Yes.

Did you and Smith then lead the way back to London?—Yes.

Where did you and Smith make for?—Beaufort Gardens.

Did you see the other car following you?—Yes.

Who was in it?—Mudie—well, at one time we were behind the car, and through the headlights you could see the shadow of Mrs. Bruce and another man; I could not be certain.

Another man besides your son?—Yes.

And you say you made for Beaufort Gardens?—Yes.

For No. 5?—Yes.

Did you and Smith arrive before the Wolseley?—Yes.

Did you go to the front door or back?—The front door. Smith opened the door with a key.

Did you see anybody inside when you got in?—Yes, Mr. Ley.

Where was he?—Just inside by his flat door.

By the LORD CHIEF JUSTICE—Wait one moment. I do not think anybody has told us this yet: you say Mr. Ley was by his flat door?—Yes.

Which was Mr. Ley's flat, the basement or the ground floor?—The ground floor. I take it that was his living accommodation, and the basement was the offices.

The ground floor was the living room and the basement was the offices?—Yes.

Examination continued—And he was waiting by his own living-room door when you two came in?—Yes.

Where did you two go; did you stay in the top part?—Smith took me down to the basement then.

What did you do in the basement?—Smith showed me the room just inside the door where I was to wait.

The LORD CHIEF JUSTICE—Members of the jury, if you look at the right-hand plan you can see where the staircase goes down to the basement. You see at the back the word "Down." (To the witness.) That is correct, is it; you go down to the basement at the

Ley and Smith.

John W. Buckingham

back of the flat?—Yes, well, it is more or less down the side of the flat.

Down the side, but it is at the end of the passage?—Yes.

Examination continued—You were saying that Smith in the basement showed you a room?—Yes.

Is there a room just to the left of the back door at the bottom of the stair?—Yes.

A room with a door which opened inwards?—That is right.

Is that the room which Smith showed you?—Yes.

What did he show you that for?—I was to wait there.

And of course, I take it this is right, that somebody coming in at the back door and walking down the steps into the basement would not see you if you were standing inside that room?—No.

But you would be there handy to the steps?—Yes.

That, of course, is the room at the top right-hand corner of the plan, the room that has got "Table with telephone." You were to wait there, and that is what Smith told you?—Yes.

Where was Smith going to wait?—In the recess in the passage.

Is that the recess where the passage broadens out a little way past the room that you were going to stand in?—That is right, yes.

You can see it on the plan?—Yes, where it says "Passage" here. That is where Smith was going to stand.

When you had been shown that did you both wait where you were?—Yes—well, no. Smith went and saw Ley again.

Smith went upstairs again, did he?—Yes.

Was he upstairs very long?—No, just a minute or two.

Then he came down again, did he?—Yes.

Had he got anything with him when he came down?—Yes, a blanket.

What did he do with the blanket?—Gave it to me.

And what did you do?—I went in the front room then.

Into the room that you had been shown?—Yes.

With the blanket?—Yes.

What was the idea?—The plan was that when Mudie came in I was to throw it over his head.

As he came in by the back door and down those steps?—That is right.

And, having given you the blanket, where did Smith go then?—He waited in the recess.

So you two had taken up your position?—Yes.

What was the next thing that happened?—The car came to the back door and Mudie came in. I heard a scuffle, and I thought it

Evidence for Prosecution.

John W. Buckingham

was Mudie running out again. I opened the door and looked towards the steps, but the door was closed, and I looked the other way and Smith had Mudie holding him round the arm.

The scuffle you had heard was Smith coming out from the recess and taking hold of Mudie?—Probably, yes.

At any rate, when you looked out he had got Mudie held?—Yes.

By the LORD CHIEF JUSTICE—What had become of Mrs. Bruce; had she come in?—No.

What happened, do you know?—As far as I know they drove right away.

Did you hear her say anything?—No.

Examination continued—Smith was holding Mudie; how was he holding him?—Just round the arm.

What did you do?—I walked up to them and Smith said to me: "All right, put it over," and I put the blanket over his head.

That completely covered him, did it?—Yes.

What did Smith do?—He tied his legs and arms up.

What with?—Rope.

Had Mudie done anything at all while this was going on?— No, nothing whatever.

Had he had any chance?—Yes, I think so.

What do you mean? What chance had he had?—Well, I thought he would have resisted.

Did he?—No.

I understand you to say that as he came into the back door Smith got hold of him and held him?—Yes.

You came out. I suppose you came out fairly quickly?—No; I think it must have taken some seconds.

You put the blanket over his head completely covering him, and then Smith tied him up with the rope?—Yes.

What happened then?—We put him into the centre room then.

Is that the room at the end of the passage on the left-hand side? —Yes; I think it is the centre room.

There is a room you see at the end of the passage on the left which is called "Room partly furnished"; is that the room?—That is the room, yes.

You say you took him down there. How did you take him?— I just got hold of him round the arm.

You were bigger than him, I suppose?—Yes.

By the LORD CHIEF JUSTICE—What sort of a size was Mudie?— Well, medium height.

83

Ley and Smith.

John W. Buckingham

As big as you?—No, not so big as me.

As big as Smith?—Yes; I should say so.

Just stand up, Smith. (The prisoner Smith stood up.) About as big as that?—Yes.

And you were a bit bigger?—Yes.

So that with the two of you he had not much chance to do anything, had he?—No.

Examination continued—You said you took him along to the room. I understand his legs were bound, his arms were bound and there was a blanket over him?—Yes.

How did you get him there?—I jumped him along there.

What did you do with him when you got him into the room?—Sat him in the chair.

Had anything happened on the way?—No.

By the LORD CHIEF JUSTICE—Did he fall over?—No.

Examination continued—No fall?—No.

Just have a look at Exhibit 13. (Handed to witness.) Have you ever seen that before?—I saw it at Scotland Yard.

Had you seen it before that?—No.

Did you see it on the night of Thursday, 28th November?—No.

So while you were there, at any rate, that had not been used?—No.

Was any violence done to this man apart from what you have already told us?—None whatsoever.

Then you had got the man where you had been told to put him?—Yes. I took the blanket off his head; I folded the blanket right off his head before I left.

By the LORD CHIEF JUSTICE—After he had been tied, do you mean?—Yes.

Examination continued—After he had been tied and was in the chair, do you mean?—Yes.

Then you had done what I understand you had undertaken to do; you had got him to London, he was tied up and in this chair?—Yes.

What did you do then?—I came out of the room and Mr. Ley was standing on——

Just a moment. Did Smith come out with you or not?—Yes. You both came out?—Yes.

I am sorry to interrupt you, only I wanted to get that clear, you both came out?—And Mr. Ley was waiting on the stairs, the

Evidence for Prosecution.

John W. Buckingham

basement steps, and he handed me a packet and told me not to get in contact with him again.

What happened then?—Smith let me out of the back door.

And you went out into Brompton Place?—Yes.

Did Smith come with you?—No, but we had made arrangements after we got Mudie there to go and have a drink like—well, the four of us. As Smith was letting me out of the back door, he said that Mr. Ley's friends had not turned up and he would have to wait with him for a bit.

So you went out, and he stayed in?—Yes.

Did he close the door or leave it open?—As far as I know he left it open.

And you passed on. Where did you go?—I went to the public-house across the road.

That is "The Crown and Sceptre"? Was anybody there?—Yes, my son and Mrs. Bruce.

And you joined them there?—Yes.

I have entirely forgotten to, and I must ask you this: can you tell me what time it was that you and Smith arrived at Beaufort Gardens that night?—Well, we were to pick up Mudie at half-past five, but we were late, I should say 20 minutes. That would make it somewhere about ten minutes to six, and I should think it took us about half an hour to get back.

You would calculate that you got there about a quarter or ten to seven?—Ten to seven—about that time.

And how soon after you got there did Mudie come in?—About five minutes.

And after you had done what you have told us, you were let out at the back door by Smith and went over to "The Crown and Sceptre"?—Yes.

How long had elapsed between the time when Mudie came in and you went over to "The Crown and Sceptre"?—Four or five minutes at the outside.

So that, so far as you were concerned, it was all over pretty quickly?—Yes.

Did you stay at "The Crown and Sceptre"?—No.

Where did you go?—We went to another public-house in Chelsea.

In the car, I suppose?—Yes, in the Wolseley.

You told me that he had given you a package on the basement stairs. Did you find out what was in it?—Yes.

When did you find that out?—In the Wolseley car.

And as you were going along from one public-house to the other?—Yes.

Ley and Smith.

John W. Buckingham

What was it?—Pound notes.

Did you count them?—No.

Did you count any of them?—Yes, 30.

What did you do with those?—Handed them to Mrs. Bruce.

Where did you go after that? You said that you went to another public-house?—We picked up a friend of Mrs. Bruce and we went to the public-house called "The Green Man" at Putney.

You went on to Mrs. Bruce's flat and finished the evening there?—Yes.

Did you finally count this money?—Yes, when I got home again.

How much was there?—Well, I gave my son £25, and gave my wife £10 and kept £15 for myself, and the rest I put in the bank the next day; it was £130 with £10 I added to it.

By the LORD CHIEF JUSTICE—You had given Mrs. Bruce £30?—Yes.

How much was left?—Actually there was £170.

So you got £200?—Yes.

And you had already had £30: you had £20 on one occasion for expenses and £10 on another?—Yes.

Examination continued—Did you ever see Ley again after he handed you that money?—No.

Did you ever see Smith again?—Yes, on the following Tuesday.

That would be 3rd December?—Actually, we made an appointment to meet on the Monday, because he said he was going to Leicester that same night and he would not be back until Monday afternoon.

He said he was going to Leicester on the Thursday night?—Yes.

And would not be back over the week-end?—Yes.

So you arranged to meet him on Monday, and you actually met him on Tuesday?—Yes.

Did he say anything about this affair to you?—Yes; the expression he used was: the old man was very pleased with the way things had gone, Mudie had signed a confession and was given £500 and got out of the country.

Of course, the last you had seen of him he was still at 5 Beaufort Gardens?—Yes.

Did he say how long he had stayed there?—Yes; he told me he stayed there about five or ten minutes. He said he heard Mr. Ley's friends come in the front door and then he went.

Evidence for Prosecution.

John W. Buckingham

By the Lord Chief Justice—You told us some time ago that Smith, when he left you at the back door, said that Ley's friends had not turned up and he had got to wait?—Yes.

Till that, had you heard anything about any suggestion of any friends coming that night?—Yes.

What had you heard?—Through Smith, that Mr. Ley had some friends that were going to take Mudie away, as far as I know they were going to take him to a 'plane; that was the impression that was given to me.

You had been told by Smith that Ley's friends were going to take Mudie to an aeroplane?—Yes. He did not say actually, but it was given me that he was going to be flown.

Examination continued—To fly him out of the country, do you mean?—Yes.

Did he say what he had done after he had left Beaufort Gardens—Smith, I mean?—Yes. He said that he could not go up to Leicester that night but he had come to look for me in the public-house, and then went over to Dulwich.

By the Lord Chief Justice—Previously he had told you that he was going to Leicester that night?—Yes.

When you saw him on the Tuesday he told you he had not been to Leicester that night?—Yes.

Examination continued—When did you see him again?—It would be about ten days after that.

Did he say anything to you about this matter then?—Yes. He said that I was not to communicate with Mr. Ley at all.

Did he say anything about Mudie then?—He said that Mudie was missing, and I took it he was out of the country, and that I was not to communicate with Ley; that was all.

Smith told you that Mudie was missing?—I am not quite clear on that point.

By the Lord Chief Justice—Did you see about the murder in the newspaper?—Yes.

Was it before you saw the newspaper or after you had seen the newspaper that Smith you say told you that Mudie was missing?—Before.

Examination continued—I want to follow this up, if I may. When was it that he said that? Was it when he said, "Do not communicate with Ley any more"?—Yes.

87

Ley and Smith.

John W. Buckingham

I think the end of the story, as far as you are concerned, is that you went to Scotland Yard on 14th December?—Yes.

Was that in consequence of seeing something in the paper and speaking to Mrs. Bruce?—Yes.

You say that the idea was that this man should be induced to sign a confession?—Yes.

Was it contemplated at all that he might refuse to sign it?—No. Mr. Ley had impressed on me that he had got sufficient evidence on him and that he would be only too glad to sign it.

Was anything said as to what, if anything, would happen if he refused to sign it?—No.

Cross-examined by Sir WALTER MONCKTON—My friend says the end of the story so far as you were concerned was that you went to Scotland Yard. The story did not quite end there, did it? You went to Scotland Yard and you made a statement, did not you?—Yes.

And also you were charged with murder?—Not at that time.

Later?—Yes.

And later you made a statement?—Yes.

And you were finally discharged?—Yes.

I want to ask you about this: for the part which you played on 28th November, and the events which led up to it, you received something like £200, on your story?—Yes.

And for that sum you were content to play the part which you say you played?—Yes.

And you have given two or three accounts of it. I want to ask you about the first. On 14th December you went to Scotland Yard and made a statement. I will just remind you what on 14th December you said about the events in 5 Beaufort Gardens: "Smith and I went to the front door. He had a key and we entered the house. We went to the back door and Mudie came in. Mrs. Bruce had been provided with a key of the back door. Mrs. Bruce slammed the door behind Mudie and remained outside. Smith was in the corridor and I was in the front room. As soon as Mudie saw Smith he said: 'Oh, yes. I know what it is all about.' We pushed him into the front room. There was no struggle and he showed no fight. We shut the door on him and left him. It was a room he could not get out of as there was a blank wall opposite the window. At this time Ley, who was on the stairs, handed me a package and I went straight out of the back door over to a pub where I met my son and Mrs. Bruce. On the way out Smith said: 'I cannot come now as the old man's friends have not arrived yet. I have got to stay in case he knocks the old man about.' We had

Evidence for Prosecution.

John W. Buckingham

one drink and drove to a pub near Chelsea." Is that what you said when you made your statement on 14th December?—Yes.

As to what happened in the house while you were there?—Yes.

You observe that you did not say at that stage anything about the tying?—No.

Nothing about your having put a rug over his head?—No.

Nothing about jumping him along the passage?—No.

And you still say there was no question of trouble while you were there?—No.

Or no gagging by you?—No.

You still say that?—Yes.

But on reflection you had come to the conclusion that he was tied up?—Yes.

And that you did put the rug over his head?—Yes.

When you were making your statement to the police you left these matters out?—Yes.

Now, you had known Minden for some little while, had you?—Yes.

And you knew him pretty well, I gather?—Yes.

And you have got to know Smith very well?—Yes.

Minden, as it were, put you on to this job?—Yes.

And you and your son and Mrs. Bruce and Smith were the people who made the journey to fetch the man?—Yes.

So far as Ley was concerned in October had he got to know you through Smith?—No.

Did not Smith introduce you to him?—No.

Thinking that some car-hiring work might be done?—No.

And is this right, after that you only saw him once again when you brought the car round to his house at 5 Beaufort Gardens?—No.

I put to you that there is not a word of truth in your suggestion that Ley was there on that night or that he made these preparations with you before?—He was, definitely.

The suggestion that I am making to you is that the interview of which I have spoken, as the occasion when you came round to 5 Beaufort Gardens, was all you ever saw of Ley?—No, I saw him on several occasions.

Cross-examined by Mr. CURTIS BENNETT—Whose suggestion was what you call the first scheme, to bring Mudie up, the scheme of acting drunk; was that your suggestion?—Yes, my suggestion.

How long about was it before the second scheme?—Just over a week.

Ley and Smith.

John W. Buckingham

Was the second scheme formulated on 26th November and finally settled what date it should be—that is, on the Tuesday?—I could not say the date.

Perhaps we will get it in a moment. The second scheme was your invention too, was not it?—Partly.

I am only thinking of what you said to the police about it. Did you not say that you thought it was your scheme?—Yes, I think it was mine.

It was invented, of course, before it was destined to be put into force?—Yes.

Invented about a week after the first scheme, was it?—Yes, I think that would be about right.

This may be important. How many days after the second scheme was invented was it decided to put it into action?—I think it must have been about a week. Do you mean actually the scheme was carried out?

No. How long after it was thought of was it agreed that it should be put into action at some time?—I should think about the same time.

It was put up to Ley and he agreed it, did he?—Yes.

If Smith says that the arrangements were made to carry out this scheme on the 28th, on Tuesday the 26th, would that be right— that the final arrangements were made to carry out this scheme two days before, namely, on the 26th?—Yes, I think it was.

The 26th is a Tuesday; I want that particularly. There was never any suggestion apart from tying him up that any violence should be done to Mudie, was there?—No, none whatever. That was insisted upon—that there was no violence.

Who by?—Well, Mr. Ley suggested that we were to use no violence whatever.

And you and Smith never heard of any suggestion of any violence being done to Mudie apart from tying him up?—No.

And that he was to be got up to London on a scheme which, although it involved deceit, did not involve any violence at all?— No.

That was the point of it?—Yes.

So that there should not be any violence?—Yes.

You and Smith had agreed, had you not, to go straight across to "The Crown and Sceptre" after taking Mudie up and tying him up?—Yes.

And have a drink?—Yes.

And Smith expressed to you his sorrow that he could not do that because he had to stay behind because Ley's friends had not turned up?—That is quite right.

Evidence for Prosecution.

John W. Buckingham

And he was there apparently to prevent Mudie from getting rough?—Yes.

Did you think that Mudie might put up a fight of some sort?—When I left him——

I mean with Mr. Ley, who is a much older man?—He definitely would have done on his own.

By the LORD CHIEF JUSTICE—How could he have done it if he was tied up?—Not because he was tied up; that is what I was trying to express.

Cross-examination continued—Did you think he would be annoyed?—Naturally enough he would become annoyed.

He would become out of temper when he was annoyed, and then he might become violent?—Yes.

And Ley is a much older man?—Yes.

You did not stay at "The Crown and Sceptre" very long?—No.

How long—two or three minutes?—Two or three minutes.

So that if Smith came out ten minutes later from Beaufort Gardens and looked for your car outside "The Crown and Sceptre" it would not have been there?—No.

Then you went to Chelsea, and then back?—Yes.

Now I want to ask you about this: from the beginning had you been told that the scheme was to get Mudie to sign a confession?—Yes.

To pay him £500 to get out of the country?—Yes.

That is what you had been told was the scheme?—Yes, right from the beginning.

Did you know there were three or four flats in Beaufort Gardens above the basement?—Yes.

I think Mr. Ley's flat is the ground floor and the first floor, the flat part and the offices in the basement?—Yes, that it right.

Three other flats as well?—I would not be certain of the number.

Well, a number of other flats in which the people reside?—I do not think there was anyone there at the time; I could not say.

By the LORD CHIEF JUSTICE—You say that you know there are three or four flats, but you do not think there was anybody living there at the time?—No; the house was under repair.

Cross-examination continued—There are houses on either side next door, are there not?—Yes.

Ley and Smith.

John W. Buckingham

Of course, you do not know about the occupancy of the upstairs flats, do you?—No.

We shall perhaps find out about that. Are you quite sure that when you put the rug over Mudie's head you did not do something else then?—Yes.

Why did you take the rug off Mudie's head in the middle room then?—Well, just took it off naturally.

What I am going to suggest to you is that you took it off quite correctly, for a very definite reason, in other words to put a gag on his mouth to keep him quiet?—No; I never put any gag on his mouth at all.

I know you said so, but you see, I am asking you about it. Did not Smith go out into the front room of the basement and bring a green cloth back for you to gag Mudie with?—No.

I do not mean severely gag him, or stifle him, but to stop him shouting?—No.

So is your story that nothing could have prevented him shouting if he wanted to?—No.

No gag round his mouth—nothing?—No.

Did it strike you that he might shout?—I did not think there was any point in it.

Never mind whether you think there was any point in it. There may be a great deal of point in it if he was tied up. Did it strike you that he might have shouted?—Well, he might have shouted. He even spoke to me, or spoke to us.

What did he say?—He said he knew what it was all about.

I am suggesting to you, and having done it I shall pass therefrom, that you were given that gag by Smith, who went and fetched it out of the next room, and you tied it round his mouth?—No.

Now, that way where you frog marched him or jumped him along the corridor is a stone floor, is it not?—Yes.

Did he not fall down, or trip up and fall down with you on top of him?—No.

Smith said he did, you know, but you do not agree?—No, I do not agree.

He was tied up right round the legs, was not he?—Yes.

I suggest you both fell down together, you picked him up, and then marched him into the room; is that not right?—No. I never fell down on him at all.

I thought you were going to say when my lord was asking you about his size, something about his weight. What sort of weight would you put him at roughly as a guess?—I should say a man about 11 or 12 stone.

Evidence for Prosecution.

John W. Buckingham

A man about, that is to say, the same height as Smith?—Yes.

Five feet seven inches, or five feet eight inches?—Yes.

When Mudie came in could you hear the Yale lock being turned?—No, I could not.

You were in the next room?—Yes, where I think there was a window leading right on to the back alley-way, and you could hear more from the window than you could——

Very well. As far as you know the mortise lock was open, or unlocked?—I do not know whether there was a mortise lock there or not.

Well, there is. As far as you know it was open?—Yes.

I want you to help me for a moment about the 27th. You live in Mostyn Road, Brixton?—Yes.

How long does it take you to get from there to Beaufort Gardens in a car?—I should say with the traffic bad about half an hour.

Did Smith on the 27th arrive at your house in Mostyn Road for tea at about half-past five?—I would not be certain of the time.

I did not ask you to be certain. I said "about." Would half-past five be about right?—I would not like to say that at all.

Did he arrive for tea?—Yes.

What time do you usually have tea—about half-past five?—I think the wife made it specially when he came.

I want to ask you not to be definite, because you cannot be expected to remember the exact time. If Smith says, for example, that he arrived at Mostyn Road at half-past five on that afternoon, you would not be prepared to disagree with him, would you?—No.

He did arrive for tea; that is quite certain, whatever the time was?—Yes.

You would agree that if he had in fact arrived at about half-past five, and if he had come from Beaufort Gardens, he must have left there about five, must not he?—Yes.

Did he stay with you? Was your son there?—Yes.

Then did you drive to Mrs. Bruce's house; is that right?—That is right.

In a place called Holmbush Road, Putney?—Yes.

Then did you go to "The Green Man," Putney?—Yes.

You arrived there about seven o'clock?—I should take it it would be.

Mrs. Bruce, yourself, Smith, and anyone else?—And my son.

And did you stay at "The Green Man" till 10.30 p.m., until it closed, about?—We stayed there for quite some time.

I expect you remember when it closed, if you were there. Did you not stay there till it closed—ten o'clock?—I think so, yes.

Ley and Smith.

John W. Buckingham

It closed I am told at half-past ten, but you stayed there till nearly ten?—Well, till closing time.

Then did Smith drive you and your son home to Mostyn Road? —Yes.

Smith lives at Dulwich, does he not?—Yes.

Just tell me, because you cannot tell us the time and I am quite aware of that, who was present at the tea party which Smith was at on the 27th besides yourself?—My son and wife.

Had Smith told you that he was going to Leicester at the week-end in that week of which the Thursday is the 28th?—Yes.

And, of course, the 29th is the beginning of the week-end?—Yes.

By the LORD CHIEF JUSTICE—You told us Smith told you he was going to Leicester on the night of the 28th?—Yes.

Cross-examination continued—What you told the magistrate in the Police Court in this case was that Smith told you afterwards that he had gone straight to Leicester that night. Here you said he went the next day, did not you? I will read you what it is said you said before the magistrate: "Then he had gone straight away to 'The Crown and Sceptre' to look for me, but not seeing a car outside the public-house he had not gone in. Then he said he had driven straight down to Leicester"?—Yes, well, that is what he told me he was going to do.

I know that is what you say now, but you see you are saying here he told you he had gone straight to Leicester?—Yes, but he told me afterwards that he did not go.

That is what I am asking you. I know you said in chief that he told you he was going to Leicester on the Thursday, and that is why I asked you. Is not what you said "Yes" to just now right, that he told you he was going to Leicester that week-end?—He told me he was going to Leicester on Thursday night.

Do you say that he told you on Thursday night he was going to Leicester?—Yes, after we had left Mudie.

Did he tell you on Thursday that he was going to Leicester, or did he tell you before that he was going to Leicester on the Thursday? Do you understand? Did he tell you on the Thursday: "I am going to Leicester," or before the Thursday did he say: "I am going to Leicester on Thursday"?—I cannot be certain about that.

So it may not be right that he told you on the Thursday he was going to Leicester on the same day?—No; it may have been the day before.

Evidence for Prosecution.

John W. Buckingham

That is why I was putting to you what I suggest is much more likely, that he said to you earlier than that that he was going to Leicester over the week-end?—Yes, but I got the impression that he was going immediately on the same——

By the LORD CHIEF JUSTICE—Did you expect to meet him on the Thursday night after you left the house?—Yes, definitely.

Why was that?—Because he had made arrangements that we would all meet and have a drink.

At "The Crown and Sceptre"?—Yes, and I took it that he was making straight for Leicester.

How long did you stay at "The Crown and Sceptre" waiting for him?—Only because he told me when I was leaving the house that he could not come and meet me and have a drink because he had to wait there with the old man.

Then did you wait for him at "The Crown and Sceptre"?—No.

Cross-examination continued—There was no waiting for him at "The Crown and Sceptre" because he had told you he could not come?—Yes, that is quite right.

Just so that we can see whether there was a murder plot here or not, the original arrangement had been that you should go and have a drink with him at "The Crown and Sceptre"?—Yes.

Only altered because Smith had told you that Ley had said his friends had not come?—Yes.

Did you hear Ley say that his friends had not come?—No.

Then you saw Smith on what you now agree is 3rd December, the following Tuesday?—That is right.

Of course, you knew by then that the arrangement had been to get Mudie to sign a confession, pay him £500 and get him to leave the country?—Yes.

You knew that?—Yes.

Was not what Smith told you on the Tuesday simply this, or something like this: first of all that he had waited talking to Ley for about ten minutes—that I think you agree with?—Yes.

And that Ley was pleased with the way that things had gone?—Yes.

You have told us that Smith told you that Mudie had signed the confession, had been paid £500, and that he had gone out of the country; you told us that just now?—Yes.

Was not that the impression you got from what he said, which was simply that Ley was pleased with the way things had gone?—Yes.

95

Ley and Smith.

John W. Buckingham

By the LORD CHIEF JUSTICE—But did he say anything about that he had been paid £500?—Yes.

Cross-examination continued—You must not agree with me just because I ask you a question, you see. I want you to think about it. It happens to be Smith's case that he did not say anything to you about the £500, or the confession, or leaving the country, but he had said so before?—No; he told me on that occasion definitely that Mudie had been given the money.

Why did you agree with me just now when I put it, as I hope quite plainly, that Smith had said that Ley was pleased with the way things had gone, and that you had interpreted that as meaning £500, the confession and leaving the country?——

The LORD CHIEF JUSTICE—You know what he said in chief, and you asked him whether he drew a certain impression from Ley being pleased with what had happened. He had already said that he had been told that Ley had given him £500 and that Mudie had left the country.

Cross-examination continued—One of the purposes of cross-examination is to try and find out the truth, and that is what I am trying to do, and I am going to put it again, because I suggest the truth is that all Smith told you was that Ley was pleased with the way things had gone, and you formed the impression that that meant all the rest?—No. He told me that Mudie had really——

What you have said in chief is right?—Yes.

Did you not understand the question?—No, I did not.

I thought it was plain enough when I asked you whether you had formed that impression, and I am suggesting, curiously enough, that what you say in chief is not always accurate?—I am trying to be as accurate as I can.

You see, that being the arrangement, if you heard that Ley was pleased, you would assume that that was what had happened, would you not?—Yes, but it was definitely told me.

Well, you say that, and you are quite entitled to say that, and that is what you said in chief, but I am just putting it to you. As Sir Walter Monckton has pointed out to you earlier, in the original statement you missed out the tying up?—Yes.

And later on you had to agree that was right; he had been tied up?—Yes.

And you missed out other things from your first statement, did you not?—Not that I know of.

Yes, the rug. You missed out all mention of the rug?—Yes.

Mrs. LILIAN FLORENCE BRUCE

Evidence for Prosecution.

You are here deliberately missing out that bit of material, Exhibit 13, are not you?—No.

And here you are missing out, as always you have missed out, the fall which you know quite well took place?—No fall took place.

Just to find out as to the various ideas, you have agreed that the first plan and the second plan were yours. Was the idea that Mrs. Bruce should go down and get to know Mudie, Mrs. Bruce's idea?—Yes, I think it was.

The idea for this plan was yours; the instructions to carry it out were Ley's; is that right?—Yes.

And Smith played a part in it?—Yes.

We have to find out in some other way, but do you know of your own knowledge when the fact that a man had been found near a chalk pit at Woldingham was published in the newspapers? —No.

By the LORD CHIEF JUSTICE—Did you see it in the paper yourself?—Yes.

How soon after that did you go to Scotland Yard?—On the same day.

Cross-examination continued—That would be the 14th, would it not?—Yes.

Was that a name or just a body found?—A name and a photograph.

It had gone further then?—Just a little piece in the *Daily Mail*.

With the name and a photograph of Mudie?—Yes.

You put this second interview with Smith afterwards at 9th December, do you not? At the Magistrate's Court it was a Monday; is that right?—On the Tuesday, yes.

Was the second occasion the time when Smith came to your house for some drink?—Yes.

Was that Monday, 9th December? That is what I suggest you swore to the magistrate; is that right or wrong?—I said he came, I think, about ten days later.

What you said here was "About ten days later." I am putting, do you think you said below it was 9th December, which would be six days later? Is that right?—He visited me the second time some days later, after the——

By the LORD CHIEF JUSTICE—I have the date, 3rd December. You remember him coming to see you on Tuesday, 3rd December? —Yes.

Ley and Smith.

John W. Buckingham

Do you remember which day it was he came after that?—No; it was about nine or ten days after that.

Cross-examination continued—On that occasion, whenever the date, did not Smith tell you that Mudie had been dropped at Wimbledon?—Yes.

By the LORD CHIEF JUSTICE—Did he tell you that before he said Mudie was missing?—Yes.

What did he say?—He said as far as he knew Mudie had been —no, I beg your pardon; that Ley had told him that Mudie had been dropped at Wimbledon.

See if you can remember. Did he say: "Mudie is missing. Ley told me that he had been dropped at Wimbledon," or did he say: "Ley told me he had been dropped at Wimbledon but he is missing"? Do you remember which it was?—No, I cannot.

He did tell you he was missing?—Yes.

And he did tell you that Ley had said that he had dropped him at Wimbledon, or he had been dropped at Wimbledon?—I think I am getting a little confused there.

Well, just try and think it out. Take your time. Do you remember him telling you that Ley had told him that Mudie had been dropped at Wimbledon?—I cannot remember that, whether I read that in the statement. I have got mixed up.

You may have read that, but do you not think he told you?— I do not think so.

But he did tell you he was missing?—Yes.

Re-examined by Mr. HAWKE—Smith came to tea on Wednesday, 27th November, did he?—Yes.

You cannot tell us the time?—No.

But you can tell us how he came; he came in a car, did he?— Yes.

What sort of a car was it?—A Ford.

Was it the same car that he drove down to Reigate the following night?—Yes.

I think you have said you did not know what the number of that car was?—No.

Did you tell my learned friend that it was insisted upon that no violence should be done to this man?—Yes.

Other than tie him up?—Yes.

By the LORD CHIEF JUSTICE—When Smith came to you on the 27th he just turned up at your house?—Yes.

Evidence for Prosecution.

You do not know where he came from?—No.

It has been put to you that of course Smith was there on that evening and took part in this tying up. Where was Ley standing at this time so far as you know?—Well, as far as I know at the tying up he was upstairs; I had not seen him then, barring the first time when I first entered.

At the time you first entered the house?—I saw him then.

And you did not see him after that?—Yes, when he handed me the package.

Was that before or after Mudie was brought in?—That was after Mudie was tied up.

Ley handed you the package?—Yes.

LILIAN FLORENCE BRUCE, sworn, examined by Mr. ELAM—Do you live with your husband, who is a 'bus driver, at Holmbush Road, Putney?—Yes.

And you work yourself as a cook-housekeeper at Putney?—Yes.

Have you ever seen, except in Court, the accused Ley?—No.

Do you know a man named John Buckingham, the elder?—Yes.

Roughly, how long have you known him?—I should think about five months now.

Did he run a car business?—Yes.

You had bought a car through him, had you not?—Yes.

Do you know his son, John Buckingham, junior?—Yes.

Do you know the accused, Smith?—Yes, I have met him twice.

Whenabouts, roughly, did you meet him first?—About a week before 28th November, I think.

Did somebody introduce you to him?—Yes, Mr. Buckingham.

Where?—At Putney, in "The Green Man."

Was there any discussion then between Buckingham and Smith? —No.

When did you see Smith again?—I am not sure; it was very near the 28th.

Where was that?—I think they came to my house first, and we went to "The Green Man" after.

Did you later go down in a car to Reigate?—Yes.

Now, going back for a minute, when you saw Smith in "The Green Man," on either time was anything said about going down to Reigate?—The second time.

Would you tell my lord and the jury what was said the second time?—I could not, because I did not speak to Mr. Smith very much.

Was there anything said about going down to Reigate?—Well, yes; I was to go down.

Ley and Smith.

Lilian F. Bruce

What for?—Well, to see if Mr. Mudie spoke to me; if he did, to invite him up to town.

Had anything been said as to who Mudie was?—Yes; he was a barman at the Reigate Hill Hotel, and that he was heavily blackmailing two ladies.

Who said that?—Mr. Buckingham told me.

In the presence of Smith?—Oh, yes.

By the LORD CHIEF JUSTICE—Was Smith present when Buckingham told you that Mudie was blackmailing, or was supposed to be blackmailing, two ladies?—Yes.

Was he one of the parties?—Yes.

Quite close to you?—Yes.

Examination continued—What was the point of your going down to Reigate; was that said?—Yes; that the ladies' solicitor wanted him to come to town to his office to sign a statement that he would leave them alone.

Who said that?—Mr. Buckingham.

Was it said at any time then where in town Mudie was to come to?—I did not know the address—Kensington.

To what sort of building, did you understand?—A house in Kensington.

Was the name of the solicitor mentioned?—I was told he was Sir Edward Ley.

Who said that?—Buckingham and Smith.

What did you say about going down to Reigate to see Mudie? —I spoke over it with them, and I agreed to go down.

By the LORD CHIEF JUSTICE—But who made the suggestion, and what was the suggestion that was made?—A suggestion was made that I should go to the hotel, not force myself on him, but if he spoke to me, ask him to come to a party in town.

Was he to come to the party as a guest or as a cocktail shaker?— Well, a guest, and mix cocktails.

Examination continued—Were you giving a party?—Yes.

But were you really giving a party?—No.

Did you ask any more about this plan?—Well, yes; I asked if it was alright; if we were doing something legal, after that.

And what did they answer?—They said yes, otherwise they would not be doing it themselves.

Who said that?—Mr. Buckingham.

Evidence for Prosecution.

Lilian F. Bruce

Had you up to that moment ever seen this man Mudie?—I had seen him, yes. I did not know who he was. I had been in there before.

But you did not know him then?—I did not know him then.

You knew the hotel?—I did not know the hotel; I did not know anything about it when I saw him first.

By the LORD CHIEF JUSTICE—When did you see him first?—I should think it was about three weeks before that time.

Who took you down?—I went with Mr. Buckingham and his wife. We were out for a ride, and we called in there for a drink.

Examination continued—When did you go down to Reigate to see Mudie about this party?—I should think it would be about the 24th, the first time; I am not sure of the date.

Who went with you?—Mr. Buckingham.

Senior or junior?—They both went.

How did you go?—By car.

Did anyone else go with you?—No.

What happened when you got to the Reigate Hill Hotel?—I went into the hotel and called for a drink.

Did the others come in?—Buckingham junior.

Did Mudie serve you with the drink?—Yes.

What was young Buckingham wearing?—His mac. and a peaked cap.

By the LORD CHIEF JUSTICE—Who drove you down that day; was there more than one car load?—No; there were just the three of us. I am not sure if Mr. Buckingham senior or junior was driving; I don't remember.

Examination continued—But the elder Buckingham on this occasion stayed outside with the car, did he?—Yes.

I am not asking you what was said, but only just the fact. Did you speak to Mudie?—Yes.

And how long about were you in the bar?—I was in there about half an hour.

Did you then leave?—Yes.

Did you all three go back to London in the car?—Yes.

When did you next go to the Reigate Hill Hotel?—The next day or the day after.

Who with?—Mr. Buckingham, the elder.

In the car again?—Yes.

Did you go into the bar again?—Yes.

Ley and Smith.

Lilian F. Bruce

Was Mudie there that time?—Yes.

Did Buckingham come in with you?—No, I went in alone.

How long about were you in the bar that time with Mudie?—About a quarter of an hour that time.

Was some arrangement made between you?—He gave me his 'phone number and asked me to 'phone him.

An arrangement was made?—Yes.

Did you then go back to London in the car with Buckingham?—Yes.

I am only asking you the fact; did you use the telephone number you had been given?—Yes.

Did you go to the Reigate Hill Hotel again?—On the Thursday, 28th November.

How did you go?—By car.

Starting about what time, roughly?—Five.

Was that from your home?—Yes.

Who picked you up in the car?—Mr. Buckingham, junior, senior, and Mr. Smith.

How many cars were there?—Two.

Which car did you go in?—The Wolseley.

With whom did you go?—Mr. Buckingham.

What was Buckingham junior wearing on that occasion?—I do not remember.

Do you remember arriving at Reigate Hill?—Yes.

What happened to the cars then and the passengers?—Mr. Buckingham got in the Ford, and Buckingham junior came in the Wolseley with me.

Did you get to Reigate Hill Hotel?—Yes.

Have you any idea of about what time?—About a quarter to six.

What happened when you got there?—Mudie was waiting and got in the car and came back.

Was he waiting outside the hotel?—Yes.

Which car did he get into?—In the Wolseley.

Did you drive back to London?—Yes.

Do you know where you went to in London?—Yes, Beaufort Gardens.

Which entrance?—The side.

Did you notice anything written up over the door or near the door?—Yes, "Ye Old Air Raid Shelter."

How many cars went to that door?—Just the Wolseley.

How were you going to get into that door?—I had a key.

A Yale key?—Yes.

Who had given it to you?—Mr. Buckingham.

Evidence for Prosecution.

Lilian F. Bruce

What happened when you got to that door?—I gave John the key—Mr. Buckingham's son—and he opened the door.

Did you get out?—I got out, yes.

What happened?—I got out, Mudie went in, the door was closed, and I got back in the car again.

By the Lord Chief Justice—Did you go on to the door?—I went to the door, yes.

Then what happened?—I asked Mudie to come in, and I called John and got back in the car.

Had you arranged that beforehand?—Yes.

You were to get him into the house and then pretend that you wanted to speak to the driver?—Yes.

Examination continued—And when the door was closed, as you have told us, was Mudie inside the house?—Yes.

Did you get back into the car?—Yes.

Was there anyone else in it?—Yes, Buckingham junior.

Did you and he go somewhere in the car?—We went across to "The Crown and Sceptre" and had a drink.

Yes; I do not think that is challenged. Did you have a drink there?—Yes.

Did you see Mr. Buckingham senior again?—Yes.

How long about were you in "The Crown and Sceptre" roughly?—Well, I should think under ten minutes.

And then where did you go?—We went on to Putney then in the car.

Did anybody give you anything in the car at any time?—Yes; Mr. Buckingham gave me some money.

How much?—£30.

How was it made up?—In £1 notes.

Did you see Mudie again at all?—No.

What did you do with the key?—I gave it back to Mr. Buckingham.

Now on 14th December did you see a report in the paper about Mudie's body having been found?—Yes.

Was that the first time you had seen anything of that kind?—It was the first time, yes.

Did you go and see Buckingham about it?—I 'phoned them straight away.

The father?—I 'phoned both of them.

Did you go that day to Scotland Yard?—As soon as they came I went straight to Scotland Yard.

Ley and Smith.

Lilian F. Bruce

That is you and Buckingham?—The two Buckinghams and myself.

Cross-examined by Mr. CURTIS BENNETT—Am I right in saying that the final arrangements to carry out the plan were fixed on the Wednesday before the Thursday—on the 27th?—To me, yes.

The day before the 28th, namely the 27th, which was a Wednesday, can you remember whether it is right that Mr. Smith and the Buckinghams called at your house at Holmbush Road; that is right, is it not?—Yes.

And took you to "The Green Man" at Putney?—Yes.

Did you get to "The Green Man" about 7 o'clock?—Yes.

Can you give my lord and the jury any idea as to what time about Smith called for you, or called in the car with the Buckinghams? How long before you got to "The Green Man" did he pick you up in the car?—I should think about a quarter of an hour before. It was between half-past six and seven.

Between 6.30 and 7 at your house?—I am not certain of the time.

No, but it was about then?—Yes.

And did you all stop there, that is to say Smith, Buckingham, father and son, yourself and your husband, until the public-house shut?—No.

Until 10 o'clock?—No. Mr. Smith went after about an hour, I think.

Did he go with the Buckinghams?—Yes.

And then you and your husband walked home?—Yes.

Re-examined by Mr. HAWKE—When Smith called for you on the evening of the 27th did he come in a car?—Yes.

He was driving, was he?—I do not remember who was driving.

Do you remember what sort of car it was?—Yes; it was a Ford.

Did you by any chance happen to notice the number?—No.

The time you say was somewhere between half-past six and seven. You could not give it any more accurately than that?—No, I am afraid I could not.

JOHN WILLIAM BUCKINGHAM, sworn, examined by Mr. HAWKE—Was it your father who gave evidence this morning?—Yes.

Do you assist him in his car business?—Yes, that is right.

How old are you?—Twenty-one.

You drive this car of his, the Wolseley, from time to time, I suppose?—That is quite right.

Evidence for Prosecution.

John W. Buckingham, jun.

Did you drive it to the Reigate Hill Hotel on Thursday, 28th November?—Yes.

Who was with you when you drove it there?—Mrs. Bruce.

Mrs. Bruce was with you in the Wolseley. Did another car go with you?—Yes, a Ford.

Who was in that?—My father and Smith.

Have you been down to Reigate Hill Hotel before 28th November?—Yes; I went down once.

Who did you go down with on that occasion?—With my father and Mrs. Bruce.

Do you remember which day that was?—Well, roughly, I should say about the 24th.

What was the purpose of that visit on the 24th?—To see a gentleman named Mudie.

Did you see this man Mudie on that occasion?—Yes, I did; in the Reigate Hotel. He was serving behind the bar.

Was Mrs. Bruce with you?—Yes.

You both went into the bar, did you?—Yes.

How were you dressed?—I was dressed in a chauffeur's uniform.

Did Mrs. Bruce have some conversation with Mudie at all?—Yes.

Did you know why you had gone down to the Reigate Hill Hotel to see this man?—Yes. At first I was told there was a man blackmailing two ladies, and that we were asked to go down and persuade Mudie to come up to London.

Were you told that Mudie was the man who was blackmailing the two ladies?—Yes; my father told me that.

When did he tell you that; how long before you went down with Mrs. Bruce?—Quite some time back; I cannot actually say when.

Some time before 24th November?—Yes.

So you went down on that day so that Mrs. Bruce could speak to him?—Yes.

And the idea was to get him back to London later on?—Yes, quite.

Was that the only other time that you went down?—That was twice; I only went twice—once about the 24th and then again on the 28th.

I see; those are the only two times you went?—Yes.

You had by this time met Smith, had you?—Yes.

When did you first meet him?—Quite some time—about a week hence.

Do you see the gentleman sitting furthest from you, Ley?—Yes.

Ley and Smith.

John W. Buckingham, jun.

Do you know him?—Yes, I met him at the Royal Hotel on two occasions.

Where did you see him?—I saw him speaking to my father in the lobby of the lounge on one occasion on which I did not speak to him.

Did you see him again afterwards then?—Yes; I saw him and spoke to him on another occasion.

Who was he with when you spoke to him on that occasion?—My father.

Was that also in the lounge of the Royal Hotel?—No; that was just outside the Royal.

Did your father introduce you to him then?—Yes, my father introduced me to him.

Did you have any conversation yourself with him?—No.

That was before your father told you that you were to go down to Reigate and collect this man and bring him up to London?—No; that was afterwards—quite a time afterwards: about a week.

By the Lord Chief Justice—Do you mean that your father told you quite a time afterwards that you had to go down so that you would meet him?—Afterwards, that is right.

You were introduced to him on one day, and quite a time afterwards your father told you he wanted you to go down on this errand?—Yes.

Examination continued—When you got to the Reigate Hill Hotel on Thursday, the 28th, was this man waiting for you?—Yes, he was waiting in the foreground.

In the forecourt of the hotel?—Yes.

What time was it?—Well, actually we were supposed to be there at half-past five, but it was late, and it was, I should think, about ten to six.

What happened when you arrived there?—We picked Mudie up, and I turned the car round and started back for London, following the Ford car.

The Ford went on ahead, did it?—Yes.

By the Lord Chief Justice—Did it go ahead all the way, or did it follow you and then pass you?—No—well, actually it was behind me at first, and I went on so far and I lost my way, and then the Ford car caught up with me and brought me back.

And then piloted you?—Yes.

Evidence for Prosecution.

John W. Buckingham, jun.

Examination continued—The Ford got to London a little before you?—Just a little time, yes.

Where did you go when you got back to London?—Beaufort Gardens.

By the LORD CHIEF JUSTICE—Had it been arranged that the Ford should get to London before you?—Yes, just a little before me.

Who had arranged that?—I could not definitely say, my lord.

Who told you that the Ford was to get there first, do you remember? Did you know you had got to let the Ford get to Beaufort Gardens before you?—No, not actually. We were to follow the Ford through to London, but actually that one of us was to be there before the others really I do not believe.

Examination continued—But it did get there before you?—Yes.

And we have heard that went to the front door; did you go to the front door?—No; I went to the side entrance of the house.

What did you do when you got there?—Mrs. Bruce gave me the key of the door and I opened it, and Mrs. Bruce went in a few steps following behind Mudie; Mrs. Bruce called out to me while I was waiting outside, and she came out and closed the door behind her. I got in the car and drove across to a public-house called "The Crown and Sceptre" where I ordered a drink, and my father came in just as I ordered the drink.

How long, roughly, after you had got to "The Crown and Sceptre" did your father come in?—I should say about four or five minutes.

Had it been arranged that Mrs. Bruce should call out when you got to the back door?—Yes, I believe so.

That evening, after your father had joined you, he has told us that you went on to another public-house?—Yes, that is right.

Then to Mrs. Bruce's?—That is correct.

You finished the evening there?—Yes.

Did you come home with your father afterwards?—Yes, I came home with my father.

Did he give you anything at all that evening?—That evening we went home; I drove my father home, and, yes, he gave me something.

What did he give you?—£10 that night.

Did you see where he got it from?—No, I did not see where he got it from, but he told me that he——

Well, never mind; you did not see where he got it from?—No.

Ley and Smith.

John W. Buckingham, jun.

Had you seen him give money to anybody else the evening before?—Yes.

Who to?—Mrs. Bruce.

When did he give her the money?—In the car as we were driving to the other public-house.

Between "The Crown and Sceptre" and the second public-house?—Yes.

How did you see that?—Well, my father brought the money out on the table.

What for?—He was counting the money.

By the LORD CHIEF JUSTICE—Where was that—at home?—At home.

Examination continued—Had your father on any previous occasion ever shown you any money?—Yes.

Could you tell me when that was?—It was once in the Royal Hotel; I did not actually see the money, but he had an envelope containing some money, which he said was given to him by——

Never mind what he said; I am afraid I cannot ask you that; but he had an envelope to your knowledge with some money in it?—Yes.

In the Royal Hotel?—Yes.

Was that one of the occasions when you saw Ley?—Yes, that was in the lounge at the time.

Cross-examined by Mr. CURTIS BENNETT—I want you to throw your mind back to the day before you drove to Reigate, the 27th. On that day were you at your father's house in the afternoon at Mostyn Road, Brixton?—Yes.

Did Smith come to the house during the afternoon and have tea there?—Well, I cannot say the afternoon, but Smith came to tea.

Let us take it by stages. Smith came?—Yes.

And had tea?—Yes, he had some tea.

The day before this expedition to Reigate?—Yes.

Would you agree with me, without being precise about it, that he arrived at Mostyn Road at about half-past five in the afternoon?—Well, I would not like to be sure.

About then? I am not asking exactly half-past five by the ringing of the church clock—say at about half-past five?—It could have been.

Well, he had some tea?—Yes.

Evidence for Prosecution.

John W. Buckingham, jun.

I do not want to worry about the rest of the evening, but I think you were present when Smith and your father and yourself went to Mrs. Bruce's house and went on to "The Green Man"?—That is correct.

And spent most of the evening at "The Green Man"?—Yes.

And then Mr. Smith drove you back home, did he?—Yes.

Re-examined by Mr. HAWKE—It could have been half-past five, could it?—It could have been.

Could it have been later?—It could have been a bit later.

Have you any idea of the time it was really?—No, I would not like to say.

WILLIAM CHARLES CARVOSSO, sworn, examined by Mr. ELAM—I am a security clerk in the Midland Bank, Sloane Street. The accused, Ley, had an account at that bank, and I know him by sight. Exhibit 2, which I produce, is an extract from his account. I have compared it with the books in daily use at the bank, and it is correct.

On 16th November, 1946, does it show that the sum of £250 was withdrawn?—Yes.

How was it taken out; in what form?—In cash.

On 26th November, was the sum of £300 withdrawn from that account?—Yes.

In what form?—In cash.

On 4th December, was the sum of £300 withdrawn from that account?—Yes.

In what form?—By payment into another account, by cheque.

And it gives the number of the cheque?—Yes.

When you say "to another account," that cheque went into the account of Lawrence John Smith?—Yes.

On 10th December, was £300 paid into the account?—Yes.

It is the bottom of page 2, the last item but one. In what form?—In cash.

And on 10th December, was the sum of £496 paid into the account?—Yes.

In what form?—In cash.

By somebody called Lawrence John Smith, who also had an account at that branch of that bank?—Yes.

Do you know Smith?—No.

Do you produce Exhibit 3, a certificated extract from it?—Yes.

Has that been compared with the books at the bank in daily use and is it correct?—Yes.

Ley and Smith.

William C. Carvosso

Can you say when and how that account was opened?—It was opened on 4th December, 1946, with a cheque for £300 drawn on the account of T. J. Ley.

That is the one you told us about just now?—Yes.

Was the whole amount withdrawn from that account on 9th December, five days later?—Yes.

In cash?—In cash.

By the LORD CHIEF JUSTICE—I do not follow that last answer. The amount was withdrawn from Smith's account on 9th December in cash; on 10th December, the same amount is paid into Ley's account in cash?—Yes.

PATRICIA BRITTAIN, sworn, examined by Mr. ELAM—I work at a car hire firm in Beauchamp Place called Howard Services. I know the accused, Ley, as a customer of that firm.

Do you know his voice over the telephone or are you familiar with it?—Oh, yes; I have heard it very often.

Did he speak to you sometime about the end of November?—Yes, over the telephone.

What did he ask you?—He asked me if I had any cars for self-drive, that was other than a chauffeur-driven car.

That is for the hirer to drive himself?—Yes. I told him we had only one at the time, which was an old make of car and rather heavy on petrol.

Did he say who the car was for?—Yes, for a friend of his, a Mr. Smith.

Did he seem interested in this old car?—Well, yes; he said could we arrange for Mr. Smith to see it, and I said yes, the following morning.

Did you know the accused, Smith, at that time?—No.

Did Ley say anything about him as he was introducing him as a customer?—He said he was a friend of his and that he could vouch for him.

Did Smith come round to Beauchamp Place the next morning as arranged?—Yes.

Was the car there?—Yes.

Did he look at it?—Yes; I took him myself.

Was some arrangement made between you and Smith as to what was to happen about the car?—Well, I said as far as the letting of it was concerned he would have to see the manager, and I would send him round as soon as he came in.

That is Mr. Normanton, the next witness?—Yes.

Evidence for Prosecution.

Patricia Brittain

He was out, and you were going to send him round as soon as he came in?—Yes.

Send him round where?—To Beaufort Gardens.

Who gave you that address?—Mr. Ley.

Cross-examined by Mr. CURTIS BENNETT—You are not clear about the date when this conversation with Ley happened?—Well, I cannot say now exactly which date it was.

I am wondering whether you could help me with regard to that. As to the telephone message you spoke of, did that happen on a Monday?—Well, I cannot say for sure; it is so long ago.

I am only trying to get some help about it. You were asked for a car on the Monday for Mr. Smith, on the 25th, that being the Tuesday. Can you tell me when the hiring was actually operative from?—Well, he did not actually have this Marmon car. It was a week later, I believe, when he did have a car.

This was a week before?—Well, it was some time before; I cannot say exactly.

By the LORD CHIEF JUSTICE—This old car was a Marmon?—Yes.

It never was let to Smith?—No.

Cross-examination continued—The conversation about that car was roughly how long before any further car was mentioned?— I should say it was at least two or three days before.

It might have been as long as a week?—I do not think it was as long as a week; two or three days.

And that was the car you sent round?—That was the one that Mr. Smith went round to look at, the Marmon.

CHARLES FREDERICK NORMANTON, sworn, examined by Mr. ELAM—You are the manager of Howard's Hire Car Service, Beauchamp Place?—Yes.

Does the last witness, Miss Brittain, work there?—Yes.

Did she speak to you about a car for a Mr. Smith?—Yes.

Is that the accused, Smith?—Yes.

Did you go round and see him about hiring a car?—Yes.

Did he eventually hire a car?—He did.

Do you know the actual date he hired a car?—I could not say off-hand now.

By the LORD CHIEF JUSTICE—Have you got any books that have got the date entered in?—We have a signing in and out slip which Mr. Smith signed.

Ley and Smith.

Charles F. Normanton

Have you got that still?—No, the police have that.

We had better have that. While that is being looked for, do you remember about when it was?—I should think it was in November.

Mr. ELAM—I am told, to save time, by Mr. Curtis Bennett, that I can put the dates to him.

The LORD CHIEF JUSTICE—Very well, if Mr. Curtis Bennett does not object.

Examination continued—Was it on 25th November last year that Smith hired a Ford car?—I should imagine so; it was a Monday, I can tell you that.

For how long?—A week.

Did he return it on the following Monday, 2nd December?—On the following Monday he returned it.

Now, going back from there, before Smith actually hired the Ford, you saw him?—Yes.

How long about before was that?—I should imagine about a week before he hired the Ford.

Where did you see him?—5 Beaufort Gardens.

There was some conversation about a Marmon car, which was rather old and heavy on petrol?—Yes.

And he did not agree to have the Marmon, and in fact never had it?—No.

Did you see anybody else at Beaufort Gardens besides Smith? —Mr. Ley.

By the LORD CHIEF JUSTICE—Was that on another occasion?— No; on the occasion when Mr. Smith decided not to have the Marmon.

Examination continued—Did Ley say anything about cars or the car?—Mr. Ley just simply said to me in these words: "Well, there you are. You have not done any business and that is all there is to it."

A day or two later did a Ford become available?—It did.

What horsepower?—8 h.p.

What colour?—Black, F G P 101.

Did you go round to Beaufort Gardens again?—I did.

The same day as it became available?—Yes, I think so.

Did you see Smith again?—Yes.

Was anyone else there then?—No.

Evidence for Prosecution.

Charles F. Normanton

Did you tell him that the Ford was available or had come into the garage?—I did.

Was he interested in it?—Yes.

As you have already told us, he hired it for a week. Did he come round and look at it at Beauchamp Place or did you take it round to Beaufort Gardens, or what?—I took it round to Beaufort Gardens.

Did Smith look at it then?—Yes.

And agreed to take it as you have told us?—Yes.

How much did he pay for it?—£15 for it and £14 rent.

Did he say, or did you ask him, where he was going in it, or what he wanted it for?—I did not ask him. All Mr. Smith said was he would only be using it locally for the first few days of the week; in fact, if I wished to borrow the car it would be there outside Beaufort Gardens; but later on in the week he was going quite a long journey in it.

Did he say actually where?—I do not think so; not at that time.

Did you have occasion to go for the car at Beaufort Gardens at any time?—No, but early in the week I saw it outside Beaufort Gardens.

And did Smith bring it back on 2nd December?—Yes.

And handed it in?—Yes.

Cross-examined by Sir WALTER MONCKTON—I suggest to you that you are mistaken in your recollection, and that in fact you did not see the defendant, Ley, on any of the occasions when you went round?—Oh, yes, I did.

Did you say it was on the occasion when the Marmon was rejected, or on some other occasion?—On the occasion when the Marmon was rejected.

Was this not your recollection when you gave evidence before: "In November as a result of what Miss Brittain told me, I went round to 5 Beaufort Gardens and saw Mr. Smith. Mr. Smith said he would probably hire the Marmon car and would come round to the office and make arrangements. He did not come round. I went to see him again."?—Yes.

"On that occasion Mr. Ley was with him"; is that the occasion? —That would be the occasion.

"But he finally decided not to have the car"?—Yes.

I misunderstood. You say you saw Mr. Ley, but I do not gather you had any conversation with him?—Well, that is all Mr. Ley said.

Ley and Smith.

Charles F. Normanton

Cross-examined by Mr. CURTIS BENNETT—Your Hire Car Service is in Beauchamp Place, just round the corner from Beaufort Gardens?—Yes.

When you hired the Ford car to Mr. Smith I presume he signed for it, did he?—He did.

There would be records in your firm that he, Mr. Smith, had taken away on that day a Ford car, F G P 101?—Yes.

You probably know something about motor cars and their numbers. Most motor cars which are new since 1939 have three index letters and then either one or two or three index numbers, do not they?—Yes.

Do you know how far the index letters had gone then, so far as the first index letter is concerned; was it down to about H?—I am afraid I do not.

Before the three letter index number came into vogue, there were two index letters and usually four figures, were not there?—Yes.

By the LORD CHIEF JUSTICE—Have you got a duplicate of the signing in and out slip?—No; there was not a duplicate.

And no entry in a book—only on the slips?—No; we have the duplicate sheet that I call the in and out sheets that the client signs when he takes the car out, and it is signed when he brings it back again; the police took that.

KATHLEEN MARY INGLESON, sworn, examined by Mr. HAWKE—I think you were Mr. Ley's private secretary at Beaufort Gardens?—Yes.

When did you start work with him?—In February last year.

Was part of your duty as a secretary to take down letters at his dictation in shorthand and then type them out?—Yes.

Just look at Exhibit 11. (Exhibit handed to witness.) Is that a letter typed by you?—Yes, it was.

Was that dictated to you?—Yes.

Did Mr. Ley dictate it and you took it down in shorthand?—Yes.

Just produce your book formally; is Exhibit 10 that book? (Handed to witness.)—Yes, that is it.

And that letter that you have before you is transcribed from that shorthand note in that book?—Yes.

The CLERK OF THE COURT—Will you check me with the original, please: "Dear Sir, we wrote you on the 19th instant and asked if

Evidence for Prosecution.

Kathleen M. Ingleson

Examination continued—Could you tell me whether he said anything else besides blackmail in connexion with other men about Mrs. Brook? (No answer.)

By the LORD CHIEF JUSTICE—Just answer the question, please. What is the answer?—Well, he did make one or two remarks.

Say what he said, please?—I cannot remember exactly what he said.

Just turn to the jury and tell them what he said about these other men or man. (A pause.) Now tell me this; what was it that he said?—Well, I cannot remember his exact words.

I do not suppose you can, but you know the sort of thing he said. What was it?—It all seemed to centre around money; that these men wanted Mrs. Brook's money.

Examination continued—Was it also a part of your duty to make out cheques for your employer?—Yes.

I see that on 26th November there is a cheque drawn on his account for £300. Do you remember a cheque for £300?—Yes.

Did you draw it?—Yes, I cashed it.

In what form did you cash it?—In £1 notes.

There is a cheque ten days earlier on 16th November for £250. Do you remember that?—Yes.

Did you cash that as well?—No, I did not.

Did you just hand that to him?—I do not think I drew that cheque.

You do not know about that one?—I do not think I actually made that cheque out.

The £300 one you cashed, did you?—Yes.

Do you know Smith, this other man *here*?—Yes, I do.

He was the foreman of the work that was going on in Beaufort Gardens, was not he?—Yes.

Mr. Smith appears to have had a cheque from Ley on 4th December; do you remember that?—Yes, I do.

Did you draw that?—Yes, I did.

On whose instructions?—On Mr. Ley's instructions.

Did he tell you what it was for?—He said he was sending it to Mr. Smith.

Just look at this cheque, which of course I am putting in. Is that the cheque you cashed?—Yes.

The LORD CHIEF JUSTICE—Members of the jury, this is a cheque drawn to L. J. Smith, drawn on 3rd December, signed "Thomas J.

117

Ley and Smith.

Kathleen M. Ingleson

Ley." "Pay Mr. L. J. Smith or order £300," and endorsed "L" something "Smith."

Examination continued—Did Smith see you at Beaufort Gardens some time after that cheque was drawn?—Yes.

What did he come to see you about?—He asked me to return the money to Mr. Ley.

Had he got the money with him then?—Yes, he had.

£300?—Yes, £300.

In what form?—In £5 notes.

Did you see Ley about that; did you speak to him about it?—Yes, I saw Mr. Ley about it and asked him to see Mr. Smith.

Did he see him?—Yes, he did.

I suppose you were in your office, were you not?—Yes; I was in my office.

Incidentally, is that the room up at the end of the passage in the basement on the left-hand side?—Yes.

Where the table and the swivel chair are?—Yes.

After Smith had been up to see Ley did he come down again to your office?—I do not think so.

Did he hand this money back?—Yes, he handed it to Mr. Ley.

In your presence?—Not in my presence, no.

You know that he did hand it back, do you?—I know he handed it back; I am not sure now whether he actually handed it to Mr. Ley or to me.

It does not matter very much. He handed the money back; and Mr. Ley took it, did he?—Yes.

Do you know what happened to it?—I paid it into the bank the following day.

You paid it back into Ley's account?—Yes.

That was on 10th December that that was paid back into his account by you. Do you remember Mr. Ley saying anything to you on 9th December, the day before, about a visit he had?—I do not remember all the actual things.

Before 10th December, when that money was paid back into the bank, having been paid back by Smith at some time, did Ley say something to you about a visit?—No.

By the LORD CHIEF JUSTICE—About someone visiting him, not a business acquaintance, but someone else?—He said that the police had been to see him, but whether that was before or after I do not know.

Examination continued—I shall be glad if you will try and think. You have got something to fix your mind quite easily,

118

Evidence for Prosecution.

Kathleen M. Ingleson

have not you? You see, on 10th December you paid this money into the bank; you may take that date. Was it before that date that you were told that the police had been to see him?—I do not think so; I think it was after that.

Did he tell you what the reason for the police visit was?—No, not at the time.

By the Lord Chief Justice—When did he tell you what the object was, if he did tell you?—Some time later.

The Lord Chief Justice—Has this witness made a statement?

Mr. Hawke—Yes, my lord.

The Lord Chief Justice—You may treat her as hostile, if you like; she is obviously hostile.

Mr. Hawke—If your lordship pleases. I am obliged. I hesitated to apply.

The Lord Chief Justice—She obviously will not tell us.

Examination continued—Did Ley in fact tell you that the police had been to visit him on 9th December, the day before that money was paid in? Just put your mind to it?—No, I do not think so.

Did you give evidence before the learned magistrate at West London Magistrates Court?—Yes, I did.

Did you take the oath?—Yes, I did.

Was your evidence written down as you gave it?—Yes.

Was it read over to you after you had given it?—Yes.

Now look at the deposition and tell me if that is your signature at the end of it? (Deposition handed to the witness.)—Yes, that is my signature.

Did you sign that after the deposition had been read to you? You must give the answer to that?—I do not remember signing that at the time.

By the Lord Chief Justice—Well, is that your signature?—It is my signature.

Examination continued—Then may I take it that you signed that document?—Yes.

119

Ley and Smith.

Kathleen M. Ingleson

The LORD CHIEF JUSTICE—I dare say you know, members of the jury, when people are brought before the magistrate in a case which has to be sent for trial to the Sessions, the depositions, that is the evidence of the witnesses that are called, are taken down in writing before the magistrates and in the presence of the accused, and after that the evidence is read over to the witnesses before they leave the Court, and the witnesses have the opportunity of correcting anything that has got down wrong, and then when it has been read over and they have had an opportunity of correcting it if they want to, they sign the deposition, and the original deposition is sent to this Court. What has just been put to this witness is the evidence that she gave before the magistrate which was taken down, read over to her and signed by her.

By the LORD CHIEF JUSTICE—Let me have the deposition. (Document handed to his lordship.) This is what is written down: "On Monday, 9th December, Mr. Ley told me the police had called on him. I think he told me he knew Mudie was missing"; this is what you said to the magistrate, is not it?—Yes.

The LORD CHIEF JUSTICE—It is a pity you could not say that before.

Examination continued—I may take it, I suppose, as you took your oath there, that that is true, is not it?—It is three months ago since it happened and it is rather a long time.

It may be three months ago, but is it right?—I expect it is true, if I said it.

After he had told you about the visit from the police did he speak to you about something that Mrs. Brook was supposed to have said to him? Look at your deposition. Do you see again that you have sworn: "A few days later 'he' "—that is Ley—"said something to the effect of that paragraph in my statement that Mrs. Brook was accusing him of having murdered Mudie"?—Yes.

Did he tell you something else about himself about the same time?—He said he had strained his back through lifting heavy packing cases.

Have you told us everything that he said to you about Mrs. Brook? You have told us so far that all he said about Mrs. Brook was that she was being blackmailed by Mudie and by her son-in-law; is that all he said?—And there was someone else as well; I cannot remember the name.

Another man as well?—Yes.

Evidence for Prosecution.

Kathleen M. Ingleson

Did he tell you with regard to all three of these that he thought that Mrs. Brook had been carrying on with them?—Well, something to that effect.

Well, that is so, is it?—Yes.

Cross-examined by Sir WALTER MONCKTON—Will you just help me about this cheque, Exhibit No. 24. Would you look at the counterfoil and tell me in whose handwriting that is? (Cheque book handed to witness.)—It is in my handwriting.

The counterfoil read: "Loan," and then it has "repaid on the 10th December" written across it?—Yes.

That is the counterfoil of the cheque to L. J. Smith?—Yes.

In connexion with that cheque, did Ley say anything about what that cheque was intended for?—He said Smith wished to start a business and he was lending him the money.

Then, as you have told us, Smith came back on the 10th, and did he then say that he wanted to return the money he had borrowed from Ley?—Yes.

Did he say why?—He said he decided not to start a business.

Not to go on with the business?—Yes.

And you cannot remember, I gather, to-day whether the £5 notes in which he returned the money were handed to you personally or to Ley?—I know Smith——

I want to ask you a question now about the transcription of your shorthand note, which is Exhibit 12, which was read out to you at the beginning of your evidence. Did you type it out?—Yes.

So far as you know was that ever signed?—Not so far as I know.

Or sent?—I do not know.

Can you tell me the date upon which it was transcribed or taken down?—No.

Can you remember whether it was in or about the month of July?—Well, about July or August.

Coming back from that, you told my learned friend towards the end of your evidence that in addition to Ley speaking to you about Mrs. Brook being blackmailed, he also said something about associations with men?—Yes.

Just let us get this clear. Were there three named men? Was it first that he said he had suspicions of Mr. Arthur Barron; is that right?—Yes.

Then did Mudie come into the picture—Mudie next?—Yes.

And then, is this right, that afterwards he mentioned the name of Arthur Romer later on?—Romer, yes.

Ley and Smith.

Kathleen M. Ingleson

So far as Mudie was concerned, he was the one he took second, as it were, when he was considering the different associations he was complaining of. After the time of those cheques which we have heard about, and after this letter which you transcribed, did he cease to complain about Mudie and turn to Romer?—I do not really remember, no.

To your knowledge, during the time you were with Ley did he ever drive a motor car?—Not to my knowledge.

Did you know of his moving packing cases at or about this time while the changes were taking place inside Beaufort Gardens?— Well, he could have done, but I did not actually see him doing it.

Were they there—the packing cases bringing in effects and furniture?—Yes, they were there.

Cross-examined by Mr. CURTIS BENNETT—By 28th November, or about then, can you tell me how many flats were being occupied at 5 Beaufort Gardens? There were to be four flats, were not there?—Yes.

How many were occupied by 28th November?—There was only one flat occupied.

Which was that?—The ground floor flat.

The ground and first floor?—Yes.

By the LORD CHIEF JUSTICE—That was Ley's own flat?—Yes.

Cross-examination continued—I suppose, as you were there, you saw Mr. Smith quite frequently working on the house, did you not? —Oh, yes; I saw him.

Can you tell me this : did he very often, or quite often, turn up in a hired car, or driving a car?—I never saw him, no—not to my knowledge.

You did not hear Smith give any reason why he had been advanced the money, but you heard Ley give you a reason?—Yes.

Did you ever hear Ley mention in connexion with Smith's business that it would be advisable for him to have a car?—No.

However, Smith paid the money back, saying he was not going on with it, whatever it was?—Yes.

You did not know the nature of the business?—No.

You know the back door in the basement of 5 Beaufort Gardens, do not you?—Yes.

Has it got a mortise lock as well as a Yale lock?—Yes.

How many keys were there to that lock?—I have no knowledge. I think there was only one key to that lock.

Evidence for Prosecution.

Well, you know, do you not? You gave evidence about this before, you know. Is this right: "On the back door there are two locks. One was an ordinary lock opening with a Yale key"; is that right?—Yes.

Now listen to this: "The other is a mortise lock. Mr. Ley is the only person who had a key to that one"; is that right?—Yes.

CHARLES FREDERICK NORMANTON, recalled, further examined by Mr. HAWKE—You told us that Smith signed for this car when he took it out?—Yes.

And it was entered again when he brought it in?—Yes.

Is this the document relevant to that car? (Document handed to witness.)—Yes; that is the in and out sheet.

F G P 101, taken out on 25th November and returned on 2nd December?—That is right.

Is the deposit paid on it £15, and the rent for the week's hire £14?—Yes.

£29 in all?—Yes.

Further cross-examined by Mr. CURTIS BENNETT—It appears that the index number of the car both out and in is F G P 101. That is from your record?—Yes.

The document bears both out and in Smith's signature?—Yes.

Obviously the £15 would be returned?—It was.

Would the £14 be for the week, or would it be an amount which would cover——?—No, that is the rent for the week.

That would be what it cost, £14?—Yes.

Not £29?—No.

DOROTHY HELEN LANE, sworn, examined by Mr. HAWKE—I started employment as a housekeeper at 5 Beaufort Gardens on 25th November. I did not start living in there until 23rd December.

Cross-examined by Sir WALTER MONCKTON—Before 25th November did you know Ley?—No. I had met him or interviewed him twice, that is all.

When you were seeking the engagement?—Yes.

When you came on 25th November did you at first have a room at 8 Beaufort Gardens?—Yes.

And go into No. 5 each day?—Yes.

At that time you were trying to get these flats, which were the basement first floor and ground floor, in order?—Yes.

Were the workmen in the house?—Yes.

123

Ley and Smith.

Dorothy H. Lane

And did you see Ley there?—Yes.

Was Mrs. Brook there most days?—She was there at times, yes.

What time used you to arrive in the morning?—Half-past seven.

And when did you leave?—Between five and half-past.

Do you remember the day you came, the 25th; do you remember Mrs. Brook coming that day to tea?—She was not there to tea, but she did come into the house.

Did she come in again on the 27th, the third day you were there?—Yes.

And did you then leave when she came? Did she come in to tea, or what?—She used sometimes to come in to tea, but I was not finished until five to half-past.

Can you carry your mind to 28th November there?—Yes.

Do you remember on 28th November whether Mr. Ley and Mrs. Brook came back to No. 5 in the early afternoon?—Yes; I remember that they came back about a quarter-past one.

Do you remember what he did?—Yes; I remember that he spent the afternoon arranging his library.

And did you see anything of him yourself?—Yes. I went up into the lounge to tell him I was going to the Food Office.

What time was that, about?—That was about half-past one or twenty minutes to two.

Did you go out on the journey you had spoken of to the Food Office?—Yes.

Then on your way back did you do some shopping with a friend?—I did meet a friend.

When did you get back to Beaufort Gardens?—It must have been about a quarter or ten minutes to four.

That afternoon, the 28th, you having got back then, were Ley and Mrs. Brook there for tea?—Yes.

Did you take it up to them?—Yes.

What is the next thing that happened?—I had my own tea in the basement with the secretary.

Did you see Mr. Ley again?—Yes. He came downstairs to go out with Mrs. Brook.

And did he go out?—He did go out, and he returned quite shortly afterwards.

About what time did he go out?—Round about half-past four.

And he came back shortly afterwards?—Yes.

When you say "shortly" what sort of period do you mean? Do you mean a quarter of an hour, ten minutes, half an hour, or what?—About ten or fifteen minutes.

When he came back did you see him?—Yes.

And speak to him?—Yes.

Evidence for Prosecution.

Dorothy H. Lane

When did you leave?—I left a few minutes after five o'clock.

Did you let yourself out or did he let you out?—It was his custom to take me through the outer corridor to the front door.

Did he do it on this day?—Yes.

About what time was that?—It must have been a little after five o'clock.

What did you do; where did you go?—I was going down to No. 8, but instead of going in to No. 8 I walked to the post box.

Is the post box further up the cul-de-sac at the Brompton Road end?—Yes.

And No. 5?—About three doors below it.

Did you post a letter there?—Yes.

Then what did you do?—I turned from the letter box and I saw Mr. Ley passing under the lamp standard.

Which way was he going?—He was going towards Brompton Road.

Had he a hat and coat on?—Yes.

By the LORD CHIEF JUSTICE—What time was this?—This would be about a quarter-past five, as far as I can remember.

Cross-examination continued—At that time you were walking back, as you have told us, towards 8 Beaufort Gardens, where you live. Did you come out again?—I came out from No. 8 about twenty-past six.

Did you come past No. 5?—I passed No. 5.

Did you see any signs of life from any floor or window?—There was no sign of life or light in the place.

If anyone had been in the drawing-room—are there any curtains there?—No, there are no curtains, but there are shutters.

Are there shutters in both the front rooms there?—Yes.

Can you tell my lord and the members of the jury this, whether with the window shutters it is possible to detect whether there is light or not?—Yes, you can see a light. There is a big gap between the top of the shutters and the top of the window.

Did you see anything more or take any further notice of the house that night, or did you see anything more of Ley?—No; not that night.

When did you next see Ley?—At 7.30 the next morning.

What did you do so that you met him?—He let me in as usual.

At which door?—The front door, as usual.

Anything unusual about him?—Nothing whatever.

Did he seem in his normal state of mind?—Absolutely normal.

Ley and Smith.

Dorothy H. Lane

Do you remember the room in the basement which has been called the middle room in which the desk was?—Yes.

Not the room right against Beaufort Gardens, nor the room right against Brompton Place—not the middle room, but the room where the desk was?—Yes; I remember.

Was there a chair there, too?—There was a swivel chair.

And any other chair?—I remember only two—literally a small typist's chair.

Was the swivel chair the chair which Miss Ingleson, the last witness, would have used when she was using that room as an office?—Yes.

Had she just begun to use the room as an office about this time in the week you came?—Yes, early in the week.

Tell me about the chair. What sort of a chair was it, apart from it being a swivel chair?—It was a heavy leather chair with a circular back.

Were there any projections from it? You say it had a circular back; had it any pieces that stuck out—knobs, or anything?—I do not remember any.

You were constantly in and about 5 Beaufort Gardens, and you know, of course, Brompton Place at the back well?—Not really well.

You know it is a cul-de-sac like Beaufort Gardens?—Yes.

It runs up into Harrods Depository?—Yes.

Do you know when people came out of that Depository from work?—Oh, no.

Cross-examined by Mr. CURTIS BENNETT—I want to know one or two things as a result of what you have just been asked. About 28th November, you say there was no sign of life in the house at 6.20?—No.

You could not see much, I suppose, in the basement on walking by?—Only if the lights were at the back. If it was in the front I should see it.

If the light was on in the middle room or the far room you mean; but if it was in the front room downstairs you would see it?—It would depend on the door being shut.

Were you looking to see if there was any light? I do not suppose you were?—Yes, but I do usually look at the house as I pass it.

Usually, but no more than any other day?—No.

When were you first asked to say what the condition of this house was at twenty minutes past six on 28th November? That is the time I am interested in. Who asked you to bring your mind out of all the other days you have been there, to the 28th? What

Evidence for Prosecution.

Dorothy H. Lane

person asked you?—Well, for a time, my mind was numbed; I could not think of very much.

That means you could not answer the question when you were first asked?—But as it clarified, so I remembered the first week of my employment.

Now let us go back. What I asked you was: who first asked you the condition of this house at about six on 28th November? —No one asked me; I volunteered.

After being so numb that you could not remember anything about it?—Yes. I was quite shocked for several weeks.

What was it that helped your memory? Who is living in the house now?——

By the LORD CHIEF JUSTICE—Who did you volunteer it to?—Mr. Ley's son.

Cross-examination continued—He is still living in the house?— Yes.

Did he help jog your memory at all?—He did not. What I told him I told him voluntarily.

What, just walked up to him and said: "Mr. Ley, at twenty-past six on 28th November there were no lights in the house"?—No.

Did he ask you himself?—No; we were discussing it.

By the LORD CHIEF JUSTICE—About when was that—a month or two ago?—It might have been, my lord; a little more than that, perhaps.

How did you remember it was the 28th?—Because I remembered starting on the 25th so well.

How do you know it was the 28th and not the 27th or the 29th?—Because I could recall most days of that week as they had passed.

I should very much like to know when it was that you told Mr. Ley, the prisoner's son, about this?—He came into the house knowing nothing about it, knowing nothing about the case, and as my mind clarified, and I remembered, so I discussed it with him.

It must have been towards the end of December, I suppose?— No; it was in January. He did not arrive until January.

Cross-examination continued—Does that mean that if anybody had asked you at the beginning of December what the condition of this house was at twenty-past six on 28th November, you would

Ley and Smith.

not have told them because your mind was numb?—No; I am afraid I could not have told them very much at that time.

By the LORD CHIEF JUSTICE—What happened to numb your mind?—I was shocked by the general event of the thing.

Cross-examination continued—What I want to know is what happened to clear it so that to-day you are able to say what was happening at twenty-past six on 28th November?—Nothing happened; I was just recovering.

A little discussion with young Mr. Ley?—I was just recovering from the shock.

Did you know when your mind clarified that it was said by some people that Mr. Ley was in this house at a quarter to seven on 28th November?—No.

Do you mean to say that no one has told you until to-day that some people are saying that Ley was in this house when Mudie and other people arrived by car at about quarter to seven on the 28th?——

The LORD CHIEF JUSTICE—It was a little later than that, you know.

Mr. CURTIS BENNETT—That was the time it was due. I have the exact time here—ten to seven.

The LORD CHIEF JUSTICE—They left Reigate at ten minutes to six, and it would take them an hour.

Mr. CURTIS BENNETT—The evidence this morning was that they arrived at ten minutes to seven. I am suggesting a quarter to seven.

The LORD CHIEF JUSTICE—This witness is speaking about twenty-past six.

Cross-examination continued—A short time before. Has nobody told you that Ley' presence or not in the house at about a quarter to seven was very important to him?—I never heard of the time of a quarter to seven. I heard of half-past seven.

Who told you that?—I could not really remember at the moment.

Mr. Ley senior was living in the house, I suppose, up to the middle of December?—Yes, he was.

Evidence for Prosecution.

Dorothy H. Lane

Did he ever speak to you about the condition of the house in the early evening of the 28th?—He told me what had happened to give me an opportunity to leave him if I wished to do so.

Did he tell you it was an important matter as to where he was at about a quarter to seven on the 28th?—No; he did not.

There would be no proof if I suggested to you that either Mr. Ley or his son, or both, had helped to clear your mind about this twenty-past six?—No.

By the LORD CHIEF JUSTICE—Do you remember 30th November? —Yes, I remember the Saturday.

What were you doing then?—I did my usual routine in the morning, and I left Mr. Ley about 11.30 and went out of town for the rest of the day and returned on the Sunday evening.

That was the first week-end you were there?—Yes.

Can you give me the date when you can remember looking at the house on any other occasion?—Yes; I looked at the house on Sunday evening when I came back to town.

Leave out the week-end when you had been away. Later on do you remember?—Yes, because I used to go over to the little café in Beaufort Gardens to have my supper, and invariably glanced up at the house both going and coming back.

In other words, you did it every day?—Every day.

Just let me see if I have these times right. Ley and Mrs. Brook had tea together and left the house at half-past four?— Yes, about half-past four.

And he came back in ten minutes or a quarter of an hour?— Yes.

You next saw him when you left a few minutes after five?— Yes.

You next saw him in Brompton Road at a quarter-past five?— Yes.

And that was the last you saw of him until 7 o'clock the next morning?—Yes.

JOHN JOWETT TAMMS, sworn, examined by Mr. ELAM—In November last I was employed at Bowles & Sons, builders and contractors. They were carrying out the conversion of 5 Beaufort Gardens, from a house into flats for the accused, Ley, who I know slightly. The accused, Smith, who I recognize in Court, was employed with us from 30th November, 1945, first at Connaught Place, and then, from 7th May, 1946, at 5 Beaufort Gardens as site foreman.

I   129

Ley and Smith.

John J. Tamms

Did he leave your employment on the night of 12th December, 1946?—Yes.

By the LORD CHIEF JUSTICE—Did he give any reason for leaving?—No.

Mr. ELAM—Would you look at Exhibit 19? (Handed to witness.) I will ask for that to be read.

The CLERK OF THE COURT—"5 Beaufort Gardens, S.W.3, 13th December, 1946. Messrs. Bowles, Hanover Square. Dear Sirs, I found last night that the foreman, Smith, who had looked after the work here under difficult circumstances during the last six months had severed his connexion with the job and the firm. I wish to place on record that he was the first foreman you sent here who appeared to be capable of doing his work, and throughout his term has been helpful and cheerful and showed much initiative and resource under the difficult conditions of shortage of labour and materials, and even of most inefficient labour. On this job I have found no one who has had any adverse comment to make on the foreman and who does not join with me in feeling that your firm has lost a first-class man. Yours faithfully, signed Thomas J. Ley"; is that right?

The WITNESS—That is correct.

Cross-examined by Mr. CURTIS BENNETT—What was your employment with Bowles?—I was looking after the accounts.
Did you see much of Smith during the time you were employed?—Approximately once a week.
Did you ever talk to him on general subjects?—Yes.
Has he ever told you in the past that he wanted if possible to get work abroad?—No.

Re-examined by Mr. HAWKE—You looked after the accounts. How much was Smith paid?—I am guessing now, but his average I should say was about £7 5s. to £7 10s. a week; that is approximate. It varied, of course, from week to week.

By the LORD CHIEF JUSTICE—Did he give you notice that he was going to leave?—About three or four days.
Before 12th December?—Yes.
He gave no reason?—Not that I know of.

The Court adjourned.

Evidence for Prosecution.

Third Day—Friday, 21st March, 1947.

FREDERICK WILLIAM SMITH, sworn, examined by Mr. HAWKE—I am a landscape gardener and work for a Mr. Nettleton at a place called Woldingham.

Were you coming away from your work on the evening of Wednesday, 27th November?—That is correct.

Does your way home lead you past the chalk pit?—Yes.

Were you with anybody else?—My mate, Clifford Tamplin.

Were you walking or riding?—At this particular time we were walking up a small incline wheeling our bicycles.

Did your way take you along the road out of which the path leading to the chalk pit runs?—It took us right by the entrance to the chalk pit.

I expect you would recognize it. Look at the first photograph in the book of photographs (handed to witness). Is that the road that you were walking along?—That is the road we came along. We were coming *this* way (indicating on photograph).

From left to right?—That is correct.

Then did you come straight past the entrance to the chalk pit?—That is correct.

Did you notice anything as you went past the entrance?—Yes; a man standing away up on the bank, roughly where there is a sort of black mark at the top of the copy of the photograph.

Could you tell me what time this was?—Between 4.30 and 4.50.

What was the man doing?—He was standing looking in the direction in which we were coming.

Did you look at him?—We looked across at the bank.

What happened then?—As soon as he saw us, he turned immediately and ran very fast down the bank.

Down the side of the pit, do you mean?—Yes.

Where did he run to?—From *there* down *there*. There is like a footpath *here* (indicating on photograph) going down behind the trees.

He ran down there. Could you see where he went to?—Yes. There was a car standing a little way, *here,* behind these bushes.

I think it might help you if you turned to the next photograph. That gives you a view of the slope down to the path. Can you show us where that car was?—Yes. (Witness indicated on photograph.)

That is above the road, is it not? The road is down *here*?—Yes.

131

Ley and Smith.

Frederick W. Smith

There seemed to be, where you are pointing, bushes and shrubs? —That is right.

Was the car, then, among those?—Not among them, but quite close to them.

What did this man do when he arrived at the car?—He was obviously flustered. He got into the car and made three or four attempts to get away. As soon as he started his engine, he revved up very hard and the engine just faded out. He tried that again. Finally he got going.

When he did get going where did he go?—If you turn to the first photograph, he came back and reversed into *there* (indicating).

Into the path?—Yes, and then turned his bonnet into the road.

That was just about where you were?—We might have been between five and ten yards past the entrance.

By the LORD CHIEF JUSTICE—Had you by this time got past the entrance?—We had got past the entrance.

Then he came past you?—That is right.

Examination continued—And went on down the road?—Yes.

Were you able to see the man to recognize him?—Only a side glimpse as he got into his car.

This being between 4.30 and 4.50, I suppose, it was getting dark?—It was just getting dusk and there was a slight drizzle.

You were, I think, called upon to see at a later date whether you could pick out the man that you had seen?—That is correct.

For that purpose you attended a parade at Brixton Prison on 13th January and endeavoured to pick out the man that you had seen?—Yes.

And you picked out a man who, in fact, has nothing to do with this matter at all?—Yes, that is correct.

As you told us, it was getting dark and you only saw this man side face?—Yes.

Was he moving pretty fast too, when you saw him?—Running down the bank.

And afterwards in the car?—In the car I should think he was doing between 15 and 20 m.p.h. by the time he passed us.

Obviously, therefore, you do not remember the appearance of this driver, but did you happen to notice the car?—Yes.

What sort of a car was it; what make?—I should say it was a Ford, an 8 horse power or a 10.

A small Ford. What colour?—Of a dark colour.

Did you happen to get the number?—We got the 101, the three figures.

Evidence for Prosecution.

Frederick W. Smith

You got the three figures; you could not get the letters?—We got the number 101.

At any rate, it was a dark car, you think it was a Ford, and the number was 101?—Yes.

Where was the number plate—at the back, at the side, or in the middle?—In the middle.

Cross-examined by Mr. Curtis Bennett—When you first saw the man looking towards you, his face was towards you?—No; sideways.

I thought you said he was looking towards where you were?—When he was standing up *here*. He was standing sideways.

I thought you said he was looking in the direction in which you were coming?—That would be about sideways to us. He was looking like *that*. (Demonstrating.)

I quite agree it is some distance away. He was more or less facing you then, was not he?—I do not know whether you would call that facing.

I suppose you had passed this place many times before?—Yes. You know it?—Yes.

I do not know whether you have gone and stood up there yourself, have you?—Yes.

Have you come down the side like that?—Yes.

It is difficult not to run, is not it?—Knowing the district like I do, no normal man would run down the bank at the pace he did.

By the Lord Chief Justice—You mean it is so steep?—It is so steep and it is very dangerous.

Cross-examination continued—It is so steep that you would either crawl very slowly down or else you would have to go pretty fast?—I do not know.

It is a very steep pit, is not it?—Yes.

It is difficult to keep control of oneself going down hill. You have experienced that, I dare say. You would agree with that, would you not? It is difficult to keep control of how fast you go down there?—No.

It really is a very steep pit?—It is a steep pit.

That is what drew your attention to the matter?—Yes.

The fact that somebody ran down the hill?—Yes.

How far does the road go before a car on it would disappear from your sight? Not so very far does it?—I should think between 20 and 30 yards.

Ley and Smith.

Frederick W. Smith

So 20 or 30 yards further down this road any car on it would be out of your sight. Did you catch what you say was the number, the figures, from the back number plate?—Yes.

We need not worry about the front number plate, then, need we?—No. All I had was just the back view of the car.

Which in 20 or 30 yards would have been out of your sight. You know that index numbers of cars are either two letters and four figures, or else they are three letters and one, two or three figures, are not they nowadays?—Yes.

You may get A B C 1?—Yes.

Or you may get A B C 111 or you may get R C 1025; something like that?—This was definitely 101.

I know you say so. What I have suggested are six things in an index number of a car—either three letters and three numbers or two letters and four numbers?—Yes.

You caught, as you say, 101 and that was all?—Yes.

By the LORD CHIEF JUSTICE—Are not the letters above the number?—No. Some are and some are not.

Which is this?—The numbers all run *that* way.

All in one?—Yes.

Cross-examination continued—They were all running along?—Yes.

Was the rear light on?—No.

You could not see whether the rear light, if it had been on, would have been on both sides of the number or on top of it?—There were no lights at all on the car when it passed us.

Could you see whether the place where the light is was above the plate or on both sides?—That I could not see.

I gather you made no note of this matter in writing anywhere?—No. It was just a mental note.

Did you discuss it with each other, you and Tamplin?—Yes.

What date did you first hear that a body had been found in the bottom of the chalk pit?—We saw this on the 27th, on the Wednesday. We read it in the paper on the Monday.

The 1st December? Between these two dates, there had been nothing to keep this date in your mind? You had not been thinking about this?—No, I had not been thinking about it.

There was no reason for you to?—No.

Then you went to the police station. When did you go there?—We went there on Tuesday evening.

The 2nd December?—Yes.

Evidence for Prosecution.

Frederick W. Smith

Do not think I am challenging your good faith; I am not, you gave me what you thought was your belief. You saw the man side face on the top of the hill, then when he came up to you going 15 to 20 miles an hour, you saw him side face again?—Yes.

Do you think that you could have quite honestly picked out the man when you went to the parade? When you got to the parade there were eight men there?—Yes.

Having seen the man side face, you did not pick out Smith, but somebody else?—Yes, but I did that only for a matter of seconds.

And in only a matter of seconds you saw the number of the plate?—Yes.

You picked out the man you thought you remembered, that is right is it not?—Yes.

You made a mistake did you not?—I did.

Perhaps the defender Smith could stand up. I do not know what height he is. He looks to me about 5 feet 7 inches or 8. You picked out a man about 5 inches taller, did you not?—I could not say that.

Did you not notice that?—No.

What I am suggesting to you is, as you were mistaken by the man, so you may well be mistaken about the number of the car?—No, I do not think so.

LORD CHIEF JUSTICE—Has the witness Normanton been released?

Mr. HAWK—Yes, my lord, I think he has. He could be sent for.

LORD CHIEF JUSTICE—He must be sent for at once, and if he happens to have the same car, bring it down. The jury shall see it and see the number plate.

Mr. HAWK—I thought this might arise. I was proposing to recall the official who took the photograph. He has the original negative in his possession.

Mr. CURTIS BENNETT—That will not be necessary.

LORD CHIEF JUSTICE—If you are satisfied?

Mr. CURTIS BENNETT—I have had an opportunity of seeing the photograph before and I am quite satisfied.

Ley and Smith.

Clifford J. Tamplin

LORD CHIEF JUSTICE—Members of the jury, would you like to see the car or are you satisfied with the photograph which everybody agrees is a photograph of the car in question?

The JURY—The photograph.

CLIFFORD JOEL TAMPLIN, sworn, examined by Mr. HAWKE—I am a landscape gardener employed by Mr. Nettleton at Woldingham. On the evening of 27th November I was walking with my friend, Mr. Smith, past the chalk pit, wheeling my bicycle.

As you passed the entrance to the pit, did you see something? —As I was approaching the entrance I saw the man up on the bank standing just above the pit.

Look at the first photograph. (Handed to witness.) Would you point out where, in your recollection, the man was standing?— *That* is where he was, just *there* (indicating).

What time was it that you saw this?—Between half-past four and twenty to five.

What did this man do?—When we got close to the entrance to the pit we stood there, about ten yards before we got to the entrance, looking up at him. Then he bolted down the bank and jumped into the car.

Where was the car?—About ten yards off the road.

Just point out, as near as you can on the second photograph, where it was?—Just about *there* somewhere (indicating).

What did he do when he got to the car?—He got in the car and he started it up. He was rather excited. He tried to reverse it three or four times before he got out.

Eventually he reversed it and turned down the hill towards the road, I suppose?—Yes, went back to the old road.

And came back on to the road?—The old road, the entrance to the pit; then he drew on to the road that went up by the pit.

That was where you were standing?—Yes, that is right.

Which way did he go down the road—past you?—Yes; turned right-handed as he came out of the pit.

Were you able to get any view of this man yourself?—Yes; I got a bit of a view of him side face.

Do you think you could recognize him again?—Yes, I think I could.

See if you can see him now?—There is the man over *there,* Smith. (Indicating the prisoner Smith.)

You also attended this identification parade at Brixton Prison on 13th January, did not you?—Yes.

Who did you pick out there?—This same man, Smith.

Evidence for Prosecution.

Clifford J. Tamplin

What sort of a car was it that he was driving?—I said it was a Ford or an Austin. I did not know which it was.

What colour?—Saloon, a dark one, black.

A large car?—No.

A small dark saloon?—Yes, about 8 h.p.

Did you see what the number was?—Yes, 101.

Could you get the lettering?—No.

By the LORD CHIEF JUSTICE—What sort of number-plate was it—a long number-plate or a square number-plate?—A long number-plate.

Examination continued—And at what part of the back of the car; on the side or in the middle?—In the centre.

Cross-examined by Mr. CURTIS BENNETT—Looking at picture No. 1, where you say you saw the man standing, it would be difficult not to run down that slope it is so steep; that is right, is it not?—I think I could walk down there easy enough.

You might be able to, but it is quite easy not to, it is so steep? —Nobody would have any need to run like that, I think.

Have you ever tried going down that particular bit?—Ever so many times.

You are sufficiently well trained not to run. It is very steep, is it not?—Yes; it is very steep.

And grassy, down the last part anyway?—Yes, the lower part.

Slippery grass?—Yes.

It was getting dark, was it not?—Yes.

Were the lights of the car on?—No.

You attended an identification parade on 13th January and picked out Mr. Smith?—Yes.

You have been asked to find him. He is sitting in the dock to-day, so it is not a very difficult task, perhaps. But let me ask you about the parade; is it right that you did not have a chance to see the man's face at the incident on the 27th?—I saw him as he passed me in the car, side face.

I am asking you that quite deliberately, as you will see in a moment. Is this right: "I did not have a chance to see the man's face"?—Not face; but side face I saw him.

Is that what you swore at the Magistrate's Court? I am reading?—I saw him from the back, neck and side face.

Let me read on. You gave evidence at the Magistrate's Court about this, did you not?—Yes.

Ley and Smith.

Clifford J. Tamplin

It was read over to you and you signed it?—Yes.

Now listen again: "I did not have a chance to see the man's face. I saw the back of his head." Is that what you swore?—As he went by I have got to see a part of his face and head.

By the LORD CHIEF JUSTICE—It is put to you that when you were before the magistrate you said: "I did not have a chance to see the man's face. I saw the back of his head." Do you remember if you said that before the magistrate?—Yes.

Cross-examination continued—You signed it, having said it. You were on oath when you said it?—Yes.

And it was true, was it?—Yes.

Then you cannot have had the least possibility of picking out the man if you only saw the back of his head, can you?—Yes.

How? I do not know, unless a man was bald or covered with hair. The back of one man's head is like the back of another man's head?—He was cut rather high up from the back of the head.

His hair?—Yes.

When did you notice that—when he was in the car, when it was darker still?—It was a matter of feet that I was away from him.

He was going about 15 to 20 miles an hour when he passed you?—About that.

That is what your colleague said. Do you agree with that?—Yes.

It would be a flash, whatever you saw, an instant, would it not?—Yes.

By the LORD CHIEF JUSTICE—Did you see him side face?—No. I just saw more or less the back of his head and a part of his side face. I had got to as he went by in the car.

The LORD CHIEF JUSTICE—He must have seen part of his side face, if he was looking.

Mr. CURTIS BENNETT—He might have—not "must." It depends which way he was looking.

Cross-examination continued—Now, about this number; you went, did you, with your friend Mr. Smith to the police on a date early in December?—Yes.

Evidence for Prosecution.

Clifford J. Tamplin

Between the 27th and the time you saw something in the papers, you had no occasion to think or worry about the number again, had you?—No.

That is what your colleague says, too. So that when you read something in the paper, you then discussed together?—That is right.

As to what the number was?—No; we did not discuss together. It was 101. It was quite simple, really.

You took no note of it in writing?—No.

You read something in December—I think it was 2nd December, the following Tuesday—is that right?—Yes.

Do you remember which day it was?—On the Monday.

That is 1st December. You cannot remember that?—It was the 3rd.

When did you read something in the paper—on the Monday?—Yes, I think it was the Monday.

That is the 1st. When did you go to the police?—We went to the police on the 3rd.

That would be a Wednesday?—A Tuesday.

Did you go to the police the same day as you read the thing in the newspaper?—No. We went there the next day.

I gathered Mr. Smith to say differently. Before you went, you had to discuss the matter together?—No.

Your colleague has told us so?—We did not discuss it.

You said so just now yourself, too. What did you have to discuss, except whether you could be sure of the number? You had to discuss the number?—Yes.

By the LORD CHIEF JUSTICE—Had you any doubt at all about the number?—No doubt at all.

Did you see anything in the paper except the fact that a dead body had been found?—Yes.

Was there anything else?—They wanted anybody to give any information. Then we thought about this car being there.

Was there anything said in the paper about a car?—No.

When you went to see the police, did you give the number of the car to the police at the time?—Yes.

At that time had you ever heard of Smith?—No.

You had never heard that Smith had had in his possession any particular car?—No.

Did you tell the police that you had seen a car?—That is right.

And you gave them the number at the time, did you?—Yes.

Ley and Smith.

Frederick Shoobridge

FREDERICK SHOOBRIDGE, sworn, examined by Mr. ELAM—I am a detective sergeant of the Surrey Joint Police Force, stationed at Caterham. I produce an ordnance map, scale one inch to one statute mile, which shows London and the journey one would take from there down to the chalk pit. It shows the section from Croydon down to the chalk pit. To get to the chalk pit from London, you pass through Brixton, Streatham, Croydon, through to South Croydon, fork left through Sanderstead, Warlingham, and on to Chelsham. Shortly after passing through Chelsham on the road to Westerham there is a fork and you take the right-hand fork, downhill for about half a mile, and the chalk pit is situate on a bank on the left-hand side of the road about 95 yards from the roadway. It is a very lonely road leading to Woldingham Village. It is approximately 20 miles from London to the chalk pit measured from Westminster Bridge, and 22 miles from Kensington. From Brixton it would be something like 18 miles. From Reigate to the chalk pit is approximately 9 to 10 miles.

At about six o'clock in the evening of 30th November did you go to the chalk pit we are talking about?—I did.

Did you see there the body of a dead man in a trench?—I did.

Did you take possession of that rope, Exhibit 12, and also that rag, Exhibit 13?—Yes.

On 5th December did you go to the offices of a firm of solicitors in London, Messrs. Denton, Hall & Burgin?—Yes.

On 7th December did you ring up Ley?—Yes, at Kensington 9951.

By the LORD CHIEF JUSTICE—By this time were certain letters in your possession?—They were, my lord.

Had you found them?—No; Sergeant Cox found them and had given them to me.

The LORD CHIEF JUSTICE—Members of the jury, you may remember that the reason why he went to Denton, Hall & Burgin would be because they were the firm of solicitors who had written to Mudie about the cheques. The letter has been read to you.

Examination continued—Somebody had been to the deceased man's room at the Reigate Hill Hotel?—That is so.

Did Ley answer the telephone?—Yes.

You are satisfied the voice was Ley's?—Yes. He told me his address: 5 Beaufort Gardens.

Evidence for Prosecution.

Frederick Shoobridge

Was an appointment made for you to see him at that address that morning?—It was.

Did you keep the appointment, getting there about 11.30 a.m.?—I did.

Did you see Ley there?—I did. He showed me into the room on the right of the hall.

Did you tell him who you were?—I did. I said to him: "I am Detective-sergeant Shoobridge, and I am making inquiries regarding these two letters." I then produced to him the two letters, Exhibits 14 and 15.

The jury will remember that one is written to "Jack Mudie, Esq., 3 Homefield Road, Wimbledon," on 25th July, and it is signed for Denton, Hall & Burgin. The other one, which is in similar terms, Exhibit 15, is written to "Jack Mudie, Esq., Reigate Hotel, Reigate" and signed in the same way. Having shown him those letters, what did you say to him?—I told him that I had been informed by Dr. Fletcher, of Messrs. Denton, Hall & Burgin that he had written the letters on Mr. Ley's instructions and that he had had no reply to the letters. I then asked him if he could tell me the reason for the letters being sent and what the outcome of the matter was.

What did Ley say?—He said: "Yes; they were written on my instructions and I can tell you about them." He then said: "But tell me, what is this all about?" I said to him: "John Mudie has been found dead at Woldingham, and I am making inquiries on behalf of His Majesty's Coroner." I then said: "Would you care to make a statement leading up to the letters being sent and what the outcome was?" He said that he was quite prepared to do that. He then made a statement, which I took down in writing, which he signed: it was taken at his dictation.

Was it read over to him, or did he read it over himself, after it had been made?—He read it over himself. He then signed it in my presence. Exhibit 16 is the statement.

The CLERK OF THE COURT—Will you follow me in the original, officer?

"Statement of Thomas John Ley, aged 66 years, of 5 Beaufort Gardens, Kensington, S.W.3., Company Director, who says: I am the Chairman and the Director of Connaught Properties Ltd., the registered address of which concern is at 82 King William Street, E.C.4. One of the co-Directors is a Mrs. Byron Brook of 14 West Cromwell Road, Kensington, S.W.5. The Secretary of the Company is Mr. G. H. Baker. In June, 1946, it was necessary to obtain money for salaries

141

Ley and Smith.

and expenses. For this purpose, I had to obtain the signature of Mrs. Byron Brook on some open cheques already signed by Mr. G. H. Baker, before signing them myself. At about this time, I knew that Mrs. Brook had been down to 3 Homefield Road, Wimbledon, S.W.18, to look after her daughter's flat. Her daughter, Mrs. Barron, had been in hospital and had gone away on holiday. I did not know whether Mrs. Brook was joining her daughter or not, but was under the impression that she was going to. I understood that Mrs. Barron was friendly with a man named Jack Mudie because Mrs. Brook, her mother, had been introduced to him. Being under this impression, I wrote a letter to Mrs. Brook enclosing two or three cheques signed by Mr. Baker. I did not seal the envelope but put a stamp on it and addressed it to Mrs. Brook at 14 West Cromwell Road, S.W.5. I then sent this with a covering letter to Jack Mudie at 3 Homefield Road, Wimbledon, asking him to hand the letter to Mrs. Brook or if she had gone from Wimbledon, to seal the envelope and post it on to her. I afterwards learned that Mrs. Brook did not go away with her daughter and was at 14 West Cromwell Road. I asked her if she had received the cheques, and she said she knew nothing about them. I explained what I had done, and she said I had made a mistake, because she had only met Mudie once on the stairs for a few seconds. I then said I would have to go after the cheques. I then instructed Dr. Fletcher of 3 Grays Inn Place, my Solicitor, to write to Mudie with a view to recovering the cheques. The letters are those which you have shown me to-day. I had one letter sent to the Wimbledon address, but I learnt a few days later that he had moved to the Reigate Hill Hotel, Reigate. I do not remember who told me this, but I asked for a second letter to be sent there. About a week or ten days afterwards, learning that Dr. Fletcher had received no answer, or taken any further action, I decided to go to Reigate and see the man myself. I hired a car from Howards Hire Service of Beauchamp Place, Kensington, and on a Saturday afternoon motored with a man who had called on me that day. This man said he was a Mr. Alfred Mollison and claimed to have been a supporter of mine for the House of Electorate, New South Wales, Australia, where I was Minister of Justice. As I was going out in the country, I asked him if he would like to come for a drive with me. I did not know him but he satisfied me that he knew my constituency in Australia. We went down to Reigate Hill Hotel where I saw Mudie for

Evidence for Prosecution.

the first time. The Manageress showed me into a room and I explained to Mudie who I was and asked him for the cheques I had sent to Mrs. Brooks via him. He said 'I have returned them.' I said 'Have you returned them to Denton, Hall and Burgin?' and he said 'No.' I said 'You have not returned them to me. Who did you return them to?' He said 'I have returned them to the proper people and I hold a receipt.' He could not produce this and I doubted his word. I told him this and that I wanted the cheques. He said 'Mr. Tommy Barron holds the receipt for me.' I said 'Will you come along and establish that?' and he replied 'Yes, but I don't want to be taken for a ride. I have got to get back here for duty.' I looked at my watch and told him I would undertake to get him back in time for his duty. There was a short man from the kitchen of the hotel present at my interview with him and I handed him my card and said 'No harm will come to him, but if he is not back on time, you will know where to find me.' We then went to Mr. Tommy Barron who at that time was at Wimbledon. I do not remember the exact address. He produced the receipt signed by G. H. Baker to whom he had handed the cheques. I was quite satisfied with the receipt. I apologised to Mr. Barron and Mr. Mudie for the inconvenience I had caused, but told Mudie that had he sealed and posted the letter as directed, all this trouble could have been avoided. I then took Mudie back to the hotel and have not seen or heard of him since. I later saw Mr. G. H. Baker and recovered the cheques, and as far as I am concerned that was the end of the matter. I do not know where Alfred Mollison is now and have not seen him since. I understood that he was on a visit from Australia. (Signed) Thomas J. Ley."

Examination continued—Did he sign it in your presence?—He did.

The jury will remember that Exhibit 19 is a reference that Ley gave to Smith, which was read last night. Looking at the signature of that, do they appear to have been signed by the same person?—They do.

Cross-examined by Sir WALTER MONCKTON — Sergeant Shoobridge, Ley made no difficulty about making the statement, did he?—Not at all.

You said would he mind doing it and he was very ready to make it?—Yes; he appeared quite ready to do so.

Ley and Smith.

We have heard in this case from some witnesses that there was a suggestion that Ley should give some financial help to the deceased man, Mudie, at some time. Did you make inquiries into the circumstances of Mudie?—No inquiries into them apart from the bank book which we found in his possession.

Did you make inquiries about Mudie generally, the circumstances?—We learnt from Mudie's brother, yes.

Did you learn of anything which might make him an anxious man?—No; I do not think so.

You did not find any financial or other anxieties?—No.

ARTHUR PHILPOTT, sworn, examined by Mr. HAWKE—I am a chief-inspector of Scotland Yard, and was in charge of the inquiries in this case. In pursuance of these inquiries and investigations, I saw Smith at Scotland Yard on the afternoon of 17th December. I told him who I was and said: "I am making inquiries with regard to John Mudie, who has been found dead. The Buckinghams and Mrs. Bruce have been here and made statements. I want to know what your part was." He said: "I am quite willing to tell you." He then made a statement which was taken down in writing.

At one point you thought it was your duty to caution him?—I did. He mentioned gagging and binding, and I thought it my duty to caution him.

And the statement proceeds from that time under caution?—Yes.

Was it written down in your presence by another officer?—Yes.

Was it read to Smith when it was finished and did he sign it?—Yes.

Do you produce it as Exhibit 20?—I do.

The LORD CHIEF JUSTICE—Members of the jury, this is a very long statement and one which you will have to consider very carefully. I will see if, before the end of this case, copies can be obtained for you, so that when you are considering your verdict you will be able to have this statement before you.

The CLERK OF THE COURT—Will you follow me in the original, inspector, please?

"Statement of Lawrence John Smith, 39 Belvoir Road, East Dulwich, S.E.22., who saith: I am a joiner by occupation, a married man with two children, aged 10 and 5 years, who reside with my wife at 15 Mowbray Street, Leicester. We are separated although I often see her because I go to

Evidence for Prosecution.

Arthur Philpott

Leicester occasionally. I was demobilized from the Royal Air Force on 28th August, 1945. In October, 1945, I commenced work with Bowles and Sons, Builders, Gladstone Street, Leicester, and 36 St. George Street, London, W., as a joiner. On 8th May, 1946, my firm commenced work converting No. 5 Beaufort Gardens, Kensington, into flats. I understand that this property belongs to the Honourable T. J. Ley, who bought the property to convert into flats and was going to live in one himself. At the present time he occupies the ground and first floor flats at the address. He uses the basement as an office. He lives there with a daily housekeeper. Ley is aged about 67, 5 ft. 8 ins. tall, well built, I think he weighs about 13 stone. Ley became very friendly with me and I have been out to dinner with him a number of times. About two to three months ago Ley commenced to confide in me with regard to his private affairs. He said that he was very worried about his cousin Mrs. Brookes,* who was also a Director of some of his Companies and who he feared was being blackmailed by a man named Jack Mudie. He was afraid that Mudie was getting money out of Mrs. Brookes which she was taking out of the Companies. Ley told me something about the blackmail. He said that one night he was called out of his bed at 1.30 a.m. to fetch Mrs. Brookes away from the address, 3 Holmfield Road, Wimbledon, where she was staying at the house of a Mrs. Evans, with Mrs. Baron, who is Mrs. Brookes' daughter. He hired a car from the Daimler Hire Service at Knightsbridge and went over to Wimbledon. He said that he found Mrs. Brookes in a very distressed state, all packed and ready to leave. Ley told me that he thought Mrs. Brookes had been interfered with. She was very distressed and although she was ill for three or four days would not let him fetch a doctor. Ley made some enquiries at the Wimbledon address and came to the conclusion that the man causing the trouble was Mudie. Mr. Ley said that what he would like to do was to get Mudie to sign a statement and get him a passage out of the country. Ley told me that he thought Mudie had been paid £150 by Mrs. Brookes in order to serve a cadetship at the Reigate Hill Hotel and later take over that business. At that time Mudie was living at the Reigate Hill Hotel. What Mr. Ley wanted to do was to get Mudie away from the Hotel up to London if possible, to sign the statement. About two

---

* The Statement by Smith is given with the spelling as taken down by the police.

Ley and Smith.

Arthur Philpott

months ago, Mr. Ley told me that he thought he had found a chap who might be able to get Mudie up to London. He said that he was meeting this person at the Royal Hotel, Russell Square (Woburn Place), and asked me to go along. He there introduced me to a Mr. Jack Buckingham who has a car hire service, and lives in Mostyn Road, Brixton. Buckingham looks about 42 or 43, 6 ft. 2 ins. in height, with a cauliflower ear. I understand that he is an ex-boxer. Mr. Ley at this meeting told Buckingham and I that he wanted the man bringing into London, who he thought was the cause of the trouble with Mrs. Brookes. This man was a Mr. Romer who was living at 3 Holmfield Road. I have led you a bit wrong about this. Although Mudie had the £150 which I have said, it was the man Romer whom Mr. Ley suspected of interfering with Mrs. Brookes and he (Romer) was the person that Mr. Ley wanted the statement from. Mr. Ley told me in the car on the way up to the meeting with Buckingham that he was in a hurry to get away and asked that when he had introduced me to Buckingham that I should explain to him how he (Ley) wanted the man Romer got hold of and the purpose and we could arrange between ourselves how it was carried out, but to let him know before we did anything. We met Buckingham at the Hotel and after the introductions Mr. Ley left. Buckingham and I had dinner together during which time I told him that the man Romer lived at 3 Holmfield Road, and that Ley wanted him brought to somewhere in London so that he could get him to sign a statement. Buckingham suggested that we go to Wimbledon and have a look at the place. He had told me during conversation that a man named Menden who had introduced Ley to him had told him he would get a year's pay for doing the job for Ley. We went to Wimbledon and went into the Dog and Fox Public House as Ley had told us that we might find Romer there. He told me what he was like and gave us a description of his car. It was an Austin 10, maroon colour. I did have the Index number, but I can't remember what it was. We had a look round Holmfield Road and made enquiries at the garage at the Dog and Fox, but could not learn anything about Romer. I did not see Buckingham for about a fortnight and in the meantime Mr. Ley had told me that the man who was the cause of the trouble was Mudie. Ley mentioned to me that some cheques had been sent to Mrs. Brookes at Holmfield Road, and had gone astray and he thought that Mudie had them. He had a

Evidence for Prosecution.

Arthur Philpott

suspicion that Romer and Mudie were working in together. About a fortnight after the visit to the Dog and Fox I telephoned Buckingham. This was on Mr. Ley's suggestion. I phoned to make an appointment to see him and tell him that the man we were after was Mudie and not Romer. I met him in the Royal Hotel. Although Mr. Ley did not mention to me any sum of money he told me that he would see me alright for my part in this business. I told Buckingham about Mudie and that he worked in the bar at the Reigate Hill Hotel. I also told Buckingham about the cheques and that Mudie was blackmailing the woman I have mentioned. It is apparent that Mr. Ley had got his information through a firm of enquiry agents as he showed me a report from them about Romer. I cannot remember the name of the agents. I always told Ley the following day what Buckingham and I had arranged or spoken about. One suggestion put up by Buckingham was that he should go to the Reigate Hill Hotel, act a little drunk and that his son should come in and ask Mudie who would be in the bar to give him a hand outside and when they got him outside to put Mudie in the car and drive him up to London. We were going to do that the night we spoke about it but Buckingham had his car stolen from outside the Crown and Sceptre, Brompton Road. The following day I mentioned this scheme to Ley but he disagreed with it, saying that there would not be time to get Mudie to London and get the statement before he would be missed at the Hotel and there would be ructions. It was this day that I knew how much Buckingham and I were going to be paid if we got Mudie to London. I saw Mr. Ley at his address and he had two bundles of notes which he asked me to count. He asked me to check each bundle and I saw that they contained £200 each. He said: 'This is here when you bring Mudie in. You will be able to collect your money and go right away.' He then put the money in two separate envelopes. The next time I saw Buckingham he said that he thought it a good idea if his lady friend made contact with Mudie to get him to London on the pretext that he go to a cocktail party as a cocktail shaker or barman. Buckingham took me to the Green Man public house at Putney and introduced me to his lady friend who he called 'Lil.' I found that Buckingham had spoken to her about it and she said that she was quite willing to go to Reigate and make contact with Mudie. Buckingham said that he would like some money to give Lil for expenses and I said that

Ley and Smith.

Arthur Philpott

I would mention it to Mr. Ley. Buckingham came down the following morning to 5 Beaufort Gardens and together we saw Mr. Ley. We explained what had been suggested and Mr. Ley was quite agreeable. It was then that the point was raised about the expenses and Ley gave Buckingham £20 to give to Lil. This was about Thursday or Friday, either 21st or 22nd November, 1946. I believe that on the Saturday or Sunday following, Buckingham took Lil and some others down to the Reigate Hill Hotel to make contact with Mudie and to find out when his day off was. At this time I knew Buckingham's son who assisted him in the Car Hire business. The elder Buckingham told me that Lil had got very friendly with Mudie and had learned that his day off was the Thursday. He said that they were going down to Reigate again so that Lil could get better acquainted—that is, Lil and young Buckingham. The idea was for Lil to show up as a woman of means with a car and a chauffeur so to impress Mudie. I told Ley what had been suggested and he was satisfied. It was Ley's idea that Mudie should come away from the Hotel on his own initiative and if on his day off all the better as there would not be any fuss about it. Ley told me to tell Buckingham to let him know when to expect Mudie at the address and he would have all the arrangements made at his end. I have been told that I need not say anything unless I wish to do so but that whatever I do say will be written down and may be given in evidence."

The CLERK OF THE COURT—Did he sign that "L. J. Smith"?

The WITNESS—Yes.

The CLERK OF THE COURT—

"Mr. Ley explained to Buckingham and I during our meetings that we were to get Mudie to his house, tie him up and gag him so that he could get the statement from him and leave him with him. On Tuesday, 26th, Buckingham told me that arrangements had been made by Lil and John the younger Buckingham to come up to the cocktail party on the Thursday. He told me this when I met him together with Lil and Lil's husband, who was in bus driver's uniform, in the Green Man public house. I told Ley the following morning the full details that Lil had arranged to pick Mudie up outside the Reigate Hill Hotel at

Evidence for Prosecution.

5.15 p.m. on the Thursday and that we would be at Beaufort
Gardens at half past six. Buckingham and I discussed plans
that Lil should be given the key to the back door of 5 Beaufort Gardens and she should come in with Mudie, Buckingham and I waiting inside the door to tie him up. This was
not what Mr. Ley wanted. He really wanted us to tie Mudie
up on the way so that he would not be able to create when
we arrived at the house. On Thursday 28th, in preparation
for Mudie I purchased a clothes line from Farmer Brothers,
Montpelier Street, next to the Crown and Sceptre for 9d. or
1s. 3d. It had two rings on it. The assistants there know
me quite well as I often go in to buy stuff for the job where
I work. I told Buckingham that I bought this and that I
would have a rug handy in the house. At 4 p.m. that night
Thursday, 28th, Buckingham and his son called for me at
5 Beaufort Gardens. They had their Wolseley car. The elder
Buckingham got in the Wolseley car and the younger got in
a Ford 8 car with me. This was the car that I had on hire
for a week from Howards, Beauchamp Street, Kensington.
We all drove to Lil's address which is near Putney Hill. The
two Buckinghams went into Lil's house and came out with
her and she got in the Wolseley car. We drove to within six
miles of Banstead where we stopped and went into a teashop
and had tea and sandwiches. Lil suggested phoning Mudie
because we were a bit late. She phoned from a kiosk on the
corner and we continued on. About half a mile from Reigate
Hill we stopped and the younger Buckingham took over the
Wolseley and the elder took over the Ford. The reason
we drove like that was because the younger Buckingham was
not sure of the road. We followed slowly behind the
Wolseley which went on to the Hotel and picked up Mudie.
As it returned we got in front of it to lead the way back to
London. We got lost from them as young Buckingham took
the wrong turning. We returned and picked them up at a
level crossing and came on through Wimbledon. As the
younger Buckingham knew his way from there we forged
ahead. We arrived at 5 Beaufort Gardens round about a
quarter to seven and entered by the front door of which I had
the key. I knocked on Mr. Ley's flat door and he came up
from the basement. We told him that Mudie was coming in
the back door. He did not say anything but I thought he
looked nervous. We went down to the basement through
the passage and I showed Buckingham where he was to
stand. This room is just inside the door on the left-hand

Ley and Smith.

Arthur Philpott

side and you have to come down three steps from the back door to it—it leads off the passage from the back door. I was going to stand in the angle formed by that passage turning right and near where the steps leading up to the ground floor flat are. We took up our positions, Buckingham was to throw the rug over Mudie's head when he entered the door. I was then going to help him to tie him up. He had the rug and I had the rope. Mr. Ley was standing on the stairs leading to his flat and he called me and said, 'Will you hang on a little while as my end has slipped up.' By this I took it that he wanted me to hang on after Mudie had been tied up as he said 'There is no need for Buckingham to stay. Let him push off.' He then handed me an envelope saying, 'Put this in your pocket. I've got Buckingham's here.' I knew the envelope contained the money. I told Buckingham that Ley wanted me to hold on as his people hadn't turned up. I told him that I didn't want to as I had made arrangements with Buckingham to go out and have a drink afterwards. I heard the car pull up at the back door and we again took up our positions. The door was opened and I heard Lil say what we had already arranged she should say, 'Excuse me, I want to speak to John,' meaning the younger Buckingham. I saw Mudie come past the angle where I was standing and the back door closed. I put my arms round Mudie's chest holding his arms down, standing in front of him, whilst Buckingham came up behind and threw the rug over him. He then held his arms down with the rug over his head, whilst I tied Mudie's ankles and then wound the rope round his body taking in his left arm but leaving out the right, pulling it tight over the top of the rug. I tied the rope in the middle of his back taking it down to his ankles again then back. The reason why I left out his right arm was purely accidental because it was raised level with the back of his head and Buckingham was holding it. If I remember rightly his left hand was in his overcoat pocket. Buckingham helped him along the passage by jumping him and at the door of the room we were going to take him into he fell forward with Buckingham on top of him. Buckingham picked him up and helped him into the room and sat him down on a swivel chair which was opposite the desk where Ley had told us to put him. Buckingham asked me if I had got a gag and I hunted round and went into the front room where I found a piece of cloth which I knew was a French polishers rag, hard in places from the polish, and

150

Evidence for Prosecution.

Arthur Philpott

gave it to Buckingham. He pulled the rug back from Mudie's face and tied the gag round his mouth. Both of us went out of the room and Mr. Ley came down the stairs and stood at the bottom where we met him. Ley handed an envelope to Buckingham. He shook his hand and said, 'Don't contact me or phone me for some time.' I then let Buckingham out by the back door and as Mr. Ley had asked me to stop behind I went and stood with him in the passage. Ley asked if we had any difficulty in picking Mudie up and I told him that everything had gone off alright; I said that I thought our plan was the best in not tying Mudie up whilst we were in the car. Ley and I stood talking for about ten minutes during which time neither of us went in to see how Mudie was. I could see from Ley's attitude that he was expecting someone to call. I heard somebody coming up the steps to the front door and Ley said 'Alright you can go now.' I went out by the way of the basement door at the front and when I got to the top of the stairs I could not see anyone. I heard the front door close and I came to the conclusion that someone had gone into the house although I did not see anybody or hear any voices. My car was at the front of the house and I got in and drove along to Brompton Road. I could not see Buckingham's car outside so I didn't stop at the Crown and Sceptre. When Buckingham put the rug over Mudie's head I heard Mudie say 'You are stifling me.' Buckingham said 'You are breathing your last.' He said this jokingly to put the wind up him. He did not struggle at all but looked scared. Mudie couldn't say anything after that because Buckingham put the gag round his face. When he was sitting in the chair he was conscious. As far as I can remember I drove straight on towards Dulwich and called in the Grove pub where I had a few drinks in the public bar. I don't know anyone in the pub and stood by myself until about a quarter to ten. I then drove home to my digs and parked the car just outside. On the following day I went to Leicester by car and came back about 3.30 p.m. on the Monday and took the car back to Howards. I stayed at the Wellington Hotel at Leicester. I saw Ley at his address on Monday afternoon and he said that everything had gone off alright and Mudie had been dropped at Wimbledon. I saw Buckingham on the Tuesday and he asked me what had happened after I left and I told him I had waited with Mr. Ley for about ten minutes, came outside, and as I could not see his car outside the Crown and Sceptre drove away

Ley and Smith.

home. I also gave to Buckingham thirty £1 notes, being my half share of what we had agreed Lil and young Buckingham should get—£30 each. I also told him that Mr. Ley had been pleased with the job but that he did not want Buckingham to phone him any more. I did not discuss this with Mr. Ley again until Saturday, 7th December, when he mentioned to me that the police from Caterham had rung up and wanted to interview him about some cheques as they had some letters which were from a Dr. Fletcher asking about them. I believe Dr. Fletcher is from a firm of Solicitors. I saw the car standing outside the address and saw a man talking to Mr. Ley. I think the man was a policeman. I left to go home to my digs. On Monday, 9th, when I got to work I saw Mr. Ley and he told me that the police had been to interview him and he had been with them for about two and a half hours, and that Mudie had been reported missing. He did not tell me what he had told the police but he asked me to go and see Buckingham and tell him not to ring up his address and that if the police saw him to say that he had not seen Mudie. He said, 'As far as I am concerned Mudie was taken to Wimbledon and left there.' I have seen Mr. Ley on a number of occasions but he has never mentioned the matter to me. This piece of rag I speak of which was used as a gag I might recognise again. It was dirty and about eighteen inches long with plenty of French polish on it. Of the money £200 I got from Mr. Ley, I put £20 in the Post Office, £30 to Buckingham; I have spent about £130 on clothes and presents, and the remaining £20 I had in my wallet which I handed to you. The money was all in £1 notes. This statement has been read to me and is true. (Signed) Lawrence John Smith."

Examination continued—Chief-inspector, did you see Smith again on the following day?—Yes, at 11 a.m.

Had you then in your possession the green rag, Exhibit 13, and the rope, Exhibit 12?—Yes.

Did you show those to Smith?—Yes. I cautioned him and showed them to him and said: "These were found round the body of Mudie."

Did he make any observation when you said that?—Pointing to the rag, he said: "Yes. That is what we used to gag him with, and the rope is like the one I bought, but I can't say for sure."

Was that also reduced to writing?—Yes.

Evidence for Prosecution.

And he signed his further statement?—Yes.
Have you got that before you?—Yes.

The CLERK OF THE COURT—
  "I have again been cautioned that I need not say anything
unless I wish to do so but that whatever I do say will be
written down and may be given in evidence. (Signed)
Lawrence John Smith. The piece of cloth you have shown
me I identify as the piece of cloth I obtained at 5 Beaufort
Gardens which I handed to Buckingham on 28th November,
1946, and which he used to gag Mudie by tying it round his
mouth. With regard to the rope you have shown me, it is
similar to that which I purchased and used at the flat. It had
two rings on then and was in one piece—not cut. This
further statement has been read to me and is true. (Signed)
Lawrence John Smith."

The WITNESS—Yes.

Examination continued—Later that same day did you go to
5 Beaufort Gardens and see Ley there?—I did.
  You told him who you were?—Yes, and that I wanted to see
him in regard to a very serious matter, and I asked him to come
to New Scotland Yard with me.
  What did he say?—He said: "That sounds bad. What is it?"
I said: "It is in connexion with a man named John Mudie, who
has been found dead in Surrey. He is alleged to have been at
your address and his death appears to have been a violent one."
  Did he say anything to that?—No.
  But he went with you to Scotland Yard?—Yes.
  What did you say to him there?—I explained to him the
allegations which had been made by the Buckinghams, Smith and
Mrs. Bruce very fully. He said: "This is very serious. I must
have my solicitor here to advise me how to meet these false allega-
tions."
  You waited until his solicitor arrived?—Yes.
  And in his presence a statement was made?—Yes.
  What did Ley say before he made the statement? I suppose
he told his solicitor what the allegation against him was?—Yes.
He explained to his solicitor what I had explained to him.
  And I suppose the solicitor advised him to make a statement?
—Yes; which he did.
  Was that statement taken down in writing?—It was.
  Read over to him?—By his solicitor.
  And he signed it?—Yes. It is Exhibit 21 which I produce.

Ley and Smith.

Arthur Philpott

THE CLERK OF THE COURT—

"Statement of Thomas John Ley, 5 Beaufort Gardens, S.W.3, a Company Director, who saith: It has been explained to me by Chief Inspector Philpott that two men named Buckingham and Smith, the latter being the foreman of the men employed by Bowles and Son on repairs at my address brought a man named John Mudie to my house at approximately 7 p.m. on Thursday, 28th November, 1946, that he was left there gagged and bound with me and that they each received £200 from me for doing this. Also that other people have said that they assisted in bringing Mudie there. I have also been told that the next time there is any evidence of Mudie being seen he was found dead. He was found dead in a quarry at Woldingham on the 30th November, 1946, at about 4 p.m. He had a rope round his neck and a green piece of cloth, death being due to asphyxia from strangulation during suspension. I have already made a statement to Sergeant Shoobridge as to my knowledge of Jack Mudie that shows that I last saw him in June, 1946, and I have not seen him since that time. I do know the man Smith who was the foreman for Bowles and Son doing reconstruction work at my house. I have known him for a few months and used to see him almost daily up till a week ago when he gave up his situation. I have never spoken to Smith about Mudie and as far as I know Smith did not know that I knew such a person as Mudie. I have never mentioned to him that Mudie used to be at the Dog and Fox or lived at 3 Holmfield Road and neither have I mentioned to Smith that Mudie was at the Reigate Hill Hotel. It is possible that Smith would know Mrs. Brook because she used to come to my address, but I have never mentioned Mrs. Baron to him. I have never mentioned a person named Romer of 3 Holmfield Road to Smith. I do know a man named Buckingham. He is a tall man, broad, aged about fifty, and I think has a slightly cauliflower ear. So far as I know he runs a Car Hire Service. My recollection is that I got to know Buckingham through Smith who introduced me thinking I would hire cars from him. I should say it is in the region of two months that I have known Buckingham. I don't think that I have ever met his son. As far as I recollect I only met Buckingham once after that. This was shortly after I first met him when he brought another car to the house in order to impress me, but his garage being too far away from my house I could not

Evidence for Prosecution.

Arthur Philpott

engage him. To my knowledge Buckingham has never been in my house. I have never discussed Mudie with Buckingham. I do know a man named Minden. He was a porter at the Royal Hotel, Woburn Place. Although I cannot remember at the moment where I was at approximately 7 p.m. on 28th November, 1946, I can say this, that if I was at my flat no other persons came in to my knowledge. At my address I occupy the ground floor and the first floor flat and part of the basement is in use by me as office premises and access can be gained to these offices in the basement through my ground floor flat. There are two doors to the house, the front door which is approached by steps out of which there is a passage leading to my flat. The rear door is in Brompton Place and I have had a sign put over the top 'Old Air Raid Shelter.' When you open the back door there are two or three steps leading down from the street level to a passage which has a very small angle. On the left immediately inside the door is a room. Then there is another room also on the left. In between these two rooms in the passage stands a fairly large safe. The passage then leads into a big room at the end which gives access to the area at the front of the house. On the right of the passage immediately inside that door is another room and further along the passage are the stone steps leading from my flat above. Access to these steps can only be obtained from my flat and the basement. The front and back door have both got Yale pattern locks. They have been on some time and I have been rather worried in trying to trace the keys. I have asked Smith about the keys and also a man named Bartlett. I have also mentioned it to Mrs. Brook. I think there are five keys to the front door. One is the original key to the lock which was the only one handed to me when I purchased the house. Four I have had cut. They have been handed—one to Sir Howard d'Egville, one to Mr. Kuppinger, two I hold myself and one is held by the housekeeper. The door to my flat has a mortice lock but this door was only put there a week or two ago. With regard to the back door, there are two keys so far as I know. I have one and my Secretary Miss Ingleson has the other. There may be other keys as the workmen may have had them cut to go in and out. I have made use of enquiry agents from time to time. I employed a firm named Conquest once and another firm the name of which I cannot now remember. I have not employed them for some time and I have not employed them to enquire

Ley and Smith.

Arthur Philpott

regarding the whereabouts of Mudie. I cannot recollect how I came to learn how Mudie was living at the Reigate Hill Hotel. Smith has never explained to me how it was being arranged with a woman to get Mudie to my address on the pretext of coming to a cocktail party. I have never given either Buckingham or Smith £20 expenses for that purpose. Neither have I given them each £200. I bank with the Midland Bank at Knightsbridge—6 Sloane Street—and I have also got an account at Barclays Bank, New Cross Gate. They are the only two accounts I have. Other accounts which I have control or part control of are at Midland Bank, 6 Sloane Street—belonging to Decorepes Company, on which cheques can be drawn to my signature only; the District Bank, Aldwych, belonging to Connaught Properties Limited, which cheques require three signatures although I am the holder of the cheque. On occasions on which I have to hire cars I deal with Howards Motor Hire Service, Beauchamp Place, Kensington. That is the only firm I can recollect. I have never given Buckingham my telephone number although he could have got it from Smith. I have never told Smith to tell Buckingham not to ring my telephone number. In fact I do not recollect Buckingham ever ringing that number. When the Police last visited me they rang up to make the appointment and said that they did not want to discuss the business over the telephone, but they had been in touch with Dr. Fletcher. I rang Dr. Fletcher and he said that he thought that the Police wanted to see me about the Inquest on Jack Mudie. I did not mention to Smith that the Police were coming. Some time later I was called to the telephone, I don't know who by, and got a message from Sergeant Shoobridge, the Police Officer at Caterham, to say he would be late. It was a Saturday that Sergeant Shoobridge called on me. My Secretary was not in that day. It might have been about 11.30 a.m. when Sergeant Shoobridge called and he stayed there until about 1.45 p.m. I know I missed a luncheon appointment through it. I did not mention to Smith on the Monday following that the Police had called on me and I did not ask him to go and see Buckingham about the matter. I did not say to Smith, 'As far as I am concerned Mudie was taken to Wimbledon and left there.' So far as my knowledge goes Jack Mudie has never been at 5 Beaufort Gardens and I have never seen him there. This statement has been read to me by Mr. P. H. Brashier, my Solicitor, and is true. (Signed) Thomas J. Ley."

Evidence for Prosecution.

Arthur Philpott

The WITNESS—Yes.

Examination continued—I do not know that a great deal turns on this now, but you went back to 5 Beaufort Gardens with Ley and his solicitor after the statement had been made, did you not? —Yes.

In the basement there is a safe, is there not?—Yes.

Was there on the top of that safe a piece of green material which is exactly similar to Exhibit 13?—Yes.

On 28th December did you see Ley again at 5 Beaufort Gardens?—I did.

What did you say to him?—I said: "We are going to take you to Chelsea Police Station, where you will be charged, with Buckingham and Smith, with the murder of John McMain Mudie on or about the 28th November, 1946." I cautioned him. He said: "I have nothing to say at this stage. I am sure that everything will right itself. I am innocent of the charge."

You then saw Smith in Scotland Yard later in the morning?— Yes.

Did you tell him that he would be charged, with Buckingham and Ley, with the murder of Jack Mudie?—Yes, and cautioned him. He said: "There is nothing further I can say. I have already made a statement."

They were formally charged with murder at Chelsea Police Station?—Yes, and cautioned.

Did either of them reply?—Mr. Ley said: "I am innocent." Mr. Smith said: "Nothing to say."

Cross-examined by Mr. CURTIS BENNETT—Smith is a man of excellent character, is not he?—Yes.

With no previous convictions or charges?—No.

He was demobilized from the R.A.F. in August, 1945?—Yes, having served about eighteen months. He came out under class B.

In this statement, Exhibit 20, Smith mentioned to you the question of the gag on his own, without you having told him anything about it?—Yes.

He told you where he bought the rope?—Yes.

Did you inquire from Farmer Brothers of Montpelier Street?— Yes, without any success as regards Smith. They do sell rope. Nobody could recollect Smith having purchased one there.

So, apart from Smith's statement, you could not have shown that?—No.

He prefaced the statement by saying in terms "I am willing to help you all I can"?—Yes.

Ley and Smith.

Arthur Philpott

And then made this long statement as to the whole of the detail?—Yes.

When did any news of a dead body having been found at Woldingham appear in the daily press?—I understand about 2nd December, but I cannot say that for certain.

What date did the witnesses Smith and Tamplin come and speak to the police?—I took up this inquiry on 14th December and at that time statements had already been taken from Smith and Tamplin. I think it was approximately 11th December when they made a statement.

Do you know when they first came?—No. It was before then.

Dealing with the question of the journey down there, taking it from London, the beginning of Westminster Bridge if you like, it would take about an hour to drive down there?—Yes; approximately 50 to 60 minutes.

You would agree that that place shown in picture No. 1, where Mr. Smith was supposed to have been standing, seen by those two witnesses, is very steep?—Yes.

So is the slope from where the trench was down to the road?—Yes.

What sort of weight do you think Mudie would have been?—Approximately 10 stone, I understand.

Is it your view that there must have been more than one man who carried the body from the road or car up to where it was found?—I would not say that definitely, because with a fireman's lift one might be able to carry it by oneself.

Either a very strong single man or more than one man?—Yes.

Because it is a very steep slope up and rather slippery grass?—Yes.

Re-examined by Mr. HAWKE—How long would it take, approximately, from the chalk pit to Brixton?—35 to 40 minutes.

KENNETH ALFRED BLANDFORD, recalled, further examined by Mr. HAWKE—You photographed a Ford motor at Scotland Yard on 27th December, 1946?—Yes.

Are *those* two prints? (Photographs handed to witness.)—Yes.

CHARLES FREDERICK NORMANTON, recalled, further examined by Mr. HAWKE—Just look at *that* photograph. (Handed to witness.) Is that a correct and true photograph of the Ford car F G P 101 which is in your possession and which you hired to Smith?—Yes.

By the LORD CHIEF JUSTICE—Was the number-plate, when you hired it to Smith, the same number-plate that is on there now?—Yes.

Evidence for Prosecution.

Charles F. Normanton

Further examination continued—And in the same place?—Yes. It is a black Ford 8, you told us?—Yes; even to the marks on the spare tyre.

FREDERICK SHOOBRIDGE, recalled, further cross-examined by Mr. CURTIS BENNETT—You know the witnesses Frederick William Smith and Clifford Joel Tamplin. When did they visit the police first?—They visited the local police about 3rd December.

Mr. HAWKE—My lord, that is the case for the Crown.

Opening Speech for the Prisoner Ley.

Sir WALTER MONCKTON—I am calling my client and other witnesses.

May it please your lordship, members of the jury, I have now the privilege of addressing you for the first time on behalf of the accused Ley. I shall have another opportunity, when the evidence in this case has been completed, of considering with you the whole of the evidence and putting before you then my submissions on behalf of Ley, and I am not going to abuse this chance by inflicting upon you a premature consideration of all the matters which I ought to lay before you in his interest before I conclude my task; but I do want, if I may, to say one or two things to you to put, as it were, the right framework in front of you into which you have to fit the consideration you will give to the pieces of evidence which all of us lay before you.

It is, is it not, an astonishing—indeed, a bewildering—story which the prosecution have laid before you in this case? You will, I know, in thinking of the case I am now dealing with, the bewildering case that I suggest it is, put out of your minds with regard to Ley the statement by Smith which has been put in. That is not evidence against me, against my client, as Mr. Hawke, with his customary fairness, made clear to you once or twice in the course of his opening speech.

The whole of the story against Ley is put before you by the witness Buckingham and his friend Minden. You saw Buckingham. You heard him and you heard him questioned; perhaps not the man for a story of this sort whom you would choose for the purpose, but it is Buckingham and Minden who alone make the allegations which are made against Ley about what he said and did in regard to the plot which is alleged—and what a story it is! Ley you will see in the box in a few minutes. He is a man of 66. He

Ley and Smith.

Sir Walter Monckton

was a solicitor in Australia, and while in Australia he served in the Government of New South Wales in various capacities, a Minister in various offices and finally Minister of Justice. He gave up that office in order to take a seat in the Australian Commonwealth House of Representatives. So that he is a person who has acquired some experience both in his profession as a solicitor and in public life in that great Dominion.

The other person most intimately concerned with his life is Mrs. Brook, who gave evidence before you here, a person with whom he has been associated for something like 24 years or 26 years, and you may think perhaps one of the oddest features in the case, a woman with whom he has not been sleeping for 10 or 12 years, on the story which the prosecution witnesses have told. So here is this man of ripe experience and considerable years and this woman with whom he has had a long association, for many years without sexual intercourse.

Who is the third person whom one has to consider in this story at this stage? It is the dead man, Mudie. Now you heard Mrs. Brook talk about what she called the protective jealousy which she found in the accused Ley. You heard witnesses speak of three men about whom he entertained suspicion. The first was Arthur Barron, the son-in-law, the second was Jack Mudie, and the third was Arthur Romer. The odd feature, you may think at this stage, is this, with Ley, this old man of whom I have given you particulars and Mrs. Brook, the woman with whom he had the association of the kind I have described, that Mudie and not Romer should be the person, if jealousy was the motive here, on the prosecution's story, he is alleged to have wanted and plotted to bring up to his 5 Beaufort Gardens address—Mudie, of whom Mrs. Brook said his jealousy ceased after the cheques incident, which itself terminated in August, and the events with which you are concerned are at the end of November.

It is, is it not, a mysterious, strange story? This man, with his experience, is said to have wished, plotted, to bring the man Mudie, tied up, into his house, into the basement of his house, in order that there he should have extracted from him a confession and should be given, according to some of the evidence, £500 to leave the country. There was a faint suspicion of a story that some other person was going to have an aeroplane ready in order to fly him away. This is all happening to a man of 66 with that experience of life of which I have spoken.

Members of the jury, when we come to consider all these matters at the end, I do not think one will doubt this, that at any rate it is a most bewildering tale. I must not leave out of account

Opening Speech for the Prisoner Ley.

Sir Walter Monckton

altogether the method by which this plot was to be brought about. Mrs. Bruce was to be sent down as the decoy. She was to represent herself as a woman of means who was going to come round with a chauffeur and a car; and what was she to do with the barman at the hotel? He was to fix the date of the cocktail party when it suited him; he was to come to mix the cocktails and to mix with the guests, perhaps not the most important, but perhaps not the least mysterious part of the story which has been unfolded to you.

As if there was not enough mystery there, when the return journey—the journey which brought Mudie, according to the prosecution's story, up to 5 Beaufort Gardens—took place and he got in there at 6.50, what happened after 6.50? What happened between the moment he got there and the moment when, two days later, he was discovered miles away down in the chalk pit of which you have seen photographs this morning? What happened?

This case at present is full of uncertainties which lead me to make this observation to you, that in my respectful submission it is not as though the first question which you have to face is: did Ley, or did Smith, or did both of them murder Mudie? The first question you will have to consider, in my submission, is: was Mudie murdered at all? In a case full of the uncertainties which I have described to you, you may find that the evidence we put before you for the defendants will in part resolve uncertainties and in part increase them, because there are some topics about this case where, even when the evidence is complete, you may be left in great doubt. It will be my submission to you later on, as it is at this moment, that nobody can safely say at this moment now that Mudie was murdered beyond reasonable doubt.

To what extent shall I relieve or resolve the uncertainties? First of all, I am going to call Ley, the accused, himself. He will give you his account of his movements at the crucial time and of the events of which you have heard, so far as he was concerned with them. Such corroborative witnesses as are available will be put before you. It is always difficult to find conclusive corroboration, but we hope that you will feel that those witnesses are more consistent with the truth of his story than you would perhaps have expected to find. If you, when you have heard him, feel that you can accept the story which he tells as being the substance of the truth so far as he is concerned, that is the end of the case against him and he would be not guilty; but in asking you to consider the framework in which the evidence will have to be weighed later on, I want to deal with it on both footings. First of all, if, when you have heard all he has got to say, you are satisfied that he had no

Ley and Smith.

Sir Walter Monckton

hand or part in any of these things which are alleged, that, as I say, means at once a finding of not guilty so far as he is concerned.

But suppose for a moment that, in the light of the evidence which you have heard, you do not accept that story, I want to deal with that, too. What, then, is the position? How then does the case for the prosecution stand? First of all, there is the question which I have already indicated as the primary one which you will have to deal with: is it proved beyond reasonable doubt that Mudie was murdered at all? That is the first point. Then, what have the prosecution proved, if the evidence which you have heard is accepted? They have proved the unlawful act of being in a conspiracy to assault Mudie by tying him up. What have they proved against Ley? That is the first thing, if you accept their evidence. Secondly, on the case which they have made, their witnesses proved that Mudie was not gagged. If you remember, he was cross-examined about it, but Buckingham stuck to it that he was not gagged. Thirdly, this Buckingham said—you may have heard it—that even on his story Ley had expressly insisted that, apart from the tying up, there was to be no violence used towards Mudie; and, fourthly, they will say they have proved that Mudie died of strangulation.

Now, there are two matters there upon which I shall wish to speak at a later stage. I shall want to argue before you that the evidence upon which they seek to prove that Mudie died of strangulation is not sufficient or satisfactory, even as it stands now. Secondly, what I submit they have not proved by evidence is who it was, if anybody, who strangled Mudie. What we shall seek to show are several propositions. We shall seek to show, by evidence of which I will speak in a moment, that it is highly doubtful whether any real violence was done, apart from the tying up, to Mudie before his death, and in the course of that to deal with what the prosecution have relied on as indicating and establishing such violence, and hope to show that the symptoms which they rely upon are symptoms equally consistent with any form of asphyxia; that is, any death by suffocation, however caused, the loss of oxygen in the blood, which is known as asphyxia. Thirdly, I shall seek to establish that strangulation could have occurred either by someone other than Ley, the hand of someone other than Ley, or indeed by accident, if Mudie were struggling to escape. I shall ask you, further, to take this view when you have heard the evidence, that the position of the rope round the neck, about which you heard a good deal, gives you no help in suggesting that the death was due to wilful strangulation.

Opening Speech for the Prisoner Ley.

Sir Walter Monckton

I have indicated to you the matters towards which my evidence will be directed. If I am right in the principal proposition which I first alleged, which is that you must first be satisfied that this is a case where murder has been proved beyond reasonable doubt, you will perhaps pay special attention to such medical evidence as I am able to lay before you. I shall not fail to deal with the suggestions about the condition found in the abdomen. You will remember Dr. Gardner speaking of the discolouration on a very great scale. I shall not fail to deal with the discoloured fluid in the brain; but I shall hope, with the assistance of my witnesses, to satisfy you that the indications which they give are indications equally consistent with a non-violent asphyxia.

Then I ought just to say this. There is a man whom we shall call before you who, as we are informed, was about this vicinity—and, indeed, in this house—during the crucial period of the evening of 28th November. We shall put him before you to see how far he can assist in this case; but finally I think it will come back to this: you will have to satisfy yourselves how did this man die, before you ask who caused his death. I ask you at this moment to bear that point in mind as you listen to the evidence which comes before you on behalf of Ley. As I say, first and foremost, we put him in to give his account, with such corroboration as we can provide. Secondly, at a later stage, after calling the man whom I last indicated, I will put before you the medical testimony upon which we rely.

There, members of jury, for the moment I leave it and I hope, at any rate, I have not detained you too long. You will realize the burden that rests upon anyone who conducts the task I have to bear to-day. Therefore, I felt bound to give at the outset of our case the way in which we feel that the approach ought to be made, and to reserve till the end, upon the basis of that approach, a consideration of the evidence which you, and you individually, will have to weigh.

Evidence for the Prisoner Thomas John Ley.

THOMAS JOHN LEY, sworn, examined by Sir WALTER MONCKTON —I think you were born in England, and when you were a small boy of eight you went out to Australia, with your family?—That is so.

Did you become a solicitor there?—Yes.

And practised your profession?—Yes.

That went on until 1929?—Yes.

Did you also take part in political life?—Yes.

Ley and Smith.

Thomas J. Ley

I think you became a member of the Legislative Assembly in New South Wales?—Yes.

During that period were you Minister of various kinds?—Yes.

I think Public Instruction, Labour and Industry, and finally Minister of Justice?—Yes.

That last post you held from 1922 to 1925?—Yes, roughly.

Did you resign it when you were elected to take a seat in the Australian House of Representatives?—Yes.

And you retained that seat until 1928?—Yes.

Then in 1929 you came to England?—Yes.

When did you first become acquainted with Mrs. Brook who has given evidence in this case?—In December, 1921, I, in the capacity of Minister of Justice, visited Western Australia and was there introduced to Mrs. Brook by her husband, who was a respected magistrate of the City of Perth.

Did her husband die in the following year?—Yes.

And did you then assist Mrs. Brook financially?—Yes, and in other ways that she wanted help.

Was that in the case both of her and her daughter?—Yes. They came to my home and stayed there for a little while until they could get settled elsewhere.

Did you give her any money at that time when you were in Australia?—I did immediately after the death of her husband, to help her over difficulties, and have done so subsequently from time to time.

Have you from time to time since then put money into her name in relation to properties?—Yes.

Can you give me a figure of the amounts which you have expended in that way on property in her name?—Roughly over £6000. It may be £8000.

Did you also pay the expenses of her home?—Yes.

When did you form an intimate association with her?—When we came to this country.

You have said that you came in November, 1929. When did she come?—She came some months afterwards. I cannot remember the exact date.

Was it thereafter that you were together in various flats and hotels?—Yes; but I would wish, Sir Walter, in view of the allegations that have been made about my insane jealousy and my suspicions of improper conduct by Mrs. Brook and the suggestion that I had been obsessed with her being blackmailed, to make a short statement, if I may, because I think my lord and the jury ought to have the background of what happened.

Evidence for the Prisoner Ley.

Thomas J. Ley

The LORD CHIEF JUSTICE—You are in your counsel's hands and your counsel will ask you such questions as he, in his discretion, thinks right. You will confine your evidence, please, to answering questions.

Examination continued—I will give you opportunities to say as much as in my discretion is in your interest and my duty to the Court is relevant. I assure you you will get your opportunities, but I wanted just to get from you at this stage whether, after her coming to England, you did in fact live in flats and hotels together? —Yes.

Did you buy her a house in Wimbledon?—Yes, wholly with my own money.

When was that—quite early on?—Yes. It was intended to be our home. I think about 1930.

Was it let during the war?—Yes.

We heard from her of a house at 16 Knightsbridge Court, Sloane Street?—Yes. It was not a house; it was a flat.

Were you there with her from 1942 until June of last year?— Yes.

Were you happily together then?—Quite happy, yes. It was roughly four years. The lease was four years; but I want to make clear that we lived there as employer and housekeeper, on account of things that had happened before, and in no other capacity.

Mrs. Brook said that for the last ten or twelve years you had not lived together on an intimate footing?—That is perfectly true. The relationship changed some twelve years ago.

In June, 1946, the tenancy expired, did it not, which you had? —Yes. I was offered a new lease, but the terms were not acceptable.

I think there was no flat which you could immediately find in June, 1946, for you both?—No.

You went, so she told us, while 5 Beaufort Gardens was being redecorated, to your Club?—That is true.

And she went to a room in West Cromwell Road?—She first found a small room in West Cromwell Road that she regarded as too small. Then her daughter had to go under an operation and I suggested that she would find it more comfortable to go to her daughter's flat, so that she would have more room and her son-in-law would be relieved of a financial burden.

Is that the flat in 3 Homefield Road of which we have heard?— Yes.

We have been told that she went there, to the daughter's flat, at or about the end of May, 1946?—I took her there on 24th May with all her luggage.

Ley and Smith.

Thomas J. Ley

She has told us that on 12th June, when she had been there about a fortnight, as a result of telephone conversations, you fetched her away from there in the middle of the night?—I did bring her away in the middle of the night.

The departure was at 2.30 in the morning on 12th June?—Yes.

During the time when Mrs. Brook was in 3 Homefield Road—that is between 24th May and 12th June—was there an incident which caused trouble between you?—Yes. It did not cause trouble between us in one way. Trouble arose out of it. It was on 8th June, 1946. I used to call for her, at her request, each evening from the time she was there right up till she left, at 6 o'clock, take her to dinner, because she said she would be lonely, and bring her back about 9, when it was her custom to retire about 9.30. That practice was observed right through.

On 8th June was there an incident?—Yes. I arrived at the house rather early and walked in with someone who was opening the door under the impression that I was going to give her some surprise that she would welcome. When I got to the top of the hall, I heard voices, her voice and another, a man's voice, both of whom seemed to be very happy, and she was calling him "Arthur." It was that name that registered in my mind.

Did you ask her for an explanation of that?—I went downstairs and closed the door, because I was quite satisfied from what I had heard that I was not wanted, and I pushed the bell ringing the electric bell in the flat. She put her head out of the window and she looked transfigured, very white, and she said she was boiling an egg.

Was that incident, when you thought you heard her in close conversation with someone, an intimate conversation with someone, the incident which caused trouble, as I put it, in June, 1946?—That caused the trouble. That was the origin of the trouble.

You heard, or thought you heard, an intimate conversation?—Yes.

By the LORD CHIEF JUSTICE—By this time I understood you to say this lady had ceased to be your mistress?—Yes; but I was not concerned on that account, and that is why I wanted to make it quite clear. I was not jealous about this thing. She had a perfect right to do what she wanted to do.

Examination continued—Then on the nights that followed 8th June, did you take her out to dine as before or not?—I took her out, but she was in such a state before we went to the restaurant that I had to get her to sit down.

Evidence for the Prisoner Ley.

Thomas J. Ley

You telephoned, she told us, every night, one or other of you?
—The arrangement was that when I got back to Knightsbridge
after taking her back, I should ring up and say a final "good
night" and just happy dreams; something of that kind.

On 12th June, the night you took her away, is there something
you remember about a conversation?—Yes, very distinctly. It was
just at the end. She said "I am packing up," and I had actually
rung off before the significance of those words dawned on me.

She said she was packing. Did you therefore ring her again?—
After undressing and getting into bed and reading for a while,
I found I could not read my book; the print was swimming before
my eyes and there was a tap, tap, "I am packing." I could not
make out what it was; so I thought I would ring her up and find
out whether I was correct that she said that, or whether I was under
some misapprehension, because I had paid the rent for a month and
I had given her living expenses.

At any rate, was it in consequence of the anxiety that you had
that you fetched her that night?—I rang up afterwards and asked
her if she did tell me she was packing, and she said "I am packed
up."

Then did you go and take her away?—I did not take her away
like that. There were incidents before that. I do not think that
anyone listening would quite understand the thing unless I went
over the incidents. She said she was packed up and she wanted
me to get fresh accommodation for her.

By the LORD CHIEF JUSTICE—At two o'clock in the morning?—
No. This was at a quarter-past ten. At half-past nine I had rung
her up and wished her "good night."

Is the story that Mrs. Brook told about this incident, in your
view, untrue?—In my view, untrue.

She gave an untrue account of the incident which led to you
taking her back to London?—Yes.

Examination continued—Whichever of you it was that wanted
her to come back to London, you did take a car down and fetch
her away in the end?—I do not want to be rude, but I think if
I might recall just two more incidents it would make everything
clear to my lord, from my point of view, and to the jury. After I
rang up at a quarter-past ten and said: "Did I understand you to
say you were packing?" she said, "I am packed up and it is up to
you to get me fresh accommodation." I said: "That is extraordinary. I cannot get fresh accommodation at this time of night.
I suggest you ring up 14 West Cromwell Road and see if there is

Ley and Smith.

a room vacant and then let me know." She rang up at about half-past ten to that place and she reported to me at about a quarter to 11 that she had got the room. Then I said: "If you are packed up, what are you going to do? Are you going to bed?" She said: "I am going to sit up all night and I am going there in the morning." I said: "That is very strange. Would you like me to come out and sit up with you?" and she said "Yes." I said: "That depends upon whether I can get a car," and I rang up Daimlers——

The LORD CHIEF JUSTICE—Sir Walter, the witness cannot go rambling on in this way. He must keep to matters which are relevant. Going into all these matters, which, if there was any relevance in them, should have been put to Mrs. Brook, I cannot allow. (To Witness.) You will please give your evidence as any other witness. I am very anxious that you should have every opportunity, but I cannot allow you to go on rambling off into matters which have really no relevance to this matter.

The WITNESS—So much has been said about my being insanely jealous that I wanted to give an explanation that someone could understand.

Examination continued—What I am seeking to do is to bring you to those matters which in this case seem directly relevant to the charge under which you now stand. I want you now, having got Mrs. Brook away from Homefield Road, to come at once to a topic which I am sure you will wish to deal with, namely, what happened with regard to the cheques in June, 1946, the same month, which you sent to Mrs. Brook, c/o Mudie, Exhibits 4 and 5. You caused a letter to be written, did you not, which has been read, of 19th June, to Mrs. Brook, c/o Mudie?—That is quite true, yes.

You wrote a letter to Mudie at the same time?—A covering letter, yes.

You said in the letter inside that there were some cheques which were essential for wages the next day?—Yes.

You say you are sending her the cheques under separate cover: "We trust they will reach you safely and that you will be able to let us have them back signed either from Wimbledon or 5 Beaufort Gardens not later than Friday morning the 20th instant"?—That is so.

And you said she could telephone, &c. That is a letter signed by Baker, the secretary?—That was signed by me per Baker, I think. One of them was.

168

Evidence for the Prisoner Ley.

Thomas J. Ley

This one appears to have been signed by Baker, but I do not think it matters. In the covering letter you say this: "Mrs. Brook telephoned last afternoon that she was going into the country." What was it that caused you to send these letters to her c/o Mudie? —I thought Mrs. Brook was leaving West Cromwell Road and going to Bournemouth to arrange accommodation for her daughter. She afterwards told me I had made a mistake. I understood both from Mrs. Evans and her that Mudie was known to her and Barron, and I understood Mudie was an insurance manager and I sent it c/o him.

By the Lord Chief Justice—Who told you he was an insurance manager?—Mrs. Evans.

What we want to know is why you sent the cheques to Mudie. What had Mudie got to do with Mrs. Brook?—Nothing at all, except that I understood from Mrs. Evans that Mudie knew Mrs. Brook and knew Mrs. Barron.

If you thought Mrs. Brook was leaving Homefield Road, why not address them c/o the landlady and ask her to forward them?— I could have done that, my lord, but I did not do it, because I know the landlady and I thought it would get more prompt business attention if I sent it to a man with business experience.

Examination continued—That was the reason you say you sent these cheques to Mrs. Brook, c/o Mudie, at the address you thought, mistakenly, she was?—Quite.

Those cheques did not come back?—No. That was the cause of their having to follow Mudie.

By the Lord Chief Justice—Did you say Mrs. Evans told you that Mudie was an insurance agent?—I gathered that from Mrs. Evans.

Mrs. Evans told us that Mudie, while he was there in her house, was a potman or barman at a local public-house?—I heard her say that, but I did not know he was a barman at "The Dog and Fox" until Sergeant Shoobridge told me when he took my statement.

Examination continued—Exhibit 11 is the document which the witness who came yesterday afternoon, the lady, said she had taken down and transcribed. I will remind you of it: "Dear sir, We wrote you on the 19th inst., and asked if Mrs. Brook was not there to post back in the enclosed stamped addressed envelope the cheques that were sent to you. Mrs. Brook reports that she has

Ley and Smith.

Thomas J. Ley

not heard from you, and that you have not returned the cheques to us. These are the company's property, and we must ask you to return them either to Mrs. Brook or to us without delay, otherwise we shall place the matter in the hands of our solicitors. We express surprise that you had the temerity to give a copy of our letter to Mr. Thomas Barron with certain information which led me to believe that there was an intrigue between you and Mrs. B. However, this is a matter apart from the return of our property which we ask you to attend to without delay. Mrs. B. reports that you said . . ."—I think it is—". . . that your signature is required. Nothing is required from you but to seal the envelope and return it as it is already stamped without delay." Ley, did you dictate a letter in those terms to Miss Ingleson, your secretary? —Yes.

Did you sign it?—No.

Did you send it?—No.

Why not?—Because on reflection I thought it should go to the solicitors to deal with.

That brings me to the letter which is Exhibit 14 of 20th July. It is a letter from Messrs. Denton, Hall & Burgin. They were your solicitors for this purpose?—That is correct.

It is a letter to Mr. Mudie in which they say: "Jack Mudie, Esq., 3 Homefield Road, Wimbledon, S.W.19. 25th July, 1946. Dear sir, On the 19th June, 1946, our clients, Connaught Properties Limited, sent to your care a certain letter addressed to Mrs. Byron Brook, one of their directors, in an envelope addressed and ready stamped. Our clients asked that you might be good enough, if Mrs. Brook had not then returned to your address, to seal and post it back to Mrs. Brook. According to Mrs. Brook you did not do this. Instead our clients' chairman understands from her that you telephoned that you would not do so because it might involve your signature coming into our clients' possession. If this is correct our clients cannot understand your attitude because your signature was not asked for, nor was it necessary in order to seal and post the letter already addressed and fully stamped. We understand that Mrs. Brook has assured the chairman of the company that she has not received the envelope with the company's cheques in it. Do you intend to retain it? Our clients know that you received the communications because, according to our instructions, without their authority you went to the trouble of seeking out the father-in-law of Mrs. Brook's daughter, Mr. Thomas Barron, and gave copies to him. It is incomprehensible to us that you should after five weeks refuse to return to our clients their cheques which were intended for Mrs. Brook, and have not been passed on to her.

Evidence for the Prisoner Ley.

Thomas J. Ley

Unless the cheques are returned to our clients by mid-day on Monday the 28th inst., our instructions are to proceed in accordance with counsel's advice for recovery thereof. In that case we shall be glad to have from you the name of the solicitor who will accept service on your behalf of any process issued. A copy of this letter has been sent to Mrs. Brook. Yours faithfully." Was that letter sent on your instructions?—Yes.

I see from Exhibit No. 15, that on 31st July, six days later, another copy of the same letter was sent by the solicitors to Mr. Mudie at the Reigate Hotel at Reigate. That was also in accordance with your instructions?—Yes.

By the LORD CHIEF JUSTICE—Are those cheques in your possession now?—They may have been used. I could not tell you off-hand, my lord, but they came back eventually; we recovered them.

Were they signed when you sent them?—When sent they were signed only by the secretary, and they required two signatures, mine and Mrs. Brook's.

Examination continued—We know from Exhibit 7 that there was a receipt which we have heard came about from Mr. Baker, the secretary of the Connaught Properties Limited, dated 29th July, 1946. You went to Mr. Barron in the end and saw that receipt?—That is quite correct.

You were then satisfied and apologized for the trouble that had been caused?—That is quite correct.

Did anyone go with you when you went to Mr. Barron for the receipts?—Yes, my visitor from Australia, Mr. Mollison.

He went with you, and did Mudie go with you too?—Yes, he led the way.

Am I right in putting that in August?—I think that is about correct.

Therefore you saw Mudie on that day in August when you went to see Mr. Barron?—Yes.

Did you ever see Mudie again?—No.

I want to come to another matter. You heard some witnesses for the prosecution speak of a meeting at Mr. Brashier's office on 10th July, 1946. Was he acting then as your solicitor?—Yes.

Mrs. Brook, Mr. Brashier and Mr. Barron were there?—Yes.

Mr. Barron told us he was there to look after Mrs. Brook's interests, and also other persons?—Yes.

He also told us that in the course of that discussion what was dealt with was the way property which had been put into Mrs. Brook's name was to be dealt with?—Yes.

Ley and Smith.

Thomas J. Ley

Tell me if this is right. He said that she said that it was true you had given her it absolutely, and you were saying something different?—Quite true.

Were you saying it was to be hers for life?—Yes.

And then?—The remainder to me and our joint appointment afterwards.

Was that matter debated between you in the office?—Yes.

When you found she was claiming the property absolutely what action did you take?—When I was quite certain of that, and she repeated that, I got up and left the room and said I wanted nothing more to do with her, as she was dishonest.

Was it after that that you engaged another housekeeper?—Yes; I started to seek another housekeeper.

By the LORD CHIEF JUSTICE—At that interview in Mr. Brashier's office, Barron said that he showed these letters to which we have been referring to Mr. Brashier in your presence?—Two copies of letters were passed. I did not see them. They were passed to Mr. Brashier through Mrs. Brook.

Did you not attempt to see them?—No; they were passed from Mr. Barron to Mr. Brashier through Mrs. Brook, and I wanted to know what they were. I did not actually see the copies, they were not handed to me, but I gathered from what they said that they were copies of the letters I had sent to Mr. Mudie and Mrs. Brook.

Did not Barron say anything about them?—Mr. Barron passed them along. I do not remember his comment, but he made some comment at the time; it was a *sub rosa* comment to Mr. Brashier.

He was your solicitor. Why did you not ask him what it was all about?—I asked, and he told me they were copies of two letters, one to Mrs. Brook and one to Mr. Mudie.

Mr. Barron has told us that you then said that this was a little bit of detective business you had done on your own?—I heard him say that, and it is not true.

Examination continued—I want you to pass on from that. Did you say that thereafter you would engage another housekeeper?—I started then to approach agencies and friends to engage another housekeeper, and I eventually did.

Was that this lady who gave evidence here?—Yes.

I think she came into your employment in November?—Yes.

She said she began on the 25th?—I think that is correct.

Did she live at 8 Beaufort Gardens when she was your housekeeper?—Temporarily, yes.

Evidence for the Prisoner Ley.

Thomas J. Ley

And afterwards went back to the flat?—Yes, when it was made ready.

She has told us that you let her in each morning at the front door?—Yes.

She came in about half-past seven, and worked until five-thirty? —Yes, those approximately were the times.

I want to come now to what you knew of the people who gave evidence, and some questions about them. First of all, there is Minden, the porter from the hotel. He said that you had been a visitor to the hotel—I do not mean staying in, but casually—over a considerable period?—I visited my wife every morning, and sometimes of an evening as well.

He says that he knew your wife well, and that he had passed the time of day with you. There is one conversation which I will put to you. He said on a date which is not quite certain, but well before the end of November, that you said to him: did he know of anyone with a car who could keep his mouth shut and look after himself, and if there was such a person he could earn a year's salary in a matter of weeks. What do you say about that? —It is untrue.

Did you ever have any conversation of that kind at all with Minden?—No.

He also says that you gave him your telephone number?—That is true. I gave him my telephone number for the purpose of ringing up in case any communication came which was urgent from my son in Hong Kong.

I want to ask you a word about Smith. Smith, we have been told, was the foreman who was in charge of those who were doing the work of converting 5 Beaufort Gardens?—Yes, he was the last foreman.

We have seen the tribute you paid him after he left?—Yes; which I thought was well deserved.

Did you see him constantly while he was the foreman there? —Yes, many times, each day, about different matters.

Did you ever entertain him to a meal or anything?—Two or three times; that was for the purpose of discussing matters affecting the house.

Did you ever mention Mudie to Smith?—No.

Or Mrs. Brook?—It might have been possible that I mentioned Mrs. Brook. She was in and out a good deal. Yes, I remember one particular occasion.

Did you ever speak to him about Mrs. Brook and yourself in relation to your private affairs?—No.

173

Ley and Smith.

Thomas J. Ley

Next I want to ask you a word about the elder Buckingham who gave evidence here. Did you get to know him before the end of November?—I could not be sure of the date; I should think I did.

How did you get to know him?—Well, Smith said he had known a man, Jack Stanley, who was a fighter, who had gone into the car hire service, and I might get a better deal from him in having my car serviced with him than at Howard's.

And as a result of that what happened?—He called and saw me, and he left his card with the telephone number.

After that did you see him again?—Yes, I think I did. He brought a second card round, a different kind of card.

Did you ever discuss Mudie with Buckingham?—No.

Did you ever say anything to Buckingham about women being blackmailed?—No.

Did you discuss Mrs. Brook with Buckingham?—No.

Did you ever discuss with any of those whom I have just mentioned plans to bring Mudie to 5 Beaufort Gardens?—No.

Did you pay either to Smith or to Buckingham any sum for the expenses for such a purpose?—No.

Did you pay to them, or to either of them, £200 for having brought him there?—No.

Or for any other reason?—No.

Did you ever arrange for Mudie to be persuaded to come there at all?—No.

Did you have any part in the idea of a cocktail party pretence to get him there?—Not at all.

Did you ever arrange for him to be tied or gagged?—No.

Did you see Mudie on 28th November?—No.

You heard it alleged that Mudie was brought to 5 Beaufort Gardens on 28th November. Were you there at any time when Mudie was there?—No.

After 28th November, did you ever say to Smith, or to anyone else: "As far as I am concerned, Mudie was taken to Wimbledon and left there."—No.

Did you see Buckingham and Smith or either of them at 5 Beaufort Gardens on the afternoon of 28th November?—No. Well, I saw Smith; he would be working about, but I never saw Buckingham.

I want to ask you about your movements on the afternoon of 28th November, your own movements. On that day where did you have tea?—I had tea at my flat.

Was anyone with you?—Mrs. Brook.

Evidence for the Prisoner Ley.

Thomas J. Ley

After tea what did you do?—I started out with Mrs. Brook, on my part to go to the Club, and her part to 14 West Cromwell Road.

Can you say about when that was?—That was roughly about twenty or a quarter to five.

Did you go along with Mrs. Brook?—Yes, I went along and tried to get a taxi, and we failed, and walked towards the Brompton entrance of the Knightsbridge Station, and she went on to the 'bus stop.

What did you do?—I went down the stairs and suddenly recollected I had not got my torch, and I went back for it to the house.

To 5 Beaufort Gardens?—Yes.

You wanted your torch, did you?—Yes; there was no electric light in the hall, and only two lights in my flat.

When you got back, having returned for your torch, did you see anybody?—Yes, I saw Miss Lane.

How long did you remain in your flat?—Not very long.

A matter of moments, do you mean?—Only sufficiently long to get the torch and see the workmen were out.

When you left, did you come out alone or not?—Yes; I came out and closed the door, and then closed the front door.

Then where did you go?—I went down to Brompton Road, and got a taxicab, and went to the National Liberal Club.

About what time did you arrive at the National Liberal Club? —I should say approximately it would be about twenty to twenty-five minutes past five.

Is there any particular day of the week when you normally go there?—I try to go there on a Thursday.

Why is that?—Originally there were three of us who agreed to meet each lunch time on a Thursday—Mr. Gilbey, Mr. Roberts and myself—and exchange views about different things.

Do you remember doing anything about an address?—Yes; first I collected two letters from my wife and son, which I was anxious to get, and I left a change of address so that in future the letters could be re-addressed to 5 Beaufort Gardens.

How long did you stay in the club?—I went down to the billiard room, and I watched a game of snooker, and I left about five-past six, I think.

Just after six?—Yes.

In what conveyance did you leave, or did you walk?—I got a taxi at the club door, and just outside the theatre in Whitehall the taxi came to a standstill owing to lack of petrol, I think, or something like that, and I got another one then.

Where did you go?—I went to the Cumberland Grill.

Ley and Smith.

Thomas J. Ley

Is that where you intended originally to go?—No, it was not.

Where did you mean to go?—To 14 West Cromwell Road at seven.

Where Mrs. Brook was?—Yes.

How did you come to go to the Cumberland Grill?—It was a lapse of memory. I had a table engaged every night.

When you got there, what did you do?—I sat down at my table, and I had a light dinner.

When did you leave?—I left about a quarter-past or twenty-past seven.

Had you by that time remembered, or had you not remembered, your intention to go to Mrs. Brook's about seven?—I remembered it when the coffee came along, and I got a bit excited and I left then.

What time did you get to Mrs. Brook's?—About 25, 20, or it may be a quarter to eight.

Did she give you anything to eat?—Yes, I had some sandwiches and coffee.

Did you tell her you had forgotten the arrangement?—Yes; it was not the first time I had done it, and I did not want to be teased about it.

By the LORD CHIEF JUSTICE—You said that at the meeting at Mr. Brashier's office, Mrs. Brook alleged that you had given her some property absolutely, while you said you had only given it to her for life?—Yes, with the understanding there should be a settlement.

I took down what you said: that you said you thought Mrs. Brook was dishonest?—I told her that in front of Mr. Brashier.

And you left the room?—Yes.

When was it that you made things up with Mrs. Brook?—I never made things up with Mrs. Brook, but she has been sick more or less from the time she left 3 Homefield Road, and I have not made it up in any other sense than we are friends for the sake of "auld lang syne," you may say, and we played gin-rummy together.

In spite of you saying she had acted in a dishonest manner towards you?—Yes.

You resumed relations with her as though exactly nothing had happened?—It was not as though exactly nothing had happened. She was waiting for her house in Wimbledon, and she used to ring me and ask me to play gin-rummy with her, and I did so, but there was no resumption of relations.

She was coming to tea with you?—Yes.

176

Evidence for the Prisoner Ley.

Thomas J. Ley

Examination continued—On this occasion when you had sandwiches with her, did you play gin-rummy at this time?—Yes.

What time did you leave her?—Roughly about 11 or 11.15; I cannot be certain. We used to play until about 11.15.

Did you go then straight back to 5 Beaufort Gardens?—Yes, by taxi.

What time did you get in there?—Roughly about half-past eleven.

Miss Lane used to come on duty about half-past seven in the morning?—That is true.

Was it your custom to let her in?—Yes, I used to be reading the paper when she arrived.

She told us you let her in on the morning of the 29th; is that right?—Yes, quite right.

I am now looking at Exhibit 2. The attention of my lord and the jury has been drawn to the fact that on 16th November you drew out of your account at the Midland Bank, Knightsbridge, £250 in cash, and that on 26th November you drew out a further £300 in cash. Can you tell us for what purpose you withdrew these sums?—For furnishings.

For furnishings at 5 Beaufort Gardens do you mean?—Yes.

Did you in fact spend it on furnishings?—Not the whole of it.

What sum about would be left unspent?—I should say roughly about £400.

Where would that £400 be?—That was locked up in my bedroom.

That, you say, as far as you know, was locked up in your bedroom?—Yes.

There is one other sum I want to ask you about which is in the same account, and that is a figure of £300 drawn by cheque on 4th December, which we are told went into the account of Smith on that day, and was withdrawn and repaid on the 10th?—I understood Smith wanted a loan of £300, and he came to me for that purpose. He was going to buy a little business of his own. Then he came to me later on and he said he had lost the business, and he wanted to pay the money back.

By the Lord Chief Justice—Did he tell you where the business was?—No, my lord.

Did you ask him?—No; I was not interested in it. You see, he had saved me a considerable amount of money.

Ley and Smith.

Examination continued—From first to last did you have anything to do with the binding up, injuring, or killing of Mudie?—No.

Cross-examined by Mr. CURTIS BENNETT—Ley, did you mean what you said in Exhibit 19 about Smith—the recommendation you gave him?—Yes, I meant that.

You found him an honest, decent, capable man?—It is not a certificate of character; it is a certificate of efficiency.

You found him an honest, decent, capable man?—While he was with me, yes.

Is there a mortise lock on the back door of your place at 5 Beaufort Gardens, in the basement?—Yes.

Is there one key to it?—Yes.

Is that door usually kept locked?—Yes.

If it is kept locked, you are the only person who can unlock it?—Yes.

So if anyone came to the basement door on 28th November, or any other day, and the mortise lock was locked, no one could get in unless you unlocked it?—Yes; there are two bolts, one at the top and one at the bottom. When I go out that way I do not lock that mortise lock, but when I go out when the day is done, I lock it——

You locked the two bolts instead of the lock with the one key?—Yes.

If the door is locked with the mortise lock, no one coming from outside can get in unless they have your key?—If it was locked; but the practice is not to lock it but to bolt it.

Did you keep the key on yourself?—Yes, I did at that time.

I suggest you kept the key on yourself so as to keep that door locked?—Your suggestion is wrong.

I am just seeing whether your statement and Smith's agree. Had Smith any reason, so far as you know, to think that Mrs. Brook was being blackmailed?—No.

Had Smith any reason, to your knowledge, to think that you thought that Mrs. Brook was being interfered with?—No. I mentioned on a certain occasion that certain things had happened on 12th July to Smith, and asked him to assist me in interviewing a Mr. Arthur Barron, my son-in-law.

Did you ask some of the workpeople working at 5 Beaufort Gardens some time in July to stay behind in case you were attacked?—No.

Did you pay them £1 each?—Yes; but not for that reason.

178

Evidence for the Prisoner Ley.

Did you ask two or three workmen in June or July to stay behind in Beaufort Gardens in case you were attacked?—No, I did not.

Did you ask them to stay behind?—Yes.

Did you pay them £1 after they stayed behind?—I cannot remember the amount, but probably that is quite right.

Is that because you were fearing some attack?—No, it was quite a different purpose.

Was that June or July?—I cannot recollect the date; I should think it would be about a week or ten days after I brought Mrs. Brook—no, it would be less than that: it would be about 14th or 15th June.

Did you ask them to stay behind as somebody was coming to see you by arrangement?—Yes.

From whom you thought you might meet with violence?—No. That part is entirely untrue.

So you had in June or July got some workmen to stay behind to help you in some purpose of your own?—Yes.

At that time were you jealous of Mrs. Brook or thinking she was being seduced?—No.

Had Smith got any reason to know that you thought Mrs. Brook had been seduced?—No.

Had Smith got any reason to think that you thought she was being blackmailed?—No.

So far as you know, did Smith know anything at all about Mr. Mudie?—No.

Did he or Buckingham have permission to use your house on the night of 28th November?—No.

Would you normally be in your house at about half-past seven in the evening?—No.

The workmen would normally go about five?—Yes.

Did you lock both bolts of the basement on that day?—To the best of my recollection.

So nobody could get in through the basement door unless they got in the front door first?—They could get in the basement by going to the area and pulling the bolts back.

By the LORD CHIEF JUSTICE—You go down the area? Who had the keys of the front area?—There were so many keys, my lord, I do not know who had them. I had one, but I know a great many others had keys.

What was the point of bolting this door at the back area if there were so many keys about instead of the front area?—We did what

Ley and Smith.

we could under difficult circumstances. There is less difficulty in Brompton Place than in the Gardens.

Cross-examination continued—You did not lock the mortise lock at the back of the basement?—No; the mortise lock was put on for my convenience when I used to go out that way.

It has been there for some time?—Yes, it has now.

For how long?—I could not tell you.

Were you at New Scotland Yard on 18th December last year? —I believe that is the date.

I put it to you that you realized by that time that allegations were being made against you by Buckingham and by Smith, and by others?—Inspector Philpott told me that, yes.

Did you know that 28th November was the day when it was supposed that Mudie was being brought to London?—I think the inspector told me that at the interview.

Is this what you said about the 28th on that day: "Although I cannot remember at the moment where I was at approximately 7 p.m. on the 28th November, 1946, I can say this: that if I was at my flat, no other persons came in to my knowledge"?—Yes, I said that.

So you did not remember then where you were?—No, I did not. I had to scratch my head and think where I had been that night. I could not tell off-hand.

But after having scratched your head, when did you remember what you had been doing on 28th November?—I could not tell you even that. I had to go over the ground step by step. One point that helped me was that I knew that I had seen a gentleman in the Cumberland Grill whom I had seen in the morning, and I looked up my diary, and I found it was the 28th, and that was my starting point. I knew I had gone to the club on the Thursday then.

There is no other statement which you made to the police which says: "I now remember where I was on the 28th November"?—That is the fault of the police, and not mine.

By the LORD CHIEF JUSTICE—Have you got your diary?—Yes, my lord, it is available.

Cross-examination continued—You could have gone and told them if you wanted to?—Yes, but the matter was in the hands of my solicitors at that time.

They could not ask you any more questions after you were arrested, could they? Have you made use of inquiry agents?—Yes.

Evidence for the Prisoner Ley.

Thomas J. Ley

For the purpose of tracking down what Mudie had been doing, if anything, to Mrs. Brook?—Never about Mudie at all, but about Romer.

By the LORD CHIEF JUSTICE—What did you find out about Romer?—I wanted to find out his financial situation, and I wanted to know whether he was a safe man or not.

Why?—Because I had come to the conclusion that there had been a relationship between him and Mrs. Brook.

On what grounds?—Well, I did not want her to get in the hands of somebody——

On what grounds did you come to the conclusion that there had been relationships between Mrs. Brook and Romer?—Because I heard the name "Arthur" on 8th June, 1946, and I subsequently found that there was an Arthur Romer, and when I saw him I recognized, as I thought, his voice.

Because you heard Mrs. Brook using the word "Arthur," when you called at the house, you thought relations were taking place? —Not from that, but from the general tenor of the conversation.

You have not said anything about any conversation?—I do not know that it would be any good, but I will tell you. (Witness then described in detail intimacies which, he alleged, he had overheard between Mrs. Brook and a man named "Arthur.") Then I went down and rang the bell.

And you saw Mrs. Brook?—Yes.

Cross-examination continued—Whoever the man was, you had no doubt about those relations, and yet you went on playing gin-rummy with Mrs. Brook in the evening?—Yes, later on I did.

Did you find out later that it was not Romer but Mudie?—No.

Did you ever suspect Mudie of having relations with her?—No.

You never told anybody that you thought that?—No.

Then it is absolute moonshine that you were jealous of Mudie? —I was not jealous of Mudie or anybody else.

You never thought that Mudie had any relations with Mrs. Brook?—No, I never thought that.

When you went round to 3 Homefield Road to fetch Mrs. Brook on 12th or 13th June, did you hire a car from the Daimler Company at Knightsbridge?—Yes.

Have you read Smith's statement, Exhibit 20?—Yes.

Did you ever tell him that you had hired that car?—Yes.

Did you tell him this: "He said that one night he was called out of his bed at 1.30 a.m. to fetch Mrs. Brook away from the address 3 Homefield Road, Wimbledon, where she was staying at

Ley and Smith.

Thomas J. Ley

the house of a Mrs. Evans, with Mrs. Barron, who is Mrs. Brook's daughter. He hired a car from the Daimler Hire Service at Knightsbridge, and went over to Wimbledon"?—Yes; I told him that on that occasion we had the men back to see Arthur Barron.

Why were you telling the foreman of this house about this?—Because I asked him on that occasion to keep the men back, and I told him a few things why I wanted to talk to Arthur Barron, because Mrs. Brook was in a very bad condition.

Did you say this: "That you thought Mrs. Brook had been interfered with"?—No, I did not say that. I was concerned about Mrs. Brook's health, and I wanted to find out from Arthur Barron, as I thought he was the Arthur, what could have happened to make it necessary for me to call for her in the middle of the night.

You say that the whole of what Smith says, he being a man who had recommended himself to you, about you speaking about Mudie is untrue?—Quite untrue.

You have no doubt, having heard the evidence of Buckingham, that Smith was a party to bringing Mudie to London?—I suppose he must have done it.

They would know what they did?—Yes, they have confessed it.

Can you suggest why they should bring this man to your house and tie him up?—I cannot suggest it, but people who will accept £200 for kidnapping a man would be quite willing to attempt that, I think. I cannot explain it in any other way.

I thought you said you had not paid him £200?—I never said I had.

You said they accepted £200?—If they accepted £200 they would find it in their conscience to frame anyone else.

Think of the danger of bringing a man to London and binding him up in your house. Why should they have brought him to your house?—I cannot explain that.

By the LORD CHIEF JUSTICE—You said just now that you never suspected any intrigue by Mudie?—I did not say "intrigue." I think I said I never suspected of there being any improper relations.

Do you know what you wrote in your letter, the letter you did not post?—My lord, I dictated that roughly, and because I did not want it, and did not approve it—the word "intrigue" in my view was underhand plotting, and the underhand plotting came to my mind because of what happened at Mr. Brashier's officer. I could not understand how the letters had been extracted.

You said: "We express surprise that you had the temerity of giving a copy of our letter to Mr. Thomas Barron with certain information which led him to believe there was an intrigue between

Evidence for the Prisoner Ley.

Thomas J. Ley

you and Mrs. B." What was the information?—At Mr. Brashier's office copies of those letters, not originals, were passed.

Which you did not see?—I did not see them. I know what they were—I found out from Mr. Brashier what they were.

What information did you have which led you to believe there was an intrigue between Mudie and Mrs. Brook?—I never sent that letter; I do not accept responsibility for that letter.

You admit you dictated it to your typist?—As a draft.

You made a very definite statement in it. If you did suspect, what was the information you had that made you suspect it?— The information I got was at Mr. Brashier's office, and the intrigue was the underplotting that came to my mind.

Cross-examination continued—Had you an obsession in your mind about Mrs. Brook and another man?—Not at all.

Which made you offer Smith and Buckingham £200?—That is a fantasy, and not a fact.

Did you want to get Mudie out of the country?—No. After I got the cheques I was not interested in Mudie.

I shall not deal with the cheques except to suggest that they were an effort to prove to your satisfaction that Mudie was in some close association with Mrs. Brook?—That is quite untrue.

Smith could not have known that you were going to be out on the night of the 26th. He could not have known that you were going to be conveniently at the Cumberland Hotel?—No, Smith would not know my movements.

For all he knew you might have turned up?—Yes, I might have, but I want you to bear in mind that it was common knowledge to everybody on the property that I was away every evening for dinner and that the place was not fit for occupation. The house-keeper would not stop there because it was not ready.

But he would not know the time you left or the time you might come back?—No, that is perfectly true.

You do not doubt that they brought Mudie there?—On their statements——

Have you any doubt?—Well, I accept the statements they made, but I never saw Mudie there.

You accept Smith's statement except where it brings you into it?—I do not know whether it is true or false. I can only take it at its face value.

You cannot account for the fact, in regard to the gagging of him——?—There has been a great deal of invention about it——

I suggestion the invention is on your part?—No.

183

Ley and Smith.

Thomas J. Ley

Did you tell us just now that you had a table reserved at the Cumberland Hotel for a long time?—Yes.

How long—three months, six months, or a year?—For months.

How often did you dine there?—Every night I dined there at that time.

On this night you only had a light meal?—Yes.

Because you had forgotten Mrs. Brook?—Yes.

When did you make the appointment to go and dine with her? —In the early afternoon.

Making it in the early afternoon, and with your experience in public life and other places, do you say you forgot it and went to the Cumberland?—Yes, and I have done that before; it is not an extraordinary happening.

You got to the Cumberland Hotel about a quarter-past six. When did you leave the hotel?—About 7.15 or 7.20, I cannot remember exactly; I remember it was about 7.15 when I got up. I saw a man I knew.

You had about an hour there having this light meal?—Yes.

If you were expecting visitors at your house in Beaufort Gardens at 6.30 of course you would have been in before and awaiting them?—Yes, if I had. Courtesy would demand it.

Are you sure you were not expecting Buckingham, Mudie and Smith at your house at about half-past six?—I am perfectly sure I was not.

And you had instructed Smith that Mudie was to be bound and gagged for you to interview him and extract a confession from him? —I did not.

And to pay him £500 to clear out of the country?—No.

I suggest you were left alone with him there?—May I suggest to you how foolish that suggestion is?

I am not answering your questions. The whole thing is more than foolish. Did you interview Mudie yourself?—No; I never saw Mudie after the cheques.

Did you ask him to confess?—No.

He had nothing to confess, so perhaps you got angry with him? —No, I never saw him.

Did anyone come to your house, do you know, at about a little after seven that night?—Not that I am aware of. I was not there.

Smith says he heard somebody walking up the stairs?—I remember that he said that in his statement.

That is all invention?—Yes, all invention.

You do not know of any motive that would drive Smith to bring Mudie to your house at all?—No, I do not.

Let alone kill him?—No; I cannot suggest anything.

Evidence for the Prisoner Ley.

Thomas J. Ley

You see, Minden says that it was he who introduced you to Buckingham; is that untrue?—Yes.

Is he telling an untruth when he says you "dropped" him £10? —Yes—I gave him £5.

That is a half-truth, then. You gave him money—£5?—Yes.

Minden has got no grievance against you?—Not that I am aware of.

Similarly you deny what Smith says as to what you said to him after 28th November about Mudie: that everything was all right, and that Mudie had been dropped at Wimbledon?—Yes; I do deny that.

Previous to all this, and quite apart from this story, did Smith from time to time arrive at your house in a car?—Yes; he used a little Austin from time to time.

Not hired from the Howard Services?—No. It was because something happened to that car that he asked me if Howard's let out "drive yourself" cars. I put the two in touch and they worked it out themselves.

I suggest he came up in a hired car quite a number of times before 28th November?—Yes, I saw him very often.

He was using the car for his business obviously?—Yes.

Did you not suggest to him that he should get a car of his own?—No.

Did he say he could not afford it?—No.

Did you not then offer to lend him money so that he could buy a car and repay you later?—No; I understood Smith was going to buy a business.

He was going to repay it?—Yes. I took the risk of his not re-paying it. He was very valuable to me.

You did not think he would repay it?—I am not here to express opinions, but I did not expect it.

You got it back?—Oh, yes.

Previous to this incident of 28th November, had you heard him talk at all of an idea of his to go abroad to one of the Dominions to get work?—Yes; I understood he had that in mind.

I do not know whether he said much to you when he paid you the £300 back?—All I can remember him saying was that he had been disappointed in the business.

He did not say anything then about going abroad to New Zealand or South Africa?—I do not recollect him saying that.

By the LORD CHIEF JUSTICE—Tell me a little more about this £300 which you say was a loan. Did Smith come one day and

185

Ley and Smith.

tell you he thought he was going to buy a business?—Yes, and he required £300 to do so.

You did not ask him where the business was?—No.

Did you not ask him what the business was?—No, I was not interested.

You just wrote him a cheque for £300?—Yes. He had been so valuable to me in saving space—more so than my architect. I think I told Miss Ingleson at the time I would take the risk of being repaid or not.

Do you lend money as easily as that?—Not to everybody, my lord, but to people who have done me services.

Were you not interested to know where the business was?—No.

Or what it was?—No. I was not interested in it.

It might have been a loss to you?—Yes, it might have been an entire loss. It would not be the first occasion on which I have lost loans.

Cross-examined by Mr. HAWKE—You were listening when my learned friend, Sir Walter Monckton, opened this case. Did you hear him say that he might be able to call somebody who went into your house that night?—I heard him say that.

Do not answer me if you do not know, but can you tell me who that is?—Well, I think I know, but I am not certain enough to answer you.

Are you in possession of the information now as to what that man found?—Yes.

Tell me what he found, will you?——

Sir WALTER MONCKTON—Is this the way to get the evidence of what the man found? I said I would call him.

The LORD CHIEF JUSTICE—It is rather odd, Sir Walter. You said you were going to call a witness who was at his house that night. Mr. Hawke is entitled to ask who it is.

Sir WALTER MONCKTON—That I am not objecting to. What I am objecting to is this: this witness, having denied that he was in the house that night, I object to what this man is going to say as to what he found.

The LORD CHIEF JUSTICE—You can ask him if he has any information to that effect.

Cross-examination continued—Have you an idea of what this man said he found?—All I have an idea of is that some man was

Evidence for the Prisoner Ley.

seeking to find something out, and what he did find out I am not clear about. He was another Australian who was looking to me for a job of some kind.

Had you heard from him or from anyone what he might say that he found?——

Sir WALTER MONCKTON—My lord, I object. I submit my learned friend is not entitled to put that question to this witness. He has not said has this witness communicated with the other, and that being so, I submit it is quite irregular to ask this witness about what a subsequent witness to be called in his defence will say.

The LORD CHIEF JUSTICE—This witness is in the box, and it has been opened on his behalf that a person who came to his house that night was going to be called.

By the LORD CHIEF JUSTICE—Have you seen that person?—I do not know, my lord.

You do not know that he was at your house?—I only heard from my solicitor that somebody had been looking for me, and what he was looking for and what he wanted, I do not know.

Cross-examination continued—I will carry it no further. You have heard that Mudie was found dead in a chalk pit in Surrey?—Yes.

He was gagged with a piece of stuff that has been identified as coming from your house?—Yes.

By the side of his body, which was in a trench, was a pickaxe that came from the work that was being done at your house?—I have heard that, yes.

Do I understand you to say that not a word of what Buckingham and Smith have said is true, or you do not know whether it is true or not?—I say that I had no part whatever in kidnapping the man that they refer to.

And therefore as regards anything that led up to a man being brought to your house, that has no reference to you whatever?—None.

Carry your mind back to 8th June; that is a day on which I understand you to say that you went down to 3 Homefield Road?—Yes.

You went into the house?—Yes.

Where did you stand when you were in the house?—I did not stand. I went up to the top floor, and stood outside the door of the lounge. I heard voices, and was attracted there.

Ley and Smith.

Thomas J. Ley

Are you telling us that that conversation which you were pleased to recount to us just now was heard by you standing on the landing?—Yes.

You recognize that what you are saying to the jury is that one voice was Mrs. Brook's?—Yes.

And the other was a man who you thought was Arthur Romer?—Yes.

And your immediate reaction after hearing a conversation like that was that you walked downstairs and rang the bell?—Yes, that is true.

Are you really asking the jury to believe a word of what you have said in that connexion?—I do, but, of course, if you do not want to, I cannot help it.

There is considerable conflict between you and other people?—What is the conflict?

You said that on 10th July you informed Mrs. Brook that she was a dishonest woman and that you had done with her—that is roughly right, is it not?—Yes.

And you then set about getting a new housekeeper?—I did.

Did you say that in order to lead the jury to think that from that time onwards it would not have interested you in the least if Mrs. Brook had been carrying on with somebody?—I had not been interested for years. All this stuff about jealousy is fantasy. It is not fact.

This woman who on 8th June, you told us, you heard in those circumstances which you have described?—Yes.

On 10th July you told her she was a dishonest woman and you had finished with her?—Yes, so far as a housekeeper was concerned.

A short time after that you were meeting her every day?—I would not say every day.

I did not hear it challenged. She said your habit was to meet her every day and have lunch, and tea, and dinner?—Yes; we met frequently.

This dishonest woman whom you had finished with, and you say you heard in those circumstances in this flat in Wimbledon?—Yes.

Do you say you were not interested in her affairs?—Yes, I am interested in her financial affairs still, and her welfare, but I am not at all interested in what she may do in sexual or other matters of that kind.

But I thought you said you put private detectives on to some of these men?—I thought Conquests were inquiry agents.

Evidence for the Prisoner Ley.

Thomas J. Ley

Let us be accurate by all means. You put private inquiry agents on to this man?—On to Romer.

What for?—For the purpose of finding out his business and financial position.

What had that to do with you?—I wanted to see if he was a man of no means, because one might expect him to take advantage of the situation. For example, he told me that he hoped to get a house that belonged to a widow.

Who told you that?—Romer.

Did you see him?—Yes.

Where?—At 3 Homefield Road.

When?—I cannot tell you the exact date, but I suppose it would be in about late July or the beginning of August.

Were you under the impression when you saw him that he was carrying on with Mrs. Brook?—No; I went to see if I recognized the voice I heard on 8th June.

Did you recognize it?—I thought I did.

Can you be sure?—I cannot be sure of identity. I think it is right, but I cannot be sure by just hearing.

It must have been somewhere about that time that Minden says you came to him in the Royal Hotel in Woburn Place and said you wanted a man who had a car and who could be trusted to keep his mouth shut; is that right?—No.

You knew Minden pretty well?—No.

Do not misunderstand me, please; I do not say that you were a familiar friend of his, but you knew him quite well as hotel porter? —Yes.

You thought he was a very worthy fellow?—I did not think about him on those lines.

You thought he was trustworthy?—No.

You gave him a tip which you say was £5 and he says it was £10?—The reason for that was that my wife had written from Australia asking me to give him something.

And you gave him something?—Yes; I carried out my wife's instructions.

Are we to take it that that man has not told a word of truth as regards you and Buckingham?—Yes, you can take it that he did not.

He says he saw you together in the lounge of this hotel more than once?—I heard him say that.

And with Smith too—all three of you?—I heard him say that.

Is that all wrong?—Yes.

Is Mrs. Evans a reliable person?—I think she is.

189

Ley and Smith.

Thomas J. Ley

Have you any reason to doubt it?—I heard her evidence, and I think she is reliable, but I think her recollection may be at fault.

Let us by all means test that recollection. You think she is quite a reliable person and a decent, respectable woman who is the landlady of a block of flats or rooms?—Yes.

Did you see her on 16th June?—It would be about that time; there were two interviews.

It was four days after you got Mrs. Brook out of this house at half-past two in the morning?—I went to Mrs. Evans to find out what could have happened.

Was it about four days after you brought Mrs. Brook to London?—Yes, it was about that.

Did you ask Mrs. Evans what men were in the house?—No. She was a little inaccurate there. I will tell you what happened if you want to know. Mrs. Brook was in a very distressed condition. She was incoherent.

I do not think that is what I am asking you?—Unless you know you cannot understand what I did, and I thought you wanted to understand——

I want to know what it was you said. Mrs. Evans has sworn that you asked what men were in the house?—No; I asked if she knew of anyone called Jack and anyone called Arthur other than Arthur Barron.

You asked her if she knew anyone called "Jack"?—Yes.

Why?—Because those two names had been mentioned by Mrs. Brook when we were taking her back to the Knightsbridge flat. You could not make head or tail of her that night. I wanted to find out the circumstances of what had happened.

Did you think it was Jack or Arthur who might be responsible for Mrs. Brook's distress?—I was quite satisfied that the name I heard was Arthur on 8th June.

Why did you mention the name "Jack"?—Because Mrs. Brook mentioned the name. I can remember that distinctly.

Mrs. Evans appears to be remarkably accurate, because she said that when she mentioned Jack Mudie your observation was: "Oh! She keeps on mentioning Jack's name"?—No, that is quite untrue, and her recollection was wrong in this respect. She confused the two interviews in one.

Let me come to the second interview then; that was on 14th July?—I cannot say for certain, but it may be.

She says it was?—I will accept her word.

By the LORD CHIEF JUSTICE—Did you ever ask Mrs. Brook who Jack was, or what she knew of him?—Yes, and she denied

Evidence for the Prisoner Ley.

Thomas J. Ley

that she ever mentioned the name, and she denied that she mentioned the name Arthur that night.

Did she say what she knew of him?—She denied using the name.

This is the only single occasion on which she saw Jack Mudie, and once she was introduced to him at the door by Mrs. Evans?— Yes, I accepted that, but that was after I sent the letters. If you take the things out of their right sequence they are apt to be misunderstood.

Cross-examination continued—There was a second visit to Homefield Road when you saw Mrs. Evans the second time?—Yes.

Did you say to Mrs. Evans that Mudie had been in the flat with Mrs. Brook?—No, I did not.

That again is a failure of recollection on her part?—Yes, quite true.

Did you say this after having observed that Mudie had been in the flat with Mrs. Brook: that Mrs. Brook was a poor old thing who could not stand the pace?—No, I did not say such a thing.

Did you say anything like it?—No.

Can you imagine this woman, Mrs. Evans, whom we have all seen, imagining an observation like that?—Mrs. Evans was confused, and I will tell you what I did say to her. When I saw Mrs. Evans on the first occasion she told me that she had heard a disturbance that night, and she wondered what had gone on. I told her Mrs. Brook was in a very bad condition, and also very worried, and I wanted to find out the circumstances in case anything happened to her. She wanted to see her, and I said it was no use because she would not see her own doctor. I tried to find out from Arthur Barron what could have happened, and he was very rude to me as a matter of fact. I tried to get him along under conditions where he would listen to me, talk, and give information.

By the LORD CHIEF JUSTICE—You wanted to get Arthur Barron along where he would talk and give information?—Yes. I wanted him to come along to 5 Beaufort Gardens and have a talk with me; but he would not come.

Why?—Why I wanted that was because I was anxious to find out what had happened, because if anything had happened to Mrs. Brook, and there was an inquest, people would have said: "Why so much indifference? You went there in the middle of the night, and you did not care what happened."

Ley and Smith.

Cross-examination continued—There were three people apparently you were seeking—Arthur Barron, Arthur Romer and Jack Mudie?—No, I was not seeking Jack Mudie at all.

You did seek two of them?—Yes, because they were both named Arthur, and I did not recognize the voice.

I do not think you have followed me. I am sorry it is difficult for you, but please try and listen. You did try and seek out two of them?—Yes, I did.

Was Arthur Barron the third one?—No, I went to Arthur Barron first because I thought he might be there, and I came to the conclusion that he was not.

Did you tell your secretary, Miss Ingleson, that there were three men whom you suspected of carrying on with Mrs. Brook?—No, I did not; she has confused entirely what happened. I used to speak of the three men, but not in that connexion at all. I often wondered about Jack Mudie, whom I understood from Mrs. Evans was a nice man.

By the LORD CHIEF JUSTICE—You said you wanted to get Arthur Barron along to Beaufort Gardens to get information from him?—Yes.

You also put private inquiry agents to find out about Romer?—Yes.

You were interested in getting information about two of these people, Barron and Romer?—Yes, I wanted to find out which Arthur it was I had heard.

Cross-examination continued—It is true that you got information about the third one as well, Jack Mudie?—No, I did not; I never searched for him at all.

Surely you got information by this process of sending those letters to him?—I got no information at all.

You went down to the Reigate Hill Hotel about 7th August, did you not?—Yes.

You sought that man out?—Yes.

You brought him back in a car then, did you not?—Yes, to see the receipt.

How did you find out that that man who, when you last knew him, was working at Wimbledon, was working at the Reigate Hill Hotel?—On my second visit to Mrs. Evans. When Sergeant Shoobridge saw me first I could not recollect, and then I learned it subsequently from Mrs. Evans.

THOMAS JOHN LEY

Evidence for the Prisoner Ley.

Thomas J. Ley

That is the first we have heard of that, but you say that is the moment you ascertained that Mudie was at the Reigate Hill Hotel? —Yes.

What brought you into touch with this man, Mudie, was the fact that you had sent those letters?—No, it was the fact that he did not post the letter and kept the cheques.

I do not think that is a clear answer. Is not it a fact that you sent him a letter when you did not get the cheque back, and you went to see him?—Through him not answering the solicitors' letters.

I still do not understand why you sent those letters and cheques? —If you do not understand I cannot help you.

Did you send them because you understood that Mrs. Brook was going to Bournemouth and had left West Cromwell Road?—I thought she had gone to Homefield Road to arrange with her daughter to go to Bournemouth in connexion with her convalescence.

That she had left Cromwell Road to go to Homefield Road?— Yes, only temporarily; she had not moved.

You thought that at the time when Connaught Properties Limited required another signature to some cheques?—Yes.

For wages: it was a cheque therefore that presumably you would want back as quickly as possible?—Yes.

Why did you send that letter and the covering letter to this man Mudie?—Because at that time I was under the impression that he knew both Mrs. Brook and Mrs. Barron—that they were tenants who were friendly.

Is that a good reason for sending something to him with which he had nothing whatever to do?—I have often done it when thinking: how can I make sure a person is there or not?

Why did you not send them addressed to 3 Homefield Road with "Please forward" on them?—Well, because I suppose it did not occur to me. There were quite a number of things I could have done differently.

Looking back on it now, does it not strike you as odd?—No.

Would it not be the first thing you would think of doing?—It did not occur to me.

Did it not occur to you it was the most sensible thing to do?— It did not occur to me that way.

You sent them to a man called Mudie, of whom you knew nothing?—Yes; I knew nothing about him except that I had heard he was a nice fellow, and so on.

You knew perfectly well that Mrs. Brook was at 14 West Cromwell Road?—I did not know that Mrs. Brook was there at

Ley and Smith.

that time. There was a misunderstanding about it for which I accept responsibility, but I did not know she was there at that time.

By the LORD CHIEF JUSTICE—Cromwell Road was less than ten minutes by 74 'bus from there?—Yes.

Why did you not go to West Cromwell Road?—Because I understood by telephone message that she had gone.

From whom?—From Mrs. Brook, but she said I made a mistake. She denies it, and so I have nothing to do but to accept it.

Cross-examination continued—So much of this is absolute news. We have heard nothing of it. Do you say now that Mrs. Brook telephoned you and said she was going down to Bournemouth?—That is what I understood.

When you spoke to her on the telephone, did you not say: "Well, just before you go there are three cheques I want you to sign"?—Well, I had not thought of that, you see.

Did she tell you how long she was going to stay at Homefield Road?—No.

Did you ask her?—Not that I recollect.

Were you not interested?—Well, it is very difficult to say what one's state of mind was at that moment. Some things slip one's mind.

I suppose you would agree that you were on the most intimate terms with this lady; you were seeing her every day?—Not at that time.

By the LORD CHIEF JUSTICE—Mrs. Brook was going from West Cromwell Road to Bournemouth?—No; first of all to 3 Homefield Road to arrange for the convalescence of her daughter at Bournemouth. She said I had made a mistake about it, and that she was going to the Broads, and she was not going with her.

Cross-examination continued—For the sake of speed and getting them back as quickly as possible, you put them in an envelope addressed to somebody else of whom you knew nothing at 3 Homefield Road; is that right?—Yes.

Are you surprised that you did not get them back again?—Yes, I am surprised. That has been done over and over again by me and others relying on persons being obliging.

That is your explanation and your final one of sending those cheques?—Yes.

By the LORD CHIEF JUSTICE—Where was Mr. Barron senior at this time?—He does not live at 3 Homefield Road.

Evidence for the Prisoner Ley.

Thomas J. Ley

Did Mr. Barron junior live there?—Not at that time.

Mrs. Evans was the landlady?—Yes, but she is very often out on charitable work.

I cannot understand why you sent them to Mudie; Mudie was a lodger in the house?—He was a tenant in the house, and I thought he knew both Mrs. Brook and Mrs. Barron.

Cross-examination continued—Is that your explanation?—Yes.

Do you think, looking at it now from a detached point of view, that it sounds a good one?—If I had to do the same thing over again, I would probably do it, except for the events into which this has been brought.

Supposing those cheques had come back signed, it would have provided you with admirable evidence that Mrs. Brook was associating with this man Mudie behind your back?—No evidence at all. Why should it? If someone obliges me by handing a letter over——

Did you tell Mr. Barron that the reason you sent those cheques was because you wanted to do a bit of detective work on your own?—No; I have already denied that, and I deny it again.

Did you pay Buckingham £200 in £1 notes?—No.

Did you pay Smith £200 in £1 notes?—No.

Did you draw £450 in 1 notes out of your bank on 16th and 26th November?—I did.

What for?—For furnishings.

May I ask why?—Yes. I wanted curtains for three rooms.

Why cash?—Because I have done so for years. In this case the velvet was going to be supplied by somebody who had been introduced to me and he wanted cash, and the estimate in one case was £300. Story of Kensington——

Did he send you a bill?—They had intimated to me that they hoped to do this thing, and when they told me it was £300 plus making up, I thought it was too dear for one pair of curtains.

Which is this firm which insists upon payment in cash?—Not a firm that you are dealing with usually, but this was a man outside who said he could get the material.

By the LORD CHIEF JUSTICE—Has he got a name?—I cannot remember his name, but I can tell you the people who introduced him to me. They were Austin of Beauchamp Place.

Cross-examination continued—They introduced you to a man you did not know, and he insisted on being paid in cash?—He did not insist on it.

Ley and Smith.

Thomas J. Ley

Then why did you draw it out?—Because I thought he would bring the velvet round, and he would want prompt payment for the velvet when he delivered it. We had never done business before, and I had it ready if he turned up.

Is there any particular reason why you should not give him a cheque?—No particular reason, except that people like that want cash.

How much do you say it was?—£300.

Are you in the habit when having a flat furnished of drawing £300 out of your bank in £1 notes?—Yes, I have done it often.

It is rather unusual, is it not?—Yes, it is, I suppose, but when you know people well, they will accept your cheque, but when it is a singular occasion and you want to get rid of people, you provide cash. I have done that often.

That accounts for £300. What about the other £250?—Story had some second-hand curtains. I saw them; Mrs. Brook and I thought they would suit. I asked her advice because I knew little about it, and they anticipated that I should want about £240. Story were not going to take cash, but their clients.

What was the name of Story's clients?—That was not disclosed to me, but it could easily be checked.

By the LORD CHIEF JUSTICE—Story are house furnishers themselves?—Yes, but people go to them to give them second-hand curtains to dispose of; another firm in Sloane Street does the same.

You were to deal with Story?—Yes, but they had to provide cash.

Cross-examination continued—I suppose you would send Story a cheque?—Well, I provided the cash; I do not know them or their clients.

You are not able to tell us the names of either of these?—In the case of Story the name was not disclosed to me, but it could be found out if you think it is essential.

Did you pay any of this £300 or £250?—What do you mean by paying it? No, not in the end. I thought the curtains were too dear and I did not buy them, and I bought some other things.

Did you buy them with part of this £550?—Yes, it was £150——

Who from?—Well, it is very difficult to say now. I have bought things, for instance, by running out in a taxi, and I have bought an electric fire.

Evidence for the Prisoner Ley.

Thomas J. Ley

By the LORD CHIEF JUSTICE—Never mind about electric fires. If you paid £150 even for curtains, how is it that you cannot remember whom you paid it to?—I do not say that, my lord. It was roughly £150, and the rest was not spent on curtains.

Cross-examination continued—I want to find out the truth about this?—I want to help you.

What happened to the £150 you did spend?—I could not tell you.

Have you a detailed receipt?—No.

Have you any evidence whatsoever, except your own word, that you paid a penny of this to any furnisher or curtain-maker, or anybody else?—There are receipts about, but for three months I have been isolated from my business.

You have been in the best of hands?—Well, I would be quite willing to exchange places with you.

The LORD CHIEF JUSTICE—Counsel means that you have had the advantage of solicitors' and counsel's advice.

The WITNESS—So far as those proceedings are concerned, but I have not had anyone who could pick up my business at the point where I left off.

Cross-examination continued—I am not concerned in the least with your business. I am concerned with a perfectly simple matter in connexion with the furnishing of your flat. You tell me that you paid £150 in cash for various matters in connexion with it. Can you produce any receipts to prove it?—I cannot produce any receipt. I am unable to identify that as I could not identify my underclothes last week.

By the LORD CHIEF JUSTICE—Before the learned magistrate at West London, you know that a witness was called from the bank who produced your bank account?—Yes, the same witness has come here.

And you know that emphasis was laid on the fact that you had withdrawn £250 in cash on 16th November?—Yes.

And £300 on 26th November?—Yes.

Therefore you have had since then an opportunity of producing any receipt to show that you spent a considerable amount of money about that time?—There was £400 or thereabout which was not spent.

Ley and Smith.

I know that. You have been asked if you can show the jury any receipts in respect of this money?—I cannot show any receipt for the money unless I get to my books.

Cross-examination continued—There is no doubt that on 4th December you gave this man Smith £300?—I gave him a cheque for £300 by way of a loan.

You got it back in the shape of £5 notes on the 9th. He was pretty quick in paying you back?—Yes, I thought so.

Has the fact that he paid it back on the 9th any bearing on the fact that on the 7th you had been visited by the police?—I have no knowledge what his object was.

Were you not visited by the police on 7th December?—You have the date there.

Will you accept it from me?—Yes.

By the LORD CHIEF JUSTICE—Cannot you remember the date?—No.

You remembered 28th November and exactly what you did every hour of the day, but you cannot remember when you saw the police?—No; I know it was a Saturday morning.

Cross-examination continued—You knew on 7th December, because Sergeant Shoobridge told you, that inquiries were being made about the dead body of a man called Mudie?—Yes.

Is there no relationship between that information being given you on the 7th and you getting that £300 back from Smith on the 9th?—I do not think so at all.

If you gave Smith £300, it must have been an act of great kindness?—Yes. I did not give it to him; I lent it to him.

You have been very civil to this man Smith; I understand that you were giving him meals?—Two or three times, yes—when we had business to discuss, purely business meals.

Treating him very decently?—Yes, I hope I did.

And this is the man who made that statement which was read this morning?—Yes.

A man to whom you had lent £300 on 4th December made that statement in the same month. Can you understand it?—I cannot understand it.

On 28th November you say you left 5 Beaufort Gardens for the National Liberal Club at about six o'clock, and then you had to go back again for your torch?—It would be before five I left originally, and then I went back, and finally I left shortly after five.

Evidence for the Prisoner Ley.

Thomas J. Ley

At what time did you leave the National Liberal Club?—Approximately five-past six.

Do I understand you to say that about five-past six you went to the Cumberland Hotel?—I took a taxi from the club, and then went to the Cumberland Hotel. The taxi broke down and I got another one.

What time did you get to the Cumberland Grill?—To the best of my recollection about twenty to twenty-five past six.

Did you see a man there you knew?—Yes, as I was coming out.

What time would that be?—About a quarter-past seven; he was standing in a queue.

Is he here to-day?—I do not see him.

Can you tell me if he is coming?—You will have to get that from my solicitor. I cannot tell you; I am out of touch.

Have you any other evidence that you were in the Cumberland Grill between a quarter-past six and a quarter-past seven?—You will have to refer to my solicitor.

Are you well known there?—Only to one or two.

Do you see any of them here?—I do not see them here; they may be hiding somewhere, but I cannot see them.

Having, as you say, been there, you went and rejoined Mrs. Brook and played gin-rummy?—Yes.

A friendly pleasant pastime, incidentally, with a woman whom you thought had been carrying on, as you so graphically described, at the flat at Wimbledon, and whom you regarded as dishonest, and whom you had finished with?—Yes.

What time did you leave her?—Roughly a quarter-past eleven.

Were you living alone at Beaufort Gardens at this time?—Yes, quite.

What time did you get in?—Well, I should say approximately 11.30; that is the time I used to get in.

Did you go in by the front door?—Yes.

Anybody else in the house?—Nobody else.

Did you find anything?—Planks and pipes.

I do not mean that. Did you find anything else that was not planks at all?—I went in by the front door, closed the door, went up to the front entrance to my flat, went to bed, got up in the morning, had my bath, and got ready to let my housekeeper in.

Is it your habit to go straight to bed without looking down below?—That was shut up before I went.

Did you not go downstairs to look round?—No, I did not; I do not now, and I did not.

It so happened that you came in about a quarter or half-past

Ley and Smith.

eleven; it might have been later?—I do not think it was much later.

I mean, any day you might have come in at any time?—No; I used to come in about a quarter to half-past eleven every night.

Are you saying if anybody wanted to bring a man trussed up to your flat that they would have a time absolutely certain in their minds when you would not be there?—Most of the people who were there knew I would come back late at night. It was a place most unfit to live in, and most uncomfortable.

By the LORD CHIEF JUSTICE—Smith would not know it, would he? He was the foreman and the builder?—My lord, we had the work——

He left at five o'clock, did not he?—We had to work in a congested place, and everybody else heard what everybody else said, and it was well-known that I went away as early as I could and came home late.

I do not know how that would be conveyed to Smith. In the ordinary way he would leave the premises at five o'clock?—Yes. I want to point out that if I were in the flat people could go in and out of the basement without my hearing.

Cross-examination continued—It all depends what they are doing in the basement?—If they were exploding bombs I would hear, of course, but ordinarily I would not hear.

Supposing they were engaged in kidnapping a man, and then tying and gagging him, and then bumping him along the passage; would you hear that?—I probably would not hear anything about it. It can be tested, if necessary.

You did not even bother to see if it was secured down below?— I did not keep my money there.

At this time Mrs. Brook was living at 14 West Cromwell Road; on 12th June she had come up to London from Wimbledon, you having gone down to fetch her?—Yes.

Did you tell Buckingham that the elder of these two women was being blackmailed, and you had to go down to Wimbledon and bring her back to Cromwell Road?—No.

Could you hazard a guess, and help me in any way, as to how Buckingham could possibly have known either of the fact that you had been down to Wimbledon, or that she was in the Cromwell Road unless you told him?—He could have learnt it through Smith. I said before, that when I asked Smith to be provided with men I gave him the information.

Evidence for the Prisoner Ley.

Thomas J. Ley

You told Smith that you had been down to Wimbledon and brought her back to London?—Yes.

Why?—Because I wanted to interview Mr. Arthur Barron about what could have happened to Mrs. Brook and put her in such a condition.

By the LORD CHIEF JUSTICE—What had that to do with Smith? —It had nothing to do with Smith, except it was an explanation as to why I wanted the men there to prevent Arthur Barron running away before I could get a chance to see him.

The men were to be there in case you got Barron there?—Yes, at 5 o'clock.

Cross-examination continued—Would your answer be the same if I asked you how you could conceivably think that Buckingham knew anything about Mudie?—No; I do not know what the answer would be about that at all.

You knew all about him?—I did not know about Mudie, except that I addressed a covering letter to him.

You knew where he was and what he was. You knew quite enough about him to locate him for somebody else if you wanted to?—Yes.

Have you any evidence at all that either Buckingham or Smith knew him at all?—No, I have no evidence.

I asked you that question for this reason: is your statement, Exhibit 21, taken by Inspector Philpott in the presence of your solicitor, an accurate statement?—There are one or two corrections I ought to make in it.

Just wait a minute, because it may be the part I am going to read you will not wish to correct. Tell me if this is right or wrong: "I knew the man Smith who was the foreman. I have known him for a few months, and used to see him almost daily up till a week ago when he gave up his situation. I have never spoken to Smith about Mudie, and as far as I know, Smith did not know that I knew such a person as Mudie." Is that accurate?—I think it is quite accurate, yes. I did not know him.

And yet, if he is right, this man Smith went all the way down to Reigate to pick up this man Mudie to bring him back to your flat. It is an astonishing coincidence?—Yes, it is; I am not able to explain it.

"I have never mentioned to him that Mudie used to be at the Dog and Fox." Is that right?—That is quite right.

He seems to know he was?—I did not know myself until Sergeant Shoobridge told me.

Ley and Smith.

Thomas J. Ley

Or that he lived at 3 Homefield Road?—No, I never told him that.

You could not tell me how he knew it?—No.

"Neither have I mentioned to Smith that Mudie was at the Reigate Hill Hotel"?—No.

Yet he went there, according to himself, with unerring accuracy? —Yes, according to him.

I wonder how he found it out?—I have no idea.

By the LORD CHIEF JUSTICE—You said just now you told Smith or Buckingham about it?—I said I thought Buckingham got to know about Mrs. Brook's removal.

Cross-examination continued—Did Smith ever tell you that by a curious coincidence he happened to know a house in Wimbledon called 3 Homefield Road?—No; I do not recollect it.

If he had said so, you would have said "That is funny, Smith, so do I." He never told you that?—No.

You could not very well have forgotten it if he had?—No, I do not think so.

May I take it he never said so?—Yes, you may.

"I have never mentioned a person named 'Romer,' of 3 Home-field Road, to Smith." How on earth could Smith know about Romer?—I will tell you. I have explained to you already the squeezed state we were in. It would be on my table among letters, and anybody could see it.

What do you mean?—The result of the search came back from Conquests, and it was on my table for anybody to read.

You think he got to know it through reading your correspondence?—I do not say that I think it, but that is possible.

We know that Smith hired a car from Howard's Services on 25th November. Did you hear that he paid £29?—I heard it in the evidence. I understood the amount he really paid was £14.

He paid a deposit of £15, and he had to pay £14, which makes £29 to get that car. Did you hear that Smith was getting £7 10s. a week?—Yes.

Did you pay for that car?—No.

Do you know who did?—No.

Is Miss Brittain right that the person who rang up saying the car was wanted was you?—She is quite right in saying I rang up. The circumstances were these: Smith had been running round in an Austin car, and he said it was broken down, or he could not get it, and he asked me if I thought my firm would provide him

Evidence for the Prisoner Ley.

Thomas J. Ley

with a car. I rang up, and put them in touch with one another. What happened after that I do not know.

Miss Brittain seems to be accurate in saying that you rang up?—Yes, I did ring up.

Is Normanton wrong when he says that when he came round to Beaufort Gardens to see you about this car, you and Smith were together?—Yes, that is probably right; we were often together.

Did you find Miss Ingleson a fairly reliable person?—At book-keeping, yes. She was not so good as a secretary, and her degree of uptake and understanding was not so good; but she was a perfectly honest person, and I do not think she would make any mistake deliberately if she could help it.

She was not going out of her way to make any mistakes yester-day?—I do not think so.

And if there was anything she could say that would help you, she went out of her way to say so?—I do not think so.

Did you say to her that Mrs. Brook was accusing you of having murdered Mudie?—I did not.

Do you mean to tell me that you did not say that to that girl? —I am quite sure that I never said such a thing to that girl.

Re-examined by Sir WALTER MONCKTON—Whatever also happened on 8th June, about which you have been asked a number of questions, was the name that stuck in your mind that night "Arthur" or "Jack"?—Arthur.

And thereafter you were trying to discover what "Arthur" it was?—Yes.

That was the episode of which you have spoken, and you have given your view about it. Then came 10th July when you went to Mr. Brashier's office, and you told my lord and the jury that you took the view, or expressed it, that Mrs. Brook was a dishonest person?—I took the view that she was acting dishonestly.

It was put to you, after the "Arthur" episode and the allegation about the dishonesty of Mrs. Brook, how odd it was that you should continue to associate with her. You had had an association with her for 24 years?—Yes.

For the last ten years it had not been of the intimate kind?—No.

In spite of what happened in June and July, were you still interested in her welfare?—Yes.

Are you still?—I shall be.

CHARLES RICHARD BREASLEY, sworn, examined by Mr. QUASS—I live at 60 Holly Road, Cricklewood, and am cashier of the National

Ley and Smith.

Charles R. Breasley

Liberal Club. It is part of my duties to enter up any change in address of members in a book called the "Alteration Book." Under the date 29th November, 1946, there is an alteration for Thomas J. Ley made in my handwriting.

What information had you before you when you entered up that change of address?—A small piece of paper came up from the Reception Office to me, and from that I entered it in this book. I do not know what time of day it was that I got this slip of paper.

Does the office close at five o'clock normally?—Yes.

When the secretary's office is closed are the entries made up the same day or the next day?—They come up next day.

From looking at this slip you cannot say when the entry on the slip was made?—No.

All you know was that it reached you on the 29th when you entered it?—Yes.

MARY RANDALL, sworn, examined by Mr. QUASS—I live at 74 King Street, Gillingham, Kent, and am the head receptionist at the National Liberal Club. I work downstairs, and from time to time members give me notice of any change of address which I write on a slip. We either take the information from the member himself or from somebody for the member.

Can you remember how you came to make this note on this slip, Exhibit 28?—I am afraid I have no recollection.

If you got a note of a change of address after five o'clock from a member, what would you do with it?—I should hold it until I got it up to the office next morning.

Cross-examined by Mr. HAWKE—I suppose sometimes when a member is changing his address he might ring you up and let you know?—Yes.

And you would make a note on a piece of paper?—Yes.

By the LORD CHIEF JUSTICE—Do you always send up a piece of paper directly it comes in?—No, sir.

If it came in in the morning, would you send it up that day or the next day?—I would send it up the same day.

What about if it came in the early afternoon?—It probably would not go up till the next morning.

LANCELOT ELLOTT BARKER, sworn, examined by Sir WALTER MONCKTON—I live at 6 St. John's Avenue, Putney Hill, and am a member of the firm of Messrs. Wontners & Sons, solicitors, High Holborn, who are engaged in the defence of Mr. Ley.

Evidence for the Prisoner Ley.

Lancelot E. Barker

On 20th February did you, on instructions from Ley, go to 5 Beaufort Gardens, along with Mr. Clive Ley, his son, and Mr. Brashier?—Yes, we all met there.

Did you make a search of the drawers of the bedroom which you were given to understand used to be occupied by Ley?—Yes.

Did you find any money?—Yes; we found a quantity of £1 notes in an envelope. They were in one of the drawers of the wardrobe in the bedroom. We took them downstairs and the three of us counted them together. There were 277 £1 notes.

On the instructions of Ley, did you attend again at 5 Beaufort Gardens with the same two persons on 19th March?—Yes.

Did you search a large canvas bag which contained clothes?—Yes. It contained a lot of clothes which seemed to be for wearing in the Middle East—hot weather clothes.

Did you find another envelope there?—Yes.

Did that also contain £1 notes?—Yes. We took them downstairs, again together, and there were 123 £1 notes.

There was £400 in all, and you produce the two envelopes?—Yes. I have the envelopes here. (Two envelopes marked Exhibit 29.)

Cross-examined by Mr. HAWKE—Did Mr. Ley at any time ask you to see if there were any receipts for payment which he had made for curtains and furnishings, and so on?—I have not got the papers in connexion with this business at all.

I was only wondering whether he had asked you, when you had access to it, to see if you could find any receipts?—No, I cannot recollect that he did.

The LORD CHIEF JUSTICE—Mr. Hawke, I think it might be necessary to have the bank clerk back in connexion with this. There were other large sums withdrawn about the material dates. If necessary you can recall the witness. This banking account, according to the entries, shows that as far back as 29th November there was £355 drawn; on 28th November there was £100; on 4th December there was the £300 that we know went into Smith's account; on the 5th, there is a debit of £370 (there is nothing to say whether it is cash or cheques); on 5th December there was £375; then there are other odd amounts which look like cheques; then on 17th December, £50; 18th December, £91; then there are other amounts which look like cheques. Except for those, there are not any other large sums drawn.

The Court adjourned.

Ley and Smith.

Fourth Day—Saturday, 22nd March, 1947.

ARTHUR HENRY STILLAWAY, sworn, examined by Mr. QUASS—
I live at 12 Cherry Orchard Street, and am the second receptionist
at the Cumberland Grill. I have been employed at the Cumberland
for about 13 years. It is my normal practice to work three days on
and one day off; another receptionist, Mr. Holmes, does the same
and neither of us is away on the same day.

Do you know the defendant, Ley?—Yes. I know him by
coming to the Cumberland Grill regularly every week-day evening
for dinner. He has done this since about July, 1946. There was a
table reserved for him.

Was he regular in his habits in the time he came, or did the
time he came vary?—No, he came between 6.15 and 6.30 and stayed
until about 7.15 or 7.30.

Did he come along with anybody?—Always with a lady.

Was she a young lady, or middle aged, or elderly?—Just over
middle aged I should think.

Was he always there with the same lady?—Always, yes.

Did he ever come without the lady?—I remember one occasion
only.

When was the last time that Ley came at all to the Cumberland?
—Well, it is rather difficult to say the last time he was there, a date.
I should say about Christmas time was the last time he was there.

When about before this was it he came alone?—I should say
about November.

Can you remember whether Holmes, the other receptionist,
was on duty on that date he came alone or not?—That I couldn't
say for sure.

I mean was he normally the other receptionist? Was he receptionist in the evening throughout 1946. and was there any occasion
when he was away apart from——?—Well, he was away for about
five months with an illness.

Do you know when it was he came back?—I would not be sure
of the exact date.

Cross-examined by Mr. HAWKE—I suppose you are a fairly busy
man, are you not?—Yes.

Do a lot of people come to the receptionist desk at the Cumberland in the evening every evening?—Quite a lot.

I expect they keep you pretty well occupied?—They certainly
do.

Evidence for the Prisoner Ley.

Arthur H. Stillaway

I was wondering, because do I understand you to say that this gentleman has never been to the Cumberland without a lady, except once?—On one occasion I can remember.

I was wondering whether you are quite sure?—I remember him coming alone.

Yes. I thought you said you remembered only one occasion which you said vaguely was somewhere in November, as the only time he came without a lady?—It would be round about November, I think.

Have you got a goodish memory?—Well, I think I have, for faces and things.

Let us try. Can you carry your mind back to June?—Possibly.

I suppose you would be on duty at the reception office in June, would you not? On one of your three days on?—Yes, I think I should be.

Was Mr. Ley visiting the hotel then?—I don't think so.

What makes you think he wasn't?—Well, I mean to say, you have got an idea when people start to come to the hotel for regular evenings.

You told us he started about July?—I think about July.

Can you give me the date?—Not the date, no.

By the LORD CHIEF JUSTICE—Did he come all through the summer, through August and September?—Yes, I think so.

He did not have a holiday?—Not that I recollect.

Every evening?—Almost regularly. There may be occasions when I was off that he didn't come either.

Cross-examination continued—Almost regularly. But you could not say he came every night?—Not to be tied down to that.

Re-examined by Sir WALTER MONCKTON—You have been 13 years receptionist at the Cumberland Grill. Have you got, as receptionist, to know the regular customers?—Yes, that is part of your business.

And to notice those who have a table regularly reserved for them?—Yes.

This was a customer of whom you said he came regularly with the same lady to dine?—Quite correct.

You recall an occasion when you saw him alone there. Is that what it comes to?—Yes, just once.

You can't fix an exact date?—No.

It is an isolated case and was in November?—Yes.

By the LORD CHIEF JUSTICE—Did he ever have a male guest with him?—No, never.

Ley and Smith.

Robert J. A. Holmes

ROBERT JOHN ARBUTHNOT HOLMES, sworn, examined by Mr. QUASS—I live at 45 Dominion Drive, West Acton, and am the first receptionist at the Cumberland Grill where I have been employed since 1934. I was away ill from the beginning of May, 1946, until 30th September, and when I came back I only worked half time, during the day from ten till three.

When did you come back to full duty?—On Monday, 25th November.

Is the practice for the receptionists to work three days on and one day off?—Yes.

If you came back to full duty on 25th November when would be your first day off?—Thursday, the 28th.

Do you know the defendant Ley from attendance at the Cumberland Grill?—I do.

Had you known him before you went off ill in May, 1946?—Not before.

Was he in the habit of coming down to dine there in the evening?—Yes.

Did he have a regular table?—Yes.

What time did he come for his evening meal?—He came about 6.15 and left between 7.15 and 7.30.

Was he regular or irregular in the hours he came and went?—He was regular.

When he came to dine did he come alone or with anybody?—He came with a lady.

Was that always so or only on some occasions when you were there?—He was always accompanied by the same lady.

Cross-examined by Mr. HAWKE—He was a regular customer then, and he had a regular table?—Yes.

And it was understood that that was Mr. Ley's table?—Yes.

I suppose that table had a regular waiter, did it not?—Well, the waiters had changed about.

I suppose some waiter was at the table for some days at any rate?—Yes.

Do you know the waiter?—No.

Do you know the head waiter?—Yes.

I suppose the head waiter would be in charge of that part of the room where Mr. Ley's table was?—Yes.

Have you seen him here to-day?—No.

ROBERT JOHN CRUIKSHANK, sworn, examined by Sir WALTER MONCKTON—Are you staying at 24 Leincester Terrace, Bayswater? —We stayed there for one night.

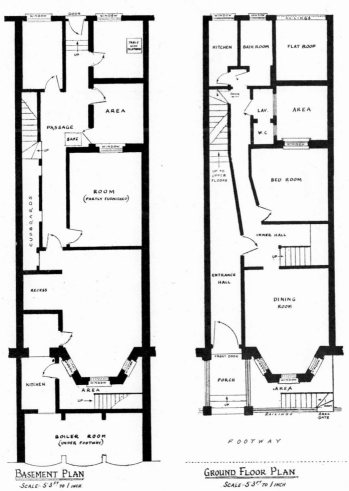

BROMPTON PLACE

BASEMENT PLAN
SCALE· 5˙3 FT TO 1 INCH.

GROUND FLOOR PLAN
SCALE· 5˙3 FT TO 1 INCH

BEAUFORT GARDENS

Exhibit No. 1. Plan of No. 5 Beaufort Gardens, London, S.W,
Basement and ground floors

Evidence for the Prisoner Ley.

Robert J. Cruikshank

Last night?—Yes.

You have been staying in a hotel somewhere else?—Yes.

Are you married, and do you have two children?—That is right.

In 1932 did you go to Australia?—I think the actual date, I can't swear to it, was about 1929.

Were you for a year or two round about that time in Australia? —Yes.

Only a year or two, I think?—Yes.

On your return to England did you find occupation of various kinds, including steward, with your wife as a stewardess, in various service flats in London?—Yes.

During the war were you called up for service?—I was, yes.

And discharged after a short time on ill-health?—Yes.

You then worked in certain war factories, and finally up till September of last year were you working in the British and American Tobacco Company as a clerk?—Yes.

I think in that month you were discharged as redundant. Since then have you been trying with your wife to go back to Australia? —Yes.

Some time after September, 1946, did you hear of Ley, the defendant in this case, and did you learn of his address?—Yes.

5 Beaufort Gardens?—I don't know exactly that it was his address; I think the actual words were that he had a house.

Did you decide to call at his house?—I did.

Can you tell me on what date you were going to go there?— Well, the decision was taken at about—as an afterthought, at a minute's notice—it was somewhere about eight o'clock on 28th November.

What day of the week was that?—To the best of my knowledge it was a Thursday.

You made up your mind to go and see him?—Yes.

To pay a visit. What did you do?—Well, I can't say exactly. I know I went to the front door, sir, and I remember hammering at the door with my hand. I was under the impression that it might have been flats, and I am not sure if there were bells there, because I have knocked at a lot of doors in the last six months, unfortunately for me, and on more than one occasion I rang the wrong bell.

On this occasion, Cruikshank, first of all you say you banged at the door. About what time was this?—To the best of my ability somewhere between quarter to nine and a quarter past.

And you got no answer. Then what did you do?—I went to the basement.

Ley and Smith.

Robert J. Cruikshank

That means you went down the area steps?—Yes, sir.

What did you do then?—Well, I found the door was open. I hammered on it. I got no answer. I wondered if there was a domestic staff there. I must say that I formed the opinion that if there was no domestic staff that might give me an opportunity to commit a felony.

What did you do?—I went into the basement.

The door was ajar and you went in?—Yes.

Then what did you do? Was there a light on?—I didn't see any lights in the house from the time I arrived to the time I left. I went into the basement. I have tried, after seeing the plans of the place, to reconstruct where I went. I can't say with any certainty. I know the length that I walked; it appeared to me that I walked the length of the passage.

Anyway, all you can say is you walked in, you don't know exactly where you went, and there was no light?—No.

Where did you eventually get—to a room?—Eventually, after bumping over some rubbish, which caused me to have the idea the place was either bombed or deserted—I didn't quite know what to make of it. Then I tried to get a light from a lighter; I didn't get a proper light, I got just a flicker, and I saw a door near me. There was no light coming from under the door. I opened the door. I tried to get another glimmer, and by the very small flicker that I got I saw what appeared to me to be somebody in a chair, tied up.

What did you do first?—Well, as you know, I was discharged from the army with neurasthenia. I was in a state of panic when I got into the basement and I didn't know whether to believe my eyes or what to believe, and I stood for a couple of moments, and I heard some sort of a moan or a grunt. I think I stood there for a couple of moments, and then went over and started pulling at some ropes.

Started pulling at some ropes?—Yes, I also felt——

By the LORD CHIEF JUSTICE—What do you mean "started pulling at some ropes"?—Well, I can't explain any more than that.

Where were the ropes?—Well, the ropes—I can't swear—they were wound round the legs, but there were some ropes round the top part of the body.

What did you do?—I just pulled at them, sir, in a sort of frenzy. I didn't quite know what to make of anything. I wasn't thinking clearly at all. I was just in a panic.

Had you gone in for the purpose of housebreaking?—I can't say definitely I did, sir; I haven't got the moral courage to do a thing like that, or the moral cowardice—I don't know which way

Evidence for the Prisoner Ley.

Robert J. Cruikshank

you put it—but one thing that was in my mind, if I had thought it was safe to housebreak I would have done, I think. I was in a very desperate situation with my family.

Examination continued—When you pulled the ropes did anything happen?—I think it was at that time that there was some sort of noise from the person who was tied up.

What sort of noise do you mean?—Well, I should call it a grunt.

You say you pulled at the ropes in the way you described, and then there was some sort of noise. What next did you do?—Well, I was trying to collect my thoughts. I was thinking all sorts of things. I was thinking about some one probably upstairs who was going to come down and beat me up. I thought it was the caretaker; all sorts of thoughts entered my mind; and some sort of a noise happened. I don't know whether it was a car, whether it was a hot-water pipe. I have got no idea at all.

Yes, when you heard this——?—Oh, no; my nerve just snapped, and I got out of the place as quickly as I could.

Which way did you get out?—As I entered.

By the area steps?—Yes.

Did you at any time think of untying the knots?—I did, yes.

You thought of it, you mean, and the noise occurred?—Yes.

You did not do it?—Never at any time, although there is one sentence in my statement which might make other people believe otherwise, but never at any time did I think this man was in danger of death.

When you got out did you go off elsewhere?—Well, I want you to understand that at the time this occurrence happened I was already worried. I had lost my home; I had lost my money; my children were in Switzerland.

By the Lord Chief Justice—Was the man alive?—He was, yes.

You left him there alive?—I already had a lot of worries; on top of that, this business happening, I can't describe clearly what happened afterwards. I got out of the place and made my way to Sloane Square. I don't know what streets I went through. I didn't go round by the main roads, I know.

Examination continued—Did you tell anybody about this at the time?—No.

Why not?—Well, the one thing you have to bear in mind with everything I say is that in 1938 I had been informed——

Ley and Smith.

Robert J. Cruikshank

By the LORD CHIEF JUSTICE—What?—In 1938 I believe there was a warrant issued against me by the police in London.

What for?—Well, something to do with getting rid of furniture before I had sold it. I just want you to understand——

Examination continued—May I just clear that up. I think this must be what you mean; you were getting rid of furniture before you had paid for it?—Yes. That was one of the reasons why I have been hesitant in this matter. I can only say that I have never made any secret of the fact from you or from Mr. Barker that I have got a criminal record.

Did you eventually say something about it to someone?—I didn't say anything about it until the day I went to Wontner's. I gave a couple of details to my wife. I didn't tell her, or go into detail; I just told her I knew something about the case.

Had you seen something about it then?—On several occasions I read about it. The trouble is that I must contradict something which you have got in writing, which is I was frightened I had killed the man. Well, in a sense that is true and in another sense it isn't. I didn't know I had killed him, and yet there was——

By the LORD CHIEF JUSTICE—Are you coming here to confess you killed this man?—Oh, no; but if there was a possibility, if he was bound in such a way—I can't say how it was done.

You said you pulled some ropes on his arms?—Yes.

That wouldn't kill him?—Well, what occurred to me——

Never mind what occurred to you. We want to know what you did, or what you say you did?—I can't add any more to what I have said.

Examination continued—You were just going to explain why eventually you came forward and what you did?—Well, I can only tell you that by—the judge has told me not to give opinions—I went over the thing in my mind, and I came to the opinion the ropes might have been tied round his neck attached to the ropes round his arms, and by pulling them I might have pulled them, and because they were round the neck I might have pulled them. That is the only reason I came forward.

You came forward and got in touch with the solicitors for the defence?—Yes.

Cross-examined by Mr. HAWKE—Did you come forward then to confess you think you may have killed this man?—I think there is a possibility.

Evidence for the Prisoner Ley.

Robert J. Cruikshank

Would you mind telling me how you did?—I can't tell anything, except by pulling the ropes.

You had better, hadn't you? You have come into the witness box now to say you think it is possible you may have killed this man yourself. Just tell us how?—Well, I can't give any opinion; I haven't said——

By the LORD CHIEF JUSTICE—You have not told us anything yet except that you pulled the rope on his arms?—Well, I can't give you anything further.

If you pulled the ropes on his arms, what reason have you to suppose you killed him?—I don't suppose, but there is a possibility. That was the reason I came forward.

Cross-examination continued—Is that all you can tell us?—That is all I can tell you.

All right. What were you doing at this time? What was your occupation?—I had no occupation.

Where were you living?—Well, at four o'clock we were living in a hotel in Berne.

What—in Switzerland?—Yes.

At four o'clock in a hotel in Switzerland on Thursday, 28th November, and at eight o'clock you were in London near Beauchamp Place?—Yes.

How did you manage that?—I have already made a statement to the police.

Never mind about that statement to the police. I am asking a perfectly plain question?—Well, I have to go back to October.

By the LORD CHIEF JUSTICE—You have just told the jury you were in Berne at four o'clock in the afternoon. You have now been asked how you were in London at eight o'clock in the evening?—I came by air.

What for?—I was engaged to bring a package.

Where is your passport?—Mr. Barker has my passport; not the original passport, he has a new one.

Where is your original passport?—I threw it overboard from the cross-channel steamer.

How did you land? You came by cross-channel steamer?—Yes. On that date?—No, this was after the case.

Cross-examination continued—Oh, it is since this episode that you thought it as well to get rid of your passport. Is that it?—I can bring a witness to swear——

Ley and Smith.

Robert J. Cruikshank

Never mind about bringing a witness?—Do you mean since? You said "since." I do not know anything?—You said "since." I would like to know what the date of my new passport is then.

I really do not mind. You know, and I do not mind?—No. You have made a statement that I got rid of it since my statement.

Simply because you said that, Mr. Cruikshank; I do not know? —The passport was got rid of long before this case, long before I came into the case.

I understood you to say you got rid of it from the steamer since this episode?—Yes, and I have got a perfectly good explanation as to why I got rid of it.

Would you tell me where you landed in England on 28th November when you came from Switzerland?—I can't tell you that.

Do you mean you do not know?—I don't know.

Where was it—in the country?—I should imagine it was somewhere near London, because I came to London by car.

Who brought you to London by car?—I don't know the man's name.

How did you find him? Just pick him up casually, or what? —It is rather difficult to answer your question.

By the Lord Chief Justice—Where did you get the money to come by air from Switzerland? It is rather expensive?—There was no money involved in the matter at all. I don't know if you are cross-examining me, or pretending you don't know I made a statement to the police, the way you are cross-examining me. I have made a full statement to the police about exactly how I came to be in London on the 28th.

Just answer the question. You say you came by air from Berne in the afternoon of 28th November?—That is correct.

How did you get a passage?—To the best of my knowledge, and without swearing to that—I can't do that—the 'plane in which I travelled was an unauthorized 'plane.

Cross-examination continued—You came from Switzerland to London in an unauthorized aeroplane?—I am not swearing that. I think the 'plane was unauthorized. It may have been a private hire 'plane.

Where did you get into it?—I got into it about half an hour's journey from Berne.

Who was the person who was bringing you over in this unauthorized aeroplane?—I don't know the name.

Evidence for the Prisoner Ley.

Robert J. Cruikshank

Could you not tell me?—No.

Were you coming over to see Mr. Ley?—Certainly not.

What for then?—I was coming over to bring over the parcel, which I believe——

You mean you were smuggling?—That is correct.

Why did you not say so?—I have already said so to the police.

I quite understand now. It is perfectly plain. You say you were engaged upon smuggling from Switzerland to London. Is that right?—I am just trying to think about the right word. There may be some other word besides "smuggling." There might be something worse.

Use any words you like; I don't mind; bringing in contraband if you prefer it. Is that what you were doing?—To the best of my knowledge.

Are we to understand that on Thursday, 28th November, you flew from Switzerland to London carrying contraband in an unauthorized aeroplane?—To the best of my knowledge, yes.

Where were you going after you had handed over your parcel? —I had this appointment at Sloane Square at ten o'clock.

What for?—To be picked up.

And taken back to Switzerland?—Correct.

Did you go back to Switzerland?—I did.

What time were you back there?—Somewhere between half-past six and half-past seven.

On Friday morning?—Yes.

So you were in Berne at four o'clock on Thursday evening and you were in Berne again at seven o'clock on Friday morning?— Somewhere around there.

All this happened on this night in London when what you were really there for was to smuggle contraband goods; is that right? —That is right.

You heard of Ley, I understand you to say, back in September of last year?—Yes.

You heard of him, as I understand it, as a man who might help you to get to Australia?—I can't explain where the September comes in.

That is what you said, you know. I do not know when you first heard of him. Just tell me when you first heard of him, will you, and then we will pass to something else?—I can't actually tell you when I first heard of him.

I do not mean the day of the week or the month; just roughly? —The only definite time I can remember was the time I stated to the police and Mr. Barker, which was some time in November.

Ley and Smith.

Robert J. Cruikshank

When in November—early part of November?—No. I should say the middle: not very far before I actually went to his house.

Were you in London at that time?—Yes.

In the middle of November?—Yes.

You have been to Berne since then?—We had been to Berne twice.

You were in London in the middle of November?—Yes.

You heard in a bar of Mr. Ley?—Yes.

What did you hear of him?—We just heard that he was some sort of big pot in the Australian Parliament, or words to that effect.

And could help you to get a passage?—Well, as perhaps you won't admit, most of these immigration things, most of these passages on ships, are wangled—although perhaps you are not prepared to admit that.

The LORD CHIEF JUSTICE—Cruikshank, just behave yourself and answer the question that you are put or else you will leave the box.

The WITNESS—I am sorry, sir.

Cross-examination continued—Would you mind answering a perfectly plain question. Did you hear of Ley as a man who could get you a passage to Australia? Answer "Yes" or "No"?—Yes, sir.

Who did you hear of him from?—I heard of it—we went into the bar; we had a drink, complained about the weather.

By the LORD CHIEF JUSTICE—Who is "we"?—Well, I don't want to drag her into it, but it is my wife.

You and your wife went into a bar and had a drink and talked about the weather?—Yes.

Who did you hear of Ley from?—Well, I don't know the man's name.

Somebody in the bar was just talking about Mr. Ley, was he?—Yes.

Cross-examination continued—You heard of him as a big pot in Australia with a house in Beaufort Gardens, and you were given his number, 5?—Yes.

That was about the middle of November?—About then.

It must have been very good news to you, was it not, that a big man in Australia might be able to help to get you a passage over there?—Well, I don't know—I had already tried a number of prominent people.

Evidence for the Prisoner Ley.

Robert J. Cruikshank

I suppose you thought it was worth trying?—I definitely thought so.

Why didn't you go and see him?—You mean that night?

Well, the next morning?—Well, for the simple reason my two children were in Switzerland. We were not at all satisfied or happy about their proceedings. We hadn't got the money to bring them back to England. We didn't quite know what was going to happen. We had no money to keep us going until the passage could be arranged to Australia.

I am very anxious not to stop you, but so far it does not seem to me you are answering the question I put to you. I asked you why, when you got this opportunity of this passage to Australia, you did not go at once and see the gentleman who might do it for you?—I can't be dogmatic about an answer to that; there may have been a dozen answers.

You see, it seems to me a funny thing that you should decide to do it for the first time at eight o'clock in the night in the middle of London when you say you were engaged in a smuggling expedition?—Well, everything I say in my statement seems funny.

It does?—It seemed screamingly funny to the gang in Gibraltar —that funny it stopped me getting abroad.

Just because it sounds funny I have the duty of cross-examining you. Do you follow that?—I quite understand you have got a job to do.

At about a quarter to nine you were at the door?—Yes, sir.

You rang the bell?—No, I never said that at all.

Did you knock on the door?—Banged on the door with my fist.

No answer?—No answer.

By the LORD CHIEF JUSTICE—What had you gone there for? What was your object in going?—I think I have said it about twenty times.

Well, say it again?—I thought if there was any chance of getting a passage on a cargo boat or by some means of that sort, that a man in a position who knew about Australia, who knew about the Australian shipping lines, he could wangle a thing like that.

Had you asked or made an appointment with Ley?—No, I hadn't.

Cross-examination continued—Having no appointment, getting no answer at the front door——?—Who is Mr. Ley that I should have to have an appointment with him?

Ley and Smith.

Robert J. Cruikshank

You thought the best way to see this big man in Australia was to walk into the basement, did you?—I didn't say that.

I thought you said you did?—I didn't.

I thought——?—I went into the basement to see if there were any servants there.

Did you go down the front steps, front area?—Those are the steps I assume I went down; as far as I know I did.

By the front door?—Near the front door.

Below the front door?—Yes.

You went down in the area below the front door?—Yes.

This door was open, was it?—It was.

And you stepped in?—Before I stepped in I banged on it.

You stepped into a dark passage, did you?—I just said before I stepped in and banged on the door.

Well, all right. And then what?—Then I went in.

You stepped into a dark passage?—Well, I have been to the place since. I have seen the place in daylight.

Have you! Oh, have you!?—And it didn't bring anything to my mind, but as far as I know I stepped into a dark passage.

I was wondering, because you say you have been to see this?—Yes, I have.

When?—Last Friday.

Who with?—With the solicitor for the defence.

I see. You went with the solicitor for the defence to go and have a look at the place?—I did.

Was that before or after you made the statement to the solicitor which he, with great courtesy, has allowed the prosecution to see?—It was after.

You were taken after that to see this place?—Yes.

Is that what made you hesitate in answering the question I have just asked you?—Have I hesitated?

Did you tell this gentleman here, the solicitor, that you got into the house and—I will put the words to you—there was no light on, you stumbled and went down a passage? Did you say that?—I said that after I saw the plan.

I suppose you saw the question I was going to ask you, did you not?—I am just trying to answer you truthfully; I am not trying to make play with words, in the way you are. You see, I am ignorant of the law.

The LORD CHIEF JUSTICE—Never mind the law. Answer the question.

Evidence for the Prisoner Ley.

Robert J. Cruikshank

Cross-examination continued—You know quite well, having seen the place, that if you come in through the front area you do not come to a passage at all, do you?—What would you call it then?

Please do not ask me questions. You have seen the place?—I should certainly say as you step inside the door you get into a passage and then go through a room.

Tell me what you get into when you open the area door?—I should call it, well, a passage, a recess, a small room, a kitchenette.

Well, just as you like?—It is much narrower than it is long. Isn't that correct?

Which would you like—a passage, a recess, a small room, or a kitchenette?—Well, seeing it is much narrower than it is long, I should call it a passage.

You know now, having seen the place of course, that you don't come into a passage at all; you come into a small room, and you have to go through a door?—Would you mind repeating exactly what I said, sir?

I think you know. Cruikshank, I will do it again. "There was no light on but I stumbled along and went along a passage"?—I stumbled along. You have just said I immediately came to a passage. How could I stumble along if I immediately came to a passage? "*And* stumbled along and came into a passage."

It is not what you said?—That is the words I used that I stumbled along and came into a passage. You are telling me I immediately came into a passage. What is the word "and" in it for?

That is what you want to say now? You went through a room? —I say the same as I said there.

You stumbled along and down a passage?—"And."

And came into a room on the right?—Correct.

And there was this live man, tied up in his chair, was he?— Well, I don't know if people make noises after they are dead. I have got no knowledge on that matter.

However, you think he was alive?—I formed that opinion; I can't swear to that.

At what you say must have been about nine o'clock?—I think I have already said it was between a quarter to nine and a quarter-past.

What you found somewhere between nine to a quarter-past nine in the basement of that house was a man apparently alive, tied up? —That is correct.

And alone?—I have got to swear that he was alone, in a dark room. If you want to be literal I can't swear he was alone. There

Ley and Smith.

Robert J. Cruikshank

may have been about half a dozen of his cronies or somebody else in the room, though I didn't see them.

Did he appear to be alone?—He appeared to me.

By the LORD CHIEF JUSTICE—How long were you in the room with him?—Well, your lordship, if you were to ask me how long a minute was I couldn't swear to it.

Of course you couldn't, but were you there an appreciable time?—Guessing at it, I should say I was there about a minute and a half, but if you were to test me on that I should probably fail.

Then perhaps we will say a minute?—It was a short time because always in the back of my mind was the idea——

You tell the jury you do not know whether there was anybody with him?—What I am trying to say is that he didn't have people round him. There may have been somebody lying hidden in the room in a recess, in a corner. I don't know about that, sir.

Cross-examination continued—It must have been a great shock to you, was it not?—No, I don't think it was.

Are you quite used to walking into empty basement rooms in the night and finding people tied up in chairs?—No, I don't think so.

Then may I venture——?—I mean to say I have just had six months walking round, and with a wife and two children——

I really cannot see what that has got to do with it. Were you shocked?—No. I wasn't shocked.

You thought it was quite a usual thing?—No; I was concerned with my own safety. I didn't really care—I know it is a callous thing to say—I didn't really care about the man tied up, because I have met so much callousness in regard to myself and my wife and children. At least he had a roof over his head.

He had a roof over his head, tied up, and gagged, and bound?—Yes.

You thought you might just as well leave him there and not say anything about it?—I don't know about that.

Is that right?—I just didn't toss it up in my mind like that.

Just answer that question?—I would like to have time to think about that.

By the LORD CHIEF JUSTICE—You see, Cruikshank, you had gone there, according to the story you are telling the jury, for a perfectly lawful purpose. You had gone to see Mr. Ley with the object of his getting you a passage to Australia. Not finding anybody at the front door, you go round to the back door which you find open; you

Evidence for the Prisoner Ley.

Robert J. Cruikshank

walk in; you see if you can find Mr. Ley. Instead of that you find a man bound and gagged—if there is any truth in the story you are telling us. You had gone there for a perfectly lawful purpose. Why not either release him, or go and tell someone that in an empty house there is a man found, gagged and bound?—I have already told this gentleman here—I am not trying to be impertinent; please understand that, sir—I told this gentleman that I understood there was a warrant for my arrest. I understood that the Metropolitan Police or the C.I.D. or anybody like that, they can be at a 'phone box in a matter of two minutes. Is that correct, or is it not, sir?

Well, go on. If you say the reason that you didn't tell anyone was because you were afraid you might be arrested that may be the answer?—That is the only thing I have done right through all this, and the reason that I kept away from the police and I eventually went to Mr. Barker was that, as is well known to the police and to the defence—I have never made a great secret of it—I haven't got a good record. My word is nothing; I am just an outcast; I have had convictions. I didn't want to get mixed up in it. It is nothing to me what happens in this case. By coming forward I have brought on myself the suspicion of my being bribed, corrupted. I have an impossible story to tell. I have got no witnesses. I have put myself in great danger by going into this box.

Re-examined by Sir WALTER MONCKTON—After you had given your statement to the gentleman sitting in front of me, Mr. Barker, at a later stage did you go round to Scotland Yard with Mr. Barker, or did the police come to you?—The police came to me.

Came to Mr. Barker's office?—Yes, sir.

And did you make to them a complete disclosure about the smuggling and your offences?—I told them everything I had done. The one offence I must have admitted to was going to the British Consul in Zürich and getting money by false pretences. I had money on me. I have laid myself open to half a dozen charges by coming forward.

Another thing I want to ask you about is this: do you know Ley personally at all?—Well, if the newspapers would like to make anything of it, I have shaken hands with Mr. Ley's son once.

You have never met Ley?—I never met anybody connected with this case, as far as I know, but if anybody can come forward and say they have seen me with or approach them, then I am guilty of perjury.

You say you had shaken hands with Ley's son?—Yes.

221

Ley and Smith.

Robert J. Cruikshank

Was that before or after you came forward to make your statement?—Afterwards. Thank you sir, I apologize if I have said anything wrong, sir.

Dr. CEDRIC KEITH SIMPSON, sworn, examined by Mr. HOWARD—I am a Doctor of Medicine, Member of the Royal College of Surgeons, Lecturer in Forensic Medicine to Guy's Hospital, and Senior Examiner in Forensic Medicine in the University of London, and have had some seventeen years' experience in that kind of medical work. Over this period I have carried out personally between 19,000 and 20,000 autopsies and examinations of this kind.

Have you seen a large number of cases of death from asphyxia caused by strangulation?—Yes, I have—a very large number of deaths from asphyxia of various kinds, including strangulation.

And we know that you were present with Dr. Gardner both at the chalk pit at Woldingham and also on the day after, 1st December, when the post-mortem was carried out?—Yes.

First of all, what do you say with regard to the arrangement of the rope round the body when it was found?—Without describing it in detail, I should say that the only part of this rope from which any sound conclusion could be drawn medically was that part round the neck.

By the LORD CHIEF JUSTICE—That was not quite what you were asked, Dr. Keith Simpson, I think. You were asked about the arrangement of the rope round the body when it was found?—I was asked what should I say *of* it, as I understood the question.

Examination continued—Are you telling my lord and the jury that the only arrangement of the rope from which you could draw any conclusion was that round the neck?—The only part from which I could draw any sound medical conclusion was, in my view, that round the neck.

What do you say with regard to the lie of the rope round the neck?—The lie of the rest of the rope, if I may complete the description of it, was that it was loose. It was tied in a series of knots, the details of which I recorded at the time. But it lay loosely on the front of and at the side of the body, and the rest of the rope lay loose either by the side of or behind the body, and there was no indication, in the lie of it, how, if it had been at all, the rope was tied round the body; no indication. There was nothing to suggest from what was seen then that it was tied round the body. It could have been, but there was nothing to suggest it was.

What about the lie of the marks round the neck?—The situation

Evidence for the Prisoner Ley.

Dr. C. Keith Simpson

of the marks round the neck was such as it not only commonly seen in suspension, but in my view speaks plainly for suspension, in this case from the left side.

By the LORD CHIEF JUSTICE—Would you say that again : "The situation of——"?—The situation, the lie——
The marks?—The marks of a noose—I can't even say it was a noose——
Of a noose?—Was such as speaks plainly for suspension. There was no mark of jerking or pulling, merely of tightening and suspension. There was nothing on the body to indicate whether this suspension was complete or incomplete.

Examination continued—Was there anything to indicate whether it was accidental, suicidal, or wilful strangulation?—There was nothing.

By the LORD CHIEF JUSTICE—But this body was lying in a trench in a chalk pit?—Yes, my lord. I am describing the conclusions I draw from this mark. One could *imagine* a great deal, but there was nothing to show—it had been lifted in some way at the left side of the neck, but how there was nothing to show.

Examination continued—Could you see anything or not to indicate whether or not the dead man had been unconscious before he was asphyxiated?—I found nothing to show that that was so, and no injury which in my view would be likely to cause unconsciousness. There were certain hæmorrhages on the surface of the brain——

By the LORD CHIEF JUSTICE—Do I understand that to mean this : that from your observation there was nothing to show he was unconscious; that the unconsciousness and death must have been caused by the tightening of the rope?—Yes, my lord. I found nothing to differ from that. If I may, I shall enlarge upon the injuries in order to substantiate that. There were certain hæmorrhages in the brain which are commonly seen in asphyxia, and which I attribute to asphyxia, and which might cause unconsciousness to develop, from asphyxia.

Examination continued—And in connexion with that, doctor, did you see the bruises and abrasions on the head?—Yes.
In your view were they necessarily the cause of the congestion of the brain or hæmorrhages of the brain which you describe?—In my view, and this was formed and recorded at the time, they had

223

Ley and Smith.

Dr. C. Keith Simpson

no connexion with it. I think it might help if I were to describe—
what I think was *not* described—the size of the bruises——

By the LORD CHIEF JUSTICE—Do you agree with Dr. Gardner
they were very small?—Yes.

Exactly?—There was none larger than an inch in diameter on
the brow. I should in my view describe them as trivial bruises and
in no sense in keeping with a rough and tumble of any violence.

Examination continued—Turning from the hæmorrhages to the
brain, did you examine the intestines?—Yes, I watched the intestines being examined by Dr. Gardner. I had every facility for
making these observation.

By the LORD CHIEF JUSTICE—I think you might just tell me,
Dr. Keith Simpson, were you there officially?—Yes, my lord. I
hold a Home Office appointment which results in my attending
autopsies for the police in that area.

Were you with Dr. Gardner?—Yes, my lord, and to make a
report in the form of a watching brief.

Examination continued—Dr. Gardner has agreed there was no
injury to the wall of the abdomen?—That is so, there was no injury
to the wall of the abdomen.

Is it possible or not in your view to attribute the discolouration
of the bowel to any particular cause?—Yes. First, I think it would
be simple and reasonable to exclude injury, local injury, being
responsible, for there was no injury to the wall of the abdomen;
there was no injury to the exterior of any part of the bowel; there
was no injury to the connective tissues of the bowel; and no injury
to the back wall of the abdomen. On those observations I could not
conceive of injury being responsible for the discolouration.
Secondly, in conditions of congestive death of many kinds, and
in particular in those accompanied by asphyxial changes, there is a
swelling and darkening of the blood vessels, the veins in particular,
a swelling of the vessels and darkening of the blood which is
pronounced where some mechanical force aids it, in this case, in
the head and neck by constriction, and less pronounced in the
stomach; and in this case I attribute this discolouration to this
common cause which was present, and I see no reason to imagine
any other cause, which had no foundation that I could see.

Finally, Dr. Keith Simpson, was there anything that you could
see or find necessarily to indicate that any serious violence had
been used before death?—No; the injuries found were in my view
trivial.

Evidence for the Prisoner Ley.

Dr. C. Keith Simpson

Cross-examined by Mr. HAWKE—Did you find in any of the evidence that you have discussed anything inconsistent with this man having been violently treated before death?—I found such trivial injuries——

Did you find anything inconsistent?—Yes; I should expect, if he was violently treated, injuries of the kind I see in beat-ups and the like.

The curious thing is, Dr. Keith Simpson—I do not know whether you were here when Dr. Gardner gave his evidence?—Yes.

Of course, we all know, but perhaps it should be said, he is a pathologist of great experience also?—Yes, he has had experience.

Did you hear him say that in his view this man showed signs —and he explained what they were—of having been beaten up before he was killed?—Yes, I did. I should describe that as a gross exaggeration, from what I found. I found only trivial bruises. I cannot see how that could be interpreted in the way described.

Did you take the view that the bruise on the head was of no consequence?—It was a trivial bruise on the brow.

Have you heard the evidence in this case, as well as Dr. Gardner's?—No; I have heard only Dr. Gardner's evidence.

We have been told by a man called Buckingham that before this man was tied up, a rug or blanket was thrown over his head. You will take that from me, I have no doubt?—I don't accept the evidence, but if you are going to base a question on it I shall answer it.

I am going to base a question on it?—What I mean is I don't necessarily accept that evidence.

By the LORD CHIEF JUSTICE—You are not asked if you accept the evidence, Dr. Keith Simpson. You are being put what has been said in this case and what you know quite well has been put in this case?—I accept that, my lord; I have not heard it.

Cross-examination continued—Supposing that had been done, and supposing with a blanket over his head that man was hit or received a blow on the head, you would expect, would you not, to find on the forehead less outward evidence of that blow, but considerable inside?—Yes, it would reduce the apparent weight of the injury to the exterior, but if the blow were of any weight I should expect to find some internal injury.

Yes, I was coming to that. Are you saying there was no internal injury consistent with a heavy blow on the head?—I saw nothing out of keeping with the effects of asphyxiation.

Ley and Smith.

Dr. C. Keith Simpson

Are you saying the discolouration of the brain fluid by blood is not evidence of head injury?—Yes, I am saying that it is commonly seen, it is accepted orthodox medical opinion, that it is likely to result from asphyxiation.

I must take that from you, with the only reservation that Dr. Gardner does not agree with you?—That is quoted commonly in the textbooks, and I am in agreement with it.

I have already said I must take it from you?—I think it is commonly accepted.

You say the view you take, that this is consistent with asphyxia and not with a blow on the head, is because the bruises and abrasions to the head were so trivial?—Yes.

Have you left something out? Please do not think for a moment I suggest intentionally. But have you forgotten something?— Perhaps you would like to put it.

I think I had better. Did you hear Dr. Gardner say the brain was bruised in two places?—Yes.

You have not mentioned that?—I think it is most misleading to describe the hæmorrhage on the surface of the brain as a bruise, under the circumstances.

He described blood in the brain fluid?—May I say——

I do not want to interrupt you. He went on to say these two lobes of the brain were bruised in two places, and he pointed out to the jury where they were?—Yes. What he and I saw—and there was no disagreement at the time—was that there was a hæmorrhage on the surface of the brain. Now a bruise is a hæmorrhage, but all hæmorrhages are not bruises. That is where I have differed, and I have not missed out anything. I am not accepting a hæmorrhage as a bruise. A bruise is a hæmorrhage, but there are many varieties of hæmorrhages.

You will appreciate that I said I was not suggesting for a, moment you missed out anything intentionally?—No. I think the misconception arises because it was not understood that this was a hæmorrage and not necessarily a bruise. Hæmorrhages on the surface of the brain are common in asphyxia, and that is in my view what they were here. Intense asphyxia was present, and I should expect the hæmorrhages I saw.

Whatever else you and Dr. Gardner may disagree about, you agree about this: that this man died of asphyxia?—Yes.

He died of asphyxia as a result of having, I would say *mainly* as a result of having, a rope tied tightly round his neck?—Drawn and lifted.

Evidence for the Prisoner Ley.

Dr. C. Keith Simpson

You can trust me not to leave anything out?—I am not trying to give the impression you are trying to trap me; I am merely anxious for accuracy.

You and I know each other too well for that. The rope had been tied tightly?—And lifted.

You want to add lifted?—Yes. That was the significant thing in this point.

Why?—Because in other cases it wouldn't necessarily cause death; it was the lifting that did it.

Quite, I agree. What caused him to be strangled was the upper lifting of the rope?—Yes.

There is nothing inconsistent with a person having come behind him or to the spot when he had the rope round his neck and giving it a pull up?—I should not agree with the word "pull." It had been lifted and maintained in a lifted position, not pulled in the sense of a jerk.

I follow what you mean because what you say is an asphyxial death would probably take some minutes?—Yes, with it maintained in that position.

It follows that it would be a sustained death?—Yes.

That is what you mean?—Yes.

If it was a sustained death, is it consistent with a sustained death by somebody pulling up the rope like that?—Not necessarily somebody.

Not necessarily somebody?—I don't think we have any evidence to show——

Not necessarily somebody?—No, I don't think there is any evidence.

Is it your theory this man was hanged?—I am not anxious to propound a theory; I am anxious if possible to draw proper conclusions from what I saw, and not to enlarge upon them.

When you made your report and Dr. Gardner his report, you did not know anything of the background of this thing at all?—No, and my report has remained the same as it was given on the day of the autopsy.

All you know was the man was found dead in this position in the trench?—Yes.

And, quite obviously if I may say so, you were there to draw what conclusion you could to assist the authorities?—Yes.

Did you find this man had been found with a rope round his neck which had been pulled tight and lifted?—Yes.

And that had killed him?—Yes.

Ley and Smith.

Dr. C. Keith Simpson

Leaving out, for the moment, if you will, anything that may or may not have happened to him before, that would be consistent with a man possibly having hanged himself?—Yes.

Knowing the facts, as you know them now, you do not think this man hanged himself, do you?—I think it is possible.

What—after he had been gagged and tied up with a rope?—I have nothing from my examination to show he had been.

We have got evidence?—I am trying to interpret my findings.

By the LORD CHIEF JUSTICE—Yes, but you know, doctor, you are being asked, as a man of common sense, having heard the facts in this case, do you think they point to suicide?—I saw nothing in the condition of the rope marks round the neck——

We are not asking you about that. We are asking you to take the whole facts of this case into account. Was there any trace of his having been hanged from a tree near where he was found?—There need be no traces left.

Were there trees there?—There were trees all round.

Was there any suggestion of that?—I made no search; a search was made. I am not suggesting there was. I am not suggesting he was hanged. I do wish to give my evidence so far as it is proper, not to give it further—not to have it drawn further.

What you are asked is, from what this man showed on his death was it consistent with his having been hanged from a tree?—From being suspended somewhere in some way; we have no evidence.

Having heard the evidence, do you think it is not inconsistent?—I say the disposition after death naturally aroused suspicion.

The LORD CHIEF JUSTICE—Well, at any rate we have got as far as that.

The WITNESS—I might make the additional statement that suspicion has often arisen where the death has been natural.

Cross-examination continued—It is not unknown that people sometimes like to tie themselves up and perhaps do it a bit too tightly and kill themselves?—Yes, I have experienced that.

I suppose what you found was equally consistent with that?—Yes.

You don't think it happened?—I say it is equally consistent.

Do you think that man gagged himself and tied himself up and put a rope round his neck?—I have no evidence——

Evidence for the Prisoner Ley.

Dr. C. Keith Simpson

By the LORD CHIEF JUSTICE—Of course you have not. You are asked from what you have heard now, do you think this man, whose body was found in a chalk pit in a prepared trench on that night, tied himself up and hanged himself?—My lord, I think the answer to that is I do not know.

Well, if you don't know, say so?—I think the circumstances are suspicious. I do not know.

The LORD CHIEF JUSTICE—I think so far anyone would agree with you.

Cross-examination continued—I think I must ask you one other matter. Dr. Gardner had the view that not only had this man an injury to his hip before he died but also a considerable injury to his abdomen?—Dr. Gardner took the view that that was an injury after death

No. Forgive me——?—May I have the evidence of the Court below?

May I put to you his evidence?—In my opinion I took the view that it was caused before death, or close to death.

Dr. Keith Simpson, you took the view that it was before death. Why do you say you formed the opinion that it was caused before death?—I thought it was in common with the other injuries sustained before death.

So did Dr. Gardner. May I just remind you of his evidence: "There was a very extreme congestion of the intestines with hæmorrhage in the stomach and upper part of the small intestine. I thought the appearance indicated that there had been a blow on the abdomen such as might occur from a raised knee in the course of a struggle." Then he goes on to talk about something else, and then he says: "In my opinion the injuries I have described had been caused before death"?—I have not heard this evidence given in Court.

Mr. HAWKE—Well, Dr. Keith Simpson, I confess I am reading from the deposition, but I examined Dr. Gardner from it, and I think I remember what he said.

The LORD CHIEF JUSTICE—He also put it that the injury could have been caused by someone falling upon him.

Mr. HAWKE—Yes, I remember asking that question—and before death.

Ley and Smith.

Dr. C. Keith Simpson

The LORD CHIEF JUSTICE—Injuries all before death.

Mr. HAWKE—There is no question, as your lordship's note has just been read.

The WITNESS—Yes, my lord, I accept it. It was the only point over which we differed at the original autopsy. I formed the opinion it was before death, and Dr. Gardner formed the view that it was after death; it was a trivial point in my view.

Mr. HAWKE—He did not say that either before the learned magistrate or here.

The LORD CHIEF JUSTICE—He described it as "like crimson velvet."

Cross-examination continued—There is one last matter that I feel I must ask you. I know you saw part of the intestine being removed, but did you see Dr. Gardner remove the whole of it?—Yes.

Did you see, when it had been removed, the whole intestine?—Yes, and I watched its examination from beginning to end.

Well, let me put his evidence to you. Do you agree that "The discolouration of the intestines was the most marked amount I have ever seen"?—Yes.

"The congestion could not have happened after death. I took out the entire intestine, opened it from one end to the other, and the whole mucuous membrane was like crimson velvet"?—Yes.

Do you agree with that?—Yes.

By the LORD CHIEF JUSTICE—Was that violence or not?—No. I see that in asphyxia deaths, and descriptions like that occur in the standard textbooks of asphyxia deaths. I should not accept that as evidence of a blow.

At any rate you and he are agreed that the cause of death was asphyxia due to that rope?—Yes.

Re-examined by Sir WALTER MONCKTON—My friend put to you that when you and Dr. Gardner examined this body by the chalk pit you did not know the background—when you saw him on the spot you did not know the background of evidence; is that right?—We knew nothing about it.

Did you both then form the views which you then expressed upon the basis of scientific medical evidence alone?—Well, I formed

Evidence for the Prisoner Ley.

Dr. C. Keith Simpson

the views that I have now expressed. They were recorded and sent to the police that day. I have not differed from them, and at that time Dr. Gardner did not disagree with them.

Are you basing your evidence, as I put to you, upon the medical symptoms and phenomena?—No; I wish to interpret what I saw fairly; the scientific evidence in my view should be quite impartial.

By the LORD CHIEF JUSTICE—Tell me this quite shortly: you differ in nothing except that Dr. Gardner thinks that violence other than the rope, other than the strangulation, had been used before death, and you think it had not?—I think that is put too broadly.

Well, I ask you?—The significant point of difference in my view is this: he interpreted the brain hæmorrhages as evidence of a blow to the head likely to cause unconsciousness, and I attribute them to asphyxia.

As I say, the only difference between you, really, is Dr. Gardner thinks there was some violence used to the body of the man before he died, and you are not suggesting——?—I think the amount of violence and the words used by Dr. Gardner are gross exaggeration. I use these words with care.

Whether or not it makes any difference in the case I do not know?—I found only trivial bruises, and the rest asphyxial effects.

The LORD CHIEF JUSTICE—The difference between you, to use a common expression, is whether he was beaten up before death.

Dr. FRANCIS EDWARD CAMPS, sworn, examined by Mr. HOWARD—I am a Doctor of Medicine, Consulting Pathologist to the Essex County Council, and Lecturer in Forensic Medicine to the London Hospital. In the course of my experience I have seen very many cases of death from asphyxia and have conducted numerous post-mortem examinations upon them.

What effects do you expect to find upon the brain surface and ventricles of the brain in deaths from asphyxia?—The whole picture of asphyxia is one of congestion and blueness, that is to say, lack of oxygen in the blood. The effect of this congestion is first of all to distend the veins, and, secondly, to increase the permeability, that is to say the power of passage through the wall of the vein, of the blood; and the result of that is that you find a picture of acute hæmorrhage, and that will occur in other organs besides the brain.

One effect of asphyxia is acute congestion and hæmorrhage in the brain?—Yes.

What do you expect to find with regard to the intestines?—

231

Ley and Smith.

Dr. Francis E. Camps

Again you will find a similar picture of congestion, and also hæmorrhages may occur.

Cross-examined by Mr. HAWKE—Did you see this intestine?— No.

Opening Speech for the Prisoner Smith.

Mr. Curtis Bennett, in his opening remarks for the defendant Smith, informed the jury that the defence of his client was a very different one from that put forward on behalf of Ley. Smith's defence was founded on the statement made by him to the police, a statement which the Crown had described as "conspicuous for its frankness, up to a point," and as a version of the kidnapping of Mudie which was "a more probable version than" Buckingham's account. Why "frank up to a point"? Why should not his whole version be accepted? Smith was now going into the witness box and would repeat that version on oath. Naturally it would be in greater detail, as there were more facts to be dealt with, but in essence the facts he would give would be the same story that he always had told. With regard to the motor car, the registration number of which contained the figures 101, and the visit to the chalk pit on 27th November, Smith would deny that he was ever at that chalk pit upon that day, and he would say where he was. But what of the "101"? To say, "I took the number of a car, and it was 101," surely was meaningless. A car's number consisted of *letters* and numerals. It was more customary now for these letters and numbers to consist of a combination of either two letters and four numerals, *e.g.*, L A 1010, or three letters and one, two, or three numerals, such as F G P 101. If someone said, "I have taken the car's number, it was F G P" one would say, "Well, what of it?" It could be F G P 1 or F G P 999 or any number in between. So here—"101"—it was 101 what? It might be anything— A B C 101, A C B 101, and so on through the alphabet. No evidence was available as to how far down the alphabet cars numbered 101 had got, but if it was worked out from the permutations and combinations of the letters of the alphabet then it was clear that there might well be a great many cars with the numbers 101, and it was not unreasonable to say that a number of them might well be "small black Fords." This, of course, left out entirely the question as to whether the two witnesses who had spoken of seeing the car at the chalk pit on 27th November had in fact taken the car's number correctly in their mind's eye at the time they saw

Opening Speech for the Prisoner Smith.

Mr. Curtis Bennett

it. One of these two witnesses had picked out a man at the identification parade who was not at the chalk pit at all, and this went to show how dangerous it was to accept such evidence from honest and well-meaning, but possibly mistaken people.

Evidence for the Prisoner Smith.

LAWRENCE JOHN SMITH, sworn, examined by Mr. CURTIS BENNETT —Do you live at 39 Belvoir Road, East Dulwich?—Yes.

Have you ever been to the chalk pit at Woldingham?—Never.

Was there ever to your knowledge a plot to murder Mudie?— Not to my knowledge.

Did you ever take any part in killing him?—No.

You are a joiner by occupation, are you not, and I think your wages are £7 5s. to £7 10s. a week?—Yes, £7 10s. I had as well a lodging allowance of £1, and travelling expenses.

Did you serve in the Royal Air Force during the war?—Yes.

Had you any gratuity when you came out of that service?—Yes, I had £32 odd.

Do you come from Leicester?—Yes.

In November, 1946, you were working at 5 Beaufort Gardens? —Yes.

Had you in mind any change of occupation?—Not in occupation, but in going away out of the country. I was thinking of South Africa.

Since when did you think about going to South Africa to become a joiner?—Quite some considerable time before.

Before you met Mr. Ley?—Hardly, no.

Did you make some inquiries about it, and also about going to New Zealand?—Yes.

On 17th December of this year you made a statement, Exhibit 20, to the police. Is the substance of it true?—Yes, definitely.

Did you express a wish to help the police all you could?—Yes.

Is your version of Ley's antipathy to Mrs. Brook's supposed lovers true?—Yes.

Is it true, as you say, that Ley wanted Mudie, whom he finally had sent along, brought up to London to his house to extract a confession from him, to pay him £500 and let him get out of the country?—Yes.

Is it true that you played your part in bringing Mudie up?— That is right.

Is Buckingham right when he says the first scheme, which was his scheme, was to be a question of drunkenness?—Yes.

233

Ley and Smith.

Lawrence J. Smith

Did Ley reject that?—That is right.

Was Buckingham right in saying that the second scheme, again his scheme, was finally adopted, of decoying Mudie up there without violence?—Yes.

Did Mr. Ley tell you how he wanted Mudie left at Beaufort Gardens?—Yes. He wanted him left tied and gagged.

So you knew that involved that?—Yes.

Is your account, and indeed Buckingham's account, of how Mudie was in fact decoyed up correct?—Yes, definitely.

First of all, when was that scheme finally settled upon and determined to operate?—On the Wednesday night, the 27th.

You say on page 3 of your statement: "On Tuesday, 26th, Buckingham told me that arrangements had been made by . . ."?—Yes; they were partly arranged on the 26th.

What time was it that Ley was to expect the party to arrive?—Round about 6.30.

At any time did you see Ley counting out money into packets?—Yes.

When was that?—Just some time before, actually—by the way, I would like to correct my statement now.

Well, correct it?—That I counted out £200 for Mr. Ley and put them into an envelope on the Monday night, either the 17th or 18th.

Let me just read what you say: "The following day I mentioned this scheme to Ley"—that was the drunkenness scheme?—Yes.

"But he disagreed with it, saying that there would not be time to get Mudie to London and get the statement before he would be missed at the Hotel and there would be ructions. It was this day that I knew how much Buckingham and I were going to be paid if we got Mudie to London. I saw Mr. Ley at his address and he had two bundles of notes which he asked me to count. He asked me to check each bundle and I saw that they contained £200 each. He said, 'This is here when you bring Mudie in. You will be able to collect your money and go right away.' He then put the money in two separate envelopes." Is that the substance of what was said? —That is what I said at the time.

Is that right?—No. There was only one envelope at that time. That was for you, was it?—No, for Buckingham, actually.

By the LORD CHIEF JUSTICE—Did you put the whole £400 in it?—No, only £200.

Examination continued—And that was Buckingham's?—Yes.

Evidence for the Prisoner Smith.

Lawrence J. Smith

When did you know you were going to get £200?—I knew then I was going to get £200.

Did you see him count it?—Yes.

When did you see the £200 for yourself counted out?—On the morning of the 28th.

I think you met Mrs. Brook. I suppose you met her through Buckingham?—Yes.

Did you know her at all?—Never till then.

Had you ever met Mudie at all?—No, never.

Therefore, it follows you had no grievance against him of any sort?—Not a thing.

You got up to Beaufort Gardens a little later than you intended, about 6.50?—Yes.

Having earlier that day purchased a clothes line from Farmer Brothers, Montpelier Street?—Yes.

Are you known there?—Yes, by sight; I go there very often.

You heard the statement read which you made yourself. Is your account of what happened when you got to Beaufort Gardens correct as given in Exhibit 20?—Yes, that is right.

I want to know a little about the back door of the basement— we know the geography about it. It has bolts on the inside, has it not?—Yes.

What about the front area door? I have not heard about that. Does that have bolts on it?—Yes, that also has bolts.

When the workmen go away in the evenings in what condition is the basement left?—Always bolted up and locked up.

That is to say, the basement door locked, the front area door bolted and the basement door bolted too?—Yes, either bolted or the two locks put on.

In other words, after the workmen went would it be possible to get into the basement unless you were let in?—Impossible.

And impossible to get into the ground floor unless you had got the key. Supposing you had the key and could get into the ground floor, could you go into the basement?—Yes.

After the workmen had gone?—Only if you had the key of Mr. Ley's flat.

Why?—Because that would be the only door leading in there to lead to the basement. There is another lock in the basement door leading down the stairs from Mr. Ley's flat to the basement.

How is that door kept after the workmen have gone?—So far as I know it was locked at night.

Did you plan with Buckingham that after the delivery of Mudie you were going to "The Crown and Sceptre" to have a drink?— Yes.

Ley and Smith.

Lawrence J. Smith

When he came in did you grab Mudie round the waist?—Yes.

Did Buckingham throw a rug over his head?—Yes.

Did you tie him up?—Yes.

How was he fetched from where he was to the room where he was left?—He was assisted along the passage by Buckingham.

Did anything happen going along that stone corridor?—Yes, as Buckingham got to the end of the passage he stumbled and fell with Mudie.

Who was beneath?—Mudie, definitely was beneath.

Mudie stumbled, Buckingham on top of him?—That is right. Mudie was being helped along, and his legs were together and Buckingham overbalanced with him.

Was he eventually taken into that room we have heard described and set down in a chair?—Yes.

What did you do then?—I went into the front room of the basement and got the rag to gag Mudie with.

That is Exhibit 13?—Yes, that is the rag.

Buckingham has said he took the rug off the man's head. What did he do then?—He pulled the rug off Mudie's head and placed the gag under Mudie's head and tied it behind his head.

Mudie was left then, was he not?—Yes.

And apart from the fall, uninjured?—Yes, uninjured.

When you came into the corridor or passage had you seen Ley? —Yes.

Where had he come from?—He was there when we came into the flat.

When you came into the passage?—We had to knock on Mr. Ley's door to get in.

You came in from the front, so you met Ley before you came into the basement to take up your position?—Yes.

He was there, and he let you down into the basement?—Yes.

Did he say anything?—No; just rather nervous, or seemed nervous at the time and that was all there was to it.

Where did you see him after that time?—He was standing on the stairs, leading through to the ground floor.

Did he say anything to you?—Yes, he told me that his end had slipped up that he would like me to hang on for a moment or two, but when Buckingham didn't stay——

By the LORD CHIEF JUSTICE—What did he mean by, "his end had slipped up"?—I understood he was having somebody come there to help him get the statement.

Evidence for the Prisoner Smith.

Lawrence J. Smith

Examination continued—You say in the statement he said: "'Will you hang on a little while as my end has slipped up.' By this I took it that he wanted me to hang on after Mudie had been tied up, as he said, 'There is no need for Buckingham to stay. Let him push off.' Then he handed me an envelope saying, 'Put this in your pocket, I have got Buckingham's here.' I knew the envelope contained the money. I told Buckingham that Ley wanted me to hold on as his people hadn't turned up"?—Yes, that is right.

"I told him that I didn't want to as I had made arrangements with Buckingham to go out and have a drink afterwards. I heard the car pull up at the back door and we again took up our positions." Then you describe what you have been telling us on oath now. After the gagging did Ley come down with anything for Buckingham?—He gave Buckingham an envelope.

Did he say anything to him?—Yes, he told him to put that in his pocket, and he shook hands with him and told him not to contact him until things had died down.

And you let Buckingham out the back door?—Yes.

How long did you stay after letting Buckingham out?—Roughly ten minutes.

Were you alone?—Talking to Mr. Ley at the bottom of the stairs where he was when he gave us the money.

Did you go into the room again where Mudie was tied up?—No.

What happened after five or ten minutes?—I heard, and also I think Mr. Ley heard, some steps coming in up the front steps. Mr. Ley told me to go along then as his friends were arriving. I went out the basement door, the front area, while Mr. Ley went back up the stairs to his own flat.

I think we know you got into your car and went and had a look at "The Crown and Sceptre" to see if Buckingham's car was there?—Yes.

And finding it was not there did not go in?—No.

Where did you go to?—I went to the public-house nearest my lodgings, the "Grove" public-house at Dulwich, and went home.

What time did you leave the public-house?—As near as I could say between a quarter to 10 and 10 o'clock.

What sort of time did you get home?—Round 10 o'clock; it was right beside the public-house.

You went to bed?—Yes.

Did you have anything to do with the taking or conveying of the live body or dead body of Mudie to Woldingham?—No.

Ley and Smith.

Lawrence J. Smith

Had you been to Woldingham the day before with this car you had hired?—No.

What were you doing on the day before, namely, the 27th?—I was at work.

What time did you stop work?—The usual time, five o'clock or just after.

Where did you go from work?—To Mostyn Road, to Buckingham's.

And you spent the rest of the evening either there or at "The Green Man"?—Yes.

So whoever's car it was at the chalk pit on the 27th it definitely was not yours?—Definitely not.

You have been in the habit of hiring cars?—Yes.

You hired this particular car, we know, on Monday, 25th, from someone whom you had not dealt with before. Why was that?——

By the LORD CHIEF JUSTICE—When did you hire cars before for your work?—Several time before, my lord.

A week at a time?—No, never a week at a time, for two days perhaps and week-ends, and that sort of stuff.

Did your employers pay you for that, give you that as an allowance?—No, it was for my own convenience I used to have it.

Examination continued—Why did you not use your usual people on this occasion?—The car I usually hired from them, or the car they had to hire, was already let out for a fortnight.

And Ley rang up his people?—That is right.

When was it that the arrangement to hire a car for a week was first spoken of on the telephone to Howard's?—It would be the week before the 28th.

Was it a few days before the actual hiring took place?—Yes.

The hiring took place on Monday, 25th. It was the week before?—The Wednesday or Thursday before.

Why for a week on this occasion and not just two odd days?—Well, I wanted a car for running about.

Were you going to do anything particular with it?—No, nothing particular at all actually.

Were you not, towards the end of the week?—At the end of the week I was definitely going to Leicester for the week-end.

By the LORD CHIEF JUSTICE—You say you had never hired one before for more than a couple of days. Why did you hire it on Monday for the whole week?—For the simple reason I was let

Evidence for the Prisoner Smith.

Lawrence J. Smith

down on the car that I used to have and I thought I would make sure of it this time.

Why did you want it for your work?—It was not for my work; it was for the week-end.

I thought you said you had hired it for your work, for a couple of days, and that sort of thing?—I used it for my work.

You were working at Beaufort Gardens?—But there are occasions when I have to go to the office for another job.

There was a 'bus I suppose?—There was a 'bus, definitely.

Who paid for this car?—I did.

£29?—Yes.

Did Ley lend you the money?—No.

A lot of money for a working man, hiring a car for a week, even if he was going to get £15 back. Had you got all that money to put down?—Yes.

Did you know at that time a large sum of money was coming from Ley?—I knew at about that time.

Examination continued—You have already told the Court you knew if you brought Mudie up to London you would get £200?—Yes.

Had you the money as well to make up the £29 and forfeit the £15?—Yes, I didn't care.

By the Lord Chief Justice—Were you hiring this car for the purpose of effecting what Ley wanted you to do?—No, not actually at all.

Examination continued—If you brought Mudie up you knew you would have access to £200?—Yes.

Had the going to Leicester for a week-end anything to do with hiring the car?—That was the main purpose.

When did you arrange to go to Leicester?—The week previous, on the Wednesday or Thursday.

Did you ask any person to fix accommodation for you?—Yes, a Mrs. Gray, and I wrote to her to book a room at an hotel for me.

By the Lord Chief Justice—Where did you keep the car?—On the Monday and Tuesday of that week it was in a garage at Goose Green, and on the Wednesday and Thursday, it was outside the house where I lived at 39 Belvoir Road, Dulwich.

Left in the road?—Yes.

Was it there when you got back at night?—It was there at night.

On the 27th did you use it to go up to London?—Yes.

Ley and Smith.

Lawrence J. Smith

Where was it during the day of the 27th?—At Beaufort Gardens.
All day?—Yes.

Standing outside?—Standing outside; there was a car park.

No one had stolen it?—Well, I had the key in my pocket.

As far as you knew it stood outside there all the day long?—
Yes.

Examination continued—Of course, you were aware that in
hiring the car you had signed your name to a document which had
the number on it, and that when you came back you signed another
document saying you had returned it?—Yes.

You got the £15 back, so in fact it cost you £14?—That is
correct.

When did you next see Ley after going away to Leicester and
returning on Monday?—Monday, 2nd December—I saw him at
Beaufort Gardens the same day.

What did he tell you, if anything, about what had happened to
Mudie?—He didn't say anything had happened to Mudie. He
only said everything had gone off quite all right. He also added
that Mudie had been dropped at Wimbledon.

By the LORD CHIEF JUSTICE—Did he say who by?—No, he
didn't.

Did you not have any curiosity to ask him?—No.

He was dropped off at Wimbledon and you didn't ask him
anything?—No.

Examination continued—Did you pass on that information to
Buckingham?—Yes.

Buckingham says that you told him that Mudie had made a
confession, had been paid £500, and was going out of the country.
Did you tell him that?—No, I didn't.

Had you told him previously that that was the idea?—Yes.

Had Mr. Ley made any comment to you about hiring motor
cars? You were hiring cars quite frequently about this time?—
Yes. He asked me if I had ever thought of having one myself. I
told him I couldn't afford one myself and he offered to lend me
the money to buy one.

That was the £300 on 4th December?—Yes.

Of course, the car would be for use in your business as well
as pleasure I suppose?—Yes.

Did you take any steps to acquire a car?—Yes, I did; I had
made one or two inquiries.

Evidence for the Prisoner Smith.

Lawrence J. Smith

By the LORD CHIEF JUSTICE—What prevented you, or what made you change your mind?—I made some inquiries about going abroad to South Africa and I had a definite arrangement, or almost a definite arrangement, for going abroad, so therefore wouldn't want the car.

When you took the £300 did you mean to use it for buying a car?—Yes.

You changed your mind very quickly?—No.

Examination continued—You changed your mind in five days. Why?—Because within that five days I had made inquiries at South Africa House.

When you originally got Mr. Ley's cheque for £300 you opened an account with it?—Yes, that is right.

You took the money out on the 9th and sought to pay it back through Miss Ingleson?—Yes, that is right.

And paid it back to Ley?—Yes.

What did you say to him?—I told him I had no use for the money, and thanked him for it and that I was thinking of going abroad and didn't need the money.

I suppose the suggestion was that—I do not know what the suggestion was—that you were paid that £300 for being a further party to the murder of Mudie. Any truth in that?—None whatever.

Were you a party to a murder plot at the price of £200, or the price of £500, or any other price?—Never.

When I said £500, I was adding the £300 on to the £200. Was your idea to go abroad to avoid the consequences of this?—Oh no, definitely not.

Did you return the money because you were frightened to hold on to it?—No.

Is all you have told us the truth?—Definitely.

The LORD CHIEF JUSTICE—Members of the jury, just let me explain one thing to you. Mr. Hawke has said to you, when he was opening the case, quite correctly, that Smith's statement was not evidence against Ley. That was perfectly true then. It now becomes evidence against both of them, because Smith has gone into the box and given evidence. A statement which a man makes before he goes into the box is only evidence against himself, because the other side has no opportunity of cross-examining, and it is not given on oath; but as soon as the person who has made the statement goes into the witness box and is sworn and says that the statement is true, it becomes evidence in the case both against

Ley and Smith.

Lawrence J. Smith

himself and against anybody else who is involved in that statement, because Sir Walter Monckton now has the privilege of cross-examining Smith. That statement is now evidence in the case against both prisoners.

Cross-examined by Sir WALTER MONCKTON—In your statement where you describe what you say happened when Mudie was brought into 5 Beaufort Gardens you say: "Ley and I stood talking for about ten minutes during which time neither of us went in to see how Mudie was. I could see from Ley's attitude that he was expecting someone to call. I heard somebody coming up the steps to the front door and Ley said 'All right you can go now.' I went out by way of the basement door at the front and when I got to the top of the stairs I could not see anyone. I heard the front door close." When you went outside did you have to unbolt anything?—No.

The door from the basement was not bolted?—Not at that time.

You went out, and that is all you know about it?—That is right.

How long had you known Buckingham?—For a matter of two months, I should say.

You had got to know each other pretty well, had you not?—Well, pretty well.

I mean, you went to his house?—Yes.

And you went about together to public-houses?—Yes, on one or two occasions.

You were frequently in each other's company?—I wouldn't say frequently.

So far as Ley was concerned, he was the owner of the house at which you were working?—Yes.

And you saw him from time to time because he was in the house and you were working there?—I saw him every day several times.

On the story that you have told now upon oath both you and Buckingham were prepared to do what you described for £200?—Yes.

And you each knew when you set about it what you were going to get?—Yes.

And you went into it together on that footing, £200 a-piece, and expenses?—Well, when we started on it we didn't know what we were going to get, the exact amount.

You knew you were going to get something substantial?—Yes.

Evidence for the Prisoner Ley.

Lawrence J. Smith

You were going to share it equally?—We were going to get the same.

For which each of you were prepared to do this—tie up and gag this man?—That is right.

You say that Ley was the man who was producing the £200 for each of you?—Yes.

You have heard him deny before my lord and the jury that he had anything to do with it at all?—Yes, I have.

Of course, to the extent to which it is thrown on him you may feel some of the responsibility goes from you?—No, I am definitely responsible for getting Mudie to Beaufort Gardens.

I put it to you that it is quite untrue that Ley had anything to do with this at all?—It is quite true.

That is what he said, and you heard it said?—Yes.

There are your stories, each told on oath?—Yes.

Cross-examined by Mr. HAWKE—It is a little difficult to follow. Did you know Mudie at all?—Not at all.

Had you any interest in Mudie?—None whatever.

Did you know, until you were told, that he was at the Reigate Hill Hotel?—I didn't know anything about him until told by Mr. Ley.

Did Buckingham?—As far as I know, no.

Incidentally, did you ever tell Buckingham, as Ley suggested in the box that you did, that Ley had been down to Wimbledon and had got Mrs. Brook at half-past two in the morning and brought her to Cromwell Road?—I told Buckingham that.

Well, I confess I am surprised at that. That was right, was it? —Yes.

Ley had told you that he had been down to Wimbledon, that he had got this woman, Mrs. Brook, out of the house at half-past two, and brought her to London?—Yes.

And put her in West Cromwell Road?—No; actually he told me he spent a miserable night at 16 Knightsbridge Court, because there was no furniture in the room.

Did he tell you anything more?—He told me Mrs. Brook was in such a very distressed state she couldn't sit down for several days, refused to see her own doctor.

Did he tell you that in connexion with Mudie then?—He didn't, no. He told me that in connexion with Mrs. Brook's son-in-law.

He told you that Mrs. Brook's son-in-law was the cause of this really shocking condition Mrs. Brook was in which caused him to bring her up to London?—He thought it was.

243

Ley and Smith.

Lawrence J. Smith

Did he tell you of any other suspicions at all he had with regard to Mrs. Brook?—Yes, he thought she was being familiar——

Yes, you said all that in your statement. I am anxious not to go over the ground again. Apparently he was telling you her son-in-law was responsible for some condition of hers from which she could not sit down?—Yes.

That is not blackmail, is it?—Well, I put it this way——

It is pretty clear what he meant, I suppose?—Oh, yes.

Did he say that sort of thing about anybody else as well as accusing them of blackmail?—Yes, he had suspicions of other people as well.

Was Mudie one of them?—Mudie was one.

As a matter of fact, he started off by having suspicions of a man called Romer, did he not?—Yes.

And then after a bit he told you that he was wrong about that, and that the man he was really after was Mudie?—Yes.

And that is how it all started?—Yes.

In your examination you said that the scheme was finally decided upon on Wednesday, 27th November, but that it was partly arranged on 26th November. What was finally arranged on Wednesday, 27th November?—The definite day that Mudie was being brought to London.

On the 26th was it arranged that Mrs. Bruce should go down and get young Buckingham to go with her, and so on?—No; that was done previously, but the final arrangements were made on the Wednesday.

What was partly arranged on the Tuesday?—The arrangements for the Tuesday were that Mrs. Bruce, I think, was waiting to hear when Mudie's day off was; she was not sure.

You were waiting to hear before you decided which day to go down, and it was finally decided on 27th November, Wednesday?—Yes.

What time on Wednesday, 27th November?—Well, we were discussing it pretty well all night, and I must say that we called for Mrs. Bruce about as near as I could say a quarter to seven to seven o'clock.

By the LORD CHIEF JUSTICE—The discussion was with Buckingham?—Buckingham was in the discussion.

Where did it take place?—In "The Green Man" public-house at Putney.

Cross-examination continued—Had you seen Buckingham that

244

Evidence for the Prisoner Smith.

Lawrence J. Smith

evening?—I had called for Buckingham at Brixton and then driven over to "The Green Man."

What were you driving?—A Ford 8, the car I had got on hire.

That is the same car that you were driving on the following day, the Thursday, and that you handed back eventually to Normanton on the following Monday?—Yes.

You were driving that car on Wednesday then?—On Wednesday evening, yes.

It is a small black Ford?—Yes, an 8 h.p.

It has got a number plate in the middle at the back?—As far as I recollect, yes.

And the numbers on it are 101?—I didn't recollect at the time the police asked me, but I have no doubt about it now.

You told us that Ley said after all this was over that Mudie had been dropped at Wimbledon?—Yes.

Mudie was living at the Reigate Hill Hotel, was not he, and you had collected him from there?—Yes.

You have heard the evidence now. You know Mudie had not been to Wimbledon for weeks and he had nothing to do with Wimbledon?—Yes.

Are you sure Ley did not say to you, "Mudie has been dropped at Woldingham"?—Yes, he definitely said Wimbledon.

You do not think you could be mistaken?—No.

You know now that Mudie had nothing to do with Wimbledon? —Mudie had.

At that time?—At that time, no. If you will pardon me, Mr. Ley told me he had heard Mudie spent his half days in Wimbledon and he had a friend in Wimbledon.

Have you ever said that before?—I have not said it before, no.

By the LORD CHIEF JUSTICE—You mean that after all this had taken place, he had been gagged and bound and so forth, he was taken back to a place where he had friends?—No.

You told us that he was taken to a place where you had been previously told he had a friend?—He was taken to Wimbledon, but it was the previous week Ley had told me Mudie had told him he spent his half days in Wimbledon.

Cross-examination continued—It goes a little further than that. You had been told by Ley that this man was blackmailing an elderly woman and her daughter who lived at Wimbledon, and he was to be brought up to London in order to sign a confession or some statement to stop him from blackmailing?—Yes.

Ley and Smith.

Lawrence J. Smith

Do you mean to say that Ley said he had been sent back to Wimbledon where he had been blackmailing two women?—Yes.

Did it strike you as rather extraordinary?—No.

Did you ask any questions about it?—No.

You are still quite certain he said Wimbledon?—Yes.

By the LORD CHIEF JUSTICE—Were you not rather anxious to know whether any harm had come to Mudie?—No, I didn't——

You had left him alone in this house in a basement room, bound and gagged?—He wasn't alone, my lord.

Well, with Ley?—Yes.

Mudie, who you regarded as an enemy of Ley?—Yes.

And when Ley tells you he has been dropped at Wimbledon you ask no questions?—No.

Cross-examination continued—I understand you to say when you left this place Mudie was in the chair, tied up and gagged?—Yes.

And that was all?—That is all.

If anybody put a rope round his neck that was later, was it?— It must have been.

You say you heard somebody coming up to the front door. Did you see who that was?—No, I didn't.

Were you not interested at all?—Not at all.

This was the man who, you told us, was there to try and get a statement?—He was to help Ley to get the statement.

Did you know what that meant—getting the statement?—Not at all.

Did it strike you that possibly it meant a little force being used to get it?—Well, that may sound callous, but it didn't interest me at the time. To be quite candid I was quite glad to be done with what I had done and get away from it.

Before this man was ever in the chair at all he had been tied up, gagged, and helped along the passage?—Yes.

How was that done?—Well, he was tied up and a rug over his head and Buckingham had held his arms from behind. Buckingham bounced him along the passage—sort of half lifted him along, and Buckingham lost his balance.

He tumbled, he lost his balance?—Yes.

Buckingham on top of him?—Yes, either on top—they fell together.

Which do you think?—I should imagine that by Mudie being lifted he was underneath.

Evidence for the Prisoner Smith.

Lawrence J. Smith

We have heard from the doctor that he did not suffer any injury to his stomach. Do you think Buckingham fell on top of him?—Well, if he fell on top of him, Mudie——

Do not say "if" he did. I said did he—you were there?—Mudie fell down definitely, and he fell face downwards with Buckingham behind him.

Do you think it is likely that Buckingham fell on top?—Either on top or at the side, because it was then at the turn at the door.

By the Lord Chief Justice—Mudie could not move at all except by being propelled?—No.

He was rigid?—No, his feet were together.

And his arms?—Yes.

He was trussed up?—Yes.

Cross-examination continued—Completely helpless. And he said, according to you, "You are stifling me"?—Yes.

And the answer he got to that was, "You are breathing your last"?—That was only said in a joking form.

Tremendously funny, do you think?—Well, it was done——

You seem to think it was. You think it was extremely humorous?—No, not extremely humorous, but it was done to frighten this man.

You were each to get £200 for your work?—Yes.

One of you had put a rug over his head, and the wretched man said, "You are stifling me"; is that right?—Yes.

Tell me if I am wrong. And then one of you said, "You are breathing your last"?—Yes.

Did you say that was just a joke?—That was said in a joking form.

By the Lord Chief Justice—You left him in a room?—Yes.

How long were you in the house after he was taken to the room?—I was in the house after he had been tied up roughly ten minutes.

Did you ever look to see if that man was being stifled?—No, but the rug wasn't over his head then, the rug had been taken off his head.

Cross-examination continued—And the gag had been put on?—Yes, the gag was there.

You know Minden, the hall porter of the Royal Hotel at Woburn Place?—I have seen him; I know of him.

247

Ley and Smith.

Lawrence J. Smith

Was he the person who was responsible for getting you and Buckingham together?—Yes.

You heard his evidence, of course?—Yes.

Is that true?—That is definitely true.

Re-examined by Mr. CURTIS BENNETT—Mr. Hawke expressed some surprise that you were saying that Ley had told you about fetching Mrs. Brook up from Wimbledon?—Yes.

Look at page 1 in the statement. I do not know why Mr. Hawke is surprised at all: "He said that one night he was called out of his bed at 1.30 a.m. to fetch Mrs. Brook away from the address 3 Homefield Road, Wimbledon where she was staying at the house of a Mrs. Evans with Mrs. Barron, who is Mrs. Brook's daughter. He hired a car from the Daimler Hire Service at Knightsbridge and went over to Wimbledon. He said that he found Mrs. Brook in a very distressed state, all packed and ready to leave." You said that right at the beginning?—Yes.

Who was the person who said, "You are breathing your last"?—Buckingham.

You or Buckingham?—Buckingham.

You are not saying that it was a joke yourself?—No.

Buckingham said it in a joking way?—That is right.

Did you believe Mudie was being stifled?—No, not for one moment.

By the LORD CHIEF JUSTICE—We have heard that you had on some occasions dined with Ley. Is that right?—That is true.

How many times did you dine with him?—I should say four or five.

When about?—It would be spreading over from October to November.

October and November?—Yes.

Where did you dine with him?—At the Normandy Grill at Knightsbridge.

You did not dine with him at the Cumberland Hotel?—No.

You knew, as I understand it, that Mudie was to make a confession?—Yes.

And to sign one?—Yes, to sign one.

When you left him he was gagged and bound?—Yes.

So far as you were concerned he was in no condition to make a confession either verbally or in writing?—When he was bound, as I said in my statement, his right arm was not bound.

Never bound?—Never bound. That was purely accidental though; I will admit that.

Evidence for the Prisoner Smith.

Lawrence J. Smith

At any rate, he was in a condition then that he might be able to write but would not be able to answer a question or make a statement?—That is when we left him.

GWENDOLINE GRAY, sworn, examined by Mr. MALCOLM MORRIS—I live in Leicester, and have known Lawrence John Smith between five and six years. I think he originally came from Leicester.

Did you hear that he was coming to stay at Leicester some time towards the end of last year?—Yes, I did.

Did he come?—Yes, on Friday, 29th November.

How do you know that he came there?—Because he rang me up between the 26th and 28th and asked me to book him accommodation.

Had you received anything in writing from him intimating that he was coming to Leicester?—Yes. He had written the week before to say he might be up the following week.

Do you know where the letter is now?—Destroyed.

Have you ever heard him talk about his future and any change of plans that he had, any particular intention with regard to his work?—Yes, he had spoken of going abroad to settle.

When did he, so far as you can remember, first speak to you on that subject?—After he came out of the R.A.F., early last year.

Did he continue to speak about it subsequently when you saw him?—He talked of it three or four times.

JOHN STREET, sworn, examined by Mr. MALCOLM MORRIS—I am employed by Bowles & Son of St. George's Street, Hanover Square. I was working under Smith, who was our foreman, on the building at 5 Beaufort Gardens, which was converted into flats last year. I first started to work under Smith somewhere at the beginning of June.

Did he ever speak to you about his plans with regard to his future—what he was going to do or what he would like to do?—He did mention about going abroad.

Going abroad to work as a builder?—Yes.

When did he first mention that?—Well, I couldn't say.

Can you say within a month or so—whether it was before the end of November?—No, I wouldn't like to say.

Do you remember a week at the end of November when Smith went away for a week-end to Leicester, went away on a Friday?—Yes.

Before that Friday can you say with regard to any of the other days in that week at what time he left work at 5 Beaufort Gardens?—No, I couldn't say at all.

Ley and Smith.

When did he usually leave?—Well, after five o'clock, because we used to go at five and he mostly stayed behind; he was always the last one on the job to my knowledge.

Do you remember whether he had left earlier on any other days?—No.

Did you say you reported to him at the end of the day?—No, he was always the last on the job because he used to lock up.

You did not notice anything particular about any of those days?—No.

MARGUERITE GATEHOUSE, sworn, examined by Mr. MALCOLM MORRIS—I live at 39 Belvoir Road, Dulwich. I know Lawrence John Smith who was a boarder in my house. He came to live there last February, more than a year ago.

What sort of a man was he?—A very straight-forward and reliable one.

I want to ask you about the week, and in particular a week-end, towards the end of November. Do you remember him going to Leicester for a week-end?—Yes, a long week-end.

When did it start?—Friday.

Is it right that that was about the end of November?—The last week in November.

That would be Friday, the 29th?—Yes.

Can you remember anything about the evening before he left for Leicester, that is the Thursday?—Yes, I can't rightly remember what time he came home because he didn't come straight from work but I do know he was home in bed before I went to bed myself.

Why is it you say he was home and in bed before you went?—Well, because for one thing he was going away in the morning.

Was he doing anything special the night before he was going away?—Only just had a bath; that was it.

When did he usually have a bath?—On Friday night, and this would be Thursday night.

He put it forward one day because he was going on the Friday?—That is right. He had his bath and went to bed before I did.

What time did you go to bed?—About 11.

Cross-examined by Mr. HAWKE—Has anything happened to refresh your memory about the time he came in recently at all?—Do you mean at that time?

Do you remember a gentleman, Detective-Sergeant Shoobridge from the Surrey Police, coming to see you?—A detective did come to see me, but I can't tell you his name.

Evidence for the Prisoner Smith.

Marguerite Gatehouse

He was very anxious to find out then if he could, was he not, what time Smith had come home on Thursday night?—I don't think he asked me the time.

Are you sure? It was just the very thing he wanted to know, was it not? Just carry your mind back and think?——

By the LORD CHIEF JUSTICE—Is that the detective? (Detective-Sergeant Shoobridge stands up.)—Yes.

What did he come about?—Well, he came to ask for Mr. Smith.

Cross-examination continued—He had been sent specially, had he not, to find out from you, Smith's landlady, what time Smith had come in on Thursday night?—Well, I expect I told him about that time.

Well, did you? That is why I asked you whether you remember. Did you not tell Sergeant Shoobridge that you could not in the least remember what time he had come in?—Not absolutely the time, but I know he was in bed before I was.

What did the officer ask you?—I don't know that I can remember really.

Did he ask you what time did Smith come in on Thursday night?—I expect he did ask that.

Did you say you were very sorry but you could not tell him?—I couldn't remember the exact time.

By the LORD CHIEF JUSTICE—Did you say the "exact time"? Just try and think. I do not suppose detectives very often come to see you?—No, that is why I expect—that is why I didn't know.

Would not that rather fix the conversation in your mind, the fact that a detective had come to see you about this decent, straightforward man?—Yes, certainly.

Was Smith there when he came?—No.

He saw you alone?—Yes.

What did he ask you, how did he start? I suppose he said he was a detective-sergeant?—No, he didn't.

Did he not? What did he say?—He asked for Mr. Smith, and we told him Mr. Smith was away.

Do you remember which day this was?—I think it was on the Tuesday night, 17th December.

What did he ask you?—Well, he asked me if I could remember if he came home that night.

What did you say?—I said, "yes."

Did you know why the policeman——?—No, I did not; I didn't know a thing about it.

Ley and Smith.

What was the next thing asked you as far as you remember?—When would he be likely to be back.

We want to know what the officer asked you when he came to see you?—He didn't come to see us until a fortnight after.

I know he did not. When he did come what did he ask you about?—Well, he asked me if I remembered what time he came home and I couldn't remember the exact time, because he didn't come straight from work that night.

Did not he ask if there was anything else you could remember?—I don't think he did.

Re-examined by Mr. Curtis Bennett—With regard to this question of time, Mrs. Gatehouse, you are not saying now you remember the time Smith came in on the night of the 28th?—No.

All that you are saying is that he was in bed when you went to bed?—Yes.

And the police officer when he came to see you did not, I suppose, ask you anything about Leicester?—No, I don't think he knew anything about that.

When you are reminded about the week-end that Smith went to Leicester you can throw your mind back to that?—Yes, that is right.

By the Lord Chief Justice—When the officer asked you if you could remember the time that Smith came in and you said no, he did not ask anything else as to when he was in the house, or if you could tell at what time he was in the house?—No; I only told him he wasn't back until the following Monday night when we saw him.

Mr. Hawke—My lord, Mr. Carvosso has been through the bank account for the purpose of verifying a matter, and I do not know if my learned friend would be satisfied if I told your lordship.

Sir Walter Monckton—I am quite satisfied. My learned friend has been good enough to show me it.

Mr. Hawke—There is no record of any large withdrawals of any large amount; there are a number of small ones between July and January totalling a sum of £287, and there are a number of small ones not exceeding £25. I do not think I need recall the witness.

The Court adjourned.

Closing Speech for the Prisoner Ley.

Closing Speech for the Prisoner Ley.

Sir WALTER MONCKTON—May it please your lordship, members of the jury, it is now my opportunity to address you upon the whole of the evidence. You may remember that some days ago I tried in a short opening of Ley's case to put before you what I suggested was the framework in which you would have to deliberate on your conclusions. I told you that, in my submission, the first question you would have to ask yourselves was whether Mudie was murdered at all, and, secondly, that you would have to consider whether Ley or Smith or both of them were a party to that murder. I did venture upon this submission to suggest to you that the case was full of uncertainties and that when the evidence was complete some of them you may think had been resolved and some of them had been increased. As I deal with the evidence as now it stands I hope to satisfy you that in certain respects, having heard the medical witnesses for the defence and having heard Cruikshank, the uncertainties have most definitely increased and in particular in that vital period between ten minutes to seven on Thursday, 28th November, when the incidents took place at 5 Beaufort Gardens, and the finding of the body in the chalk pit on the afternoon two days later some miles away at Woldingham.

I suppose I should deal first with the problem of whether Mudie was murdered at all, but with your permission I shall not do that. I will deal first with the evidence of Ley because he came before you to give on oath his account of the events so far as he was concerned. He denied, you will remember, all knowledge of the plot and all complicity in it. He denied any suggestion that he had paid Buckingham or Smith to do what they described as having been done by them at his request and for payment by him. He gave an account of his own movements over the evening of 28th November and, of course, the evidence which he gave brought him into conflict with the witnesses for the prosecution. First of all, there was a conflict between what he said and what was said by Minden. Minden, you will remember, was the hall porter from the Royal Hotel in Woburn Place who spoke to a conversation in which he said Ley made this remark, that anyone with a car who could keep his mouth shut and look after himself could earn a year's salary in a matter of weeks—something you will remember which was repeated in the evidence of Smith. Now, that conversation was challenged. There is that conflict between them, and you will judge between them.

So far as Ley's acquaintance with Minden was concerned it was for Mrs. Ley, you will recollect, that Minden had done work when

Ley and Smith.

Sir Walter Monckton

she stayed in the hotel. Ley had only passed the time of day with
Minden. He had had no conversation of that kind with him. So
far as Buckingham and Minden were concerned, Minden knew
Buckingham well. He saw him day by day and gave him most
of the car hire work which he got from clients of the Royal Hotel.
There was one other incident to which some attention was paid,
namely, that at one stage it was said that Ley gave £10 into the
hands of Minden. That is according to Minden. Ley said it was
£5. However, you will recollect what Minden said about that
sum of money. He had done a lot of jobs of work for Mrs. Ley
when she was in the hotel, she was not coming back, and he was
expecting that present of money to be made by her to him. It
was during some unimportant conversation that he received that
present. So you may think there is not much in that. I said there
is that conflict between Minden and Ley, but apart from that
conversation and saying, as I think Minden said, that he saw Ley
and Buckingham together once, and going after him into the
lounge on another occasion in the Royal Hotel, he does not carry
the matter further. Apart from that, the true conflict of testimony
in this case so far as Ley's account and everything is concerned,
rests between Buckingham and Smith on the one side and Ley on
the other.

Now, are you prepared to accept as clear and certain what
Buckingham and Smith say? On their own showing they came
before you as having played a part in this conspiracy to kidnap;
for £200 apiece they were prepared to do what they have admitted
in the box. You start with that—as being accomplices in the
crime; and it is upon their evidence that confidence is put. Is
Buckingham, the witness called for the prosecution, a man upon
whose word in this matter you are prepared to rely? You saw
and heard him. There was one thing which was very clear, that
at first when he made a statement, which was put to him in the
box, he admitted nothing which drew him into the picture of
putting hands upon Mudie. There was nothing in his first statement about the tying up of Mudie at all. If he was telling a truth-
ful story you would think that that could hardly have been left out,
but there was nothing about that. Then there was the incident
about putting the rug over the head of Mudie which he says—and
Smith says—that he himself did, but that was left out of his first
statement. Was that because he was seeking to cover up anything
he had done and anything which would implicate him in putting his
hands upon Mudie? At that time he was saying not as we now
have heard "I jumped him along the passage," but "We pushed
him into the front room," and even now when he has been dis-

Closing Speech for the Prisoner Ley.

Sir Walter Monckton

charged, when he has seen Smith's statement, when his present evidence and Smith's are brought into accord—even now he says "I did not gag him; he was not gagged when I was there; I did not fall with him; he did not fall as far as I know." You have heard Buckingham and you have seen him, as I have said. Is his evidence that upon which you can implicitly and confidently rely?

You will remember that when Mrs. Brook was before you she spoke—I will quote her exact words—about the order in which, according to her, Ley entertained suspicion, first, of Arthur Barron, secondly, of Jack Mudie and, thirdly, of Arthur Romer, and you will remember, without my troubling you in detail, that it was the name of "Arthur" which stuck in Ley's mind, according to that which he himself has said. She said that he kept on about her son-in-law—that was Mr. Barron—and then it was Mr. Mudie for some time, and then those two were dropped; then it was Mr. Romer for some time. You will recollect that she went on to say this in cross-examination in relation to the incident of the cheques: (Q.) "After the incident of the cheques did Ley refer to Mudie any more as someone about whom he entertained any suspicion? (A.) No, after that he started on Mr. Romer. (Q.) By that time he had stopped as far as Mudie was concerned? (A.) Apparently he had stopped."

I mention that to you for the moment for this reason. You will remember all about the incident of the cheques, how they were sent to Mrs. Brook, c/o Mudie, and how Ley went down and went with Mudie to Mr. Barron's in order to see the receipt which at the very end of July had been given for those three missing cheques; and you have Mr. Barron's evidence that when in August Ley saw the receipt for those cheques he expressed himself as satisfied and apologized. So that dates for you the incidents of the cheques and the closing of the incidents of the cheques. And, says Mrs. Brook, it was then when that was over that he ceased to entertain any suspicion of Mudie and turned to Romer.

Let us look at the statement of Smith to which he has sworn. In the fifth paragraph of the statement Smith says this: "About two months ago, Mr. Ley told me that he thought he had found a chap who might be able to get Mudie up to London. He said that he was meeting this person at the Royal Hotel, Russell Square (Woburn Place), and asked me to go along. He there introduced me to a Mr. Jack Buckingham who has a car hire service, and lives in Mostyn Road, Brixton. Buckingham looks about 42 or 43, 6 ft. 2 ins. in height, with a cauliflower ear. I understand that he is an ex-boxer. Mr. Ley at this meeting told Buckingham and I that he wanted the man bringing into London, who he thought was

255

Ley and Smith.

the cause of the trouble with Mrs. Brookes. This man was a Mr. Romer who was living at 3 Holmfield Road. I have led you a bit wrong with regard to this. Although Mudie had the £150 which I have said, it was the man Romer whom Mr. Ley suspected of interfering with Mrs. Brookes and he (Romer) was the person that Mr. Ley wanted the statement from." He is speaking of a conversation some two months before the statement was made.

He goes on to say: "Mr. Ley told me in the car on the way up to the meeting with Buckingham that he was in a hurry to get away and asked that when he had introduced me to Buckingham that I should explain to him how he (Ley) wanted the man Romer got hold of and the purpose and we could arrange between ourselves how it was carried out, but to let him know before we did anything. We met Buckingham at the hotel and after the introductions Mr. Ley left. Buckingham and I had dinner together during which time I told him that the man Romer lived at 3 Holmfield Road, and that Ley wanted him brought to somewhere in London so that he could get him to sign a statement. Buckingham suggested that we go to Wimbledon and have a look at the place. He had told me during conversation that a man named Minden who had introduced Ley to him had told him he would get a year's pay for doing the job for Ley."

Then he describes how they went to Wimbledon: "We went to Wimbledon and went into the Dog and Fox Public House as Ley had told us that we might find Romer in there. He told us what he was like and gave us a description of his car. It was an Austin 10, maroon colour. I did have the index number, but I can't remember what it was. We had a look round Holmfield Road and made inquiries at the garage at the Dog and Fox, but could not learn anything about Romer."

Now, members of the jury, see how it goes on to bring Mudie in: "I did not see Buckingham for about a fortnight and in the meantime Mr. Ley had told me that the man who was the cause of the trouble was Mudie. Ley mentioned to me that some cheques had been sent to Mrs. Brookes at Holmfield Road, and had gone astray and he thought that Mudie had them. He had a suspicion that Romer and Mudie were working in together." In that last paragraph you will observe that cheques had been sent and he thought that Mudie had them. It is obvious from August onwards that the matter was completely open, as it were. So it would be idle to say that the conversation which is recollected and spoken to there refers to something happening in November. The truth is, is it not, that having heard what Mrs. Brook had to say and having heard what Barron said about the cheques, the Mudie

256

Closing Speech for the Prisoner Ley.

Sir Walter Monckton

incident, as she says, had finished and the Romer suspicion came later? If so, what a muddle this statement makes of the true events which are being described by Smith there. After all it was, according to the evidence of the other witness I have referred to, "Arthur" whom Ley was supposed to be suspicious of, not "Jack." The cheques incident was over in August. Am I not entitled to say that there is a muddled piece of testimony?

There is a more serious matter about Smith's evidence to which I should like to draw your attention. Do you remember how Smith described about ten minutes after Buckingham left, he left Beaufort Gardens and the conversation in which Ley is supposed to have said "My end has slipped up"? Smith said: "I was waiting because I thought other men were coming to help to get the confession Ley wanted." He did not see anyone. You will recollect he went out through the basement stairs and thought someone was coming in through the front door. The door was closed and he was gone.

If Ley was in this plot, if he was plotting to kidnap Mudie in order to wring a confession from him, if he wanted help in persuading Mudie to make the statement that he desired, does not one ask oneself this: why enlarge the circle of those who would know about the plot; why bring more people in? If you wanted someone to persuade Mudie to make a statement can you think of a more persuasive person than Buckingham, whom you have seen, and Smith, whom you have seen? Can you really accept that he went out after those ten minutes because of someone else coming in, or is the truth this, that he has to bring someone else in to make his story sound true, and for this reason: nobody would suppose that Ley, a man of 66, a man who on the evidence is not accustomed to driving a car, would be able to take a man or the body of a man from 5 Beaufort Gardens down to the chalk pit in Woldingham, pull him up that steep slope of which we have heard so much and put him in the trench. So somebody else had to be introduced to make that story sound true.

Well, members of the jury, you have seen these witnesses. I do not want to spend time in going into that part of the matter in great detail. This old man of 66; the old woman of 66 with whom there had been no intimate relations for more than ten years; jealousy of Mudie so great as to make him wish to bring him up to London; the suspicion starts with Arthur and not Jack; the cheques incident is all over in August, and yet does he want to bring him up there in November?

Remember, on 10th July, 1946, the incident at Mr. Brashier's office. There was Mr. Barron senior, whom you have seen in the

Ley and Smith.

Sir Walter Monckton

box; there were Ley and Mrs Brook; what they were discussing themselves were certain properties which had been made over by Ley to Mrs. Brook—had been made absolutely over to her, as she claimed, and they parted in anger. He said, according to his statement in the box, that she was dishonest; and they parted in anger. Some months later, before this incident happens on 28th November, he replaces her with another housekeeper, Miss Lane. Intimate relations stopped ten years ago. There was a break over the money in July. She was replaced as housekeeper before 28th November. Yet the cause of the jealousy is over Arthur and he is said to have kidnapped Jack. Perhaps it is inconsistent with that story that after July, 1946, when he regarded her as dishonest he should have been seen with her constantly and dining in her company, but you may think, after an association which had lasted for over 20 years and which had been intimate beforehand, that he might care for her welfare and her company, but how hard it is to reconcile what I have been saying to you with that acute jealousy which drives a man to crime. I ask you to say with regard to that, on the evidence of these accomplices who go out after they have done it and drink on it out of the money they got, that you are not prepared to say that Ley played the part which they said he played.

I want to summarize his account of what he did on 28th November, how he left 5 Beaufort Gardens with Mrs. Brook after tea—and Mrs. Brook says "Yes, he did." He went out to the club, returned for his torch, left again shortly after five, went to the National Liberal Club about half-past five, a place he used to go to on Thursdays when he could, and gave the porter, as he says, a slip, or caused the porter to write a slip, containing information about his change of address so that letters should come to 5 Beaufort Gardens; and there is much corroboration, members of the jury. You saw that a slip was prepared and on 29th November was the first of the two matters of change of address dealt with in the office of the club. You have heard if after five o'clock a change of address was notified it would not be taken up to the office till the next morning. I do not say it is conclusive, but it is consistent and, I hope you will think, helpful.

Then he leaves the club, has a break-down in one taxi, takes another one, and goes on to the Cumberland Grill, forgetting he has an engagement with Mrs. Brook; he has a meal and then he leaves. Whilst there he is seen by the receptionist who knew him as a regular customer, who says: "Well, he was a man who came in always with the same lady, but I do remember an occasion at or about this time when he was there alone." There was some cross-examination to say "Is not there a waiter or head waiter who is

Closing Speech for the Prisoner Ley.

Sir Walter Monckton

regularly on duty?" but you may think that it is not everybody on duty who notices which particular customer is in on a particular night, though you would rightly expect, would you not, that they would observe the customers who have regular tables and whether a customer is accompanied by his usual accompanist or is alone. Nobody is going to say it is proved for certain on this evidence that it was this night, but you may think it is helpful in support of the story which Ley has told you about his movements on that evening. Then after leaving the Cumberland about quarter-past seven he goes to Mrs. Brook's, has sandwiches and the usual game of cards, and arrives home at Beaufort Gardens about half-past 11. Having spent the night in his room he comes down the next morning and lets in Miss Lane as usual, and she notices nothing unusual about him.

If you take the view when you come to deliberate upon this case that Ley's own account of his movements that night may reasonably be true, then he is entitled to be acquitted at your hands. I want to deal before I close with the possibility that you do not accept that story. What happens then? Then still the two main questions remain for you to consider: Was Mudie murdered? Did Ley murder him or take part in the murder? You are back at what happened at Beaufort Gardens on the afternoon and evening of the 28th and what happened at the chalk pit.

You have two lots of evidence which I want to consider with you for a moment: the medical testimony called for the defence and the evidence of the man Cruikshank. First of all, as to the medical evidence, Dr. Keith Simpson was called. Nobody doubts that he is a man of great experience in pathology. He was called in originally in this matter not by the defence. Originally he was called in by the police. He was there with Dr. Gardner on both occasions at the chalk pit. He had the same opportunities of observation as Dr. Gardner. He was present at the autopsy. He saw everything presumably that Dr. Gardner saw. He was a person who was called in by the police for that purpose, and you may feel you cannot lightly turn aside what someone who has been selected for that duty has come and told you in the box. His approach to the matter might be criticized by those who say "Well, even a doctor has to look outside medical symptoms," but is not he entitled to say "I come here as a witness in regard to symptoms which, as a doctor, I can deal with as a matter of science"? Outside that it is, of course, for a jury to say that in the light of other evidence this piece of evidence must fit in its place. "I am a doctor and a doctor only; I can only tell you what the medical symptoms show."

Ley and Smith.

Sir Walter Monckton

When you deliberate on the case you may think that that is a matter of primary importance. What can he as a doctor tell you from the medical evidence alone? After all you know you may get a case in which an innocent person comes along and finds a body and disposes of a body because he loses his head and he has not got an explanation. What does he say about the medical symptoms? He says this, that the medical symptoms, in his view, do not indicate a beating up or violence. You may think it important to notice that whatever else may be in dispute between the doctors this much is agreed: there were no external bruises upon this body except trivial bruises. So says Dr. Gardner as well as Dr. Simpson. If there was a beating up would you not expect something more than trivial bruising? As to the abdomen, there was no injury to the abdominal wall. In Dr. Gardner's view, the beating up is proved by the discoloration in brain fluid and the discoloration in the intestines. With regard to that you have the evidence of Dr. Simpson, reinforced by the evidence of the other doctor, that those symptoms are perfectly consistent with asphyxia. May not that be the right view of the medical evidence? After all, Dr. Gardner first of all did not take such a very different view. I will come to it in a moment.

There is another thing which Dr. Simpson said to you, and it was that the situation of the marks round the neck speaks plainly for suspension in this case; there is nothing to indicate whether it was accidental, suicidal or foul play. I asked Dr. Gardner, not having in my hands his original report, what his view had been when he was there with Dr. Simpson, and he told me, and I have since seen his report, that he then thought "the rope mark differs in no way from that commonly seen in self-hanging, but I am not satisfied that death was due to suicide," for reasons which he then gives. So at the time he made his first report his conclusion was not "This is a case of foul play." He says: "The rope mark differs in no way from that commonly seen in self-hanging, but I am not satisfied that death was due to suicide," for reasons which he has explained in this Court and which he gave in this report. Earlier he states: "Death was due to asphyxia," &c. (reading to the words), "but there may have been some rough handling before as shown by the bruises on the head and hip." How far do the medical symptoms go to show that there was a beating up? There may be evidence of rough handling, but the bruises were trivial and, with regard to the bruises on the hip, were something done after death, according to his opinion.

He says he thought that death was due to suspension but not to a drop. Is there so much difference between him, Dr. Simpson

Closing Speech for the Prisoner Ley.

Sir Walter Monckton

and Dr. Camps, when you look back and see what he originally thought and what Dr. Simpson still thinks? "The discoloration of the brain fluid," &c. (reading extract). What you do not find is a vital thing. You do not find external bruising and you do not find a bruising to the abdomen or abdominal wall. Therefore, with that evidence before you, can you say that there was violence and a beating up in this case? I felt bound to draw attention to that evidence.

I will now say a word about the witness Cruikshank. He has given an account of what you may well think could well have happened on the night of 28th November. He came before you as a man with a grudge against society. He has a wife and two children. Since September he has not had a job; he has not had any money, and he has not had a roof over his head. You may have a grudge like that, and it does not mean to say he is a liar because he has a grudge like that. He was a smuggler, on his own story. He was concerned with smuggling goods from abroad by aeroplane by an irregular route. Is that so fantastic? Do not we hear of small aeroplanes which fly from one country to another, and does not one realize that nowadays there is a good deal of money in smuggling? That man Cruikshank might be prepared to earn a pound or two in bringing a package back. Is it fantastic? Is not it a possibility that that story which he describes to you is accurate from first to last?

Members of the jury, do not disregard him because he has a grudge against society. Do not disregard him because he is a smuggler. That does not make him a liar. Further, he has confessed his record. He said "I have had convictions." He said "I am a person who has a warrant against me because I sold furniture," or something of that sort. That does not make him a liar. Ask yourselves this, will you : why should he come here and take the risks he has taken if he is not telling the truth? It is not, you know, a case of exhibitionism. We all know of people who come forward and say "I did a murder" to draw the attention of the public and the spotlight upon themselves. He does not say that. He says that he read about the case in the newspapers and he felt that he must come forward, and he came to the solicitors who instruct me. You may say, "What a careless man he was when he went there," but his opinion was : "I could not let this fellow stand his trial without giving my version; it was always at the back of my conscience that I was there and it might be something I did which caused him his death."

My learned friend Mr. Hawke knew what he was going to say when he went into the box because we gave him a statement.

Ley and Smith.

Sir Walter Monckton

Cruikshank had given to the police all he said in the box. They had ample opportunities for inquiry. Nobody has suggested, nor is there the slightest indication, that he was to be rewarded in any way to say something which was not the truth. Indeed the evidence is that he does not know Ley, and that once only he shook hands with Ley's son. Think earnestly, I beg you, when you look at this story and say whether this story does not ring true. Why should anybody but a madman come forward with that story to tell unless it is true? What is it that he said? He says that he decided to go round to Ley that evening in the hope of getting some help to get him to Australia. You may think that if he had found anything round there worth taking he would have taken it. He goes there and he finds the door ajar. You will remember that there was cross-examination to show whether the door to the basement was kept bolted, but we know now from Smith's own statement that on this evening Smith had gone out after the ten minutes interval which he speaks of by the door up the area steps, so there is no question of the door being bolted this night.

Through that door then left ajar he makes his way. He goes in. He stumbles along down a passage. He says he found in the room at the end somebody tied up in a chair. He says: "I pulled the ropes in a frenzy. There was a moan or grunt from the man who was there. I thought about untying the ropes properly, but there was a noise, and I panicked and went away." You may think he was callous, but he went away. If that evidence may reasonably be accepted, we know that Mudie was alive and alone about 9 o'clock on the evening of the 28th. Who can ever know if that pull in a frenzy at those ropes caused his death? Who can tell now whether the rope round his neck was connected with the ropes round the body as it was when the body was found in the chalk pit at Woldingham? Nobody can know. You cannot, can you, in the light of that evidence exclude the possibility that that happened? That evidence increases the mystery—increases the uncertainties with which in this case you are beset.

Now, members of the jury, what is the case which the prosecution endeavour to make against Ley? It cannot be, can it, that they say that this was deliberate murder, that Mudie was brought up to this place to be murdered? That can hardly be. It is inconceivable, is it not, that anybody who intended to murder would use these means? As I understand it, it is not really put like that. It is rather that there was an intentional beating up of Mudie which in the result caused his death.

Mr. Hawke opened the case in this way: was it contemplated that such treatment was to be meted out to him as might result

Closing Speech for the Prisoner Ley.

Sir Walter Monckton

in serious bodily harm? Then he went on to say that some person or some cause pulled that rope tight about his neck. I can accept the second of those statements, that some person or some cause pulled that rope tight about his neck, but the first part I challenge, where he asks whether it was contemplated that such treatment was to be meted out to him as might result in serious bodily harm.

The evidence against Ley as to what happened that day is the evidence of Buckingham and the evidence of Smith, the accomplices about whom I have said all I wish to trouble you with, but this much they would have you believe, that Ley expressly wanted no violence to be used. It was Ley they thought, being an old man, who might get knocked about. Let me remind you of an answer or two which Buckingham made to my learned friend Mr. Curtis Bennett for Smith. He made this answer: "There was never any suggestion of violence apart from tying up." Then he went on: "Ley suggested and wanted no violence," and then a little later: "The point of the scheme was there was to be no violence," and again: "I thought he must be untied for confession and he might have offered violence." Those are the witnesses against me. It is Buckingham who made those answers in answer to questions by Mr. Curtis Bennett. The witnesses do not say Ley wanted violence. On the contrary, the point of the scheme was that there was to be no violence. I shall ask you to say, even if you are satisfied there was a kidnap and even a tying up, that no bodily harm was intended or done by Ley on the occasion that has been described in that room, and I shall ask you to say firmly that this was not a case in which a beating up was carried out.

I have been dealing with a charge of murder against Ley, the murder based upon the doing of grievous bodily harm intentionally. I must also deal with this in a few words, that it might be said if you take the view I ask you to take, that there was no intention of grievous bodily harm intended, you may say that the kidnapping was an unlawful act and if you think Ley took part in it he would be a party to that unlawful act, and if you thought that he was inadvertently killed during that unlawful act then, subject to my lord's direction, you might have to bring in a finding of manslaughter.

I want to say two things about that. First of all, about the tying up. The tying up was very wrong. Nobody could possibly excuse it. But if there was no beating up—I have dealt with this matter—and if you accept what I have said to you, you may think that the mere tying up in itself was not a dangerous thing. That is the first thing. The second thing is this. On the evidence that we have put before you we submit that you ought not to find that

Ley and Smith.

Sir Walter Monckton

the kidnapping caused his death. Nobody can say definitely how he came to die. That is a matter, in my submission, which is left in uncertainty and doubt. You cannot disregard as not even a reasonable explanation or a possible alternative those things which the doctors have said to you, and the suggestion which Cruikshank came here to make, that he himself might, however inadvertently, in his frenzied pulling, have pulled the ropes tight and killed the man. You cannot disregard those alternatives as to how Mudie came to his end. How can you say that it has been proved beyond doubt that Mudie was murdered, and murdered or killed by these men? The cause of the death might have been quite extraneous to any of them.

I am very conscious of the burden I must carry in regard to the imperfections and the shortcomings of what I lay before you. If considerations occur to you which I have missed, take them into your deliberations and give such weight to them as I should have given them. Your burden will increase under my lord's direction as to the law. It will be your decision upon which the issues hang in this case. It will be the decision of each one of you. You will never have a more anxious or a graver burden. The scales are in your hands, the scales of justice for these two men, and it is not as if you had to say on balance on a nicety of a decision: I think that this explanation is more likely than the other. That is not your task. The task of each one of you is this: am I satisfied in my conscience beyond reasonable doubt that the prosecution's case is right against these men? If it is not then they are entitled to be acquitted. Suspicion will never do. It is proof to a reasonable certainty that must be had before a man is convicted for a crime such as this.

I have had to make the first speech. I shall be followed by my learned friends who in the course of their duty will have in varying degrees to criticize Ley and his conduct. Then my lord will sum up. He will direct you as to the law and he will marshal the facts for your consideration. The law you will take from him, but he will say, I know, that the decision is yours upon these issues upon which I have tried to address you. I shall not have another opportunity of speaking to you or of repelling suggestions which I have now got to listen to against my client, but this much I ask of you: to remember these appeals and the claims I make upon each one of them.

Members of the jury, however critical you may feel, however outraged you may have been by some of the things you have heard and which you will hear described again, if you feel at the end of the case in your hearts and consciences an honest doubt as to

Closing Speech for the Prisoner Ley.

Sir Walter Monckton

how Mudie came to die, whether it was by violence, whether an accident intervened, or whether there was some other intervention —if you have an honest doubt as to whether Ley had any part in causing the violence, if it was violence from which the death came, then stand fast and firm by the honesty of your doubt, and remember that it is only if you are satisfied beyond that reasonable doubt that you can find a verdict of guilty. I have said little about Ley. I only say this. He comes before you in the evening of his days, after some service to the State, to the family of nations in which we all belong. He comes before you with all his faults, and who is there among us who has none? He only asks one thing of you, and it is this, that when you decide all these issues you should faithfully deliberate and not condemn him unless you are sure.

Closing Speech for the Prisoner Smith.

Mr. CURTIS BENNETT—May it please your lordship, members of the jury, it now becomes my turn to address you on behalf of the defendant Smith. There is a great deal which Sir Walter has said with which I shall agree, but there is a certain amount with which I do not agree. I will assume that you are satisfied, and you must be satisfied unless the evidence called means nothing, that the story which Smith told as to how Mudie was brought up to London must be right, because unless he was brought up for Ley and on Ley's behalf what sense is there in this case at all? Why should Smith and Buckingham bring Mudie up? They did not know him. They were not interested in him. They had no grievance against him. The statement Mr. Hawke in opening spoke of as being one which was conspicuous for its frankness up to a point, if you will remember, and which he described later on as more likely to be true, was Smith's statement.

Smith is not an important man. Smith is a humble joiner. He had until this case a decent character. I shall not put that too high because we all start life with a good character. You may think it is one thing for him to have agreed to have taken part in this kidnapping for £200 and quite another thing to say he is a hired assassin for £200. Members of the jury, there he is. You saw him. He is not a very distinguished looking person, not very robust, not very dangerous, not very rough looking, not a person of whom Mudie or anyone else would be afraid, not a violent man or a violent looking man. He is just a simple ordinary joiner.

Smith for £200 has taken part in the disgraceful episode of just bringing Mudie up to 5 Beaufort Gardens. Why 5 Beaufort

Ley and Smith.

Mr. Curtis Bennett

Gardens unless it was on behalf of Ley? Why Mudie unless it was on behalf of Ley? Why all this unless it was on behalf of Ley? You will remember what Ley said when I cross-examined him, that if a man accepted £200 for kidnapping he would not hesitate to frame him. Do you believe those words? Do they come well from a man or on behalf of a man who obviously paid that sum? Who else paid Smith £200? It does not help him (Smith) to say he was paid £200. It damns him on a charge of conspiracy to assault. Why should he invent that in regard to Ley? He (Ley) might have been able to prove he was somewhere else at the time. You may think he has not proved that he was not there when this cavalcade was expected on the 28th.

I say, of course, Smith and Buckingham are telling the truth about why Mudie was brought up. Mudie was suspected of being a lover of Mrs. Brook by the arrogant, vain, ruthless man Ley, you may think, who cares for nothing provided he can say he was not there. I shall not criticize what Sir Walter says. You may think that Ley was not a party to a plot to murder at all. I was flattered when Sir Walter drew attention to the cross-examination of Buckingham when Buckingham said there was never a plan of that sort. It may well be that you are not at all satisfied that there was murder here by Ley or anybody else. Of course, there are only a few things in this case you can be certain of. This building has heard so many amazing stories, probably more extraordinary stories than any building in the world, but it can never have heard a more extraordinary tale than has been unfolded before you since Wednesday morning last.

What can we say is certain? One thing that is certain is that Mudie was found dead on 30th November. Another thing that is certain is that Mudie was brought to London by Buckingham and Smith and deposited in Beaufort Gardens, the reason being that Ley should force a confession out of him, whether by violence or not who knows, and that is a thing Ley had been wanting to do in June or July in regard to Barron junior. When he was cross-examined you will remember he said he asked some men to stay behind. He was asked some questions with regard to that matter which you will remember. It is quite certain, is not it, that Smith's statement is true for a very long way? Just consider this, members of the jury, if Smith was a party to this murder—if this be murder indeed. Ley is not unintelligent, is he? He is no fool. No one has said Smith is mad. He is perfectly sane, but he has not the intelligence of an ex-Minister for Justice for New South Wales. Do not you think they would have planned a similar story if they were in a murder plot together? Is not that the most extraordinary

Closing Speech for the Prisoner Smith.

Mr. Curtis Bennett

thing in this case? His first words to the police are "I am willing to help you all I can." "I am willing to help you all I can." But Smith and Ley could not have told each other what to say, their stories are so different.

Murders are frequently committed in this country without the murderer being discovered. In my submission, there is eloquent proof that there was no murder plot at all. You will remember what Buckingham has told you with regard to the gagging and the rug. He denies the fall. That part was described in Mr. Hawke's opening as being true. Mr. Hawke relies upon Smith. Indeed you may think while Smith was giving evidence he was a good witness for the Crown. He is not very dissimilar from Buckingham. Of course one is in the dock and one is a free man, but he is not in a very dissimilar position from Buckingham on the evidence, is he?

If there was a murder plot, Buckingham was in that plot; if there was not, then he was not, and I suggest there was never a murder plot. Obsessed as you may think that man Ley is, quite imaginarily obsessed as you may think he is by the misdoings of Mrs. Brook, you cannot think, can you, that that is sufficient to conjure up a murder plot? He says he was not obsessed. While he was being asked questions he came out in a torrent with a vivid description of what he said he heard on 8th June, what he said happened between Mrs. Brook and Arthur. I will not repeat it. Did not that show festerings of jealousy in Ley's mind? Can you imagine why he would be saying those sort of things about that lady at this time of her life? It is the festerings of jealousy which caused the bringing of Mudie up, but which did not cause him or Smith to enter into a murder plot.

You see, Smith went and bought that rope—Exhibit 12, I think it is—from a place in Montpelier Street, opposite Beaufort Gardens. He got the gag from downstairs. You will remember the rope and the cloth were on the dead body. Would Smith have done that if he had been guilty of murder—leave the rope there? He would know that an intelligent police inspector would be employed on the task. The police are not unintelligent, as you know. They do not find ropes round bodies and burn them or throw them away. That rope came from Farmers of Montpelier Street where Smith is known. There was the gag hung like a garland round Mudie's neck. Would not Smith realize that anyone could find out where that cloth had come from? Members of the jury, that is a powerful argument which you must bear in mind, in my submission to you. Before passing from what I was saying, how can they have left Mudie ungagged in the room downstairs when he could have

Ley and Smith.

shouted his head off? That is why I think Mr. Hawke suggested that Smith's story is more likely in those particulars.

So we can pass to other matters. You know what happened after Smith left. Why should you disbelieve that he left? If he left just after seven then something happened between then and some time at which Mudie died. Somebody of course may have come to assist in the taking of the statement, as it was gently put—the forcing of the confession from the wretched Mudie who was a completely innocent man with nothing to confess at all.

Cruikshank comes on the scene. He may have been telling the truth, for all I know. He talks about being in the house at 9 o'clock, when Smith was two hours away from there. You may not believe Cruikshank, but if you believe him it is plain that both Ley and Smith ought to be acquitted. You will not necessarily believe all you hear. You are not as gullible as that. If you are looking round for someone to play the part of the tough, strong person who was going to assist Ley—and you may think this was probably the truth—if you were to cast that part, can you think of a better person to cast in that part than a tough angry criminal who had been smuggling? Who for? Nobody seemed to worry much about that. Who paid for the aeroplane in which he came? Why does he seek out Ley directly he arrives in London? No one knows. Was it drugs? No one knows. Why did he come to Ley? Did he go to Ley with a parcel of contraband? There are the footsteps, the missing link in Smith's case; the man who went up the steps who was a bit late. Perhaps the aeroplane was a bit late. Those are the matters you must consider. You saw the personality of Cruikshank. Was he putting himself into danger? It is one thing to be charged with smuggling; it is another thing to be concerned in murder or manslaughter. Why does he come here? Is he still expecting a passage to Australia from Ley? I could not help looking through the papers over the week-end. We do not know what other assets Mr. Ley has, as to whether he is engaged in smuggling with Cruikshank or not, but we do know that on 31st October in Exhibit 2 there is £5127 to his credit. That is the first entry.

The Lord Chief Justice—I thought it was overdrawn.

Mr. Curtis Bennett—No, my lord. It looks like it. "Credit plus overdrawn O.D."

The Lord Chief Justice—I understood that. I may be wrong about that. It does not matter. You say it is a credit balance.

Closing Speech for the Prisoner Smith.

Mr. Curtis Bennett

Mr. HAWKE—Your lordship will see there is "Credit plus," then "Overdrawn O.D."

Mr. CURTIS BENNETT—It is confusing. The point I was seeking to make was this, that if you look at 7th December, before the £300 was paid back by Smith, it had gone down to £1500. He had spent a good deal of money by that time. Of course he was repairing his house or having it turned into flats, and he was willing to pay £150 for a pair of curtains. He was spending a good deal of money. He drew £550 out. £150 he spent on curtains or furnishings, and £400 is found by Mr. Barker. Of course, it was found by Mr. Barker in two lots. Was not that most extraordinary evidence? Two lots which added up exactly to £400; that is to say, he never paid Buckingham and Smith £400. Mr. Barker said he went along with Ley's son. If you take £550 out of the bank and spend about £150 would you have exactly £400. Of course. It is not £400 and 6d. or £396. How did that come about? Mr. Barker, of course, found it there. He was asked to go along with Ley's son. Somebody has put that money there nicely so they can say to you that Smith and Buckingham never received £400.

There is no limit to which Ley will operate to get himself out of the mess he is in. It may not be murder. You may wonder why it is that Ley cannot tell you the truth. He is a lawyer and he knows what murder and manslaughter are, and he knows if he told you the whole truth it may be a confession to one or the other and that possibly something happened which deprived the unhappy Mudie of life.

Smith left about 7 o'clock, with the rope not round Mudie's neck and, therefore, not in a dangerous position. There was a gag tied round his mouth only. In my submission, he died from the rope being changed into a different position after he left, and he is neither guilty of murder nor manslaughter.

Dr. Gardner said "There was the impression of the rope round the neck, well marked behind on the right side under the angle of the jaw and in front above the larynx. There was an open angle below the left ear. There was another horizontal mark on the left side of the neck corresponding in position to the edge of the collar. It was 2½ inches long and very distinct. There were hæmorrhages in it. The collar mark suggested to me a hand grip on the opposite side of the collar, pulling it tight." In other words, somebody went like *that;* somebody inserted their hand in the collar band of Mudie and somebody, probably the same person, pulled that rope up and up. Can you see that happening when the wretched Mudie is not able to confess to something he had not done? Ley is 66, but a big

Ley and Smith.

Mr. Curtis Bennett

man still, or equally there may be an angry sullen criminal like Cruikshank. Either might have done it, or some third person, because you have not seen all Ley's friends here. If he had some ulterior motive in getting Mudie there, you may think the last person he would tell about that would be the humble joiner Smith. "I will give £500 to get him out of the country."

I have nothing more to say about Cruikshank except to say, if you believe him, he may have accidentally caused his death. Until Cruikshank came into the box, who was the man who, as Smith said, came up the steps? I say to you there is one man at least for whom it would be perfect casting who walked up the steps a little later and who tried to extract a confession from Mudie. Ley spent in that period £3613 9s. 4d. I do not suppose you will believe Cruikshank when he says he has never met Ley. There is a lot more in that. Is there not a lot more than that?

You cannot convict either of these people of murder unless you are absolutely certain that you know the answers. Need I worry you about the so-called alibi with reference to the National Liberal Club and the Cumberland? If Ley was not at Beaufort Gardens at about 6.15 or 6.30 that evening, this case means nothing.

There is a test here which, in my submission, will prove that Smith cannot have been the man or one of the men who took the body down to Woldingham. You may think that Ley helped with the body out of that room into a car. You know the size of a Ford 8. Whether you can get a body into the back of a Ford 8 I leave to you. You will remember that Ley had told Miss Ingleson he had strained his back carrying packing cases. I suggest either Ley himself or somebody else with him went to Woldingham. If Smith was there he had to get back from Woldingham to Dulwich, and he was there at 11 o'clock because his landlady has told us so. If Dr. Gardner is right, Mudie cannot have been buried until one o'clock, and Smith was back at home then. Mrs. Gatehouse does not remember exactly, but she says: "I went to bed at 11 and Smith was in. I know that because the next day he went to Leicester and he had his bath night changed." Taking 7 as the earliest that Mudie was killed or murdered and taking four hours that elapsed between the death and the burial, Smith could not have got back until the early hours of the morning.

Members of the jury, there is not very much left for me to deal with, but there is a most important point with reference to Howard's Garage. That hiring was done the week before, or the arrangements by Ley for the hiring, the telephoning, was done a week before the plan was fixed. Smith hired a car to go to

Closing Speech for the Prisoner Smith.

Mr. Curtis Bennett

Leicester in during the week-end. Is there anything suspicious about that? If he was going to hire a car to do a murder with you might think he would hire it for a very short time. You will remember that the Leicester visit was fixed a week before. He goes away from the garage knowing the car is registered, and he signs for it in that number: F G P 101.

Now we come to a thing which unless you are satisfied about there can be no verdict against Smith here in respect of murder or anything else on this indictment: F G P 101 and the two land-scape gardeners, the witnesses Smith and Tamplin. My learned friend Mr. Hawke said when he opened this case that the Crown asked you to attach no importance whatsoever to the identification of an individual in these circumstances, it being dark, &c., yet when Mr. Tamplin was in the box Mr. Hawke said: "Do you see the man you saw then?" and Mr. Tamplin looked at the dock—where else could he look?—and said: "Yes, that is the man." That is insignificant evidence. Smith, the witness, on 13th January picks out another man and not this Smith at all, and Tamplin picks out the man whose back of the head he had seen. Try and pick out a man by the back of his head among those whom you know. I suggest it is quite impossible. You will remember that I suggested to Smith, the witness, that he had picked out somebody much taller than the accused, and I think the witness said he did not know. I wonder who that was at Woldingham in the afternoon of 27th November. Of course, Cruikshank is a man who is a little taller than Smith. With regard to the number, I leave it to your common sense. The evidence is that it was just 101. That car is *F G P* 101. There are probably hundreds of cars numbered 101 in this country.

They are honest witnesses. You heard them both say that they had discussed it together before going to the police. What did they discuss? Cannot you hear them saying: "Was it 101?" "Yes, it was." "By Jove, we will tell the police." Perhaps they are right. Perhaps they are wrong. "101." It was a Ford car. I cannot give evidence, but I suppose it is common sense and knowledge that there are more Fords in this country than any other make of car. It might have been 1010. They might have been missing the last "o." It might have been A G P 2101 and they might not have seen the first figure. It is a coincidence that three days after that on the 27th in the chalk pit or in the trench there was the body of Mr. Mudie, dead. It is of course a very unfortunate coincidence, but is it proved not to be a coincidence? Is it proved as a statement of fact? Does it sound to you reasonable? Are you going to convict a man of murder because those men are sure it was number 101

Ley and Smith.

and because he had a car number 101? I submit it was taken in semi-darkness. It is very weak.

You get the evidence of the accused man himself, Smith, who is entitled to be believed as much as anybody else, that he was not there. You will recollect that he says he left at five, got to Mostyn Road about half-past five, and was then with the Buckinghams and Mrs. Bruce at Putney, and so forth, for the rest of the evening. I was very grateful when my lord asked the question of Smith as to whether the car could have been taken away during the day. Smith says he left Beaufort Gardens at five. It is an hour's ride to Woldingham. You heard Mr. Normanton from Howard's Services say that Smith said when he hired the car that he, Mr. Normanton, could borrow it back during the week if he desired. Would the car be left outside the house when a murder plot is being hatched?

Supposing Smith is wrong about the times. Supposing he has made an honest mistake about that and supposing he did not leave at five at all but left at five-thirty, or quarter-to six; or something like that. There may have been time for somebody else to take the car from the front of the house and bring it back, and it could have gone away in the afternoon and it could have got back, could not it? Of course, if you were going to do something dangerous to Mudie and you wanted to prepare the ground and wanted to throw the blame on somebody else when the time came, that is what you would do.

Ley actually rang up the garage in the first place for the car. Again it is one of those things which I suggest you cannot possibly disregard. It is another uncertainty. If it was Smith who was there at the chalk pit at half-past four he must have left Beaufort Gardens at half-past three at the latest to be there. I have not called people before you to say Smith was there until five. People would not remember as far back as that. I think it was Street who said he was there until five-thirty as a rule and there was nothing odd about that actual day. I will read his actual words: "That week I noticed nothing extraordinary about Smith leaving earlier." So the assumption is surely that Smith was there as usual.

There are three things about this evidence. The proposition that this car was there on the 27th driven by Smith is in the highest degree unlikely as a proposition, is not it? It is hardly likely that Smith would be there if he was plotting a murder, having signed for the car in its registered number. I have not reminded you of this, that as well as the time it must have taken from the house to Woldingham, it must have taken a long time to take the body out of the car and carry it up to the trench. Why was the pickaxe taken

JOHN McMAIN MUDIE

Closing Speech for the Prisoner Smith.

Mr. Curtis Bennett

there? Was it done possibly to put the blame on Smith? There is the rope put round his neck. Does not the same thing arise there?

We come to the back door of this basement. The only person who had a key was Ley. Secondly, the £300 which Ley paid admittedly to Smith by cheque on 4th December and which was given back on the 9th. I did not hear Mr. Hawke when he opened this case mention that fact, and I was listening very carefully as you may imagine to what he was saying. Neither did I hear my learned friend ask Smith any questions about that £300. I suggest therefore that it is not a serious part of the Crown's case that this £300 had anything to do with the events of 28th November. You have heard the evidence that Smith had a conversation about going abroad. People do nowadays. You heard that he talked about going to New Zealand. There is this man spending over £3000 in November. It would be nothing for him, would it, to lend a man £300? "Why not have a car of your own?" says Ley. Smith says, "I cannot afford it." Ley says, "I will lend you the money." Ley says it was a different story. He says it was for a business. However, on the 9th he pays it into the banking account. It can be seen. It is an exhibit in this case. He tries to pay it over to Mr. Wilson and hands it back to Ley. I do not know what you think about it. Would it have been wise for him to have kept it or handed it back? With respect, I should think that you will probably think that it was an honest and ordinary thing to do if someone lent you money you did not want to pay it straight back, not because you had come to the conclusion that the money was too hot to hold. No point has been made by the Crown about this £300 at all. So therefore I suggest I am entitled to say it cannot really have much to do with this case or, of course, a point would have been made of it.

Ladies and gentlemen, there is an onerous task on one's shoulders in defending a man on a charge of this nature. No one who has not undertaken such a task can know what it is like. Sir Walter said not long ago that his burden passed, and so now my burden passes, and after the Crown's speech and after my lord's summing-up the burden passes upon your shoulders. I am not asking you to find a verdict against the weight of the evidence. I am asking you to say that no one comes into a dock in this country and is expected to find a complete answer. That is putting the onus upon him. The onus is completely and squarely upon the Crown.

I say, with respect, whatever you may think of Smith's part in this very unhappy episode of kidnapping—it was done by deceit on the part of Mrs. Bruce and not by force, and that has nothing to do with this case—you will not convict Smith of murder unless you are

Ley and Smith.

sure that he actually killed him, subject to my lord's direction, or that he was a party to killing him or was a party to doing him grievous bodily harm from which he subsequently died. You will not convict him of the crime of manslaughter unless you are satisfied beyond all reasonable doubt that he was guilty of some unlawful act, not of gagging him from *here* to *here,* but of some unlawful act from which he died. If you think, having been tied up by Smith and Buckingham, not up to the neck but up to *here,* he was left in the house bound and gagged so that Ley and probably his confederates could try to extract from that man a confession which he could not make, you will not convict Smith, in my submission, of manslaughter. You have seen and heard him. May I suggest to you that without the evidence of the "101" there is plainly no proof of murder. That evidence is so uncertain. With such issues at stake as we have here you could not say as a matter of certainty that that car was the car which belonged to Smith or that Smith was in it, and that Smith was reconnoitring for a place to put the body on the 27th. I submit, on the whole, the evidence is fantastic.

Therefore, for the reasons I have stated and for other reasons which you may think of yourselves, bearing in mind this man's statement made at the very first—"I will help all I can," said Smith —I submit he ought to be found not guilty because no one has satisfied you of his guilt upon this indictment.

Closing Speech for the Crown.

The LORD CHIEF JUSTICE—Before you address the jury, Mr. Hawke, I should like to be reminded what Dr. Gardner's evidence was as to the rope on the body. As I understood him, there was a rope tied in a half-hitch round the neck, and then there was another rope which passed over that. There were two ropes.

Mr. HAWKE—Yes, my lord, that is so. May it please your lordship, members of the jury, both my learned friends very naturally and very properly indicated to you what responsibilities lay upon their shoulders. Well, I am sure you will not be at any loss to understand just the extent of the responsibility that lies upon counsel for the Crown. It is my duty, with my learned friend Mr. Elam, to put before you such facts and all the facts which bear upon the issue which you have to decide, to endeavour to assist you to the best of my ability to consider those facts now that they are before you as they affect each of the two accused men here.

Closing Speech for the Crown.

Mr. Hawke

You will no doubt consider the case against each of them separately, and it is no part of my duty to indulge either in theories or speculation. It is my duty to put, as I say, the facts before you. You have been told that this is a very extraordinary case. I venture to ask you whether, when stripped of any emotional background, it is not really a very simple case. The body of a man is found dead, dead by strangulation. I will deal in a moment with the medical evidence. I am just giving you the skeleton of what you may think is not a very complicated matter. The body of a man is found dead by strangulation in a chalk pit in Surrey, undoubtedly transported to that chalk pit from a house in Kensington to which he had been decoyed, if that be the right word, as the result of a plot engineered by the defendant furthest in the dock from you, the defendant Ley.

In many of such observations, and I hope they will be reasonably short and concise, that I have to make to you about that defendant I may inevitably trespass upon ground much more ably covered already by my learned friend Mr. Curtis Bennett. If I do, I apologise. I shall endeavour to avoid it, but I must deal with the case as it affects him on the facts now put before you both for the prosecution and for the defence. Let me deal as far as I can with those facts now.

Members of the jury, this man who was found strangled had, if you accept the evidence of Dr. Gardner, been not only strangled but subjected to violent treatment. He was so injured before his death, according to Dr. Gardner, that the mucous membrane of his intestines presented the appearance of crimson velvet. You have heard from Dr. Gardner that that man's brain was bruised in two places, indicating that he had been struck upon the head, and you will not, I imagine, necessarily cast aside those opinions of an eminent pathologist merely because another pathologist goes into the box and indulges, if I may say so with all respect to him, in wild speculations and not upon fact, and who describes Dr. Gardner's evidence in his opinion as gross exaggeration. Dr. Gardner said in answer to a question by my lord that this man bore every appearance of having been beaten up. Let us avoid controversy between pathologists. Let us stick to something which is not in controversy at all between them. Dr. Keith Simpson, if he agrees with nothing else, agrees with this: that this man died of asphyxia caused mainly by the fact that a rope was pulled tight about his neck with an upward movement. Dr. Keith Simpson said that was consistent with hanging. Members of the jury, may I most respectfully agree? Of course it is consistent with hanging. As one knows, there are people who tie themselves up and who go

Ley and Smith.

too far in the course of doing so and strangle themselves. Of course it is consistent with that as well, as a mere speculative theory, but it is equally consistent, is it not, with a rope having been pulled by a human agency, a rope that had been placed round the neck of a man who was helpless to prevent it and pulled in such a way as to be an upward pull, such a way, you may think from the nature of the mark to which both these doctors have referred, as a pull that came from behind.

There are three states of affairs with which this man's injuries are consistent: hanging, self-infliction and what I have just described. I almost hesitate to ask you this: do you think, now that you have heard the evidence, that that man tied himself up? Do you think that that man, now that you have heard the evidence, a man who was bound hand and foot and gagged, then proceeded to put a rope round his own neck and hang himself? Members of the jury, those theories have only to be stated in the light of the facts to show—I hesitate to use the word—how ridiculous they are. It is not theory and is not speculation, and I assume you will accept it that this man was brought into a room, bound and gagged. You know now that somebody or some cause pulled the noose tight about his neck and strangled him.

I only say this one word more before passing from the doctors' evidence altogether, and this Dr. Keith Simpson's evidence entirely disregarded—you may have observed this—that it was not only the mark of a rope which this man had upon his neck. There was a mark which indicated that somebody had from the other side exerted pressure upon that man's collar before he died. As I say, this man, as both doctors agree, died of asphyxia. If a man dies of asphyxia as a result of a rope being pulled tight round his neck and by his collar being pulled tight round his neck, then any person who is taking part is, if that man dies, guilty of his murder. This I say with respect before his lordship, who will tell you the law and from whom you will take the law. It matters not who pulled the rope. It matters not who tightened this man's collar. If you are satisfied that at the time these injuries occurred which resulted in this man's death Ley or Smith, or either of them, were present, assisting or acquiescing in what was being done, then I venture to submit to you that your verdict, one which you will only arrive at after due and careful thought, weighing all the facts, and only if proved by reasonable certainty in the minds of each one of you, would be one of murder.

It has been said that you can doubt whether this man was ever murdered at all. I do not know whether that, in the light of the evidence which you have before you, commends itself to you. Have

Closing Speech for the Crown.

Mr. Hawke

you any doubt that this man died, whether as a result of violent treatment or not beforehand—have you any doubt that he died of strangulation? If there is no doubt of that then the question arises: who took part in the operation which resulted in his strangulation, and the question which arises from that of course is how and where was that bodily harm done to him. Smith and Buckingham both said it was at Beaufort Gardens. Have you any doubt in your minds that that is true? I shall mention Cruikshank later, but not at any great length. Have you any doubt that Smith and Buckingham have told you the truth when they say that this man was tied up and trussed and left in the chair in the room in the basement of Beaufort Gardens? If that is right, who was responsible for the events which led up to that being done in that basement far away from the chalk pit, far away from Reigate, but in London, in a flat in Kensington?

When I had the task of opening this case to you, Buckingham was the only witness as to the person who was responsible, with one exception which I will deal with in a moment. Smith's statement was not then evidence against Ley. Members of the jury, it is now. Have you, as I say, any doubt whatever, now that you have heard the evidence of both those men, that the instigator, the promoter and the financier of the plot which brought that man to London and deposited him in the chair at the end of the passage was the defendant Ley?

It may still be said, and it has been said, that Smith and Buckingham are witnesses who from the very nature of their evidence must be open to criticism and must be treated with caution. Well, be it so, but they have sworn to things which you may think they could not possibly have known except from one source only. What interest had either of those two men in Mudie? How did they know that he was to be found at the Reigate Hill Hotel? Certainly not, according to him, from Ley. He says "I have mentioned it to Smith that Mudie used to be at 'The Dog and Fox' or live at 3 Homefield Road, but I never mentioned to Smith that Mudie was in the Reigate Hill Hotel." He says that with regard to Buckingham also that he never told Buckingham. How do they know that a man called Mudie lives and works at the Reigate Hill Hotel? That is another remarkable coincidence if they did not hear it from Ley, is it not? What a coincidence it is, is not it, if from some completely different angle these two men, Buckingham and Smith, also knew Mr. Mudie who was living at the Reigate Hill Hotel and acting as barman there, and in order to put some pressure or vengeance of their own upon him they

Ley and Smith.

brought him back, again by an amazing coincidence, to the flat of the other man who knew so much about him?

A certain amount has already been said about coincidence in connexion with this case. Coincidence is so strong sometimes that it ceases to be coincidence. It has often been said that facts by undesigned coincidence are capable of proving a proposition with the certainty of mathematics. Smith and Buckingham in their evidence do not stand alone, because there is the porter Minden at the Royal Hotel, an entirely independent person, a person who knew that man Ley as a visitor at the hotel, a witness, if I may say so most respectfully, lightly passed over by my learned friend Sir Walter Monckton. Is Minden not to be relied upon, an independent person who only knew this person Ley as a visitor to the hotel? Is it to be suggested that he is suffering from faulty recollection or that he is deliberately trifling with the truth when he says that this man actually approached him and asked if he, Minden, knew of a person who could hire a car and at the same time keep his mouth shut, a person who if he did what he was told would earn more than a year's salary in, I think he said, a matter of weeks?

Members of the jury, have you any doubt at all that that evidence is true? If you have none, well, then there is the beginning of this plot emanating from the source of the defendant Ley. If you want further independent evidence you have only to consider the fact that on 16th and 26th November this same man drew from his banking account £550. Smith and Buckingham both say they were paid £200 each. Ley's explanation of that is that he drew those two sums out for curtains and furnishings. As to why he should draw sums of that size out for that purpose in cash he did not appear to have any convincing explanation. You have only his own word that that is what the cash was for. He had no receipt to support it or evidence of any kind. You have the evidence, on the other hand, of Buckingham and Smith themselves and also of Mrs. Bruce, who in the car, you may remember, passing from "The Crown and Sceptre" to another public-house said that she was handed £30 by Buckingham, he having counted them out of the envelope which he had just brought out of Beaufort Gardens, and young Buckingham's evidence was that when they got back from Mrs. Bruce's that night he counted the rest of that envelope and it contained £150 or £160.

I have dealt with this evidence quite shortly because I feel it would be a waste of your time if I went into it in detail. I have given the essential part of it, I hope, which affects the case here. I now come to the fact that there are two witnesses who give an

Closing Speech for the Crown.

Mr. Hawke

answer to the question why was this deed done at Beaufort Gardens and who was responsible for it. They are the two witnesses Smith and Buckingham. Now I venture to say this, and this is a matter for your consideration : is there not now a third witness who has provided evidence which supports the evidence of those two men? I mean by that, Ley himself. You may think that in spite of overwhelming evidence to the contrary it is impossible to believe a man of his obvious intelligence and ability could sink to the level to which this man has sunk if this case is proved against him. It may be difficult of comprehension. I would respectfully accept that. Members of the jury, I would also preface what I am going to say quite shortly with this, that it is no part of the Crown's duty or onus to search for motives. The Crown has quite a sufficient burden in the burden of proof without speculating as to motives unless there is a motive which can be proved and proved with reasonable conclusiveness.

Now that Ley has given evidence himself do you think—I think this is the best way I can put it—do you think I was justified in saying to you in first presenting the facts of this case before you, that the beginning of all this story lies in this man's obsession upon one particular subject? Has any evidence which has been called negatived that? Most of all, has anything he said himself in the witness box or anything in his demeanour in the witness box negatived that suggestion? If you are satisfied upon the evidence that Ley instigated this plot and that he insisted in the tragic final carrying out of the plot, it matters not what his motive was, but, you know, he denies ever having accused this unfortunate lady Mrs. Brook of having been her son-in-law's mistress; however, Miss Ingleson, his secretary, who was not, you may think, disposed to put any obstacles in the way of helping this gentleman, says that he did tell her so.

It is perhaps no part of my duty to go further than this, than to ask you what you think of a person who accuses that lady of being her son-in-law's mistress. He is a man who admits putting inquiry agents on to Romer, this man Romer living at 3 Homefield Road, because he thought Romer had relations with Mrs. Brook. He was asked by Mr. Curtis Bennett what made him do that, and you heard his answer; you heard him describe a conversation which he says he overheard behind a shut and locked door. If I described that particular moment in his evidence as a nauseating performance, should I be overstating it? I suggest that on one particular subject this man *is* obsessed, obsessed, you may think, almost to the point of being unbalanced. If that is right, have you any doubt at all that by the middle of the summer Mudie had become the

Ley and Smith.

focus of that obsession? It is all very well to say that at one time he is mentioning his son-in-law and at another time he is mentioning Romer. That may be so. But by mid-summer has not that suspicion, a poisonous suspicion you may think, become centred and focused upon this man who was conducting his work first of all in Wimbledon and then in Reigate, Mudie? It is shown, is not it, with the greatest possible clarity?

There is the performance of sending those cheques to Homefield Road, addressed to Mudie, asking him to get Mrs. Brook to sign them. You will remember them, and I shall not trouble you with those letters. They will be very fresh in your minds, I am sure. The explanation that he gave you of that extremely odd performance was that he understood that Mrs. Brook had gone out of London and was going down to Bournemouth, and he thought that that was a sensible way of getting her signature to the cheques, by sending them to somebody whom he had been told was living in the same house.

Members of the jury, that is an explanation which you may think is quite unbelievable. But there is a perfectly reasonable explanation, you may think. This may have a bearing on the proposition that this man's obsession was becoming focused on Mudie. The position was this. If he had got those cheques back signed by Mrs. Brook it would be evidence that he could lay before her that she was associating with this man behind his back. That plan misfired miserably because this wretched man who subsequently died gave the cheques to Mr. Barron. You have heard Mrs. Evans's evidence—the landlady at Homefield Road—that Ley told her that Mudie had been in the flat with Mrs. Brook and that the poor old thing could not stand the pace. You will remember that he dictated the letter, Exhibit 11, to Miss Ingleson, addressed to Mudie, to the effect that there was reason to believe there was an intrigue between Mudie and Mrs. Brook.

You may think those things give you a picture of a man who is obsessed on this subject and whose attention is focused upon one particular person. Is not it a short step from such performances as these, the sending of the cheques, and so on, and from such observations as I have reminded you of to Mrs. Evans—is not it a short step to evolving a plot such as has been sworn to in the evidence of Buckingham and Smith, a plot which was carried out with complete success inasmuch as it landed Mudie there in the chair bound and gagged and trussed?

You have heard that at that point Ley was there. Smith and Buckingham have told you so. I have indicated reasons based upon evidence why you may think there is no doubt about it.

Closing Speech for the Crown.

Mr. Hawke

So, upon that, it only remains for me to consider the evidence that Ley himself has called to displace that he was there awaiting them when they came back to 5 Beaufort Gardens, shortly followed by Mudie, at about 6.45 on the night of 28th November.

Ley's evidence is that he left Beaufort Gardens after tea that evening and went to the National Liberal Club. He said that later that night, I think some time after 8.30, he joined Mrs. Brook. Members of the jury, no doubt he may have done both those things, but does that help you to answer the question where he was at the vital time, the time when Mudie arrived at 5 Beaufort Gardens and the subsequent events took place there?

He says that he was dining at the Cumberland Hotel, and to support that two receptionists of that hotel were called. I venture to suggest that those two witnesses proved nothing beyond the fact that Ley was a regular customer at the hotel. But where are the people who could have proved that he was there that evening if he was? You heard that Ley was in the habit of always occupying the same table. If that was so, surely the best person to prove that he occupied it on the night of 28th November would be the head waiter in that part of the room, who would of course, one supposes, know him. More than that, Ley himself said that he saw a person of his acquaintance in the Cumberland at 7.15 that night and yet that gentleman, whoever he may be, has not been called to give evidence that he saw the accused. Therefore it comes to this that as regards the vital time you only have Ley's unsupported word that he was at the Cumberland Hotel and not at Beaufort Gardens.

If the evidence drives you to the conclusion beyond reasonable doubt that he was in fact at Beaufort Gardens when Mudie was brought there, can you have any doubt that he was concerned in the events which followed? Those events were that in the basement some person or some cause tightened the rope round Mudie's neck so that he met his death by strangulation, and more than that (if Dr. Gardner's evidence be accepted) some person or persons did violence to him before he died. This brings me to another witness called by the defence, Cruikshank. I gather he was called for the purpose of showing that by some well-meaning action of his in pulling at the ropes round Mudie's body he might himself inadvertently have been the cause of his death. But he was quite incapable of giving any explanation of how such a thing could have happened, and as I followed his evidence the ropes he pulled were round the man's body. How pulling at them could have caused his death you may think is obscure. I venture to wonder whether you believed a word that Cruikshank said. He explained the curious fact that

Ley and Smith.

Mr. Hawke

he was in the middle of London by 8 p.m. although he was still in Switzerland at 4 o'clock, by telling that story of a journey by aeroplane on what was apparently a smuggling expedition. You may think it is curious to say the least that a man who had carried out an adventure like that successfully and was waiting to be carried back to Switzerland again should have suddenly thought of paying a call upon someone whose name he had been given in a public-house as a person likely to be able to find him a job in Australia. Apparently too, if this story is true, he took no steps whatever to go to the police or give the information to anyone that he had found a man trussed up and helpless in that basement. You may think this story of his a fabrication from beginning to end, told, as sometimes these stories are, by a person with a perverted desire for attracting publicity, but if you think it may be true you may also think that it at least corroborates the case for the prosecution to this extent that it does show that this man Mudie was tied up and helpless and evidently injured in the basement of Ley's house on the night of 28th November.

Now, members of the jury, up to the time when Mudie was tied up and slumped in the chair Buckingham was equally responsible with Smith for all that had happened. But at this stage Buckingham says that he left the house and Smith agrees with him. From that time there were two men in the house besides Mudie—Smith and Ley. If Smith left soon after that and before anything else had happened, then I entirely agree with what my learned friend Mr. Curtis Bennett said to you that there could be no case against him upon an indictment for murder, though admittedly he was guilty of conspiracy to assault, and assault. The question is, did he leave? Or was he a party to what the evidence shows happened to Mudie in that flat after he was placed in the chair? The answer to that vital question may lie in one of those trivial incidents which by some curious chance contribute to the elucidation of the truth about matters which are very far from true. I mean the incident that two ordinary people happened to pass by the chalk pit on the evening of 27th November. Of the two men who, if Buckingham and Smith are right, were left alone with Mudie at Beaufort Gardens, one was Ley and the other was a man who had during that week been the temporary owner and driver of a small Ford car with the index number F G P 101. If those chance passers by, Smith and Tamplin, the two landscape gardeners, are right, the car they saw driven out of the chalk pit on the evening of 27th November was a Ford which bore the number 101. Tamplin went further and identified Smith as the man they saw run down to the car when he attracted their attention and drive the car away. As

Closing Speech for the Crown.

Mr. Hawke

I said to you before that personal identification having regard to the circumstances in which it took place would not for one moment be safe to act upon and by itself would be quite useless. But both these men agree that the car was a small Ford, both agree that it had the number 101, and we now know from Buckingham, Buckingham's son and Mrs. Bruce that Smith *was* driving a Ford car bearing the number 101 on the evening of 27th November because they too say that he arrived at Buckingham's house at Brixton in it that evening at a time which none of them can place with any certainty.

You will have no doubt (Smith admits it) that on the following day, 28th November, he drove that Ford with the number 101 to Reigate, where Mudie was picked up, and back to Beaufort Gardens. At Beaufort Gardens Mudie met his death. After his death Mudie's body was by some means conveyed to the chalk pit where later it was found, the same pit at the side of which the driver of a Ford with the number 101 was, if Smith and Tamplin are right, standing on the evening before Mudie was brought from Reigate to London. Can there be any reasonable doubt on that evidence that it was the same car that did the journey to the chalk pit on 27th November and the journeys to Reigate and back on the 28th. If there is no doubt of that then as we know that Smith did the journey in it on the 28th and we know that he was driving it on the evening of the 27th, the inevitable must be, must it not, that Smith was the man who on 27th November was reconnoitring the chalk pit in which Mudie's body was laid after his death by strangulation on 28th November? If that is right, the question then arises for what purpose was he reconnoitring it? And the answer to that question may provide the answer to the question how was Mudie's body conveyed there. If Smith and Tamplin are right about the number and the make of the car, which is the same as the number and make of the car which Smith was, according to the evidence, using on the night of 27th November to visit Buckingham at Brixton, and the car which he was admittedly using on the night of 28th November, it reasonably follows that Smith knew the locality of the chalk pit, the place to which Mudie's dead body was conveyed. Smith's evidence is that he left Beaufort Gardens soon after Buckingham did, and heard no more about the matter until he was told later on by Ley that Mudie had been dropped at Wimbledon. In the light of this evidence about the Ford car and its number do you think that that can possibly or reasonably be true?

There is one other matter I ought to deal with, as it was raised by my learned friend Sir Walter Monckton in his speech. He said,

Ley and Smith.

if I followed him correctly, that you might come to the conclusion upon the evidence that Mudie died by accident when he was struggling to escape. Members of the jury, if a struggle resulting in such an accident as that followed directly upon an assault consisting of tying and gagging, those responsible for that assault might in law be guilty of manslaughter subject to my lord's direction upon the law, but in that connexion you should surely ask yourselves what evidence is there of any such accident having occurred when all the injuries suffered by the dead man indicated violent treatment resulting in bodily injury and culminating in strangulation? Members of the jury, may I end by pointing out to you that there is evidence, and cogent evidence, for you to consider that the two accused men were present at the place where these injuries were caused and for the reasons which I have communicated to you there is, I submit to you, also evidence that one of them conveyed the body to the place where it was eventually found. If that is right and they were engaged upon a joint enterprise which resulted in this man's death, then it matters not whose hand it was that pulled the rope which caused the man to die, and both of them would be guilty of murder, which is the charge in the indictment against them.

Charge to the Jury.

The LORD CHIEF JUSTICE—Members of the jury, these two men, as you know, are charged with murder. This does not appear to me to be a case in which I need enlarge at any length upon the law with regard to murder or what constitutes murder beyond telling you this. A man is guilty of murder if he deliberately kills another. If he inflicts on him grievous bodily harm, does an act, that is to say, which a reasonable man must know will cause the other person grievous bodily harm, and the dead man has died as a result of that act, even if the person may not have intended to kill him, he is still guilty of murder. If for instance, to take a simple illustration, I stab a man meaning not to murder him but only to wound him and do a grievous wound to him and that man dies from that stabbing, why of course I am guilty of murder.

Now one reason why it seems to me that it is not necessary to enlarge very much upon this topic beyond what I have done is this. If you accept the medical evidence, and on this point the medical evidence called for the prosecution and the defence are entirely at one, the death of John Mudie was caused by strangulation, it was caused by strangulation with some degree of suspension.

Charge to the Jury.

The Lord Chief Justice

You know what suspension means—the doctor has illustrated it—some upward movement. When his body was found, in addition to the rope with which he had been bound, according to the witness who found him and according to the admission of the prisoner Smith, there was found round his neck another piece of rope and that rope had what is called a half-hitch—you know what a half-hitch is, just one turn, so that it could be drawn across his throat. In the opinion of both doctors that was the cause of death, and I do not suppose that you have any doubt that that was how this unhappy young man met his death. Someone tightened that rope round his neck till he died and of that he died.

Something has been said, and I rather regret it because it seems to me to bring in almost a fantasy into this case, about suicide. It may be that if a man hangs himself you would find the same marks on his neck as you find if he is strangled in the way it is suggested in this case that man was strangled. But anybody who sat in this Court and heard the evidence that has been given can, I suppose, have no lingering suspicion in his mind that Mudie committed suicide. Why should he? Where did he commit it? How did he commit it?

Another faint suggestion has been thrown out which would have some bearing, I suppose, on the question of manslaughter. I agree and tell you that if Mudie was left bound up merely as Smith and Buckingham have described, so that he had one arm free, there was some rope round his body and round his legs, and in some way, though I cannot visualize it, manage to get the rope entangled round his neck when no person would consider there was the smallest chance of his being able to do so, that might reduce the case to manslaughter if you thought fit to do so. But you see that overlooks the fact that on the uncontradicted evidence in this case where that body was found there was a second piece of rope round his neck. You have to ask yourselves as people of ordinary common sense, what is the significance of that piece of rope round his neck, the marks of which show that he was strangled by it, if it was not that some person pulled that rope and thereby caused Mudie's death.

The second general observation I want to make to you is this. It is not only the actual killer who can be guilty of murder. An accessory before the fact to a crime is equally guilty with the person whose hand commits the crime. An accessory before the fact is, in the language of the old law, one who procures, counsels or abets the commission of a crime, commission of a felony, though he is not present actually at the moment when the felony is com-

Ley and Smith.

mitted. If he is actually present at the commission of the felony which he procures, counsels or abets, he is called in law an aider and abettor. But according to our law either an accessory before the fact, which means some one who counselled and procured though he was not present; or the aider and abettor who counsels, procures and abets and is present, are both equally guilty of the crime, provided that they were accessories and aiders and abettors either at or before the commission of the crime and they can be tried, indicted and convicted in the same way as the principal offender. They are what is called principals in the second degree.

The third general matter which I want to say to you is this : you probably well know that in all criminal cases the burden of proving the offence is on the Crown and they have to prove the case to your satisfaction, and when you hear the words used about doubt, benefit of doubt or anything else, it means only this. It means that if you are left in doubt upon a matter, then the prosecution have not proved the case to your satisfaction and the prisoner is then entitled to be acquitted. You may then ask yourselves what is the point of evidence being called for the defence if it is not that the prisoner should prove he is innocent. It is this. If the Crown present a case which requires an answer, that is to say, if the Crown proves a case upon which a jury could in the opinion of the Court, and that is a matter for you, properly find a verdict of guilty, if it has not been answered the defence may call evidence by calling the evidence of the prisoners and any witness they choose to call and once that evidence is given it becomes part of the totality of the evidence, of the whole evidence. The evidence that is called for the defence may have one of three different effects; it may convince you of the prisoners' innocence; it may throw such doubt on the evidence that has been given for the Crown that you may no longer feel satisfied that the prisoners are guilty; thirdly, it may and sometimes does strengthen the evidence which was given for the Crown.

Now here at once I want to say a word to you about the evidence of the Buckinghams and Mrs. Bruce. You have heard that Buckingham senior was in the first instance charged with murder and that no evidence was offered against him and that the Crown have called him, his son and Mrs. Bruce as what is sometimes called in popular language King's evidence. It is always open to the Crown in the interests of justice to call those whom they may think took but a minor part in any particular incident or matter; to call them against the other actors in the crime who are the more responsible for the case. No doubt those people who are called as King's evidence, as it is called, are accom-

Charge to the Jury.

plices at least to some extent. In this case there is no doubt that Buckingham and possibly young Buckingham and Mrs. Bruce took part in the conspiracy of luring Mudie to Beaufort Gardens. It does not at all follow that though they were accomplices in that matter they were accomplices to murder. I want you to observe a very good reason in this case why the Crown should accept their evidence and put them forward as King's evidence and not charge them with murder. Buckingham and Mrs. Bruce made statements to the police on the 14th of December, very soon after the murder had got known. There is no suggestion that they saw Smith after the 1st of December, before the fact of the murder was notoriously public property. There is no suggestion that at the time they last saw Smith they knew of the discovery of this murder. Now Smith was seen by the police three days afterwards, on 17th December, and his statement was taken that day and all Smith was told by the police was that Buckingham had made a statement—I dare say they said Mrs. Bruce too—but he was not told what was in it. Smith entirely corroborates in his statement what Buckingham had said, namely, that Mrs. Bruce never entered the house and that Buckingham left the house immediately after the tying up. Therefore the position was that Smith, who was vitally interested in this case, entirely supported Buckingham, saying that Buckingham had no part in anything after the tying up. Therefore you can see for yourselves that there was a good reason for the Crown acting as they did and deciding to call Buckingham and Mrs. Bruce so that they could give their evidence upon this most mysterious matter and to see in the interests of justice whether their evidence would not assist the jury in coming to a just conclusion.

But of course it is my duty to warn you that they should be regarded as tainted witnesses whose evidence must be looked at with great care by a jury, and therefore evidence a jury would not be wise to rely on unless it was corroborated. With regard to Smith you do not need corroboration, because Smith's statement— and you see he is himself a person against whom the evidence is given—corroborates Buckingham almost word for word and line for line, except on that one small matter, and of course corroboration is never necessary of everything. If you can prove a fact without out calling the witness whose evidence has got to be corroborated, if you can prove the whole case, then there is no need to call the witness who ought to be corroborated. Smith of course corroborates Buckingham entirely, except on the one point as to whether it was Buckingham or whether it was Smith who gagged the deceased man. Smith says Buckingham did; Buckingham said Smith did. That is a very small matter. But with regard to the

Ley and Smith.

plot, the luring of this young man to the house, to the tying up, so far as Smith is concerned you need not trouble about any corroboration about Buckingham because Smith has admitted it all. The question as to whether Buckingham's evidence is corroborated with regard to Ley is always a matter for you. But there is abundant evidence here, if you believe it and if you accept it, that corroborates Buckingham's story in regard to Ley. The evidence of Minden alone was of course of the highest and most vital importance in the case. There is also the evidence of Mrs. Brook. How could Buckingham have known of this, you will ask yourselves, without it being passed on to him either by or through Ley? There is also the matter with regard to the cheque which becomes of great importance in this case. So I do not think you will have any doubt that when you are looking for corroboration there are plenty of facts which do corroborate Buckingham's evidence if you consider the evidence he has given is true.

The last thing I need say to you before I turn to the facts of this case is that the facts and the inferences to be drawn from them are entirely a matter for you. My duty is now to lay the evidence before you, to remind you of the salient points. If in so doing I seem to express any opinion of my own, please remember this. Any opinion, if I do express one, I express only for the purpose of assisting you. You are not bound to follow my opinion, but pay just as much or as little attention to it as you think fit. The duty of deciding upon any question of fact is not for the judge: it is entirely for the jury. I must also tell you that it is your duty to consider the cases of both of these men separately. You must consider of course the two cases together because the charge is a joint charge. It is said that they both were concerned as principals either in the first or second degree in this murder. But if you come to a conclusion that one was guilty you have still got to come to a separate conclusion as to whether the other is guilty. You must consider the two cases therefore both jointly and severally.

Now, members of the jury, let us come to the facts of a story in some respects, I suppose, as remarkable as has ever been told even within the somewhat grim walls of this Court. At half-past five on the afternoon of 30th November, a man named Coombs was walking home from his work and passed by a chalk pit on a high position in the North Downs, not far from Woldingham, which lies on a steep slope and is some 200 yards from a lane which runs from Warlingham to Woldingham, or runs off the Croydon western road in the direction of one of these villages. It is a lonely spot, an unfrequented lane. There as he passes along he sees something lying which attracts his attention. What was it? Is was the body

THE LORD CHIEF JUSTICE OF ENGLAND
(Rt. Hon. Lord Goddard)

Charge to the Jury.

The Lord Chief Justice

of a young man, a comparatively young man, who we know now was John Mudie, aged about 30 to 35, lying there strangled. He was lying with his body in a trench dug in the side of this pit. His legs were out of the trench. There he lay, his body cast away and left, I suppose, to rot in the wilderness. He went to the police at once and Police-constable Hearn arrived and there he saw what I have described to you. He also says that there was an overcoat pulled over the head, which you may think if you were considering how that man met his death to be of some significance. The man's body was tied with rope in the way in which you have heard, and which I need not again describe, and round his neck was another piece of rope which you can see for yourselves in the photograph which was taken of the body as it lay there. One arm we know was not bound. That we find out afterwards from Smith. In the pocket of the coat was found a card bearing the name of Mudie, which assisted the police at once to identify the body, and it is discovered that it is the body of this young barman who at this time was earning his living at an hotel at Reigate, some 12 miles away, where he was last seen on the afternoon or the early evening of the 28th of November. The doctor who was called finds the condition of the body, taking into account the degree of *rigor mortis* which he found—estimated that the body had been in that trench something over 40 hours, which, as you see, will bring the time when that body was deposited into that trench to some time on the 28th of November. By that time, strangely enough, was found a pick-axe. We know now where that pick-axe came from. It has been positively identified by two men who had used that pick-axe at 5 Beaufort Gardens. Beaufort Gardens, you may know, some of you, is a large cul-de-sac opening out of Brompton Road quite close to Harrods Stores.

The doctor examines this body and finds, as I told you, the cause of death. A second doctor was present at that examination, whom you heard give evidence on Saturday. I do not propose to take up time with you in discussing which of those two doctors' opinions is correct with regard to marks which are found upon the body or indications from the condition of the intestines as to whether or not violence had been used before death or not. It seems to me that can have but very little bearing upon the case. The cause of death we want to know. The cause of death we do know. What caused death was not any violence that was used before—blows or anything of that sort—he was killed by being strangled by a rope with some upward movement of suspension. You can picture for yourselves, can you not, how a man might be sitting in a chair and someone behind him, in front of him or at his side, drawing the rope and strangling him that way? That would be a degree of suspension, or he might be lying on the ground and a rope put round him and his head jerked up in the noose. At the time the body was found the knots of the rope were loose. Perhaps you will not think that very extraordinary. You have heard that the rope which was round the neck was in a half-hitch, that is to say, just one turn, so that if a person strangled him by pulling the rope, tightening the rope round his neck so as to strangle him, when that tension was relieved, then of course it could go loose. No further violence before death, although in the opinion of Dr. Gardner considerable signs of violence were on that man, was the cause of his death and the indication of strangulation, the doctor told you, was before the death. So at any rate we know what the cause of death was. You will also remember that, as I told you, one arm was not bound, and Smith, when he came to give his evidence, told us he did not bind one arm, and you can see for yourselves, I suppose, that if a man were left bound with his right arm free, if he were left in a room with his right arm free, as Smith has told us, if that were all that happened, that is to say, if the only rope upon him was the rope round his chest binding his left arm, his chest and his legs, what would be the man's first inclination to do? Why, to try to loosen his bonds. That may assist you in considering, if you believe Smith's evidence, as to the time, and that this arm was left free, how soon after that man was put into that room strangulation must have taken place, because you see, as I say, his inclination would be, would it not, to loosen his bonds? But for my own part I fail to see, though it is a matter entirely for you and not for me, if he was trying to loosen the knots that bound him how he could have hanged himself in so doing. It seems almost grotesque to suggest it, but it is a matter to be taken into account. But it is certainly remarkable that it is found in this case that one arm is bound and the right arm is free, and yet that man was strangled.

His identity being established, the police make inquiries and visit the place where he worked. He was, as you know, at this Reigate Hotel in decent occupation. So far as is known or we have heard in evidence, he does not appear to have been a man of loose life. He had previously been living in the house of the Mrs. Evans, who gave evidence before you, where she found him a quiet, inoffensive young man. It may be, I do not know, he did not know he had got an enemy in the world. There does seem to have been one person who was taking a most exceptional interest in Mudie, for a strange reason as you may think. That man was the prisoner Ley. In the room at the Reigate Hotel, where Mudie had lived, the police find a letter from a firm of solicitors demanding the

Charge to the Jury.

return of some cheques—a curious thing that the Connaught Properties, Limited, should be employing their solicitors to write to a young barman demanding the return of cheques said to have been sent to him for the purpose of sending on to someone else. Accordingly that leads them, having visited the solicitors who wrote the letter, to visit Ley, whose statement you have now got before you, which he made on the 7th of December. This statement discloses the story, or part of the story, with regard to the cheques about which you have heard, and for the first time introduces into this case the name of Mrs. Brook. Mrs. Brook was a woman who had lived with Ley as his mistress for a great number of years. She was still, as I understand, or had been up to a quite short time before the events into which we are inquiring, acting as his housekeeper. At any rate, as she said, he was paying the rent where she lived and she had lived with him at Knightsbridge Court. We know now that by the 8th of June she had gone to Wimbledon where she was occupying the flat in which her daughter, Mrs. Barron, lived with her husband, and young Mrs. Barron having had to go to hospital for an operation, her mother had gone down to live in the flat.

Two other men were living in this house besides Mr. Barron, a man whose name has been freely mentioned in the case but about whom we know nothing, of the name of Romer. It is a matter of regret that people's names sometimes should happen to be mentioned in this case, and I hope with all my heart that Mr. Romer has not been put to any inconvenience about this case, for any suggestions against Mr. Romer seem to be from what we have heard as groundless, as they apparently were against young Mr. Barron or Mudie. Mudie also lived in this house, and if you believe the evidence of Mrs. Brook and the evidence of Mrs. Evans, and Mrs. Evans, I think, must have struck you as a careful, decent, and reliable witness, Mrs. Brook had spoken to Mudie on one occasion. It so happened as she passed up the staircase on one day Mudie was there, the door of the bedroom which he occupied was open and he was standing there, and Mrs. Evans just said, as was the natural thing to a fellow lodger in the house, "This is Mr. Mudie." Mrs. Brook passed the time of day with him and Mrs. Evans was there the whole time. Mrs. Brook then passed on her way and she says that was the only occasion on which she ever spoke to Mudie at all.

On the 8th of June it appears that this man Ley goes down to this house at Wimbledon and whether he had some conversation that day or not, at any rate at that time he was obviously having suspicion of young Mr. Barron, Mrs. Brook's own son-in-law, Mr. Romer, and young Mudie. He had believed, he tells you, that on that date

Ley and Smith.

when he went down to visit his former mistress—I say "former mistress" because his evidence is that sexual relations had ceased between them for 12 years—he heard Mrs. Brook and Romer under such circumstances that obviously showed that sexual intercourse was taking place between them. Whereupon, he says, he goes down the stairs to the front door and then rings the bell and then he goes upstairs and sees Mrs. Brook. I do not know whether you believe that story at all. You may believe that he has persuaded himself that it is true. You may think that it is evidence of a diseased imagination on his part.

But a more strange episode takes place four days later. On the 12th of June, according to Mrs. Brook, and here she and Ley are about as opposed on the matters as one can well imagine, Mrs. Brook says Ley rang her up at night, 10 o'clock at night, that he seemed very agitated or excited about something, so much so that he said he was coming down to fetch her up to London. Thereupon she thought, I suppose, being still somewhat influenced by the insistence and importunities of her former keeper, that she had better pack up, and she began to put some clothes together, and at half-past two in the morning Ley arrived to take her to London and took her to London. Ley, on the other hand, says that somewhere about midnight, I think he said, though that does not matter, Mrs. Brook rang him up and said she was in great distress and indicated that she was being, I suppose, in some way molested or ill-treated by one of the men in the house, whereupon, so anxious was he for her protection, he got into a car, hired a car from the Daimler Hire, and went down to bring her up. He did get down there about half-past two. So far he agrees with Mrs. Brook and only so far—that he then found her in a very distressed condition, so distressed, maltreated, or whatever it may be, that she could not sit down, and when he got her to Knightsbridge that she spent the rest of the night in the Knightsbridge flat, and the next day she went to Cromwell Road, where she had already taken a room, from where she had gone down to her daughter.

Members of the jury, what is the next thing in this astonishing story we are told? We know both from Mrs. Evans and from Ley that on the 16th of June Ley goes down and sees Mrs. Evans and wants to know what he can find out about the "high jinks," as he calls it, that have been going on in the house, but according to Mrs. Evans nothing had gone on in the house. According to Mrs. Brook, nothing had gone on in the house. Mrs. Brook knew by this time that accusations of one sort or another were being made with regard to the three men who lived in the house, for which, she says, and you may think also Mrs. Evans supports her upon this,

Charge to the Jury.

that there was no foundation at all. But by this time Ley had got interested in regard to Mudie, and he asks Mrs. Evans about Mudie, and Mrs. Evans told you that he said something to the effect, "Poor young . . . I am sorry for Mudie," that he did not like to think that a man like that was involved in these affairs—in what affairs? —and he would like to help him. Why should he want to help Mudie—Mudie, whom he had never seen—Mudie, according to Mrs. Brook, about whom she had made no complaint, who had never caused her any anxiety or offered her any insult? And as to blackmail, because blackmail gets introduced into this, you remember, Mrs. Brook says it is fantastic—Mudie never asked her for any money. Nor did Ley tell us in the witness box, so far as I remember—I shall be corrected on this point by learned counsel—it has slipped my memory if he did say anything—I cannot remember that Ley gave us any indication as to where he had got the idea into his head that Mudie was blackmailing Mrs. Brook. She told us something about £150 to set him up in business. Ley says there is not the least foundation in that. Do you think the suggestion which the Crown puts forward is the right one, that for some reason this man had got an unreasonable jealousy of Mrs. Brook? She herself, you know, made use of the words, "He seemed to have a protective jealousy," in other words he was the person to look after her and nobody else and, it is true, at some time or another, found very considerable sums of money for her. But why this curious and sudden interest in Mudie, unless that is the fact?

Then there comes the extraordinary thing about these cheques. I make no apology to you if I go into the question about the cheques in some little detail in reminding you about one or two matters which by this time it is possible may have escaped your memory. You remember, I think it was in answer to a question I put to him, Ley said that he thought Mudie was an insurance agent. Do you think he thought anything of the sort at all? I said, "Where did you get that idea from?" Mrs. Brook had never told him he was an insurance agent. If Mrs. Brook had told him anything about Mudie it would be that at that time he was acting as a barman at the public-house in Wimbledon. But at this time, you know, on the 19th of June, Mrs. Brook was living in West Cromwell Road, no more than 10 minutes away from where this man Ley was at 5 Beaufort Gardens. Well, on the 19th of June, this letter was written by the prisoner's instructions: "Jack Mudie, Esq., 3 Home-field Court, Wimbledon, S.W.19. Mrs. Brook telephoned last afternoon that she was going to the country about some arrangements in regard to the convalescence of her daughter who is still in hospital"—I pause there for a moment to say Mrs. Brook

Ley and Smith.

never said in her evidence she ever told him she was going down, as far as I remember, to Bournemouth, as he said, or going any-where; she was in Cromwell Road—"and as we want some cheques signed and returned to us not later than Friday next we asked for her instructions. She directed us to send the cheques to her in your care."—Now, you know, that is absolutely untrue, according to Mrs. Brook, and I do not know whether Ley really says that is true or not—"with the request that if she did not reach Homefield Road by 4 p.m. on Thursday to ask you to be good enough to seal up the enclosed addressed envelope and post it to her new flat at 5 Beaufort Gardens, London, S.W.7, so that we can send up on Friday morning by taxi and obtain them"—if she had a new address at that time it was West Cromwell Road and not Beaufort Gardens —"We enclose stamped envelope addressed to her and marked as she directed 'Strictly private' "—why all this mystery about sending some cheques through the post?—"her instructions being that we were not to open the envelope on any account until she returned on Friday morning." If you accept Mrs. Brook's evidence, it is pure fantasy. At the same time he writes a letter and sends it also to "c/o J. Mudie," addressed to Mrs. Brook, "Dear Madam, We refer to your telephone message and as the cheques are essential for wages to-morrow, payable on Friday, we have sent the cheques under separate cover addressed as directed. We trust they will reach you safely and that you will be able to let us have them back signed either from Wimbledon or 5 Beaufort Gardens not later than Friday morning the 20th instant. If you care to telephone we will send someone to Beaufort Gardens, but you will appreciate that the distance from here to Wimbledon might make a special journey awkward. The only other director available is Mr. Ley"—who was at 5 Beaufort Gardens—"or we should not worry you at this time."

Ladies and gentlemen, the particular importance of these cheques and these letters seems to me to be this. When Mudie got those letters, what do you suppose he thought? I should think he thought that some madman was writing to him. But at any rate so puzzled was he about it that he, wisely enough, consulted a man older and more experienced than himself, a Mr. Barron, senior. Mr. Barron, as you know, was a gentleman who came into the box, a welfare officer, and helped Mudie with regard to this by taking the cheques, later, it is true, and returning them to the person who purported to have written them, a man named Baker, I suppose the secretary of one of Ley's companies. He took them back to him and took the precaution to get a receipt. Meanwhile Ley, and he has never told us how, traced Mudie and discovered that he was

Charge to the Jury.

at Reigate, because we know that a little later on he had brought Mudie along to Mr. Barron and there was an interview, and Ley afterwards was shown by Mr. Barron the receipt which he had got and he then said he was sorry he had given all this trouble.

Members of the jury, a matter which I ask you to bear in mind is this. Shortly after that Mr. Barron had an interview with Ley at the office of Mr. Ley's own solicitor, the gentleman by the name of Brashier. Mr. Barron has sworn that Ley said at that interview with reference to these cheques that that was a little bit of detective work on his own. Now, Ley heard Mr. Barron give that evidence at the Police Court, and it is on his deposition. Ley was therefore not taken by surprise when Barron said that in the box before you. He denied he had ever said anything of the sort. He gave you his explanation as to why he had sent those cheques. He did not call Mr. Brashier. Do you believe Mr. Barron's evidence or do you not, that Ley said at that interview that he had done this as a little bit of detective work on his own? If he did not, why could not he call Mr. Brashier to support him on that point, because, you see, it is beginning to get vitally important? He tells us, as he told Mrs. Evans, when he saw Mrs. Evans in June he said, "A young man I should not like to see mixed up in anything unpleasant. I should like to help him." In June he is sending those cheques addressed to his mistress care of Mudie. Do you think with this extraordinary obsession on his mind, or as suggested by the prosecution, was in his mind by this time—do you think that he was doing that to better Mudie, or do you think he was doing that to get some evidence against Mudie and that by this time he had got some obsession in his mind against him?

We now pass on to the month of September, late in September or the beginning of October. Ley's wife, who was in Australia, had been in the habit when she came to London, apparently, to England, of staying usually at the Royal Hotel in Woburn Place. At the end of September or the beginning of October he visited that hotel and saw the porter. Now the porter knew Ley, probably knew he was a man of some position and at any rate knew he had been a solicitor or was a solicitor. He was a solicitor, as he has told us, in Australia. He asked Minden, if you believe Minden's evidence, and you will ask yourselves what possible object Minden could have had in coming and giving the evidence he did unless it is true—he asked Minden if he knew of a man with a motor car who could be trusted to keep his mouth shut. Minden said that did not raise any particular suspicion in his mind, because he knew Ley as a solicitor and he thought he might be wanting a man for some service in connexion with his profession. Well,

Ley and Smith.

perhaps you may not think that altogether unusual. Solicitors have to conduct divorce cases and other cases sometimes of an unpleasant or suspicious nature, and they may want to find something out and someone who can provide a car or something like that with a driver on whom they can rely not to talk. So far that is all right. I think it was either the first or second time he did speak to Minden and said if he did think there was such a man he would earn as much as he did in a year. Well, that probably was only meant as a figure of speech, meaning if he did the thing satisfactorily and did keep his mouth shut he would get a sum of money.

Minden says he introduced Ley to Buckingham. Now, you will remember that Ley says there is not a word of truth in this. He has contradicted Mrs. Brook upon many points, most important points, he has contradicted Mr. Barron on that very significant matter, as to whether he said those cheques were a little bit of private detective work, and he now says Minden is a liar. There is no question of mistake. Either Minden when he went into the witness box and told you what he did was committing the most deliberate perjury or he was telling the truth. Ley says there is not a word of truth in Minden's evidence at all, and not only that, he says there is not a word of truth in Buckingham's evidence, and not a word of truth in Buckingham's evidence as to meeting him at the Royal Hotel. Minden, on the other hand, says, and this of course strongly corroborates Buckingham, if you believe Minden, that he not only did introduce Buckingham, not only did he give Buckingham Ley's telephone number, but that he saw them have interviews on more than one occasion at the hotel. More than that, he saw Ley have interviews with Smith and Buckingham at the hotel, all the three together. Buckingham says, I think I am right in saying, that at the very first opportunity he had with Ley, that Ley told him the story about a lady being blackmailed. Well, you know you will consider that and consider whether that fits in with the other evidence that you have heard in this case, and all this mysterious business for which you may think Ley gave no explanation at all about the cheques.

Smith now appears on the scene. Smith seems to have been a man very much taken into Ley's confidence. It seems, you may think, rather a curious friendship. Smith is a joiner who is acting as foreman of the works at Beaufort Gardens where Ley was converting a house into some flats. Ley and Smith are not, you may think, quite of the same social standing. Ley is a man who has been a Minister in New South Wales and a solicitor. You find him dining on several occasions with Smith. Of course there is no

Charge to the Jury.

reason why you should not take the foreman who is doing work on your house out to dinner, but you may think it is not a very usual thing. You might expect a casual lunch being stood to a man, taking him to a snack bar, buying him a drink and some bread and cheese, but on more than one evening, if you believe Smith, and I think Ley agreed with it, you find him taking him out to dinner. You will ask yourselves why: Why this sudden interest in the foreman of the works? Thereafter matters proceed between Smith and Buckingham, but there were at least, according to Minden, and I think according to Buckingham, at least two further interviews at which Ley was present. I do not think I need pause to turn up Minden's evidence to be quite accurate on this point. I am not sure Minden spoke of seeing Buckingham with Ley on more than two occasions, but he certainly saw Buckingham and Ley and Smith together on at least one occasion. You see that corroborates Buckingham and Smith. Certainly there is one occasion of which Minden speaks when he saw all three together.

Now, according to the evidence that has been given before you, Ley told the story to Buckingham about Mrs. Brook being brought to London in the middle of the night, and Ley at one time, according to Buckingham, told him that he had now got enough on Mudie, whose name had been brought into the conversation, to get a confession out of him and that he wanted him brought to London. Again I remind you, Ley says that there is not one word of truth in this matter at all, and of course you will ask yourselves this—there are only three people up to now involved : Smith, a joiner, Buckingham, the proprietor of a hire car, and Ley. Do you think that Smith or Buckingham knew Mudie or had the least interest in Mudie? Do you think they thought they could get anything out of Mudie or that they had any reason to suppose they could get anything out of Mudie or that they would have any reason themselves for getting Mudie to London? You see, I say that because Ley says, and of course you are bound to consider this, that this was a frame-up on the part of Smith and Buckingham; in other words, it was Smith and Buckingham doing something to Mudie and then trying to put the blame on Ley. Yet Ley, we know, is the man who has been taking this curious and, I think one may say, very sinister interest in Mudie, a man whom he seems, if you believe the evidence, to have suspected was trifling in some way with his former mistress and for whom, again if you believe the evidence, he laid a deliberate plot or trap, and by means of those cheques tried to trap him. According to Smith and according to Buckingham, the suggestion was made to them that they were to get Mudie to London, and of course when that was made clear to

Ley and Smith.

Buckingham we at once see where the reward which was to be equivalent to a year's wages was coming in, because you do not do these sort of things, you do not act as a hired driver for nothing. Thereupon the plot begins to thicken.

Now you will remember that both Smith and Buckingham have told you that they at first suggested that the thing to do would be to go down to Reigate, and you may think they could only have known Mudie was at Reigate if Ley had told them, and by shamming drunk get Mudie out to help push one of them into the car and then to push Mudie into the car. But that was not approved by Ley, so they say—Ley of course says he knows nothing whatever about it. Then they formed the plan of bringing a decoy, and the decoy that is taken is Mrs. Bruce. Mrs. Bruce is to be taken down and get to know Mudie, and apparently she goes down to the hotel and enters it on one or two occasions. It was on the third occasion, I think, that she went on at once to suggest to Mudie that she was going to have a cocktail party and she would like him to come up and act as a shaker. I need not take you through all the long story about this. That is the way, as we know, the plot was hatched. If you believe Smith and Buckingham and young Buckingham and Mrs. Bruce, that was how the plot would work. Mudie was enticed into the car—there were two cars in this plot, one of which I shall have a great deal to say about later on—and Mudie having been got into that car, at some time on the journey home Mudie is in the car with Mrs. Bruce and young Buckingham, and the car that Smith was hiring, the Ford car, is leading the way, and that car at some times accelerates and gets away, drives off fast so that it gets to Beaufort Gardens before the other one and goes to the other entrance, goes to the front entrance. It having gone to the front entrance, the other car is brought to the back entrance. Then, as you know, and I do not propose to go through the story again, Mudie unsuspectingly enters the house. Smith, who admits he was waiting for him, grips him round his arms, Buckingham emerges from the back of him and puts a rug over his head. Then Smith ties him up and one or the other, and I do not think it is worth taking up your time in discussing which, gags him. He is taken into the room and left there, and then Buckingham admittedly leaves the house. Buckingham has taken part in a gross assault and no doubt has committed the offence of what is called falsely imprisoning a man, but both according to Buckingham and according to Smith, Buckingham then left the house and Smith stayed behind.

Before I say any more about Smith, let us see what we know, if anything, with regard to Ley's movements, because you see we

Charge to the Jury.

have got now to a state where Ley denies all knowledge of anything that took place. He has contradicted Mrs. Brook, he has
contradicted Mr. Barron, he has contradicted Buckingham, Smith,
Mrs. Bruce, everybody connected with that plot, and says he knew
nothing about this whatever. If you come to the conclusion, and
I suppose you have really no doubt about it, that that unhappy man
who met his death that night was taken to Beaufort Gardens, the
first and most obvious question you will ask yourselves: why was
he taken to Beaufort Gardens? If Ley knew nothing about this
and was no party to the plot, surely they were running the most
enormous risk in taking him to Ley's premises, into Ley's flat and,
if you believe it, leaving him bound there. But Ley says he can
give you an account of his movements on that night. He had tea
with Mrs. Brook—very likely he did—Mrs. Brook left that house
before five o'clock, so she says. I think she said that Ley went out
with her. He is also able to say he was seen at a quarter-past five.
After that there is no evidence before you, except the evidence I
shall mention in a moment, of his movements at all that night,
except Mrs. Brook says and professes to be able to remember this
night quite distinctly, but how she does remember anything to
mark out that night from any other night I do not know, but she
remembers he came round to her rooms much later, somewhere
about half-past eight, I think, and stayed there till quite late in the
evening and went home after a game of cards. Of course the
material time in this case is ten minutes to seven or seven o'clock.
　　Ley's account of the matter is that he went to the National
Liberal Club and then went to the Cumberland to dinner. He has
called certain witnesses. You may think they help you, you may
think they do not throw the least light on the case. The young
woman from the National Liberal Club, in connexion with Ley's
change of address, said that if any address was handed in it would
be passed on the next day, but the cashier does not necessarily get it
next day. She does not remember any day she got it. Ley may
have handed it to her at any time of the day, including of course
five or after five, as he said he did. Then you get the evidence of
the two receptionists from the Cumberland Hotel. It is possible,
you may think, that their evidence shows they know Ley as a
regular diner, a man who frequently used the grill room for a meal.
They told you he always came accompanied by a lady, though once
they remember he came alone, that he came every night. We know
he did not, because we know that he dined at the Normandy on
occasions with Smith and he did not take Smith to the Cumberland.
If you think there is anything in it—I do not suggest it to you at
all—one thing is perfectly clear: wherever Ley dined that night

Ley and Smith.

he did not dine with Mrs. Brook, he did not take Mrs. Brook to dinner that night. Mrs. Brook has told you that and he has told you that. Yet the witnesses that he relies on as coming from the Cumberland Hotel say that whenever he came to the Cumberland Hotel, except on one occasion, they can remember he always had a lady with him. As I say, Mrs. Brook did not dine with him that night. She admittedly was in the habit of dining with him most nights. You may ask yourselves why she was not dining with him on this all-important night. There may be a very good reason that she did not.

Let us see how far we have got. You will also remember that until she was about to leave the box Mrs. Brook did not say a word, had not said a word up till then in her evidence about how she remembered all the movements of herself and Ley on that all-important night. You will ask yourselves whether you think her evidence really can be relied upon about that, but, you see, whether you think it can or whether you think it cannot the most material time that we are dealing with is from 10 minutes to seven till, say, a quarter-past or half-past. Nobody has come here to say that they saw Ley at that time that night, unless you think on the evidence of the receptionists that he was always there and therefore must have been there that night. I do remember that Ley said in his evidence that on this all-important night as he left the Cumberland Hotel he saw a person he knew, a man he knew, and nodded or spoke to him. We have not seen that man. But at any rate that is what you have to consider here : where was he between 5.15 and 7.45, if you accept Mrs. Brook's evidence that he went round there at 7.45?

Now you know, it must have struck you as remarkable, although it is not impossible, that in this case this curious body of evidence that has been led here is met by him with simple, positive, flat denials. There is no question of his saying "Yes, so far that is true. I engaged Buckingham for some purpose and he misunderstood the purpose," or whatever it is. He has simply given a flat denial of this and says there is not one word of truth in it from beginning to end. Of course to that you will give such weight as you think fit. You see, one of the things which he has most positively sworn to is that he never knew Mudie was brought to that house at all. Members of the jury, do you remember one piece of evidence that Ley gave while he was in the witness box? You will remember there were three people of whom he had suspicions with regard to their conduct with Mrs. Brook—Romer, young Barron, and Mudie—and he said in the course of his evidence, and I took it down, "I wanted Arthur Barron to come along somewhere where I could get information to Beaufort Gardens." Is not that exactly what Smith and Buckingham say he wanted with regard to Mudie? You may possibly think, members of the jury, that it was lucky for Arthur Barron that he was not induced to go along to Beaufort Gardens. But if he was wanting, as he has told you in the witness box, that Arthur Barron should go to Beaufort Gardens to get a statement from him, does it strike you as altogether remarkable that he should have procured Mudie to be brought to Beaufort Gardens? If the motive of this man, you know, was jealousy, and jealousy is one of the most powerful emotions and leads very often to the most incalculable and unhappy results—if you think what he said to young Barron shows that he was suffering from this, shall I call it insane—that only means unreasoning, it does not mean he was mad, no one suggests he is mad, but unreasonable—jealousy in this case, you may think, throws a flood of light upon the whole of this story.

You know there came into the witness box, called for the prosecution, but obviously showing herself a witness who wanted to do all she could for Ley, that young woman his secretary, Miss Ingleson. She was a most reluctant witness, and she told you he had told her of his suspicions of Romer and of Barron and of Mudie. Then there is another piece of evidence which I call to your attention, because I think it is right it should be in your mind. That young woman Miss Ingleson told us when the police called on Ley—I think she put it at the 9th of December, it may be the 9th or the 7th—that matters not—but a few days after the police had called on Ley, Ley said to her, "Mrs. Brook is accusing me of murdering Mudie." Now Mrs. Brook says she never accused him of murdering Mudie, it never entered her head he had murdered Mudie. Why did he tell Miss Ingleson he was being accused of murdering Mudie at a time when nobody was accusing him? Do you think perhaps that was the uneasy conscience he had, or why should he make that remark to his confidential secretary when nobody had ever accused him of it at all? It may be that he knew of the deed that had been done on the 28th of November, but up to that time nobody had accused him of it. Yet you heard from that witness what she said he told her.

Members of the jury, before I leave Ley it is right, I suppose, that I should say one word to you about the witness Cruikshank. I have dealt with the other witnesses that were called in this case, but with regard to Cruikshank, that man who, we know, was an ex-convict, came and told you a story which you may or may not believe to have any truth in it at all. It is not uncommon, you know, that people of bad character come and tell these various

Ley and Smith.

stories. You will remember that it was put to Cruikshank in a test of whether he was telling the truth or not that in his statement he said that he came down, nobody having answered him at the front door, he came down and found the door of the area was open and he went into the passage and stumbled along the passage. You have seen the plan of the house, and you know he does not come into a passage when he comes in through the area door: he comes into the kitchen. It is not for me to express any opinion as to the wisdom of his being called, but you know he tells you he saw a man sitting bound up in the room and he saw him with the aid of a cigarette lighter that he had got in his pocket and he said he fumbled with the cords. Well, supposing he did, how could that have mattered? But you know if there was any truth in his evidence at all it shows that about nine o'clock that man tied and trussed up, as you have heard, had been in that house for two hours, in Ley's house, left there for Ley to come back and find him at any minute, an astonishing thing for people to do if they were doing it without Ley's permission and knowledge and encouragement and incitement.

Members of the jury, you will probably think that there is not much truth at all in Cruikshank's evidence. He comes and tells you that he pulled the ropes. Well, supposing he had, he could not have done that man any harm. To do any harm to that man you had got to pull that noose round his neck, not to go up and pull at some ropes that might have been round him. But it is asked, why should Cruikshank come here and tell this story if there is no truth in it? Members of the jury, you have probably formed your own opinion about it, but I should have thought you have not very far to seek. This case after it was seen here, seen before the Magistrate, has been published in the papers. Possibly some of you may have seen it yourselves. If an ex-convict of that description sees a man in trouble who, according to the evidence, has been willing to give £200 to one, £200 to another, might not he have thought if he, finding that man in trouble, comes forward and tells some story, that man might help him afterwards and he might be the recipient of that man's bounty? I do not think you need seek very far, but it is for you to say whether you do or whether you do not believe his evidence.

Now, ladies and gentlemen, I should tell you this, I think, before I go on any further. If, of course, you believe Ley's denial, then there is no more to be said in the case against Ley, and equally if you believe Smith, with whose case I am going to deal now, if you believe Smith's story and his evidence, that all that he did was to leave that man bound in that room, well, then he is not guilty,

Charge to the Jury.

The Lord Chief Justice

because if somebody else came and strangled that man, Smith certainly would not be guilty of murder. He would be guilty of no more than having assaulted Mudie by binding him and leaving him in that house. We must indeed look very carefully at Smith's evidence, because it seems to me very likely that if you disbelieve Ley you may feel: Well, Smith at any rate has been telling us the truth. You may feel that you can rely very much more strongly on what Smith says than on what Ley says. But that may not be enough for you to dispose of the case against Smith, because there are some matters in regard to Smith which do require the most careful and anxious consideration at your hands.

Let me first point out to you, because I think I must, that in one respect his conduct after this business differed very materially from Buckingham's and Mrs. Bruce's. Buckingham—I do not want to use slang expressions, but I think I might use the very common expression applying to him—he appeared to you probably to be what is commonly called a "tough." He at any rate says, "I always agree I took part in the decoying of this man and the leaving of him bound in this place, but I was no party to murder and as soon as I saw and as soon as Mrs. Bruce saw in the paper that this enterprise, wrong as it was, had had such a terrible ending we went straight to the police and told them." Smith did not. In that respect you may see, although it may be said that up to a point he was no worse than Buckingham, Buckingham and Mrs. Bruce at any rate were not going to let it be said against them, "We were party to this murder." They went and told the police at once as soon as it was known. They went to the police and said, "Look here, we did take part in this business with regard to Mudie. We lured him to London. We did illegal acts for which we are liable to be prosecuted, and were, for assaulting and for kidnapping him," or as the law would call it "falsely imprisoning him," "but we had nothing to do with murder." Now Smith did not do this. He told nothing to the police until the police came to him, and we have now got to see very carefully how the evidence stands in regard to Smith after this time when Mudie was brought into the house.

You will remember, as I have told you, that Smith has said, and no one knows better than Smith, that in tying up Mudie he left his right arm free, so would it be extraordinary if Mudie was using his right arm to try and get out of his bonds? Would it be altogether beyond the bounds of possibility that whoever was in that house afterwards would have taken precautions or steps to see that Mudie did not get himself free? He stayed behind. He told Buckingham that he stayed behind because he was waiting

Ley and Smith.

until some friends that Ley expected arrived. That would indicate to you that what he was thinking was going to happen was that he had done all that he was hired to do and that somebody else was coming on the scene. He told us that he talked to Ley for some time, some few minutes, some ten minutes. Neither he nor Ley went to see this man who was tied up in another room, not merely tied up but gagged—he was left. Then says Smith—by this time he means, I suppose, Ley was no longer there—he says, "I heard something," just as Cruikshank said he heard something. "I heard someone, I think it was some steps coming up to the front door and so I left by the area door." So that if the person had not been admitted at once they might easily have seen each other because, you see, they would both be at the front of the house. His car was standing out there all the time, and he got into his car, so he says, and drove away, and he heard someone else go into the house and the front door shut as he just came out. You will have to ask yourselves whether you believe that and whether you think there was some third or fourth person brought into this matter.

But what I think you ought to pay particular attention to is this. One might have supposed that after these two men had done their rough work on Mudie, if all that was to be done was that Mudie was to be left tied up there, and Ley or any of Ley's friends cross-examine him and try to get a confession from him, you might have thought, I suppose, that these men would have gone possibly to discuss this business in which they had been engaged and to congratulate themselves on it and have a drink together. But that was not the plan. Buckingham said, and on this matter he was not challenged, he was not cross-examined, that Smith told him that he was going to Leicester that night. As I said, Buckingham said that and he was not cross-examined. Therefore, you may take it, if you choose, that this is true. Did he go to Leicester that night? Of course he did not. He says he did not. Not only he says he did not, but he has called his landlady. He did not go to Leicester that night. Why did he tell Buckingham that he was going to Leicester that night when he was not? Why was he going to put himself 130 miles or 120 miles away from what he had done in London? He tells Buckingham "I am going away; I shall be in Leicester." He was in London, in the outskirts of London.

The next time that Smith saw Ley was on Monday, the 1st of December, and he spoke to Ley about this matter. It would have been remarkable if he had not. What did Ley tell him? Ley told him that Mudie had been dropped at Wimbledon and he says he never asked him any other questions about it, never asked

Charge to the Jury.

whether Mudie had confessed, never asked whether Mudie had got the money to go out of the country, because, you know, another instance of Ley's generosity in this case was that he was to pay Mudie, the blackmailer—if only he signed the confession—he was to pay him to go out of the country. Why not hand him over to the police for blackmail, I do not know, but that was what he was going to do—pay him money to get out of the country. Smith said Ley told him Mudie had been left at Wimbledon, Wimbledon where he had been previously living, Wimbledon because his house was there, Mrs. Evans's—he had lodged at Wimbledon. What was there to show he would not go to the police, tell the police how he had treated him? If Smith had gone on to say Mudie was in a blue funk and signed a confession that he was a blackmailer and so on, that might have been something. But he was content—he had taken part in this outrage, because it was nothing short of an outrage he had taken part in—he is content when he is told that Mudie was dropped at Wimbledon. Later on it comes to Smith's knowledge that Mudie is missing. Again he asks and all he is told is, as far as I am concerned, he was dropped at Wimbledon. You might think that is a very astonishing state of affairs.

Now, ladies and gentlemen, of course I have got to deal with one other matter. Before I come to that I just remind you of one thing. According to Smith's own evidence he did receive his £200. He received it that night on the 28th of November. We heard a great deal about Smith going to South Africa. Well, you cannot go to South Africa with nothing. If he goes to South Africa a man may want something to start himself with when he gets there. It may be that that was the reason why Smith was taking this money or anxious to get this money. But you know there is another curious incident here with regard to money. On the 4th of December, three days after Smith has come back from London and Ley has told him that he had dropped Mudie at Wimbledon, Ley gives Smith £300. Why? According to Ley and according to Miss Ingleson it was because Smith was thinking of starting a business. No questions asked—"What business?"—no question asked: "Where is your business?" Oh no, just £300: "I am starting a business, would you mind lending me £300?" No mention of paying it back or any interest at all. Very generous conduct, you may think. Smith, I think, says, "No, that was not the purpose of it at all. He lent me £300 to buy a car, and in two or three days I found out I should probably be going to South Africa." Well, you can use your own knowledge of the world. Is it so easy

Ley and Smith.

to get passages to South Africa at the moment? Having been lent £300 to buy a car, it may be some months before you get a passage to South Africa, and one would have thought that you might have bought the car, because if you were lucky enough to get one for £300 you could use it and probably be able to sell it at any rate for the same as you paid for it, if not at a profit. At least there was a question about it being for a business. He says it was not for a business, it was for a car, but anyway it may have been a mistake. The money was repaid in an extremely short time. If money is lent for the purpose of a business or a car, not a particular car he had in view but to buy a car, you do not usually think it would be returned in four days. Had anything happened within four days that might cause the money to be paid back? The police had come. You may think that the visit of the police was not altogether unconnected with the return of that money, but even then one must be perfectly fair to Smith on this matter, even if he had not told the truth about that he could quite well say even then, "Well, I knew I was engaged in this enterprise and the police were on the matter and I knew I should sooner or later have to disclose what part I took. I had better get rid of that money." That is quite possible.

Now, members of the jury, I must take you to the last and so far as Smith is concerned by far the most important piece of evidence. Members of the jury, I go as far as this. It is on the next matter that I am going to deal with that I should advise you— I cannot direct you because it is a matter entirely for you, but I should advise you to let your verdict for or against Smith depend. We know Smith was there at the house. We do not know positively what happened afterwards. Somebody took that body from Beaufort Gardens, if you believe the evidence that it was at Beaufort Gardens. Somebody took it from Beaufort Gardens to that chalk pit near Woldingham, and that man was dead when he was put in the chalk pit, if you believe the evidence which has been given, and you have heard that his boots were clean while his clothes were stained as they would be through lying in the chalk. The boots were clean, so he did not walk. Probably you will think that more than one person carried that body up. Now was it Smith?

Members of the jury, on the Monday before this murder Smith hired a Ford car and he hired it for a week. He had never hired a car for a week before. He paid down £29 and he says that was his own money. £15 he would get back when he returned the car. But he had to pay down £29, no inconsiderable sum for a

306

Charge to the Jury.

man in his position, but a sum which he might be willing to pay if a considerable sum of money was coming to him almost immediately. That car was a Ford 8, a dark saloon, and it had its number plate on the back of the car, not one of the square number plates you see on some cars but a long number plate. You have seen the photograph FGP, I think it was, 101. He says that he hired that car for business purposes. Why? What business purpose was there for which he required that car? His employers gave him no car allowance. He had not hired a car for a week before this for his business, although he says he has on occasions hired a car for the day. His business in London was not to be a foreman at half a dozen places where he had to run about; he was a foreman joiner at 5 Beaufort Gardens. You would expect a man of that sort to go to his work by omnibus or by rail. But he says that he got it for the purpose of his business. On the Monday and the Tuesday he did not use it for the purpose of his business. It was in the garage at Goose Green which is down somewhere near Dulwich. So he was not using it for his business then. On the Thursday we know what that car was used for, at any rate up to 10 minutes to seven. It was used for the kidnapping of Mudie. That car which had not been used on the Monday or the Tuesday, on the Wednesday and the Thursday was used by this man and was taken by him in the morning, because he said it stood outside Beaufort Gardens all day. I was careful to ask him what had become of it, where that car had been kept, so that there should be no question as to whether it had been stolen or anything of that sort. He said it was outside Beaufort Gardens all day on the Wednesday and the Thursday and he had the keys in his pocket. We know he used it on the Wednesday, not only because he must have used it to get it to Beaufort Gardens, but somewhere about half-past five he called on Buckingham at Brixton—I think I am right in that—he called on Buckingham at Brixton in his car. At 20 minutes to five the men whom you have seen in the witness box before you, were walking down that lane which adjoins the chalk pit. Smith at any rate had no legitimate interest to be in that neighbourhood at all. They see a car and they also see a man up by that chalk pit. They said he seemed flurried when he saw them and he ran down to the car. Do not take too much notice as to whether he ran or walked, because if it was a very steep bit people do not as a rule run down because they may fall, because it was a very steep ditch, but at any rate that is a small point. At any rate he got into this car and by then they had got past the entrance of the drive that goes up to the chalk pit and saw the car come past them. They had therefore an opportunity of seeing the number of the car as they passed it and when it passed them and they say the number of that car was 101 and it was a dark saloon car and one of them said it was a Ford or an Austin and the other said it was a Ford.

Members of the jury, can coincidence go as far as this, that some other car, a Ford 8 with the number 101 attached, a dark saloon, should have been the day before this murder at the scene where the body was disposed of, that a car bearing that number and of that description was hired by Smith, hired by the man who kidnapped Mudie, and the car was used in the kidnapping of Mudie? Is not that a matter of most intense importance in this case and a most deadly matter for the prisoner Smith? You will remember that there has been no evidence in this case which should show that the times were in any way impossible, unless of course he stayed at Beaufort Gardens that night until five o'clock. At 20 minutes to five—those two men were positive of the time and remembered they afterwards went, so careful were they, they went and told the police—they knew of course from the papers where the body had been found—they told the police of the car and they told the police of the number—at 20 minutes to five that Wednesday afternoon, if you think it was that car, that car with the number 101 was at that position near Woldingham. You heard the distances from the Chief Inspector. There would be no difficulty whatever, would there, in that car being at Brixton at Buckingham's house by half-past five?

Now take the times on the next episode. Smith brought Mudie to that house in Beaufort Gardens at 10 minutes to seven. Assuming that Mudie was put into a car and this car 101 was standing outside the front door, assuming that Mudie, dead or alive, was put into the car, we will say if you like, at 20 or half-past seven, you have got to get to Woldingham which would be somewhere about 22 miles. It would be less than an hour's run—half-past eight, a quarter to nine if you like. The body has then got to be taken from the car and dropped where it was found. Give 20 minutes, another half hour if you like. He has then only to drive back to his lodgings at Dulwich, and the evidence of the landlady was, although she did not know when he came in, he was in bed when she went to bed, which was 11 o'clock. Members of the jury, so far as times are concerned they at any rate do not show there was anything impossible. Something has been said about the identification by Tamplin of the driver. You will remember that he explained how he saw the back of the head and turned towards you and showed what he meant. I entirely agree that if the matter depended on that for the identification of the man it would be unsafe to act it, but you cannot overlook altogether the fact that at the

Charge to the Jury.

identification parade at Brixton Prison Tamplin did pick out the man who had hired the car which was a black saloon car, which was a Ford 8, which did bear the number 101 and which was engaged in the kidnapping of Mudie.

Members of the jury, I think now I have covered all the ground that I need cover. It is a terribly serious case. When you go to your room and consider the case you will remember of course that you owe a duty, and a grave duty, to the prisoners, but you owe an equally grave duty to the State and to the dead man. That man's life perished through some cruel and wicked act. If the evidence has brought home to these men to your satisfaction that they were guilty of that cruel murder it is your duty to say so, and if you are not satisfied it is your duty to acquit them. I will now ask you to consider your verdict.

(At 25 minutes to five the jury retired and returned into Court at 28 minutes to six.)

THE CLERK OF THE COURT—Members of the jury, are you agreed upon your verdict?

THE FOREMAN OF THE JURY—We are.

THE CLERK OF THE COURT—Do you find the prisoner, Thomas John Ley, guilty or not guilty of murder?

THE FOREMAN OF THE JURY—Guilty, my lord.

THE CLERK OF THE COURT—Do you find the prisoner, Lawrence John Smith, guilty or not guilty of murder?

THE FOREMAN OF THE JURY—Guilty, my lord.

THE CLERK OF THE COURT—You find both prisoners guilty of murder?

THE FOREMAN OF THE JURY—Yes, my lord.

THE CLERK OF THE COURT—And that is the verdict of you all?

THE FOREMAN OF THE JURY—Yes, my lord.

THE CLERK OF THE COURT—Prisoners at the Bar, you severally stand convicted of murder. Have you or either of you anything

Ley and Smith.

The Lord Chief Justice

to say why the Court should not give you judgment according to law?

PRISONER LEY—I would like to say two or three words, my lord. First, I am not surprised at the verdict of the jury after the biased summing-up. Secondly, I am not surprised at the exploitation of the allegations of jealousy, suspicions, obsessions and such like nonsense when you refused to allow me to state in the box what I wanted to say to refute that. I am perfectly innocent. I have said it from the beginning and I say it now, and I regret very much that I at my time of life have to suffer an injustice of this kind that is utterly unfounded and based on anything but real fact. I have nothing more to say.

(Proclamation.)

Sentence.

THE LORD CHIEF JUSTICE—Thomas John Ley, Lawrence John Smith, you both stand convicted of murder and I say no more than that I agree with the verdict. The sentence of the Law upon you and each of you is that you be taken to a lawful prison and thence to a place of execution. That you be there each of you hanged by the neck until you be dead, and that your bodies respectively be buried within the precincts of the prison in which you shall have been last confined before your execution, and may the Lord have mercy upon your souls.

310

APPENDIX*

REX v. LEY
REX v. SMITH

COURT OF CRIMINAL APPEAL, 21ST-22ND APRIL, 1947,

BEFORE

Mr. Justice Atkinson, Mr. Justice Oliver, and Mr. Justice Cassels.

Sir Walter Monckton, K.C., Mr. Phineas Quass, and Mr. Gerald Howard, appeared for Ley; Mr. Derek Curtis Bennett, K.C., and Mr. M. Morris for Smith; and Mr. Anthony Hawke and Mr. Henry Elam for the Crown.

Sir Walter Monckton, in opening the appeal, made a preliminary application to call Mrs. Evans to give additional evidence on two points. At the suggestion of counsel the Court agreed to keep the application open pending his proposed criticisms of the summing-up.

The case, said counsel, was full of uncertainty during the period from 6.50 p.m. on 28th November at Ley's house at Beaufort Gardens, Kensington—the moment when Mudie was brought there —and 9.30 p.m. on 30th November—when his body was discovered in the chalk pit. The first question in the case was not whether Ley or Smith had murdered Mudie but whether he had been murdered at all. The gap in time between 28th November and 30th November had been filled by the assumption, made by the Lord Chief Justice, that Mudie had been murdered, without regard to other possibilities, including accident and manslaughter.

Criticizing the summing-up on the issue of manslaughter, counsel said that if there was a question of an accident causing death which in the circumstances might constitute manslaughter, the jury ought to have been directed that they had to consider whether the accident occurred in the performance of a dangerous act as well as an unlawful act. Unless such violence were established as would constitute murder if death resulted even unintentionally, or

---

*Reproduced by courtesy of the Editor of *The Times*.

Ley and Smith.

deliberate murder were established, there was no case here of murder at all.

Concluding his argument, counsel submitted that the case which was made on behalf of Ley did not really go to the jury—namely, that what was found to have happened between 6.50 p.m. on 28th November and 9.30 p.m. on 30th November was consistent, on the evidence, with slow strangulation by Mudie's tugging at the rope himself, or a sudden pull in a frenzy or panic by someone other than Ley or Smith on the rope which was round Mudie's neck, in each case causing strangulation by accident. Further, the issue of manslaughter should also have been put to the jury.

Mr. Curtis Bennett, addressing the Court on behalf of Smith, said that, with regard to him, the summing-up left a very wide hiatus with regard to manslaughter. If, after Smith had brought Mudie to Ley's house for cross-examining, which was what had happened, and while Mudie was there someone, even in Smith's presence, in an excess of temper pulled the noose, which was round Mudie's neck, tight and killed him, that did not make Smith guilty of murder. The fact that he was given money afterwards was immaterial.

Criticizing the part of the summing-up relating to the alleged presence of Smith's car at the chalk pit on 27th November, counsel said that if it was not established that the car was there on that day there was no case of murder at all against Smith, only a case of assault with violence.

Smith having brought Mudie up to London for interrogation by Ley, something had happened to Mudie for which he (counsel) submitted Smith might at the most have been responsible in manslaughter, but might not have been responsible at all.

Mr. Hawke called upon to address the Court with regard to the complaints of misdirection in the case of Smith, submitted that after a trial lasting five days it would be impossible to find any summing-up by any judge which did not contain some inaccuracies of fact. That was no ground for saying that the jury had been misdirected on the essential points of the case. He (counsel) submitted that the evidence of identification of Smith coupled with the evidence identifying his car at the chalk pit on 27th November, justified the verdict against him.

As for the question of manslaughter, he (counsel) submitted that there had been no misdirection. If the Lord Chief Justice had erred at all, he had erred in favour of the appellants by exploring avenues which, on the evidence, were not really open to him.

Sir Walter Monckton and Mr. Curtis Bennett replied.

Judgment.

Judgment

Mr. Justice Atkinson, giving the judgment of the Court, said that Ley's main complaint was of insufficient direction to the jury on the possibility of manslaughter, accident, or suicide as having been the cause of Mudie's death; and that the case had merely been put to them as one of murder. It was argued that there was no certainty as to what had happened between 6.50 p.m. on 28th November, 1946, and the evening of the 30th, when Mudie's body was found in the chalk pit, and that the Lord Chief Justice had assumed that it was a case of murder. The Lord Chief Justice, it was clear, had directed the jury with perfect accuracy as to the matters on which they had to be satisfied before they returned a verdict of murder. He was under no obligation to direct them on the law of manslaughter unless there was some evidence on which a verdict of manslaughter might reasonably be given.

The main facts proved were: (1) That on the evening of 28th November, Mudie had been bound and helpless in a chair with no rope round his neck; (2) that two days later he was found near a chalk pit dead with a cord round his neck, tied in such a way that it had only to be pulled to strangle him, and with a deep mark of that cord on his neck, which indicated that it had been pulled from behind and upwards; and (3) that according to the medical evidence on both sides, death was caused by strangulation through that cord.

His Lordship discussed the law relating to murder and manslaughter, and said that, on the facts, it was quite impossible for the jury to take the view that the act done which caused death was of such a nature that a reasonable man would not contemplate that death could result from it, and to return a verdict of manslaughter on that basis. The same applies to the suggestion that death might have been due to accident.

The rope with a noose and a slip-knot in it must have been deliberately put on Mudie's neck, and had been pulled with such violence as to show the mark on the neck. There was therefore no obligation on the judge to direct the jury as to manslaughter. The suggestion of suicide was fantastic. How could a man, tied up as Mudie was, get a rope, tie it round his own neck and pull it from behind?

With regard to Smith, Mr. Curtis Bennett had suggested additional possibilities which, he said, the Lord Chief Justice might have left to the jury. The Court could not accept that view because there was no evidence on which these possibilities could be based. The appeals would be dismissed.

Tehin.
9 Sept. 1947.